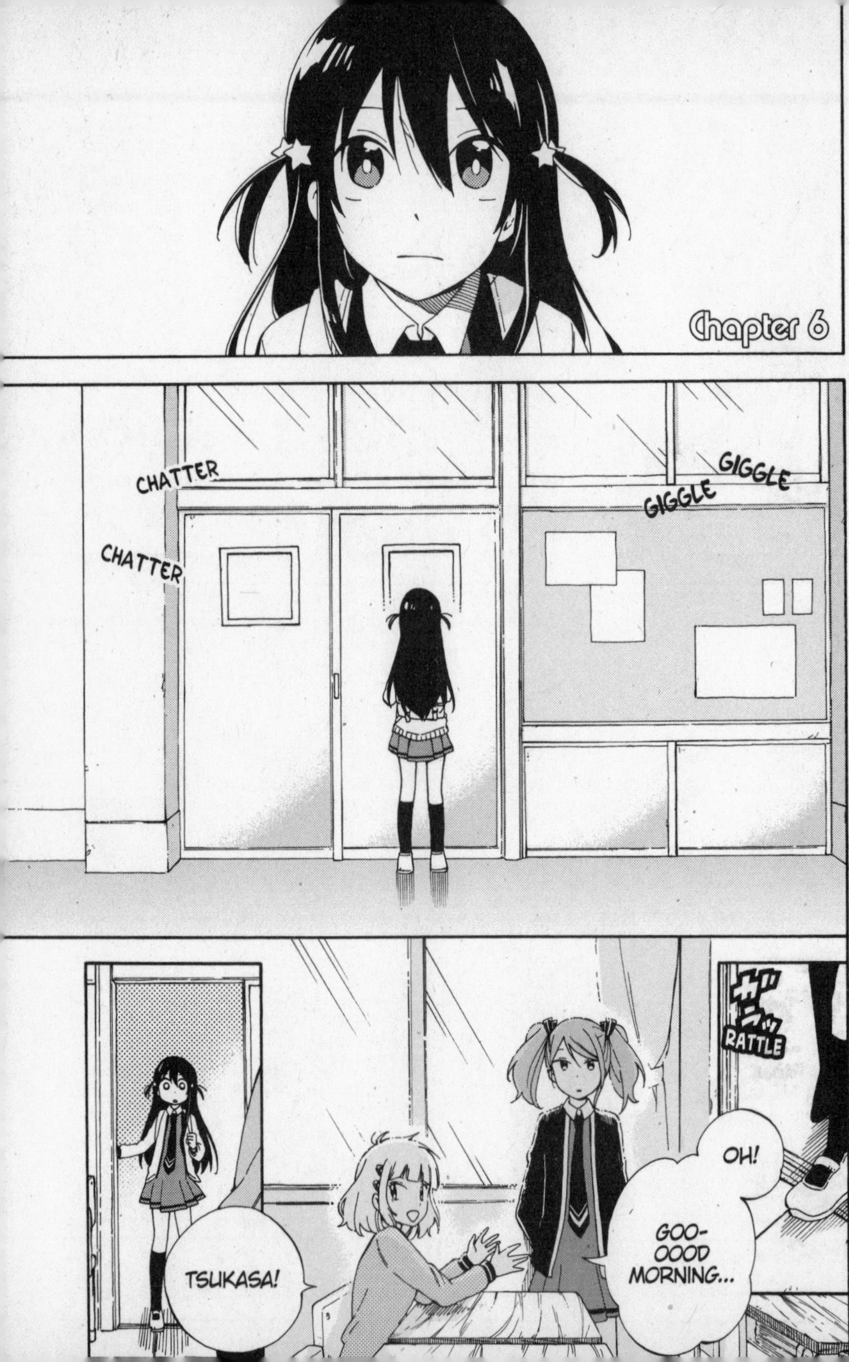
Chapter 6
GIGGLE
GIGGLE
CHATTER
CHATTER
ガラッ
RATTLE
OH!
GOO-
OOOD
MORNING...
TSUKASA!

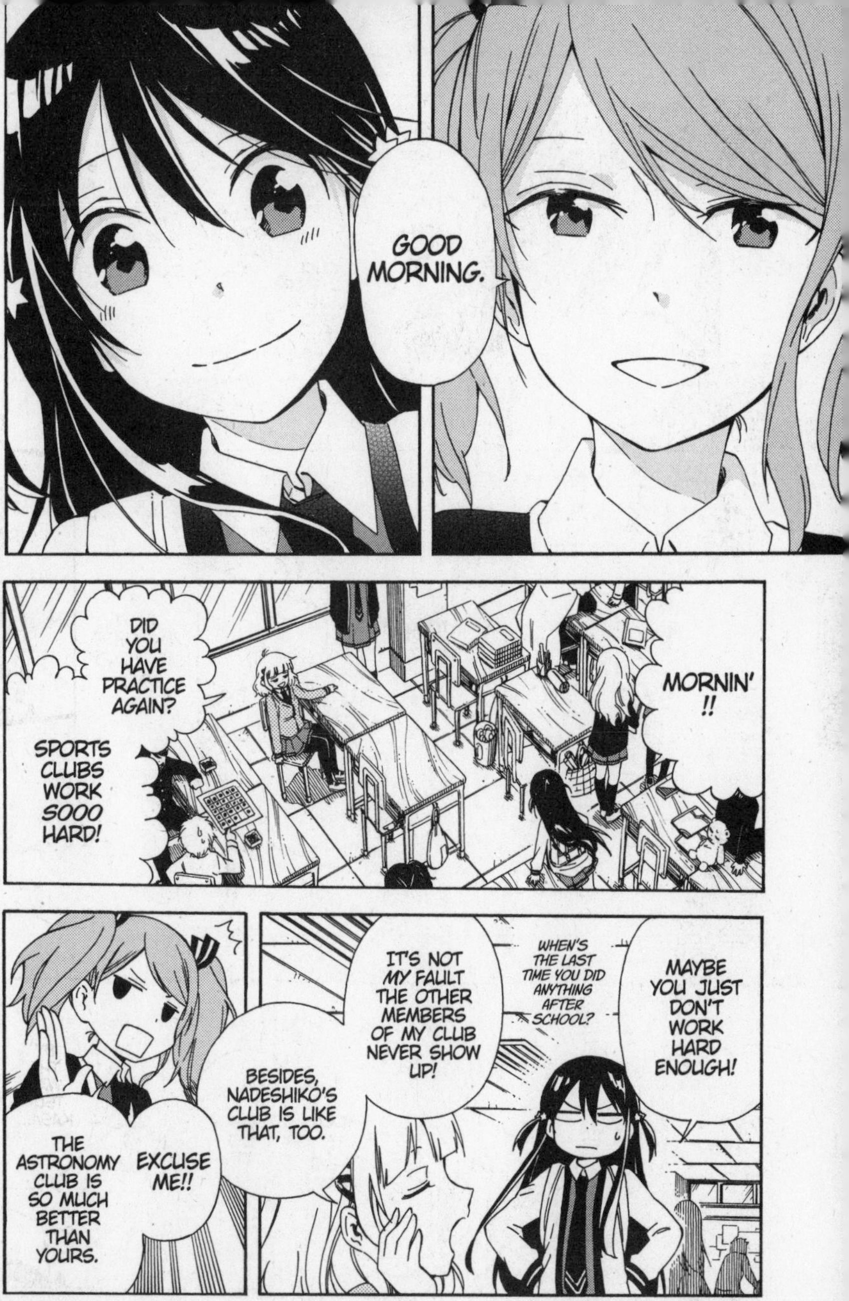
GOOD MORNING.
MORNIN' !!
DID YOU HAVE PRACTICE AGAIN?
SPORTS CLUBS WORK SOOO HARD!
MAYBE YOU JUST DON'T WORK HARD ENOUGH!
WHEN'S THE LAST TIME YOU DID ANYTHING AFTER SCHOOL?
IT'S NOT MY FAULT THE OTHER MEMBERS OF MY CLUB NEVER SHOW UP!
BESIDES, NADESHIKO'S CLUB IS LIKE THAT, TOO.
EXCUSE ME!!
THE ASTRONOMY CLUB IS SO MUCH BETTER THAN YOURS.

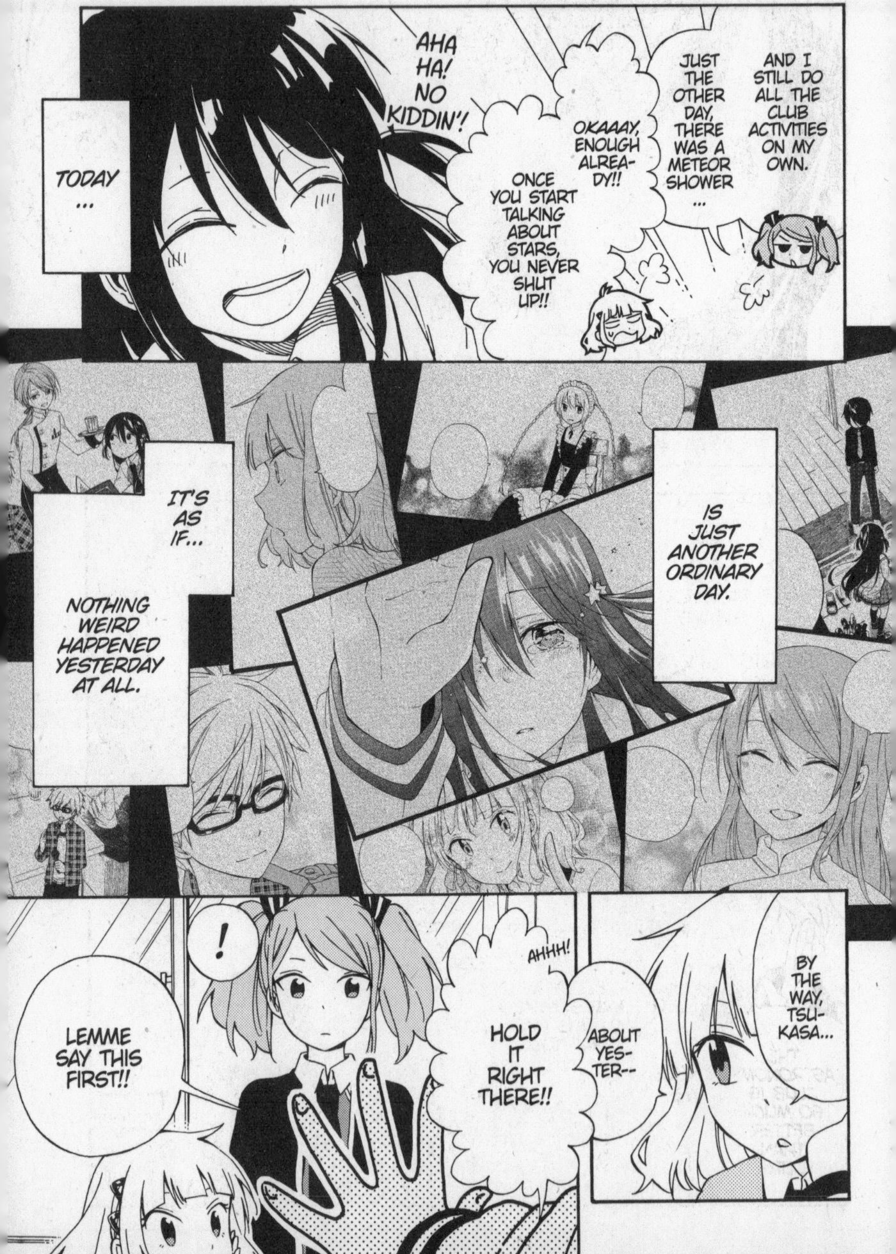
AND I STILL DO ALL THE CLUB ACTIVITIES ON MY OWN.
JUST THE OTHER DAY, THERE WAS A METEOR SHOWER ...
OKAAAY, ENOUGH ALREA-DY!!
ONCE YOU START TALKING ABOUT STARS, YOU NEVER SHUT UP!!
AHA HA! NO KIDDIN'!
TODAY ...
IS JUST ANOTHER ORDINARY DAY.
IT'S AS IF...
NOTHING WEIRD HAPPENED YESTERDAY AT ALL.
BY THE WAY, TSU-KASA...
ABOUT YES-TER--
AHHH!
HOLD IT RIGHT THERE!!
!
LEMME SAY THIS FIRST!!

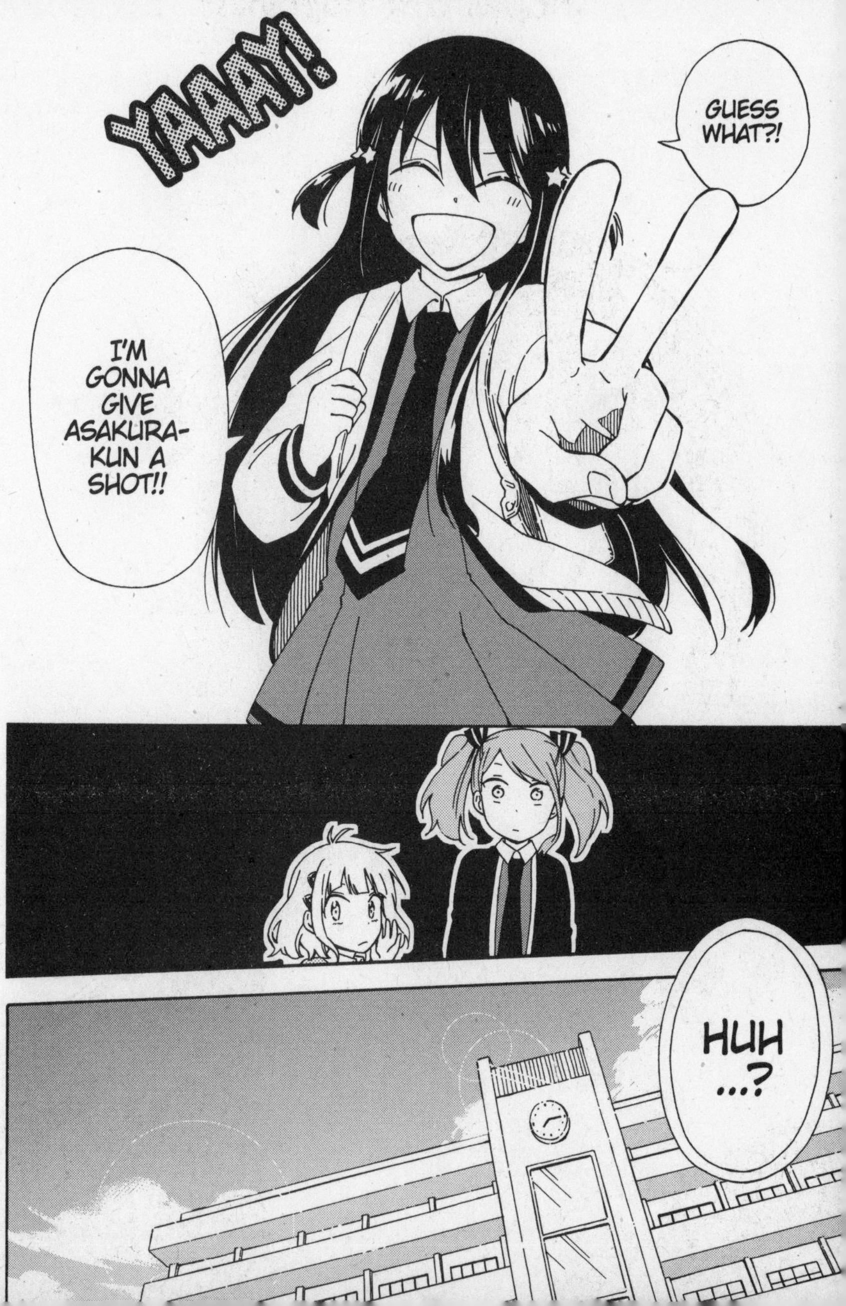
GUESS WHAT?!
YAAAY!
I'M GONNA GIVE ASAKURA-KUN A SHOT!!
HUH ...?

Chapter 6 ★ Happiness

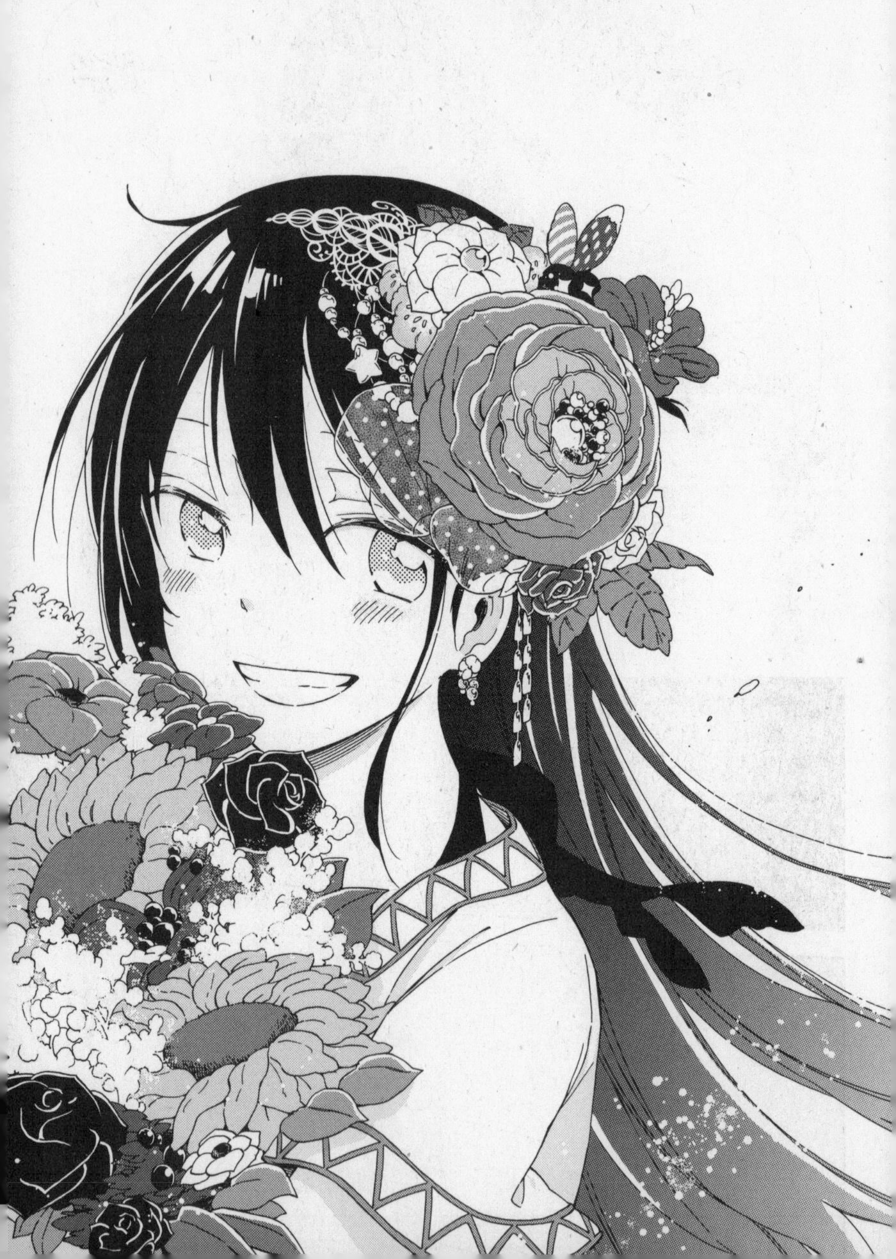

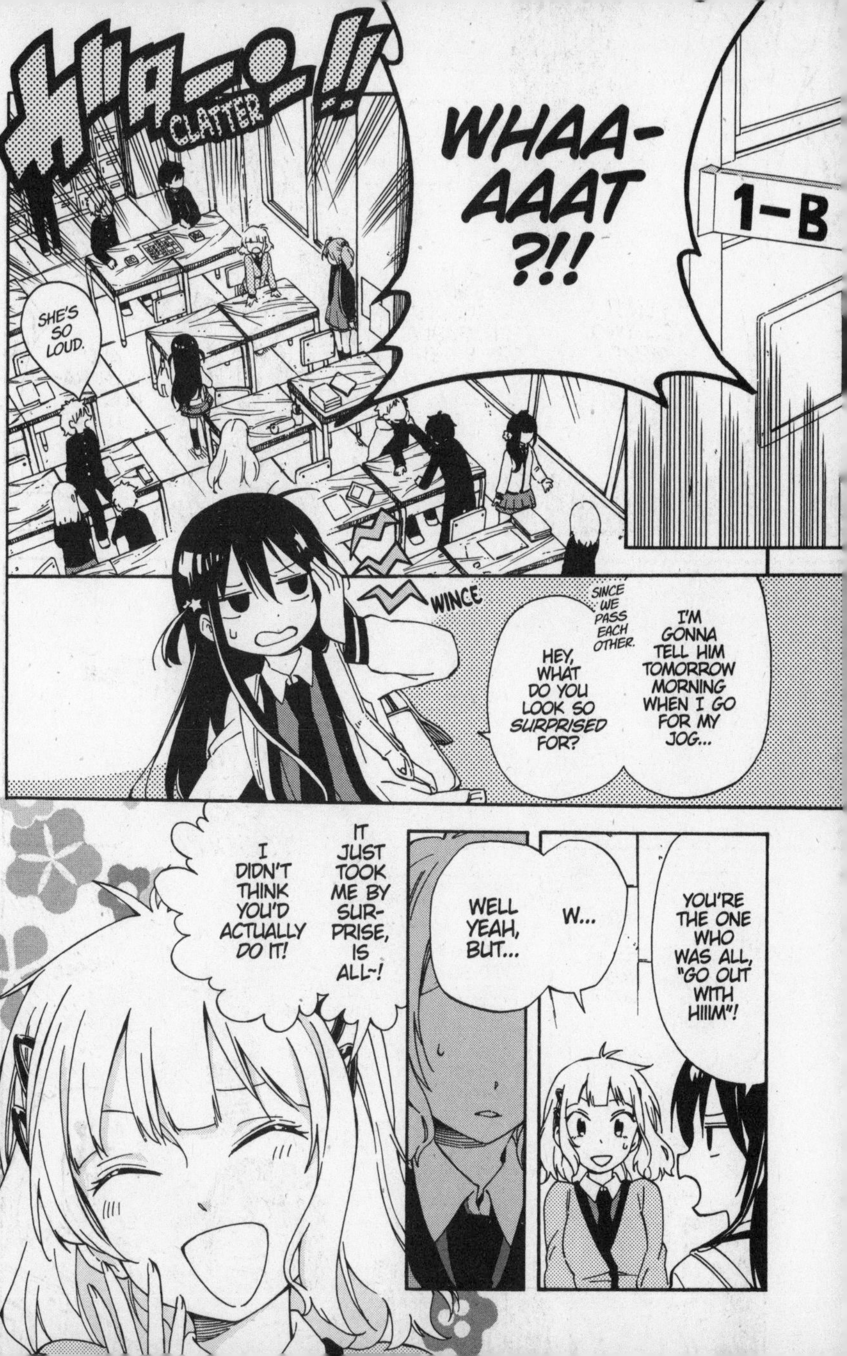
1-B
WHAAA-AAAT ?!!
CLATTER
SHE'S SO LOUD.
I'M GONNA TELL HIM TOMORROW MORNING WHEN I GO FOR MY JOG...
SINCE WE PASS EACH OTHER.
HEY, WHAT DO YOU LOOK SO SURPRISED FOR?
WINCE
YOU'RE THE ONE WHO WAS ALL, "GO OUT WITH HIIIM"!
W...
WELL YEAH, BUT...
IT JUST TOOK ME BY SURPRISE, IS ALL~!
I DIDN'T THINK YOU'D ACTUALLY DO IT!

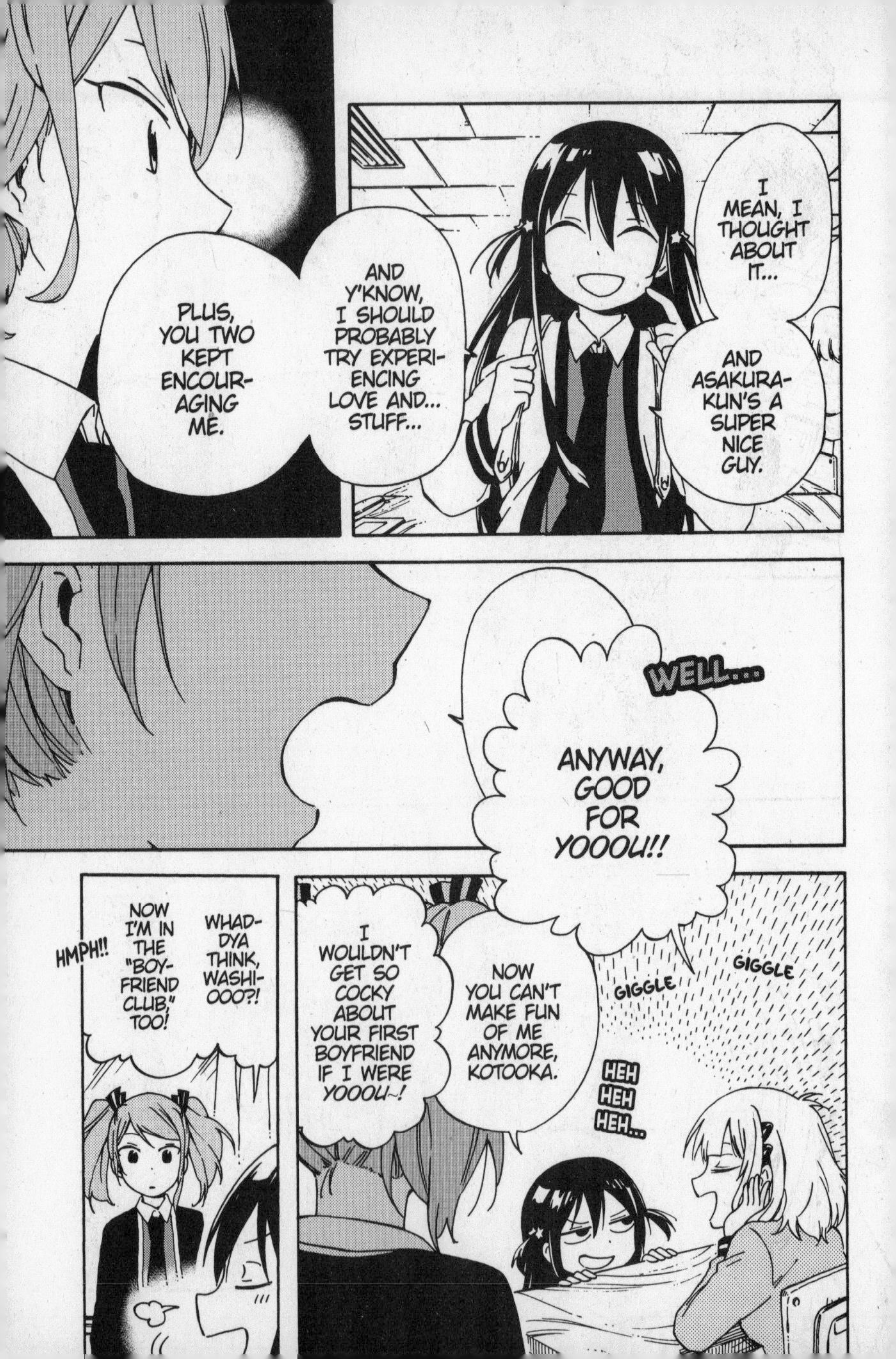
I MEAN, I THOUGHT ABOUT IT...
AND ASAKURA-KUN'S A SUPER NICE GUY.
AND Y'KNOW, I SHOULD PROBABLY TRY EXPERIENCING LOVE AND... STUFF...
PLUS, YOU TWO KEPT ENCOURAGING ME.
WELL...
ANYWAY, GOOD FOR YOOOU!!
GIGGLE
GIGGLE
NOW YOU CAN'T MAKE FUN OF ME ANYMORE, KOTOOKA.
HEH HEH HEH...
I WOULDN'T GET SO COCKY ABOUT YOUR FIRST BOYFRIEND IF I WERE YOOOU~!
WHADDYA THINK, WASHIOOO?!
NOW I'M IN THE "BOYFRIEND CLUB," TOO!
HMPH!!

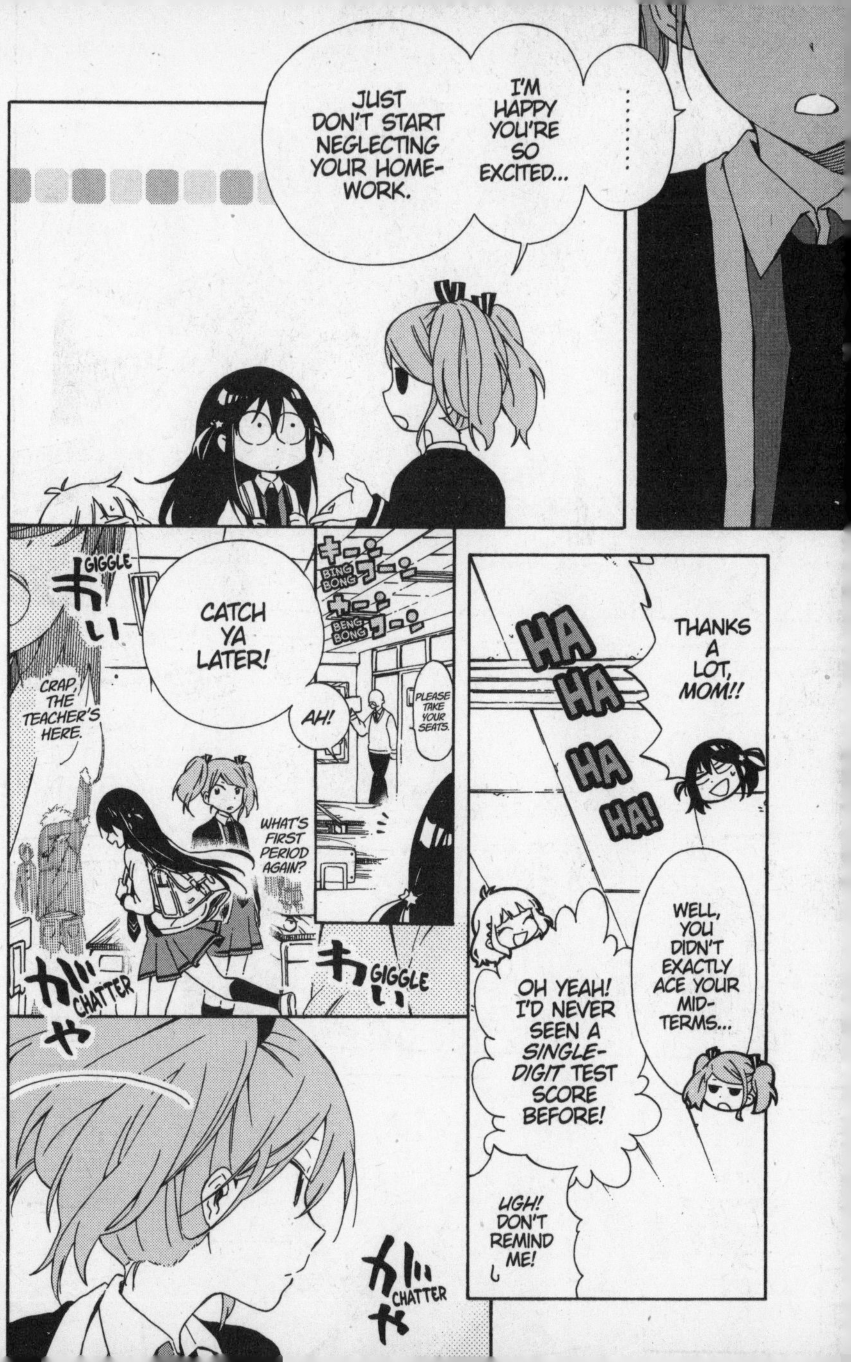
......
I'M HAPPY YOU'RE SO EXCITED...
JUST DON'T START NEGLECTING YOUR HOME-WORK.
THANKS A LOT, MOM!!
HA HA HA HA!
WELL, YOU DIDN'T EXACTLY ACE YOUR MID-TERMS...
OH YEAH! I'D NEVER SEEN A SINGLE-DIGIT TEST SCORE BEFORE!
UGH! DON'T REMIND ME!
BING BONG
BENG BONG
PLEASE TAKE YOUR SEATS.
CATCH YA LATER!
AH!
GIGGLE
CRAP, THE TEACHER'S HERE.
WHAT'S FIRST PERIOD AGAIN?
GIGGLE
CHATTER
CHATTER

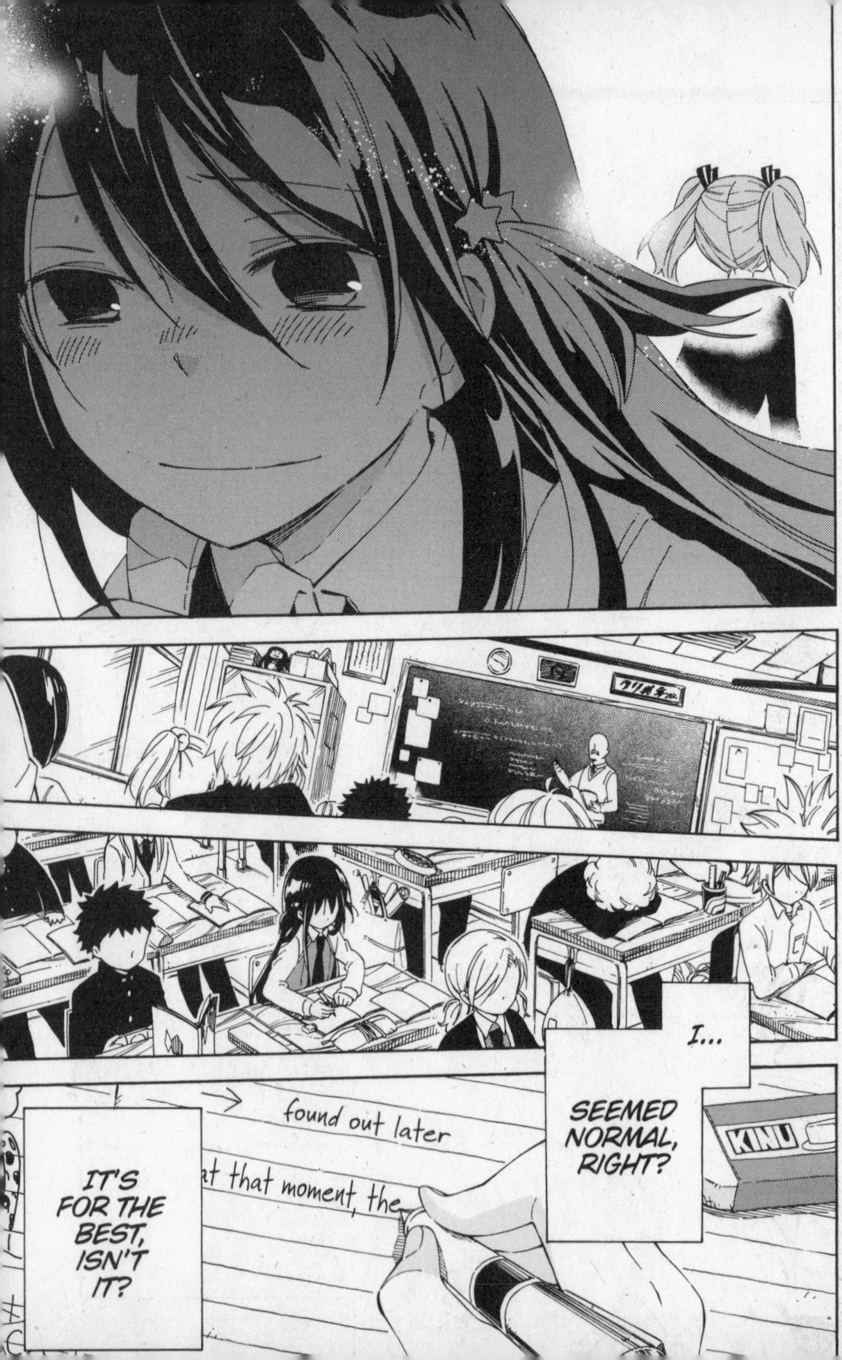
I...
SEEMED NORMAL, RIGHT?
KINU
found out later
at that moment, the
IT'S FOR THE BEST, ISN'T IT?

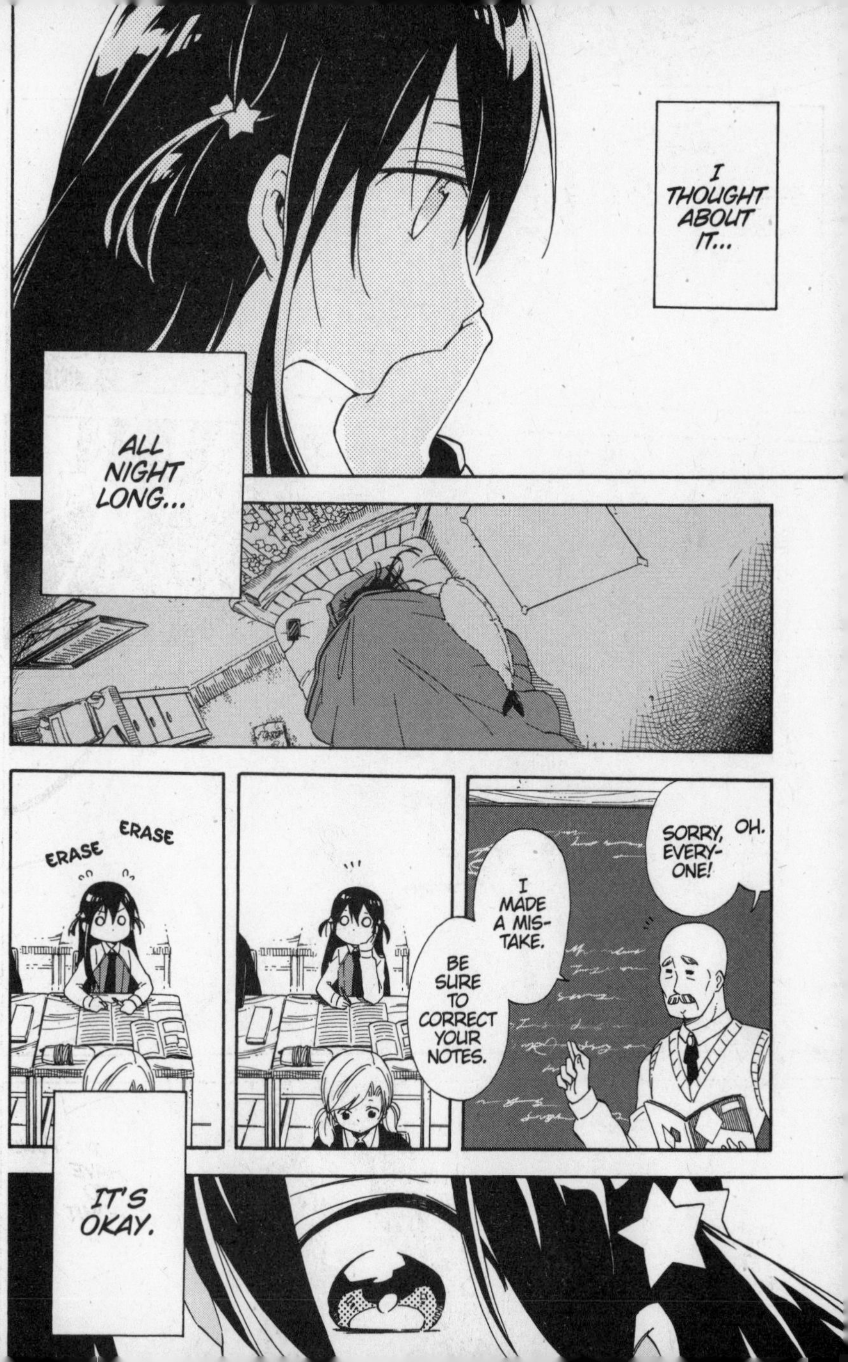
I THOUGHT ABOUT IT...
ALL NIGHT LONG...
OH.
SORRY, EVERYONE!
I MADE A MISTAKE.
BE SURE TO CORRECT YOUR NOTES.
ERASE
ERASE
IT'S OKAY.

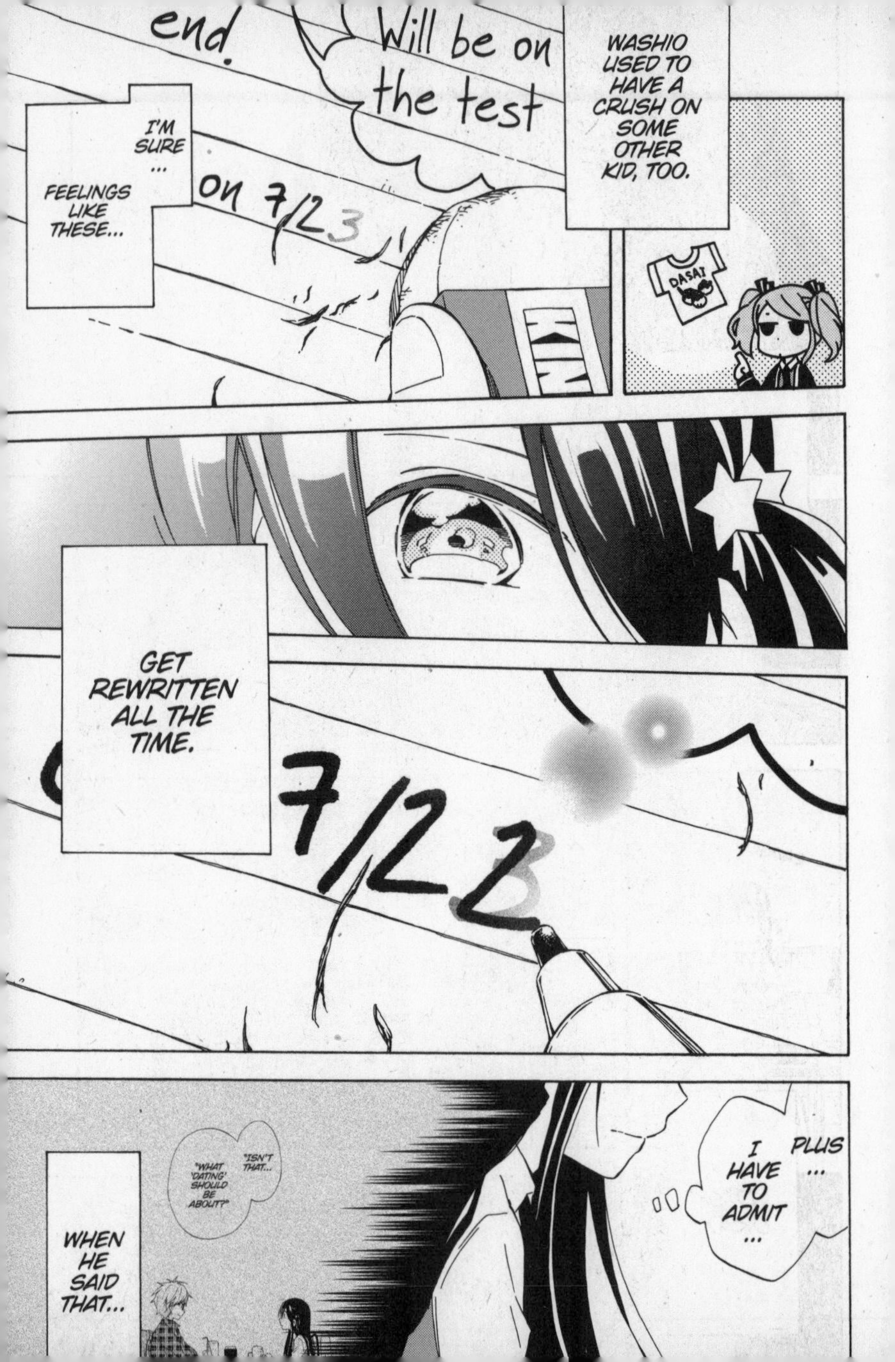
WASHIO USED TO HAVE A CRUSH ON SOME OTHER KID, TOO.
DASAI
end.
Will be on the test
on 7/23
I'M SURE ...
FEELINGS LIKE THESE...
GET REWRITTEN ALL THE TIME.
7/22
PLUS ...
I HAVE TO ADMIT ...
"ISN'T THAT...
"WHAT 'DATING' SHOULD BE ABOUT?"
WHEN HE SAID THAT...

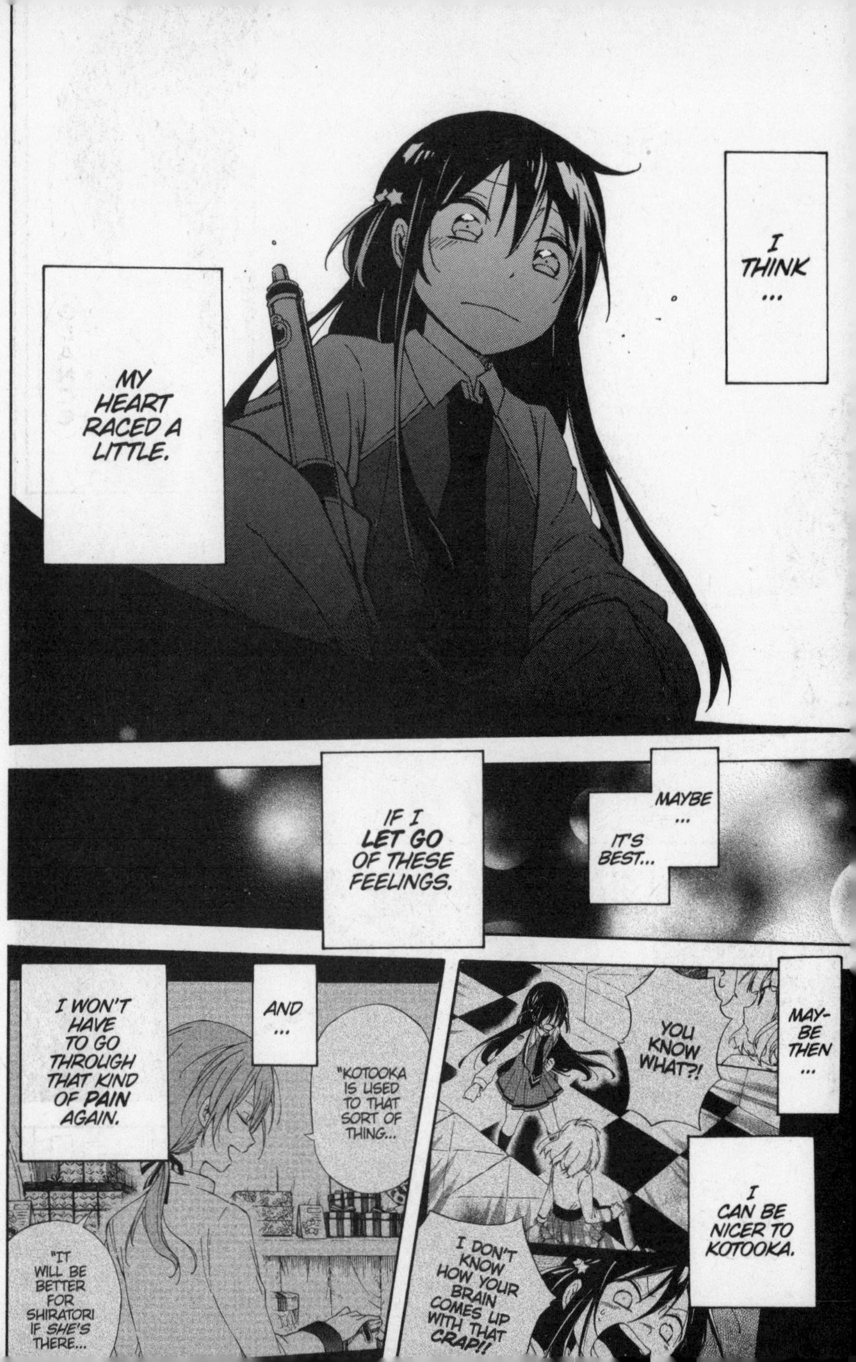
I THINK...
MY HEART RACED A LITTLE.
MAYBE... IT'S BEST...
IF I LET GO OF THESE FEELINGS.
MAY-BE THEN...
YOU KNOW WHAT?!
I CAN BE NICER TO KOTOOKA.
I DON'T KNOW HOW YOUR BRAIN COMES UP WITH THAT CRAP!!
AND...
I WON'T HAVE TO GO THROUGH THAT KIND OF PAIN AGAIN.
"KOTOOKA IS USED TO THAT SORT OF THING...
"IT WILL BE BETTER FOR SHIRATORI IF SHE'S THERE...

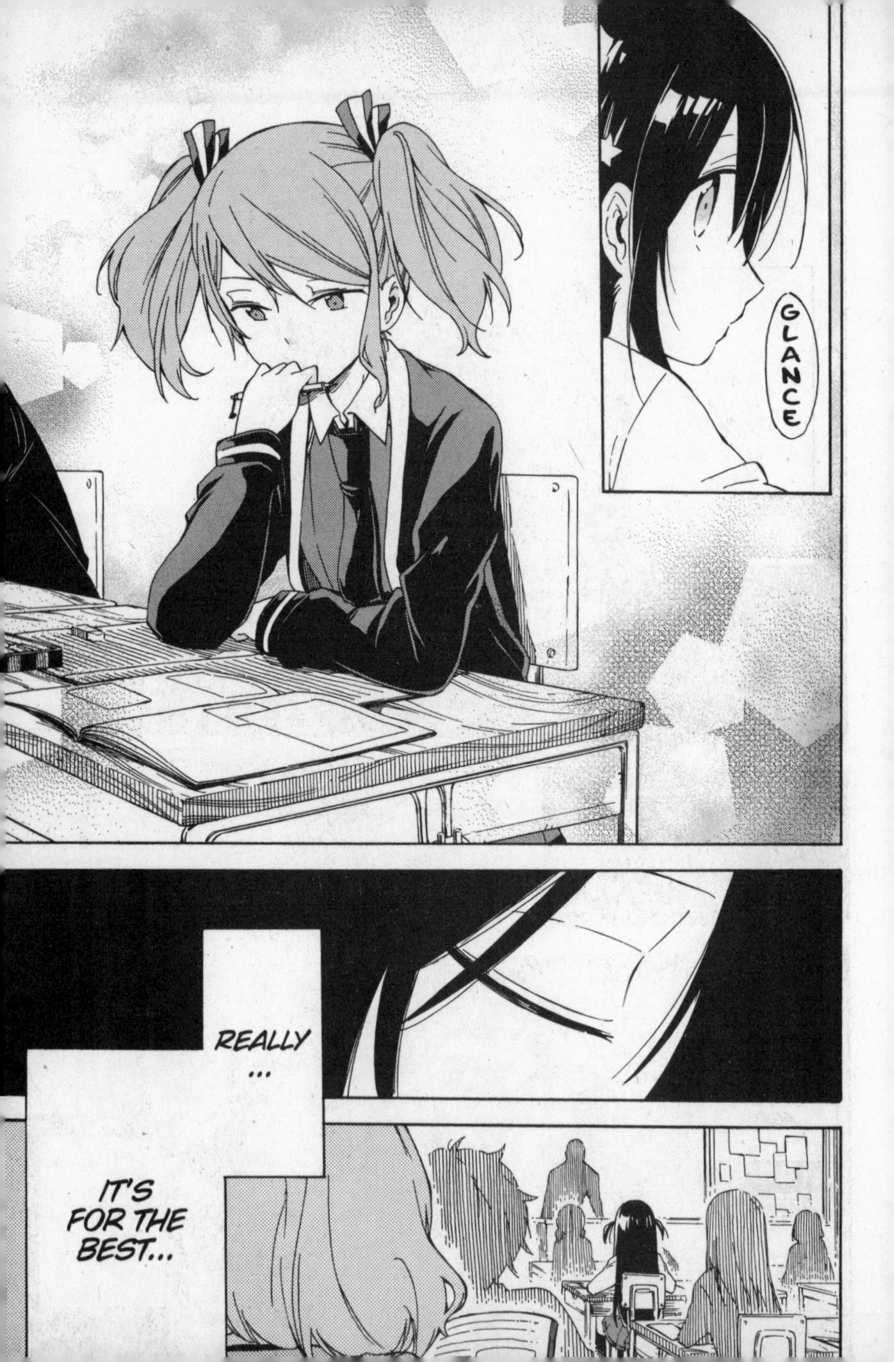
GLANCE
REALLY...
IT'S FOR THE BEST...

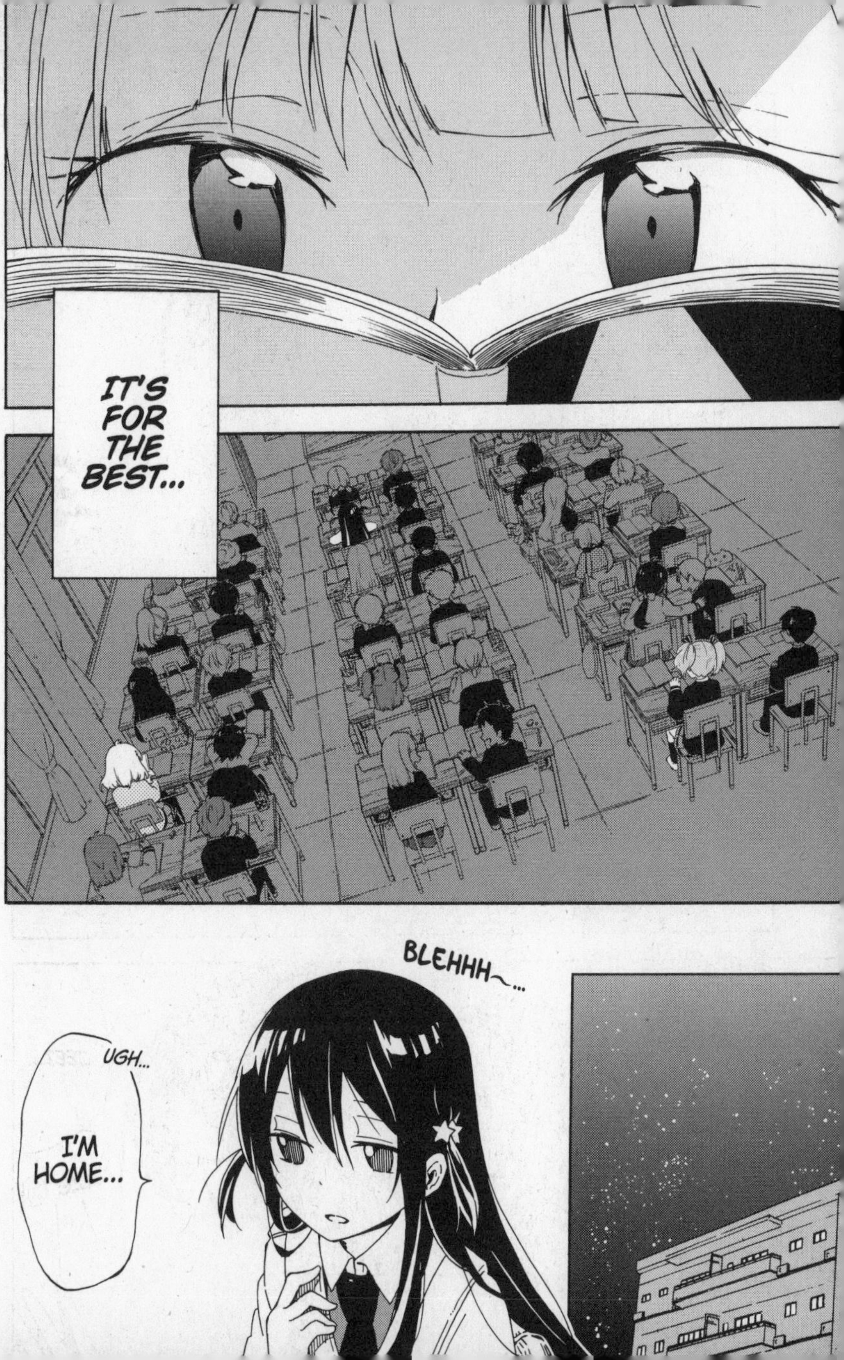
IT'S FOR THE BEST...
BLEHHH~...
UGH...
I'M HOME...

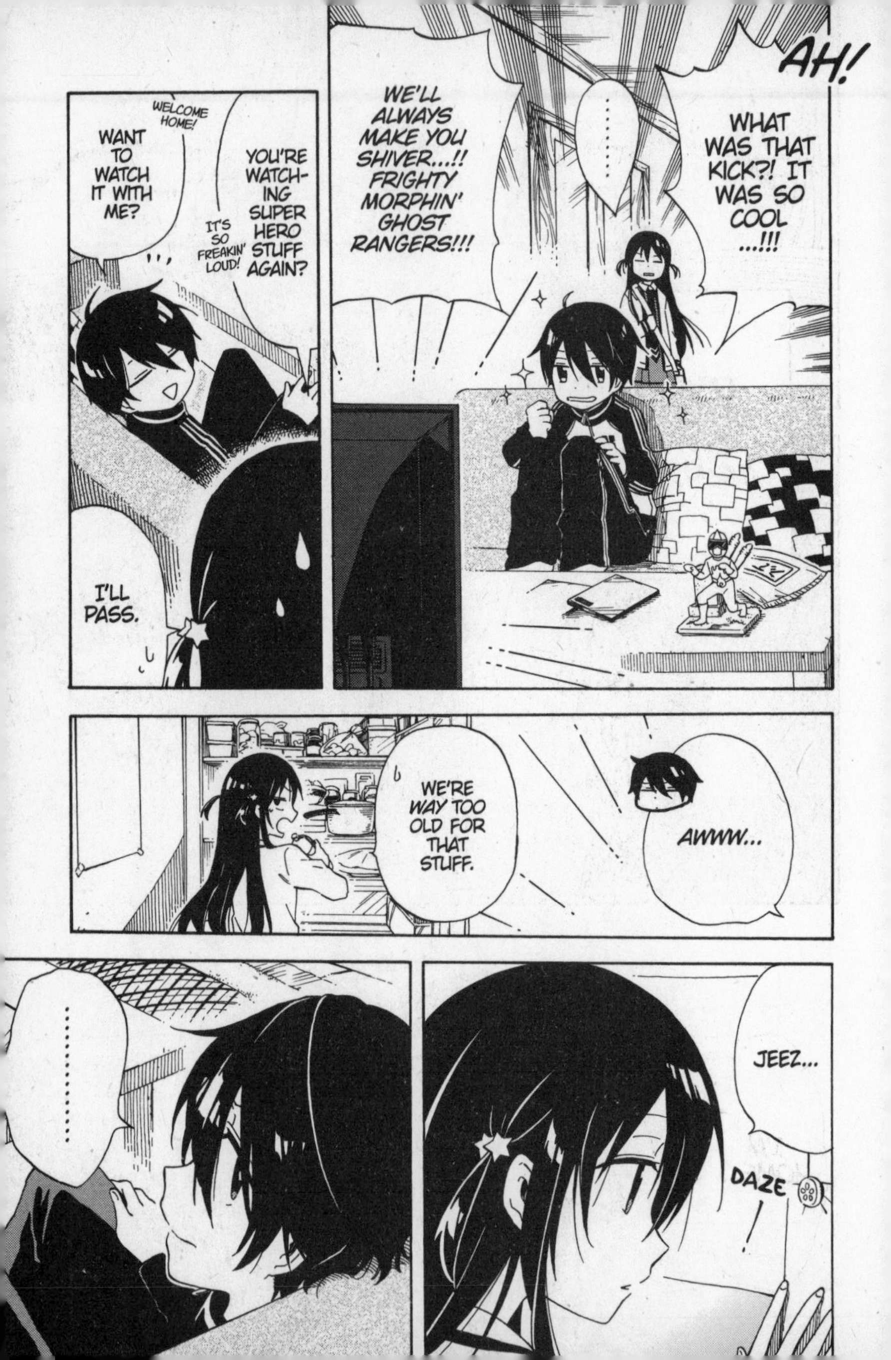
AH!
WHAT WAS THAT KICK?! IT WAS SO COOL ...!!!
...
WE'LL ALWAYS MAKE YOU SHIVER...!! FRIGHTY MORPHIN' GHOST RANGERS!!!
YOU'RE WATCHING SUPER HERO STUFF AGAIN?
IT'S SO FREAKIN' LOUD!
WELCOME HOME!
WANT TO WATCH IT WITH ME?
I'LL PASS.
AWWW...
WE'RE WAY TOO OLD FOR THAT STUFF.
JEEZ...
DAZE
......

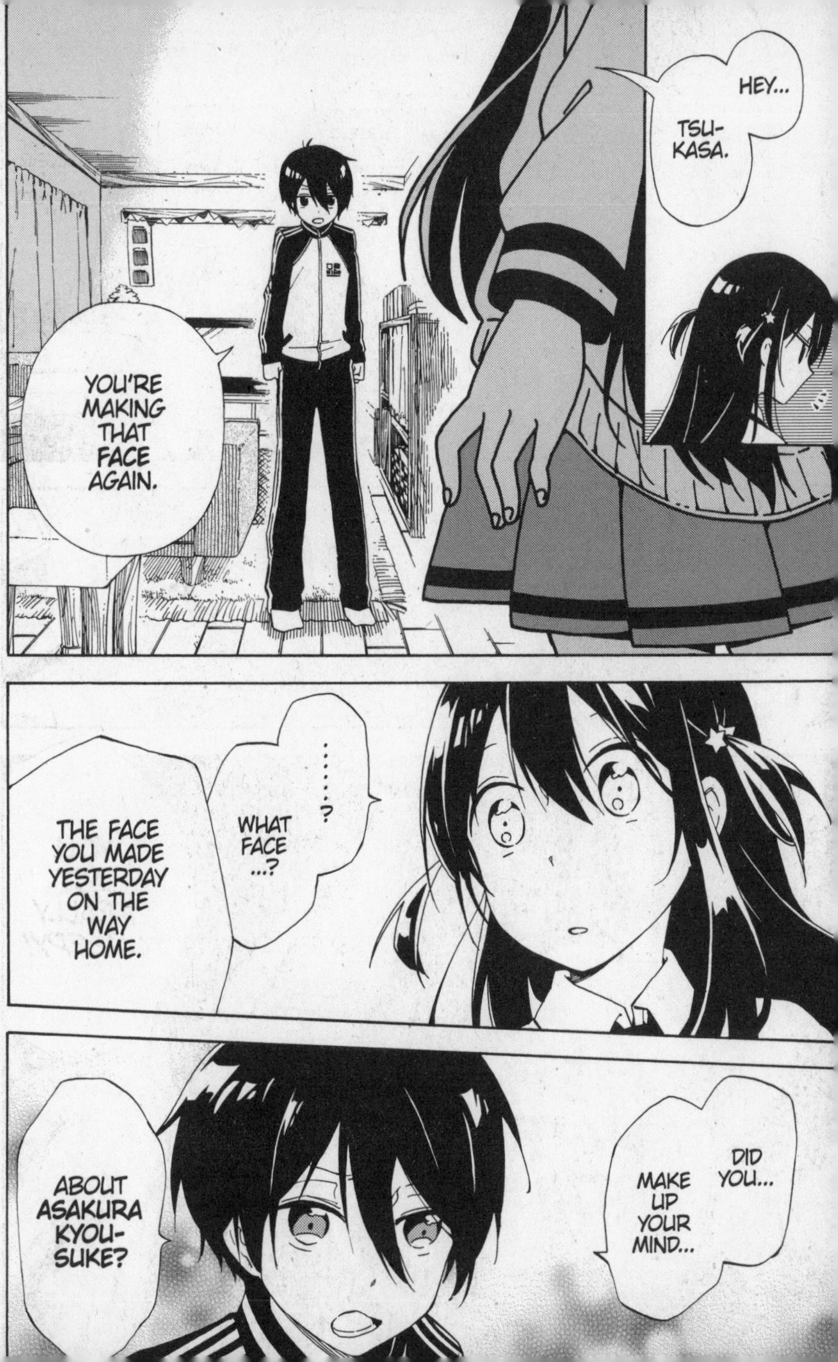
HEY... TSU-KASA.
YOU'RE MAKING THAT FACE AGAIN.
......?
WHAT FACE ...?
THE FACE YOU MADE YESTERDAY ON THE WAY HOME.
DID YOU... MAKE UP YOUR MIND...
ABOUT ASAKURA KYOU-SUKE?

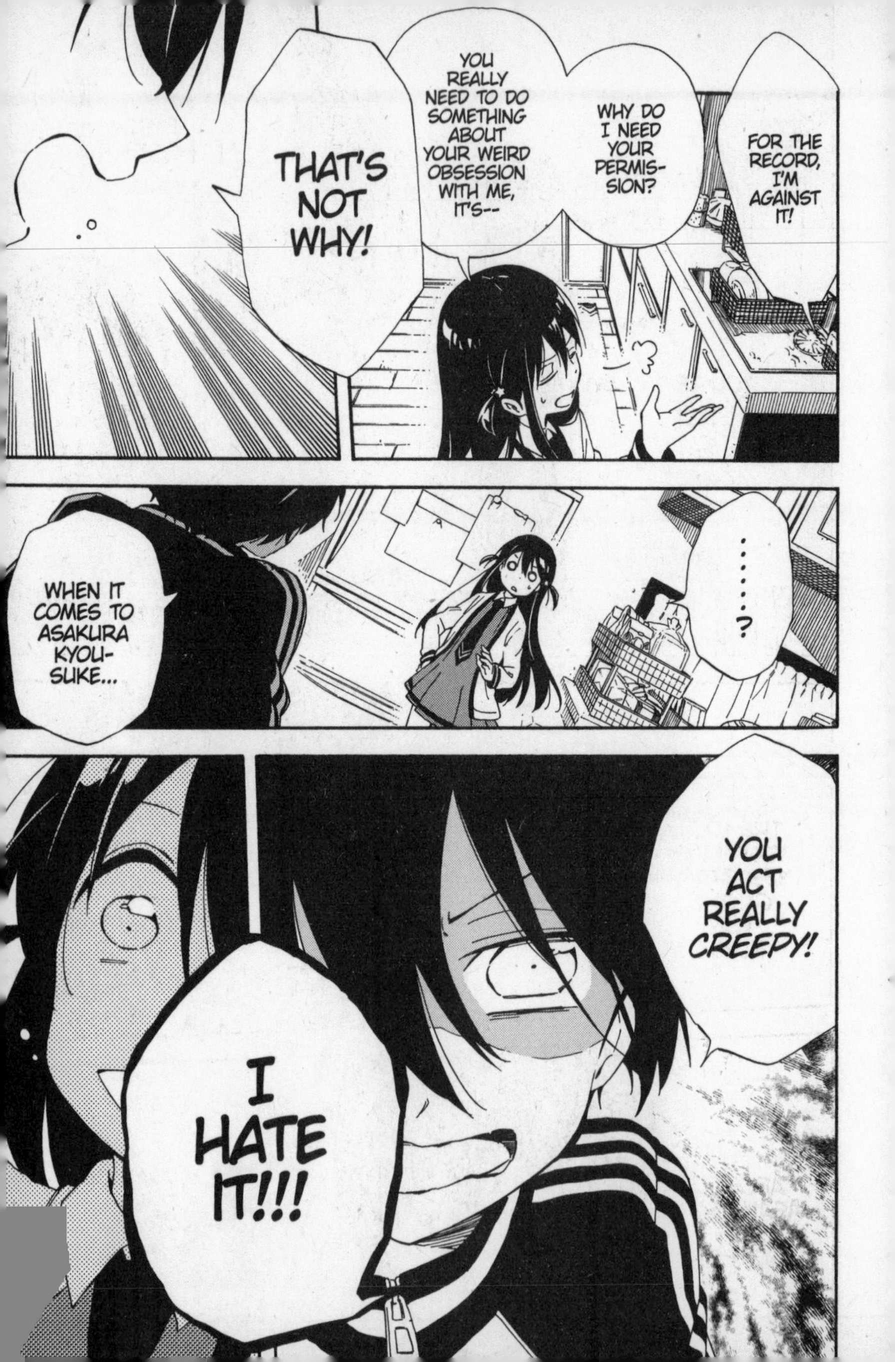
FOR THE RECORD, I'M AGAINST IT!
WHY DO I NEED YOUR PERMISSION?
YOU REALLY NEED TO DO SOMETHING ABOUT YOUR WEIRD OBSESSION WITH ME, IT'S--
THAT'S NOT WHY!
......?
WHEN IT COMES TO ASAKURA KYOUSUKE...
YOU ACT REALLY CREEPY!
I HATE IT!!!

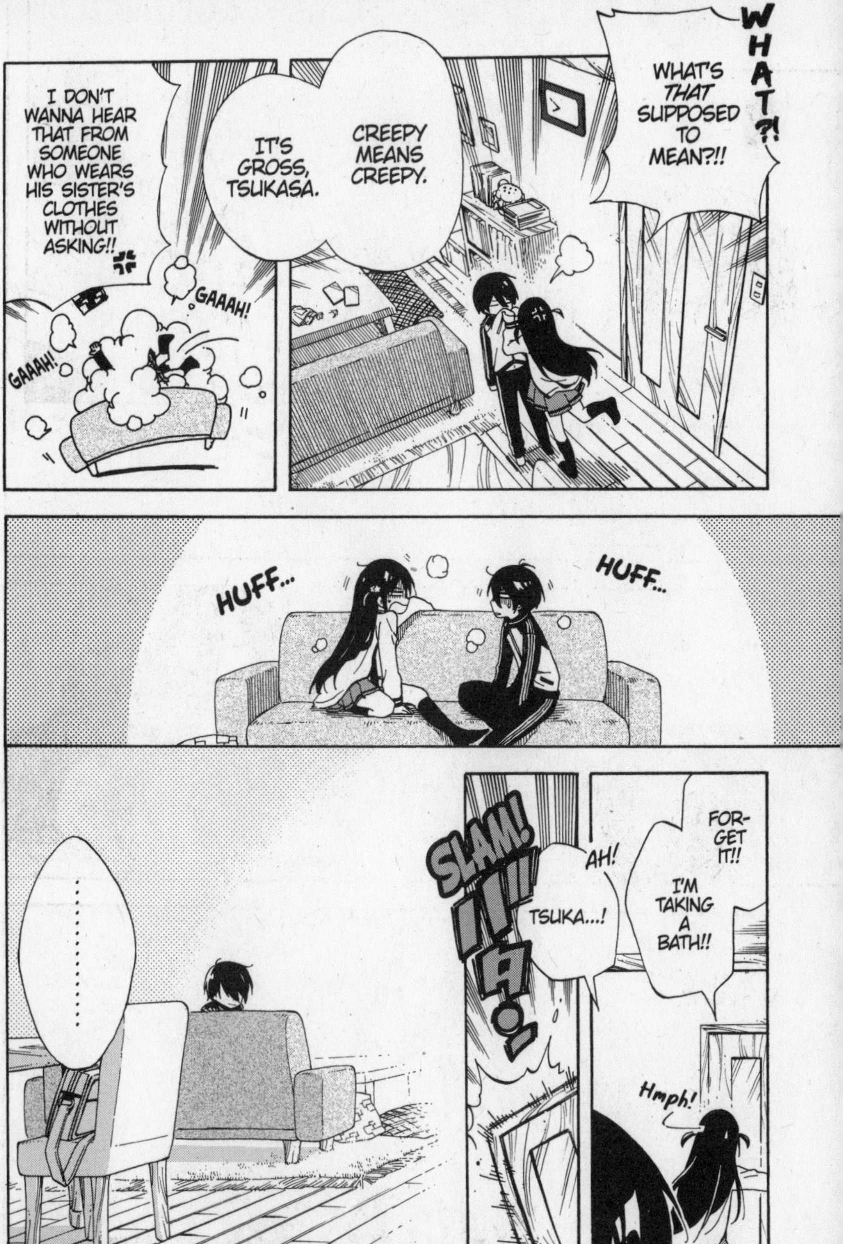
WHAT'S THAT SUPPOSED TO MEAN?!!
WHAT?!
CREEPY MEANS CREEPY.
IT'S GROSS, TSUKASA.
I DON'T WANNA HEAR THAT FROM SOMEONE WHO WEARS HIS SISTER'S CLOTHES WITHOUT ASKING!!
GAAAH!
GAAAH!
HUFF...
HUFF...
FOR-GET IT!!
I'M TAKING A BATH!!
Hmph!
SLAM!
AH!
TSUKA...!
......

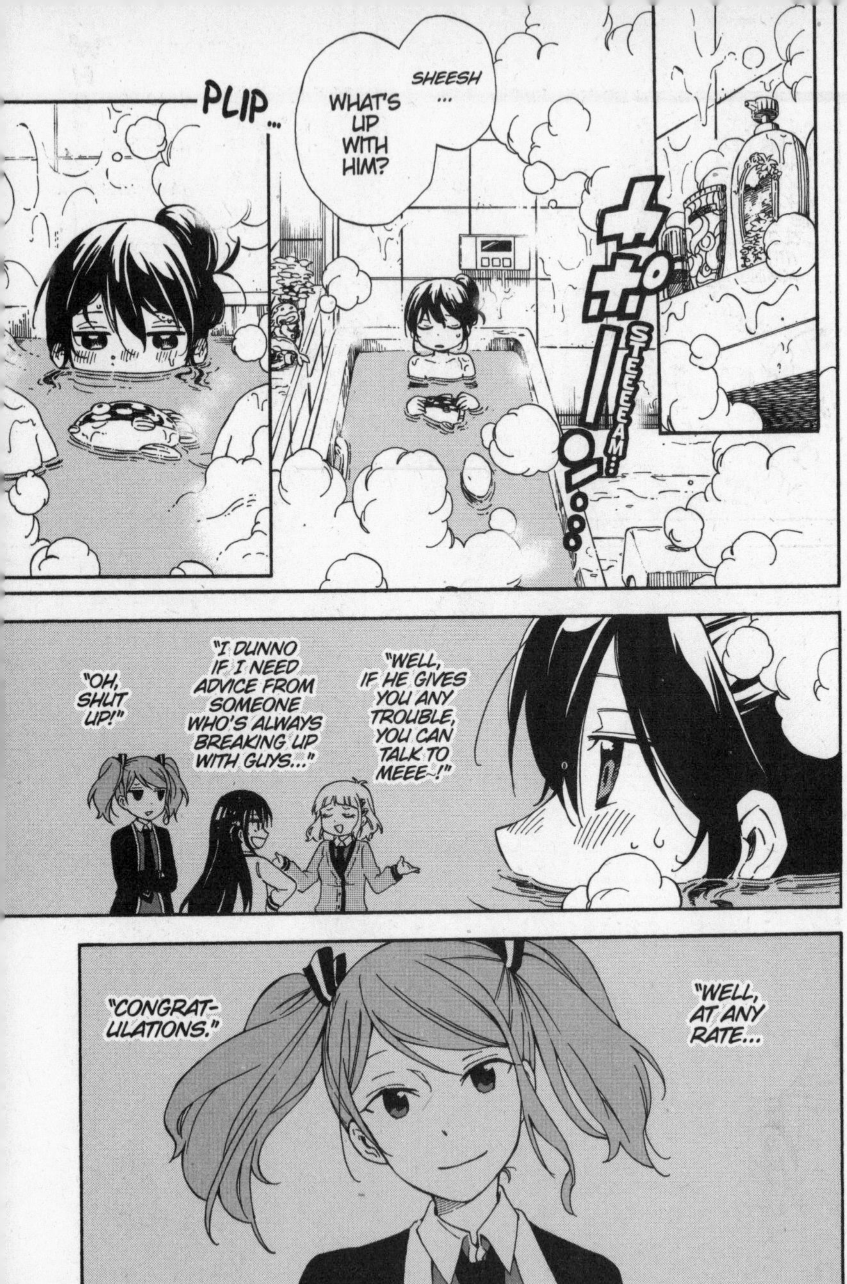
SHEESH...
WHAT'S UP WITH HIM?
STEEEAM...
PLIP...
"WELL, IF HE GIVES YOU ANY TROUBLE, YOU CAN TALK TO MEEE~!"
"I DUNNO IF I NEED ADVICE FROM SOMEONE WHO'S ALWAYS BREAKING UP WITH GUYS..."
"OH, SHUT UP!"
"WELL, AT ANY RATE...
"CONGRAT-ULATIONS."

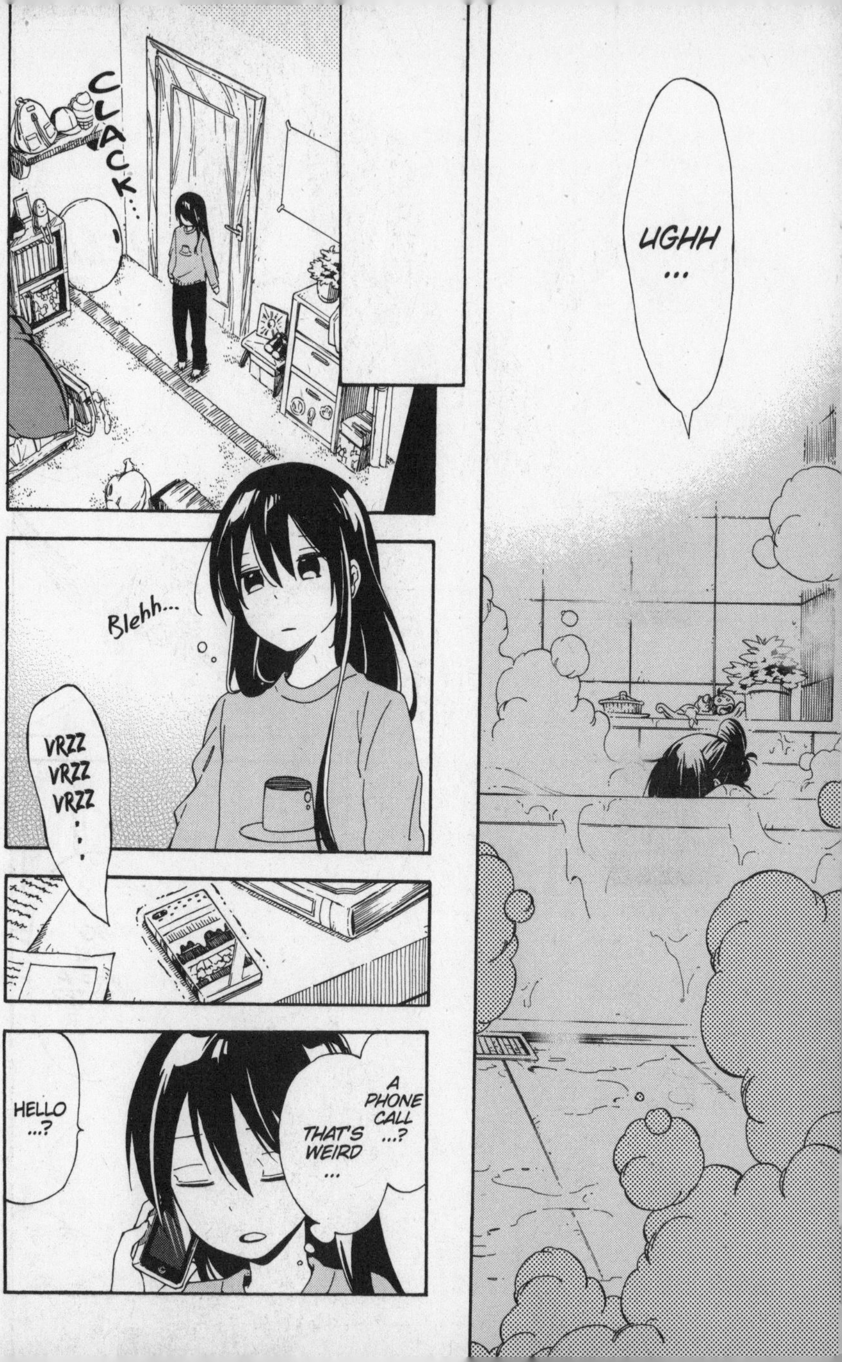
UGHH ...
CLACK...
Blehh...
VRZZ VRZZ VRZZ ...
A PHONE CALL ...?
THAT'S WEIRD ...
HELLO ...?

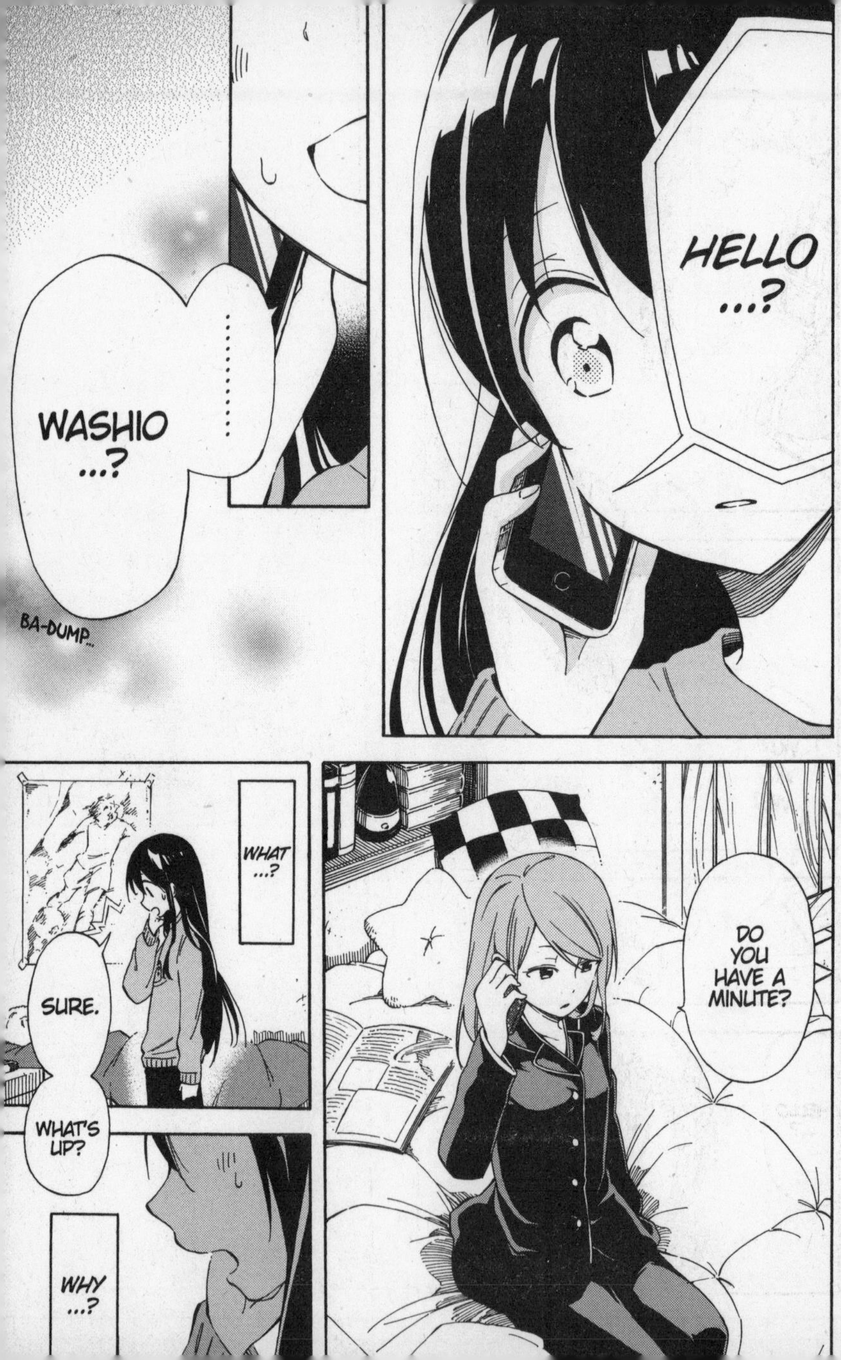
HELLO ...?
......
WASHIO ...?
BA-DUMP...
DO YOU HAVE A MINUTE?
WHAT ...?
SURE.
WHAT'S UP?
WHY ...?

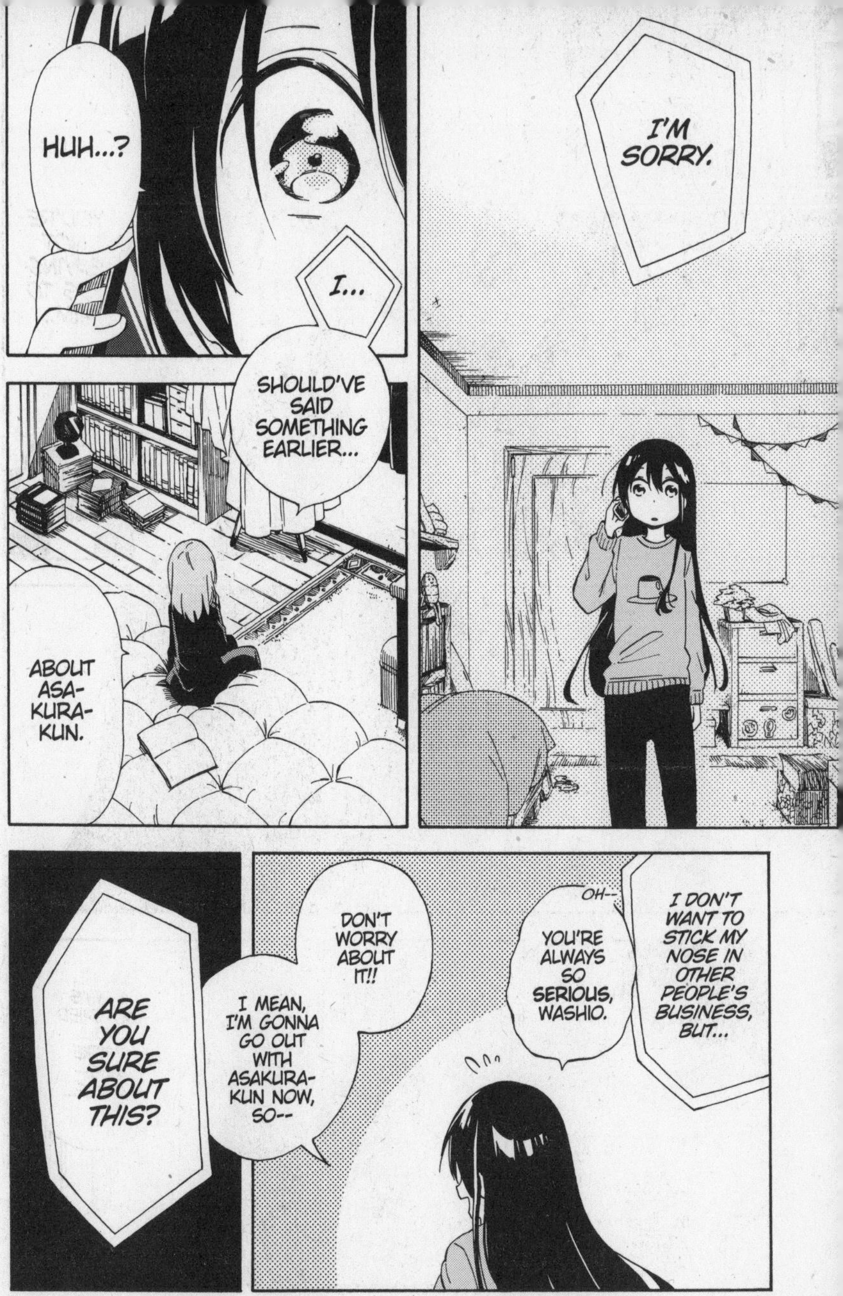
I'M SORRY.
HUH...?
I...
SHOULD'VE SAID SOMETHING EARLIER...
ABOUT ASAKURA-KUN.
I DON'T WANT TO STICK MY NOSE IN OTHER PEOPLE'S BUSINESS, BUT...
OH--
YOU'RE ALWAYS SO SERIOUS, WASHIO.
DON'T WORRY ABOUT IT!!
I MEAN, I'M GONNA GO OUT WITH ASAKURA-KUN NOW, SO--
ARE YOU SURE ABOUT THIS?

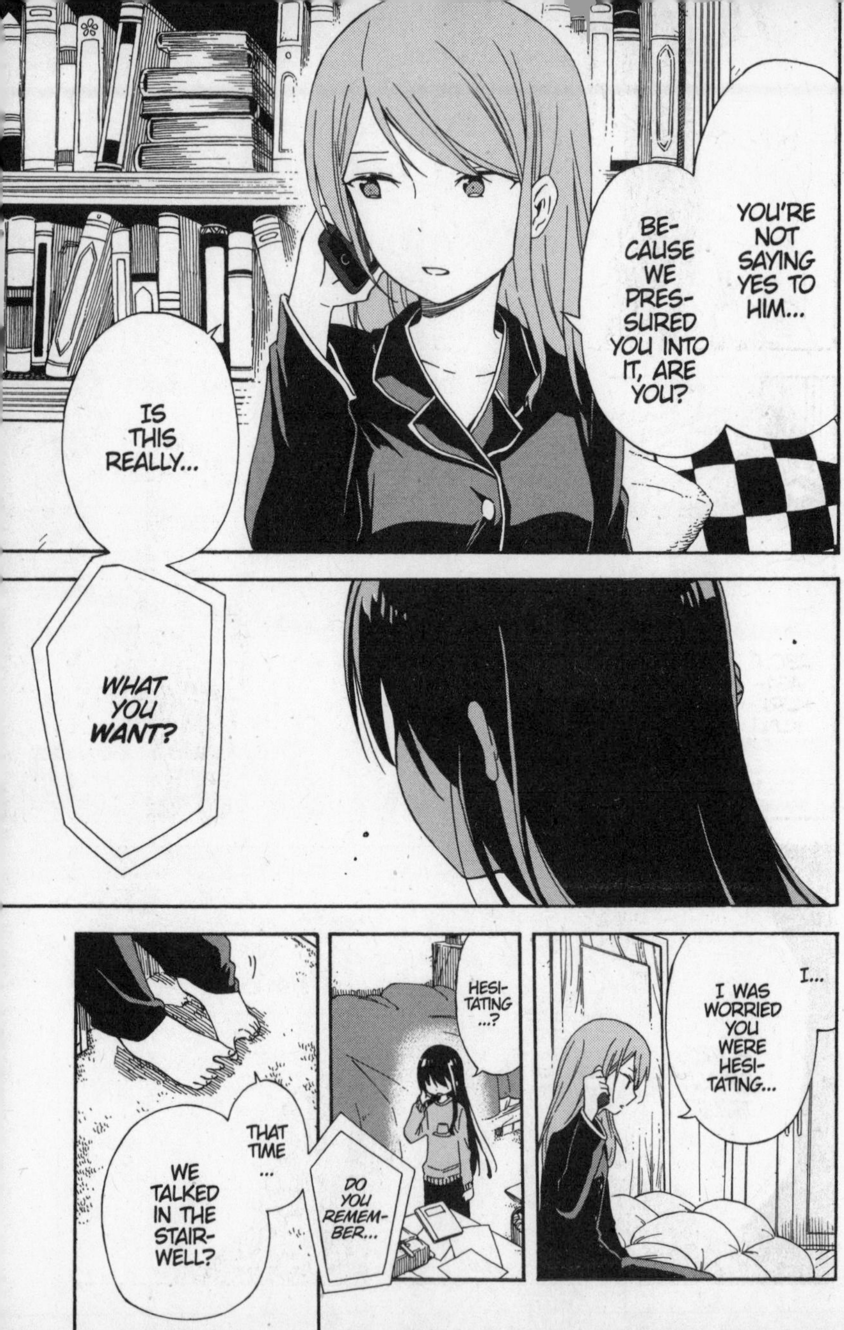
YOU'RE NOT SAYING YES TO HIM...
BECAUSE WE PRESSURED YOU INTO IT, ARE YOU?
IS THIS REALLY...
WHAT YOU WANT?
I...
I WAS WORRIED YOU WERE HESITATING...
HESITATING...?
DO YOU REMEMBER...
THAT TIME...
WE TALKED IN THE STAIRWELL?

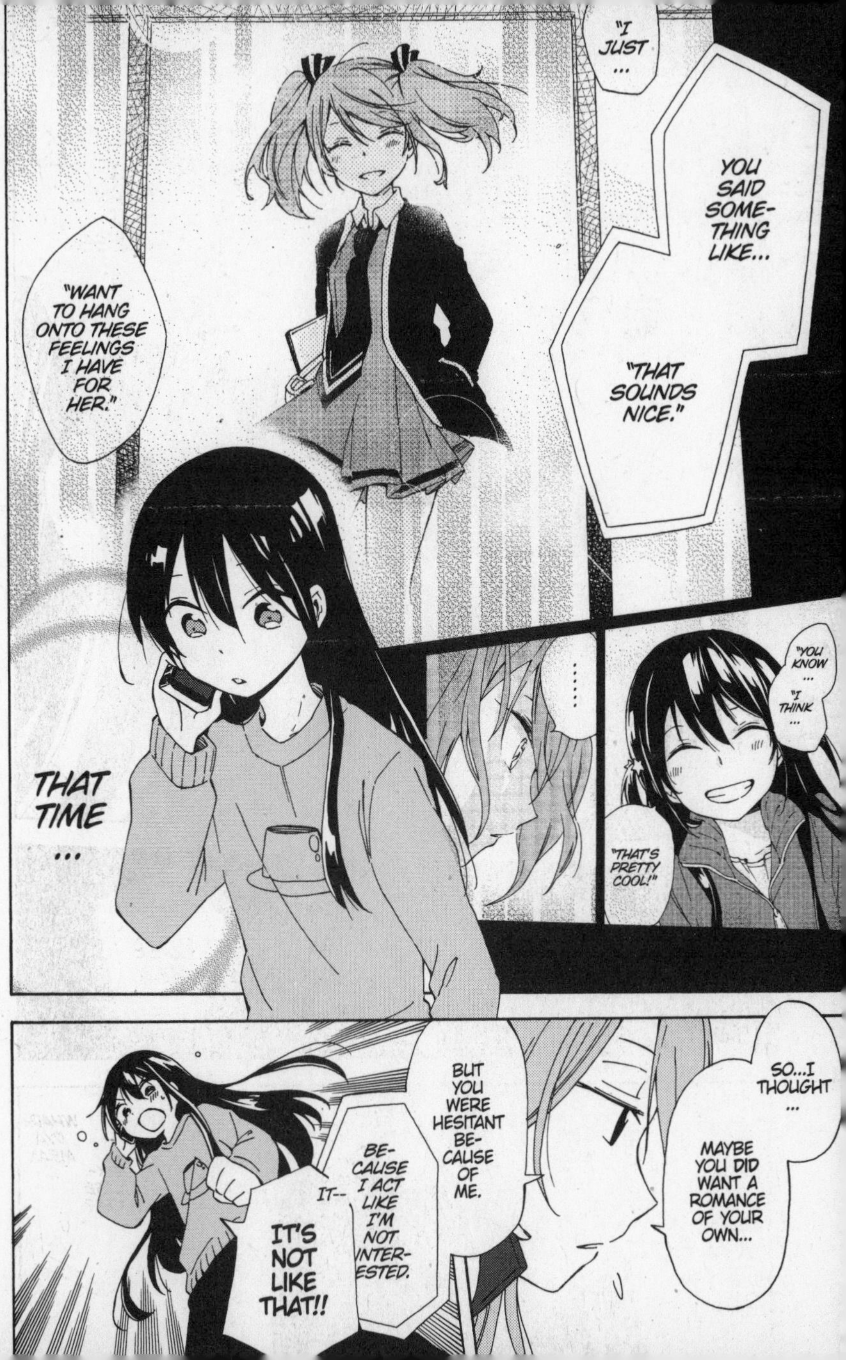
"I JUST ...
YOU SAID SOMETHING LIKE...
"WANT TO HANG ONTO THESE FEELINGS I HAVE FOR HER."
"THAT SOUNDS NICE."
"YOU KNOW ...
"I THINK ...
"THAT'S PRETTY COOL!"
......
THAT TIME ...
SO...I THOUGHT ...
MAYBE YOU DID WANT A ROMANCE OF YOUR OWN...
BUT YOU WERE HESITANT BECAUSE OF ME.
BECAUSE I ACT LIKE I'M NOT INTERESTED.
IT--
IT'S NOT LIKE THAT!!

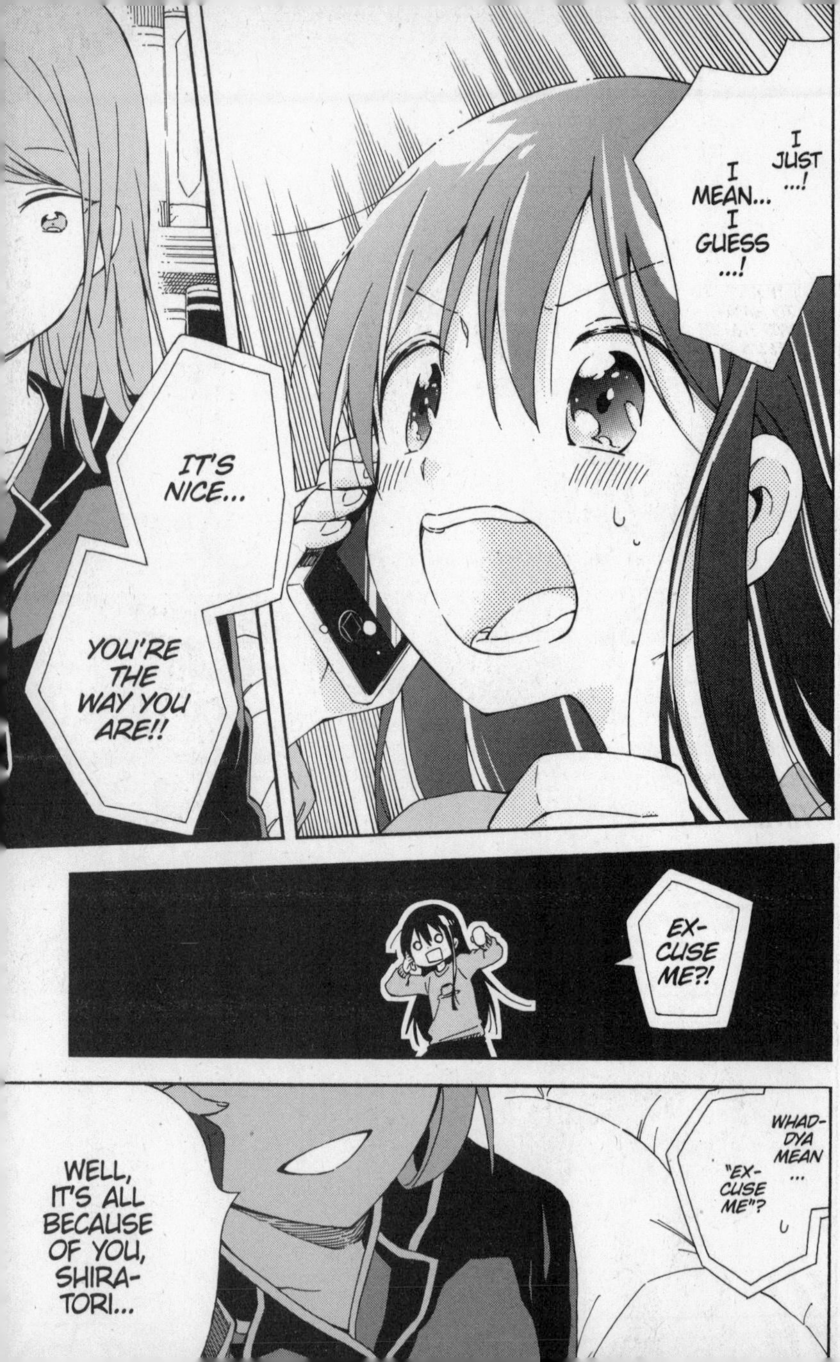
I JUST ...!
I MEAN... I GUESS ...!
IT'S NICE...
YOU'RE THE WAY YOU ARE!!
EX-CUSE ME?!
WHAD-DYA MEAN ... "EX-CUSE ME"?
WELL, IT'S ALL BECAUSE OF YOU, SHIRA-TORI...

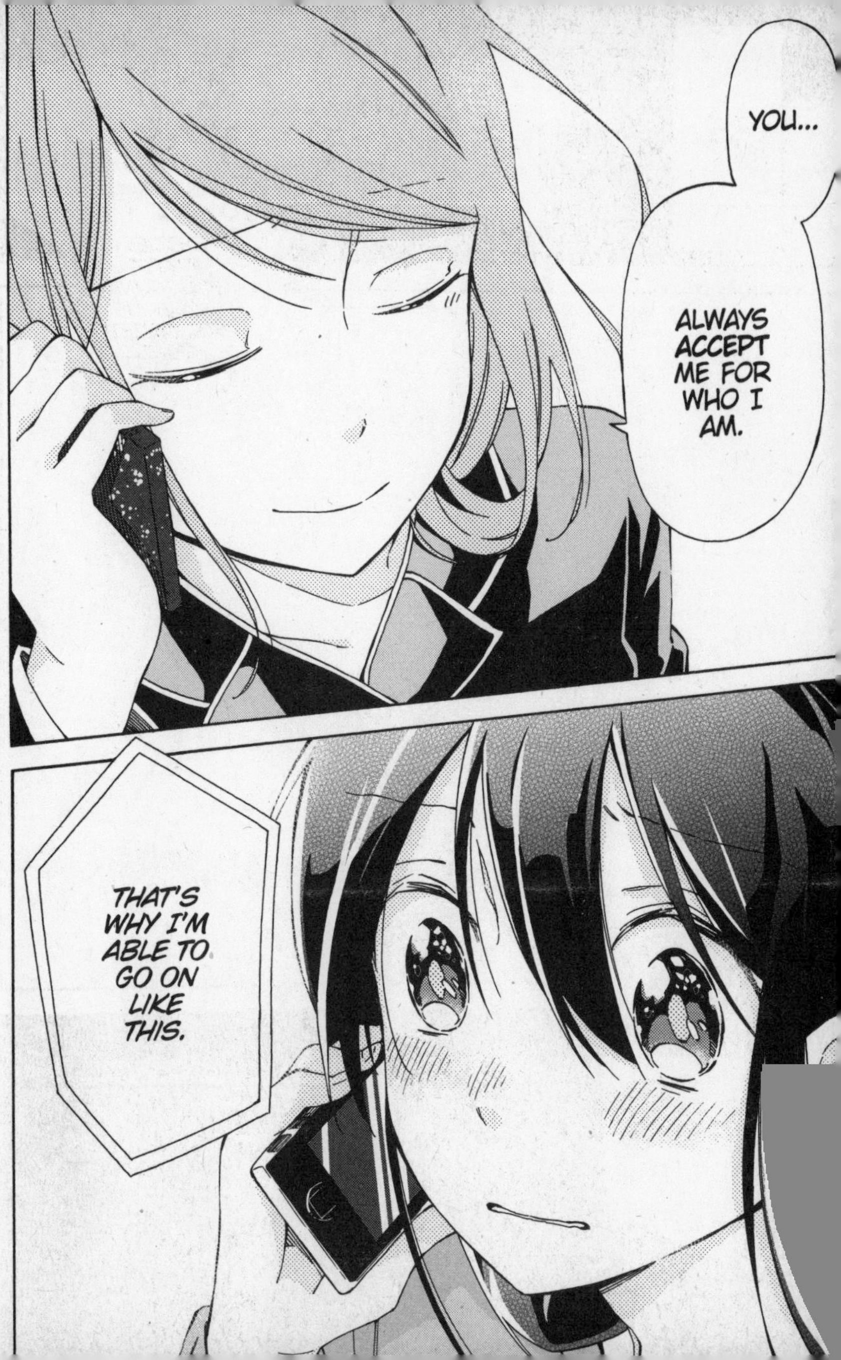
YOU...
ALWAYS ACCEPT ME FOR WHO I AM.
THAT'S WHY I'M ABLE TO GO ON LIKE THIS.

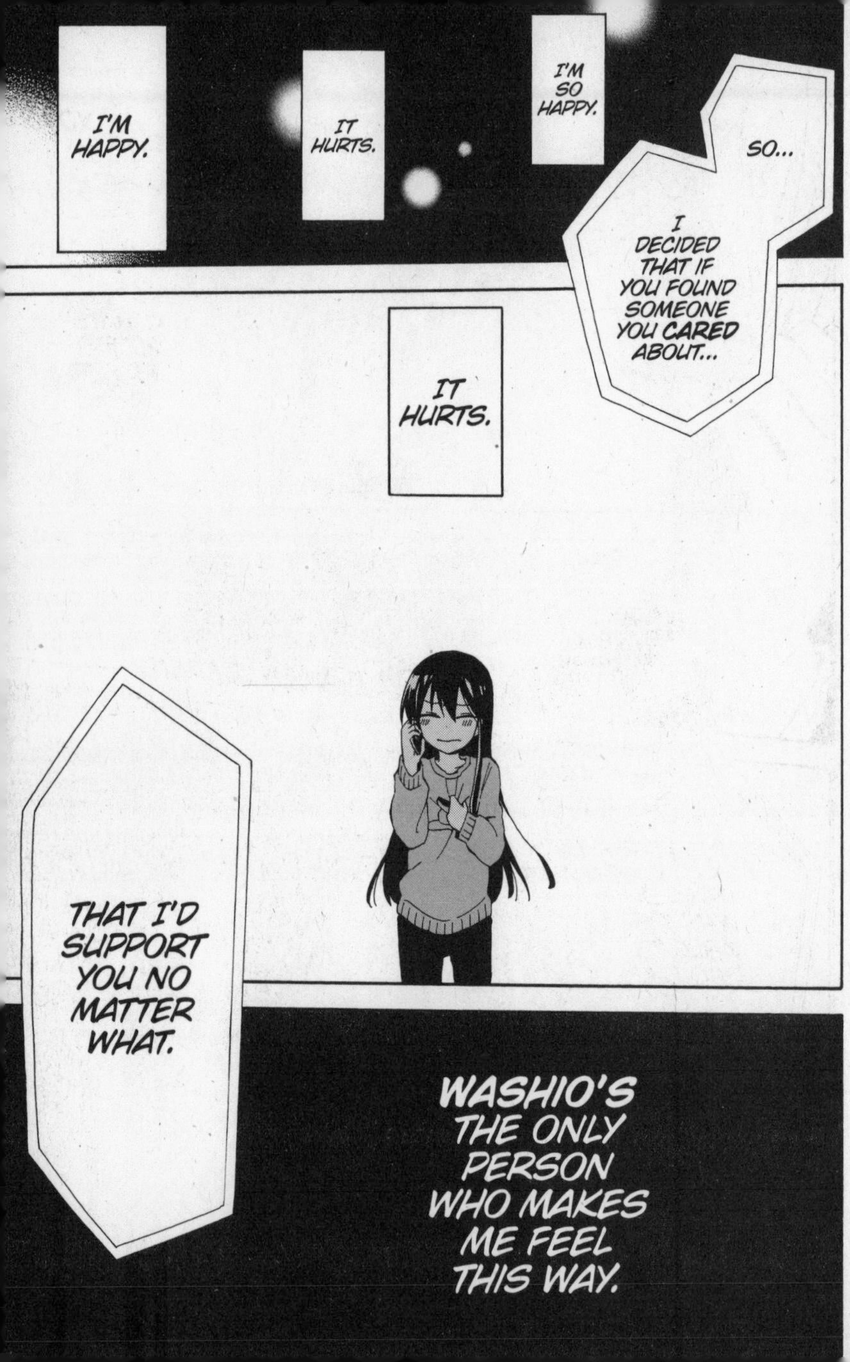
I'M SO HAPPY.
IT HURTS.
I'M HAPPY.
IT HURTS.
SO...
I DECIDED THAT IF YOU FOUND SOMEONE YOU CARED ABOUT...
THAT I'D SUPPORT YOU NO MATTER WHAT.
WASHIO'S THE ONLY PERSON WHO MAKES ME FEEL THIS WAY.

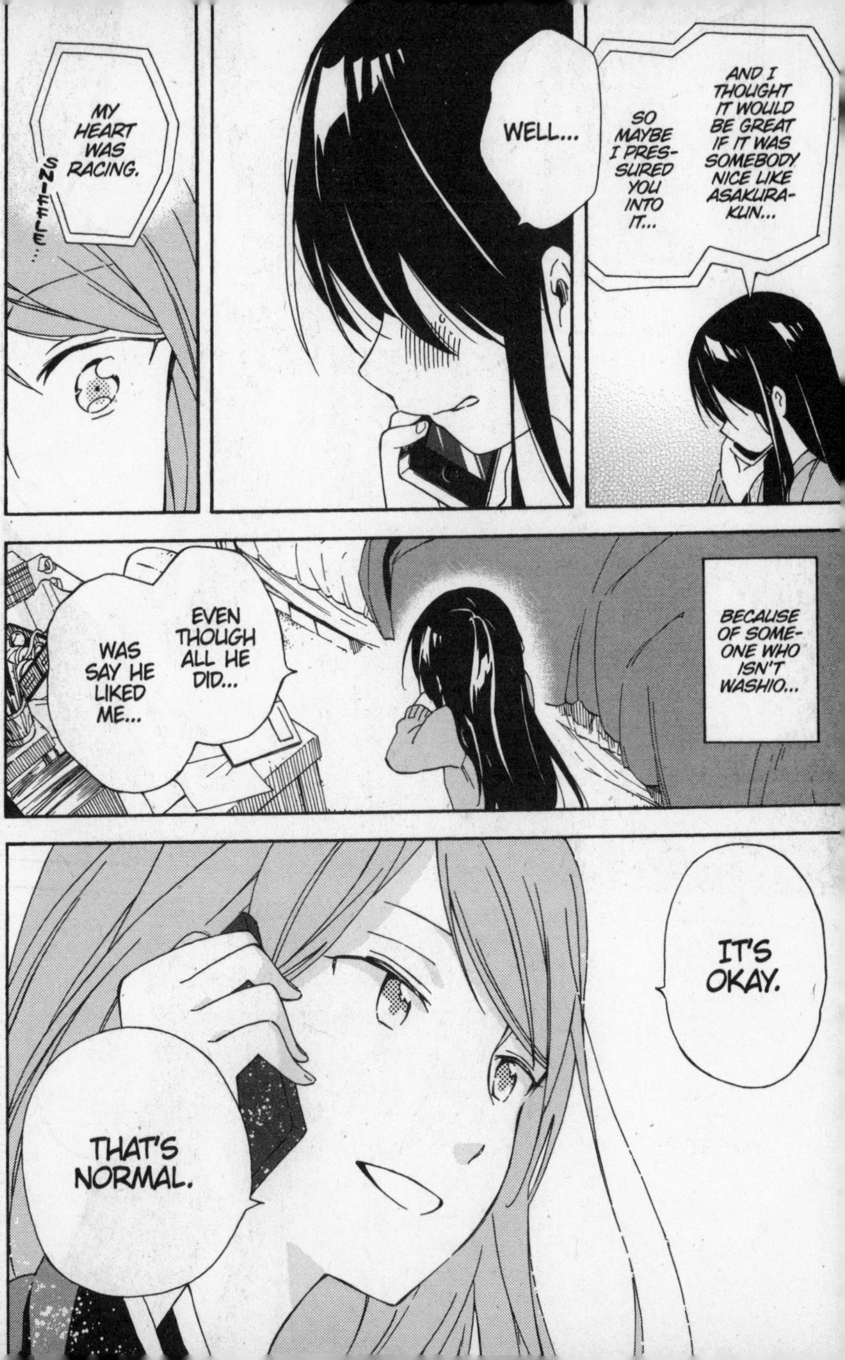
AND I THOUGHT IT WOULD BE GREAT IF IT WAS SOMEBODY NICE LIKE ASAKURA-KUN...
SO MAYBE I PRES-SURED YOU INTO IT...
WELL...
MY HEART WAS RACING.
SNIFFLE...
BECAUSE OF SOME-ONE WHO ISN'T WASHIO...
EVEN THOUGH ALL HE DID...
WAS SAY HE LIKED ME...
IT'S OKAY.
THAT'S NORMAL.

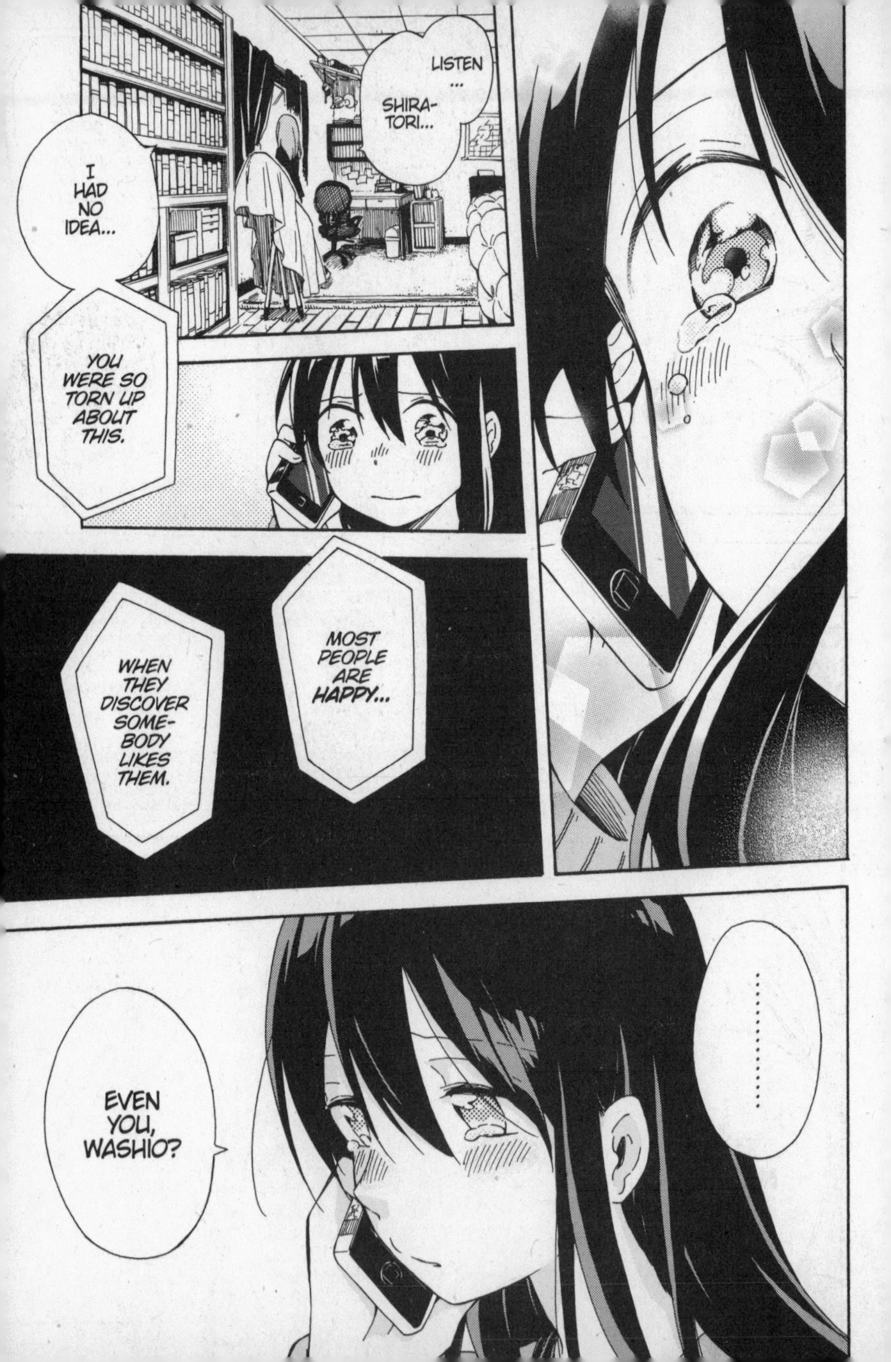
LISTEN... SHIRATORI...
I HAD NO IDEA...
YOU WERE SO TORN UP ABOUT THIS.
MOST PEOPLE ARE HAPPY...
WHEN THEY DISCOVER SOMEBODY LIKES THEM.
......
EVEN YOU, WASHIO?

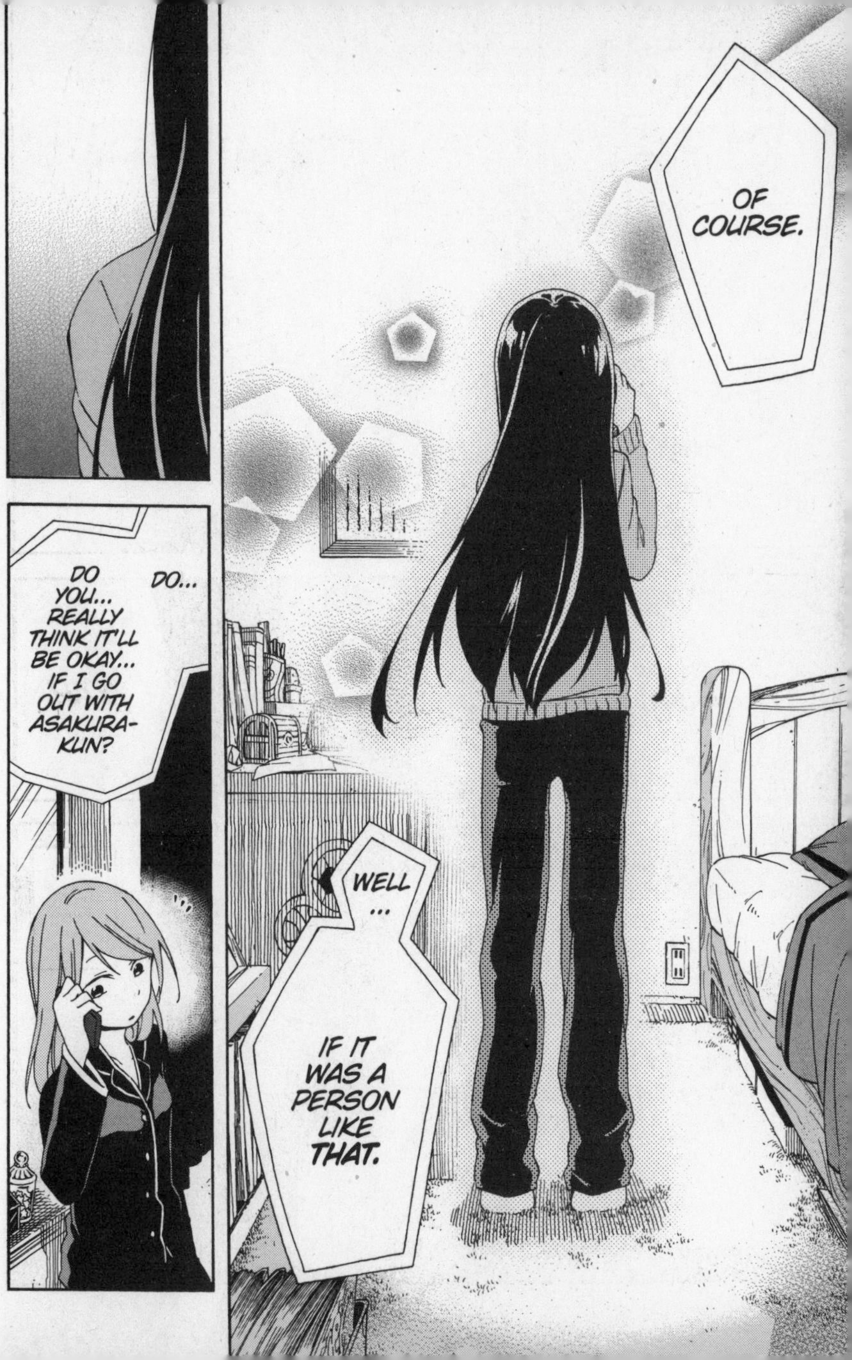
OF COURSE.
WELL...
IF IT WAS A PERSON LIKE THAT.
DO... DO YOU... REALLY THINK IT'LL BE OKAY... IF I GO OUT WITH ASAKURA-KUN?
...

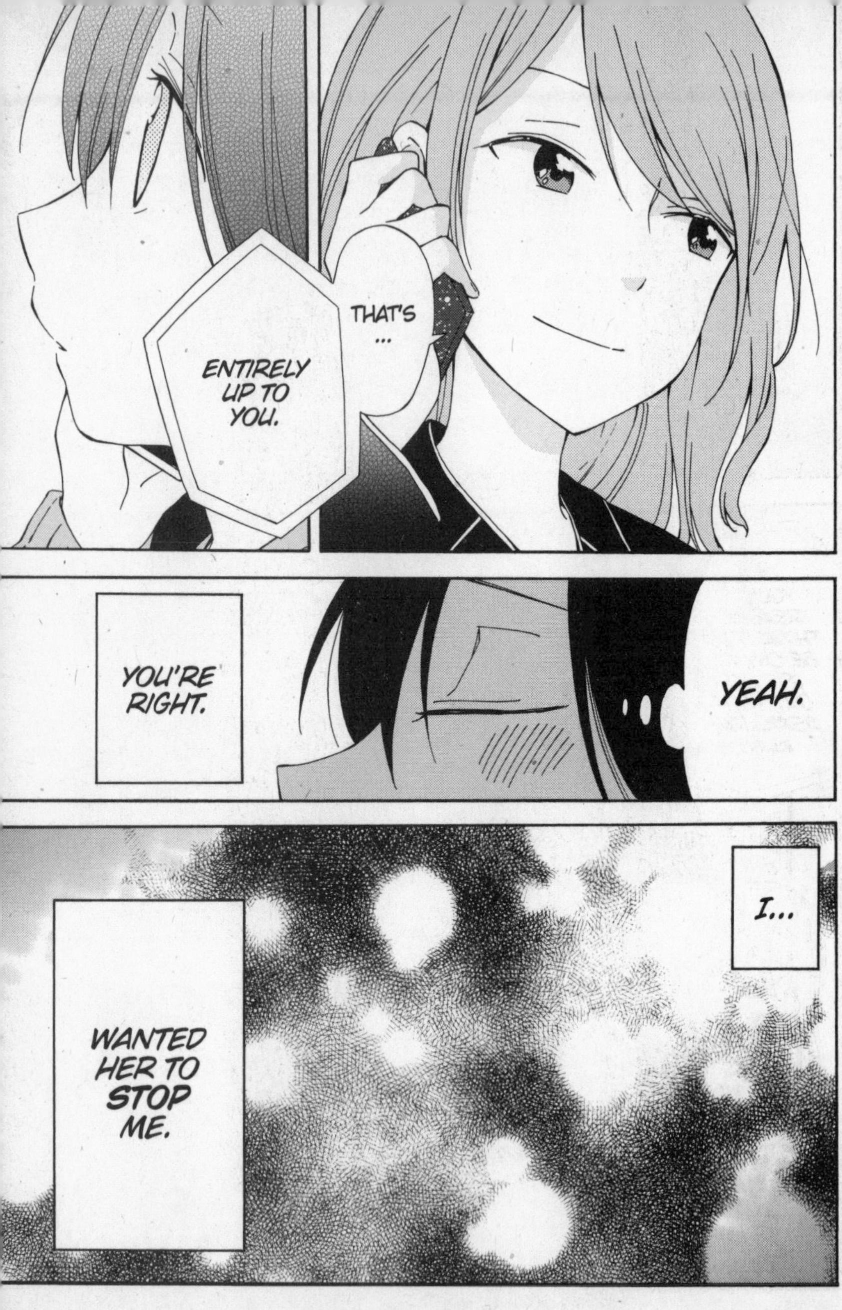
THAT'S ...
ENTIRELY UP TO YOU.
YEAH.
YOU'RE RIGHT.
I...
WANTED HER TO STOP ME.

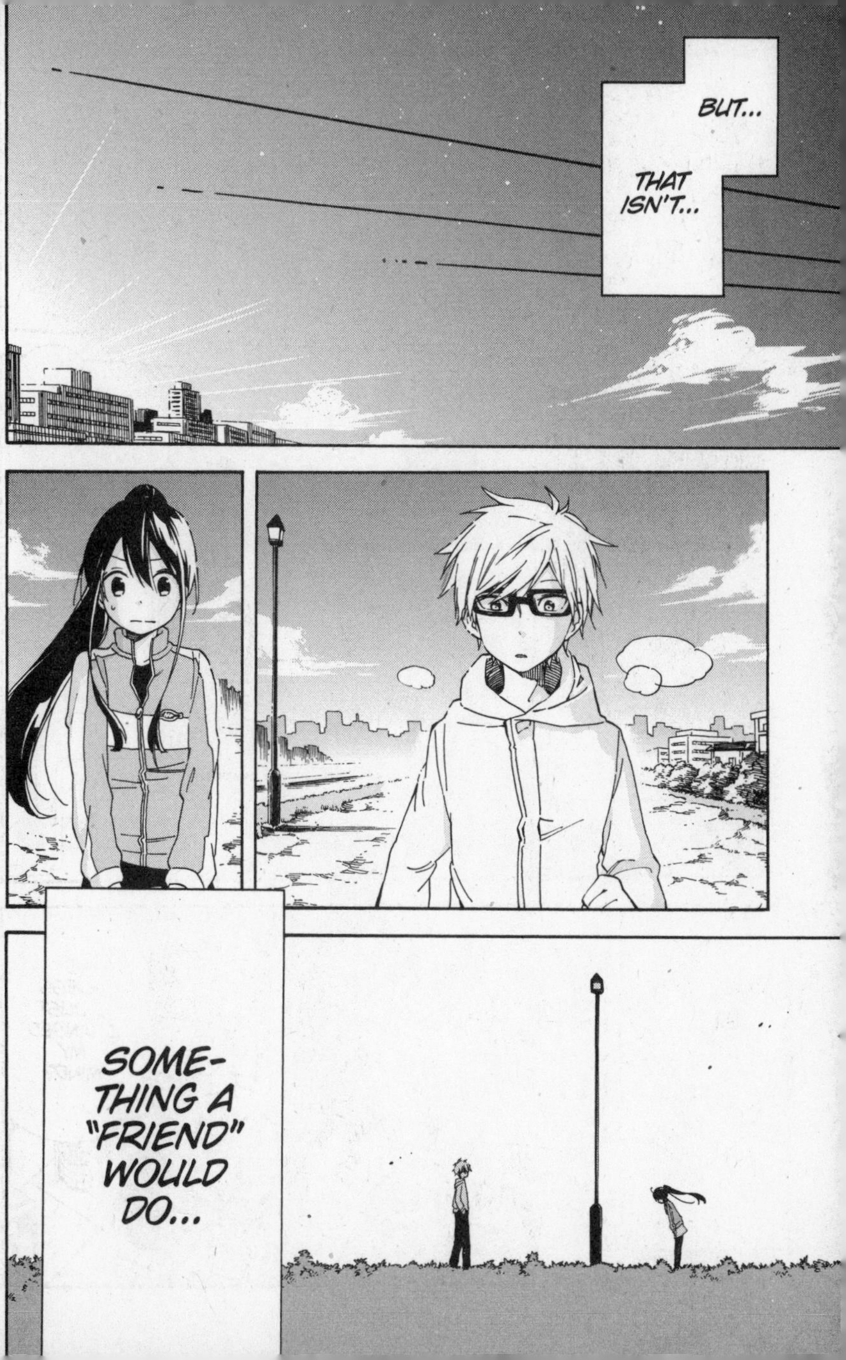
BUT...
THAT ISN'T...
SOME-THING A "FRIEND" WOULD DO...

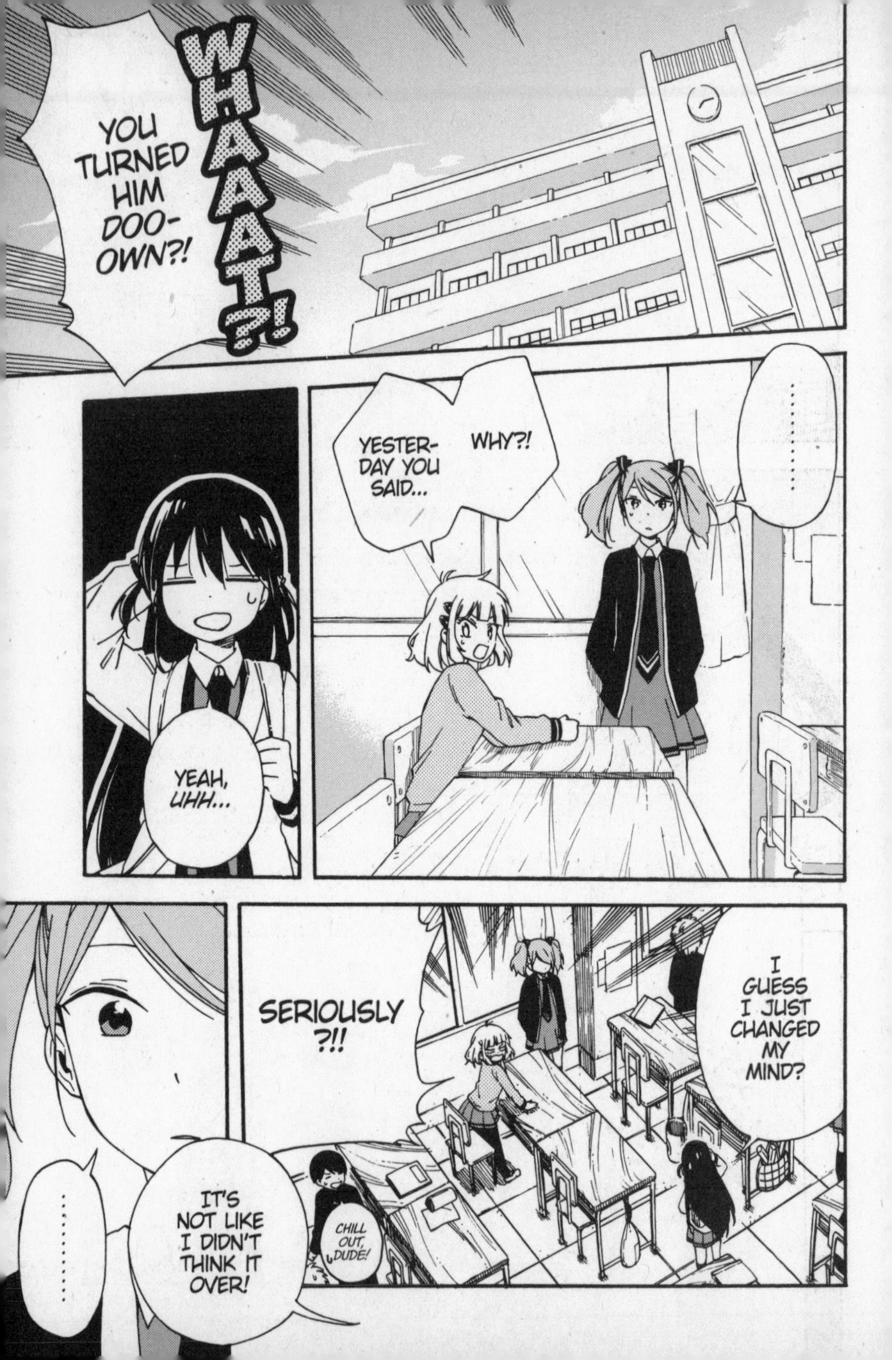
WHAAAT?!
YOU TURNED HIM DOO-OWN?!
......
WHY?!
YESTER-DAY YOU SAID...
YEAH, UHH...
I GUESS I JUST CHANGED MY MIND?
SERIOUSLY?!!
IT'S NOT LIKE I DIDN'T THINK IT OVER!
CHILL OUT, DUDE!
......

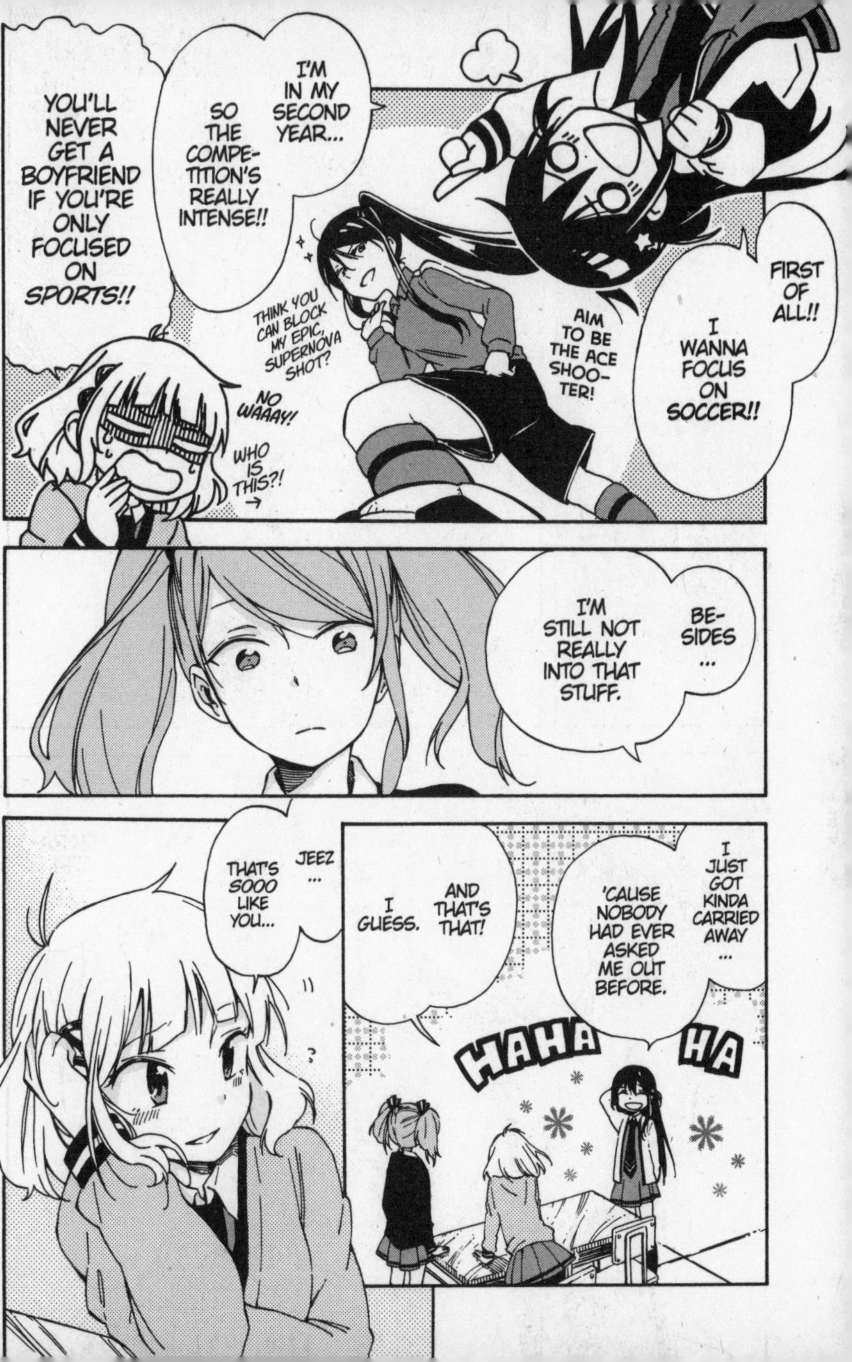
FIRST OF ALL!!
I WANNA FOCUS ON SOCCER!!
AIM TO BE THE ACE SHOOTER!
I'M IN MY SECOND YEAR...
SO THE COMPETITION'S REALLY INTENSE!!
THINK YOU CAN BLOCK MY EPIC, SUPERNOVA SHOT?
YOU'LL NEVER GET A BOYFRIEND IF YOU'RE ONLY FOCUSED ON SPORTS!!
NO WAAAY!
WHO IS THIS?!
BESIDES...
I'M STILL NOT REALLY INTO THAT STUFF.
I JUST GOT KINDA CARRIED AWAY...
'CAUSE NOBODY HAD EVER ASKED ME OUT BEFORE.
AND THAT'S THAT!
I GUESS.
HAHA
HA
JEEZ...
THAT'S SOOO LIKE YOU...

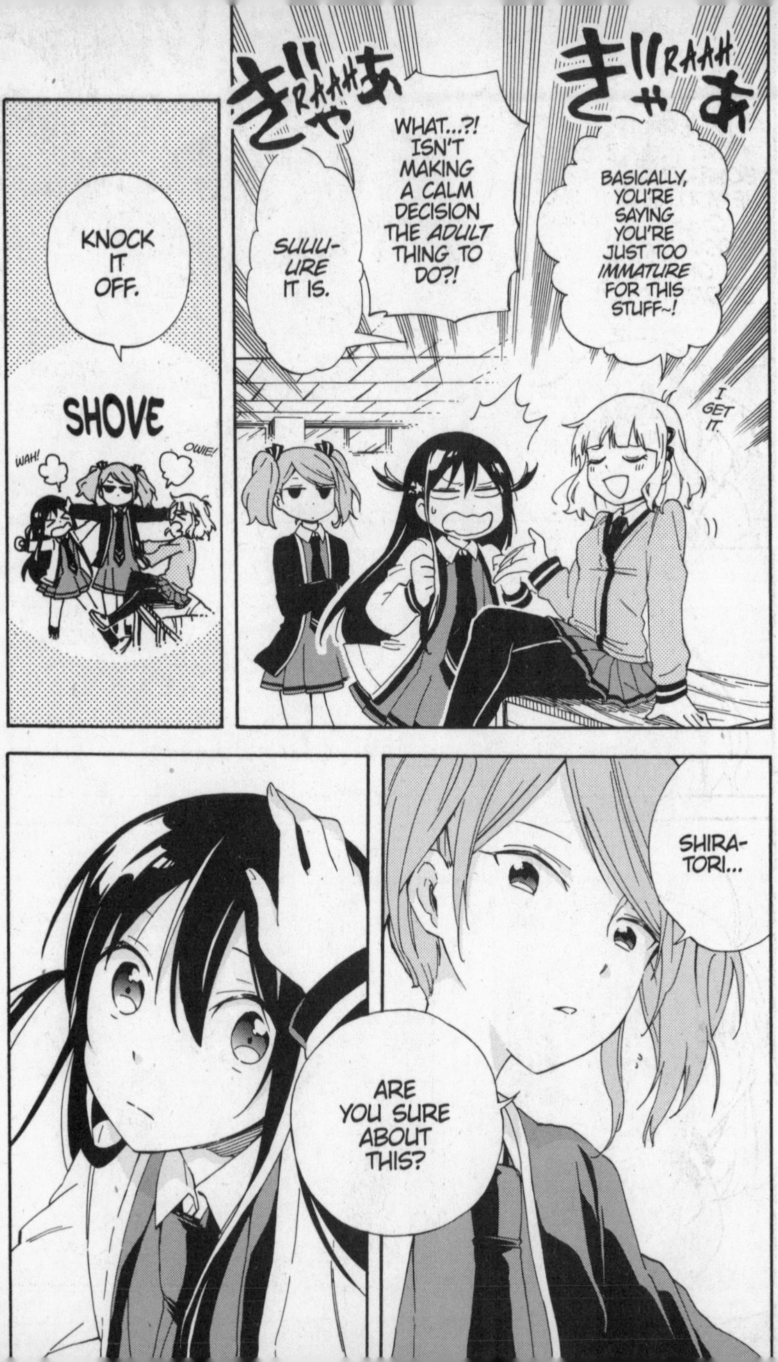
きゃあ
RAAH
BASICALLY, YOU'RE SAYING YOU'RE JUST TOO *IMMATURE* FOR THIS STUFF~!
WHAT...?! ISN'T MAKING A CALM DECISION THE *ADULT* THING TO DO?!
きゃあ
RAAH
SUUU-URE IT IS.
I GET IT.
KNOCK IT OFF.
SHOVE
OWIE!
WAH!
SHIRA-TORI...
ARE YOU SURE ABOUT THIS?

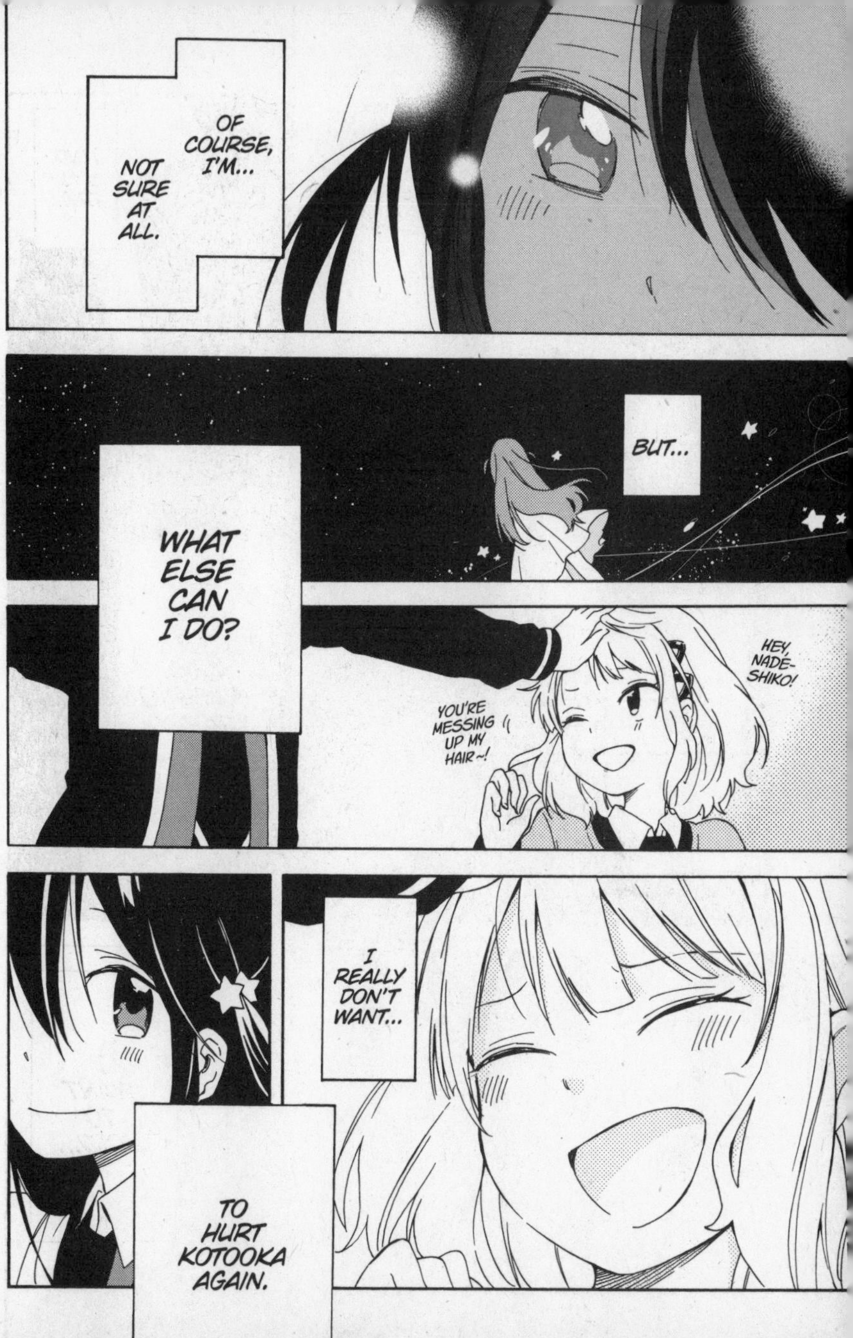
OF COURSE, I'M...
NOT SURE AT ALL.
BUT...
WHAT ELSE CAN I DO?
HEY, NADE-SHIKO!
YOU'RE MESSING UP MY HAIR~!
I REALLY DON'T WANT...
TO HURT KOTOOKA AGAIN.

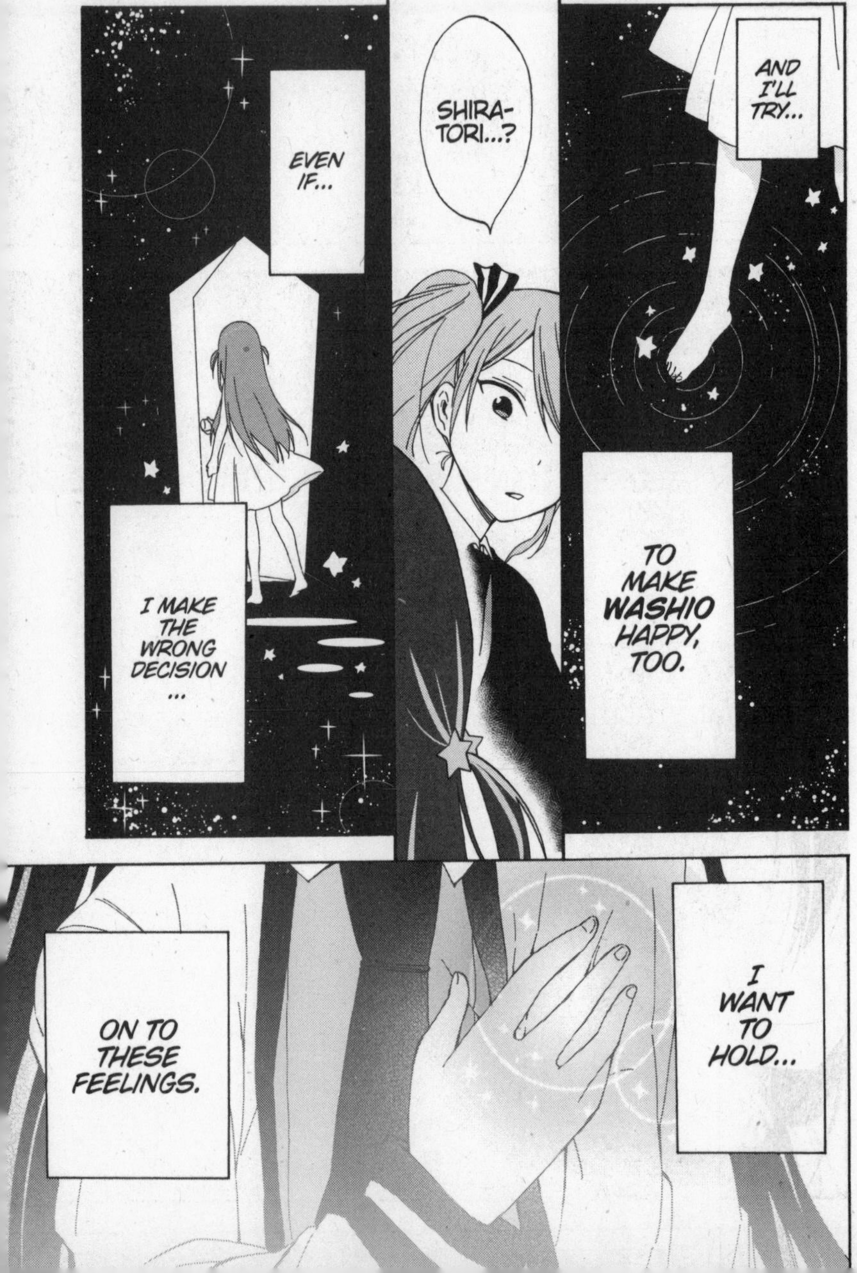
AND I'LL TRY...
TO MAKE WASHIO HAPPY, TOO.
SHIRA-TORI...?
EVEN IF...
I MAKE THE WRONG DECISION...
I WANT TO HOLD...
ON TO THESE FEELINGS.

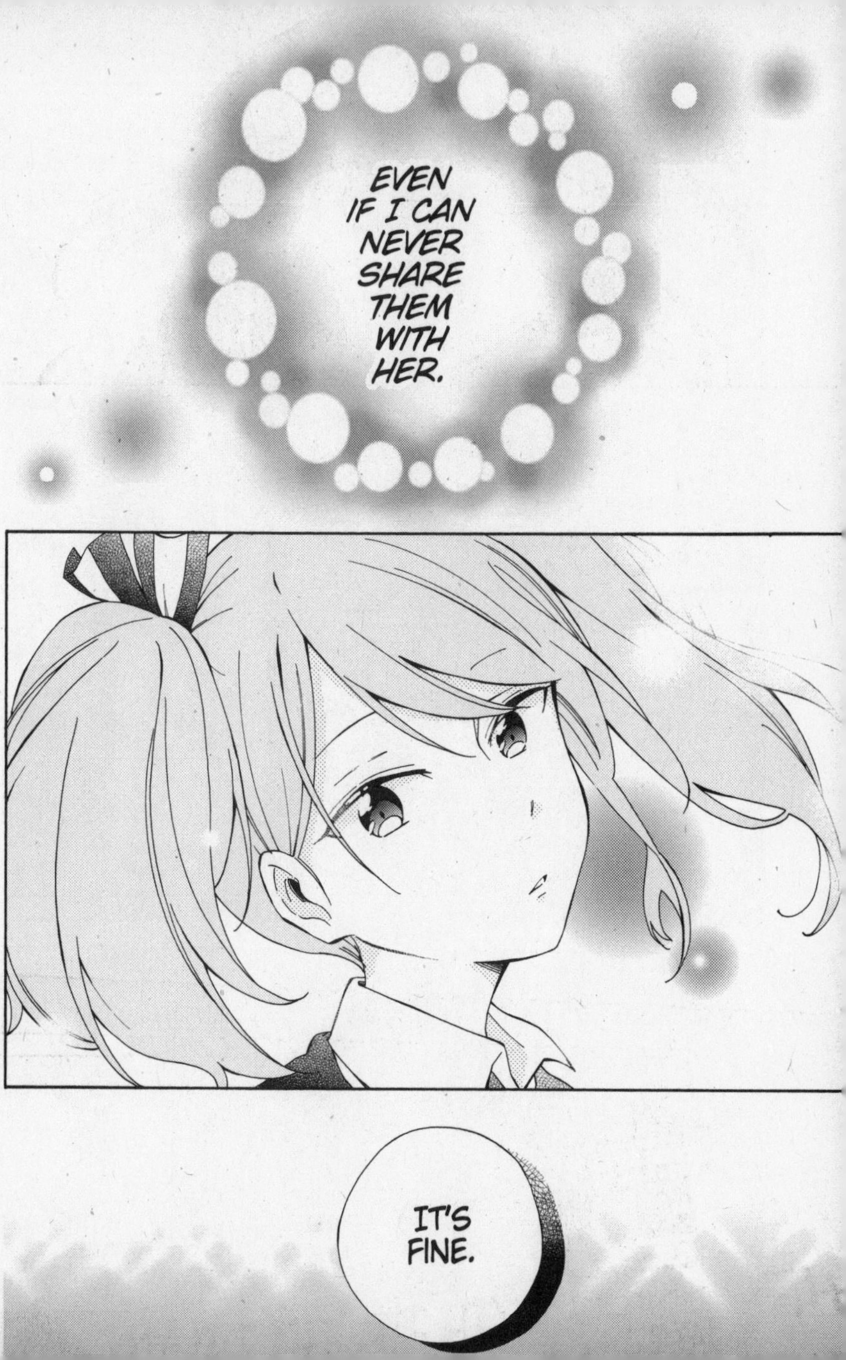
EVEN IF I CAN NEVER SHARE THEM WITH HER.
IT'S FINE.

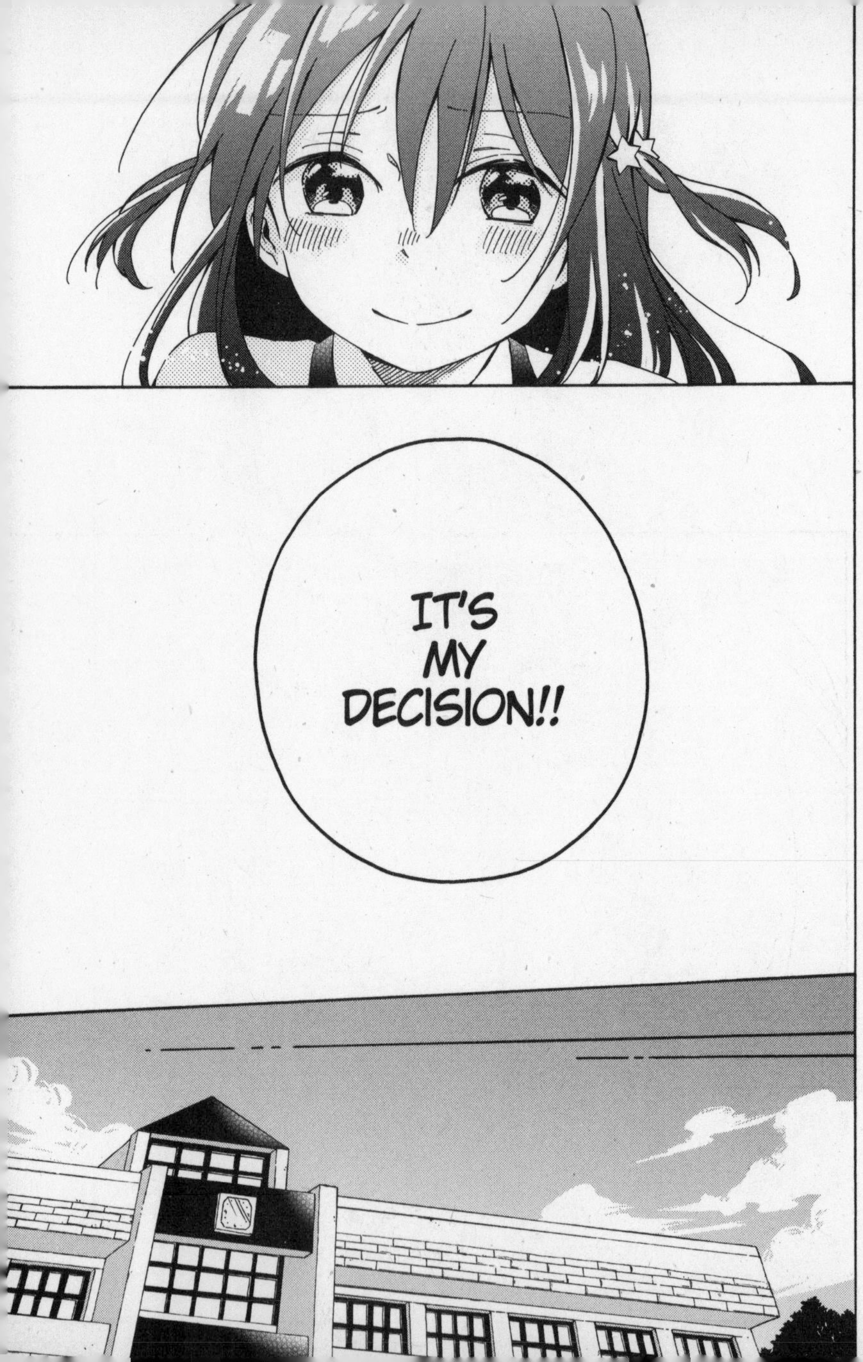
IT'S MY DECISION!!

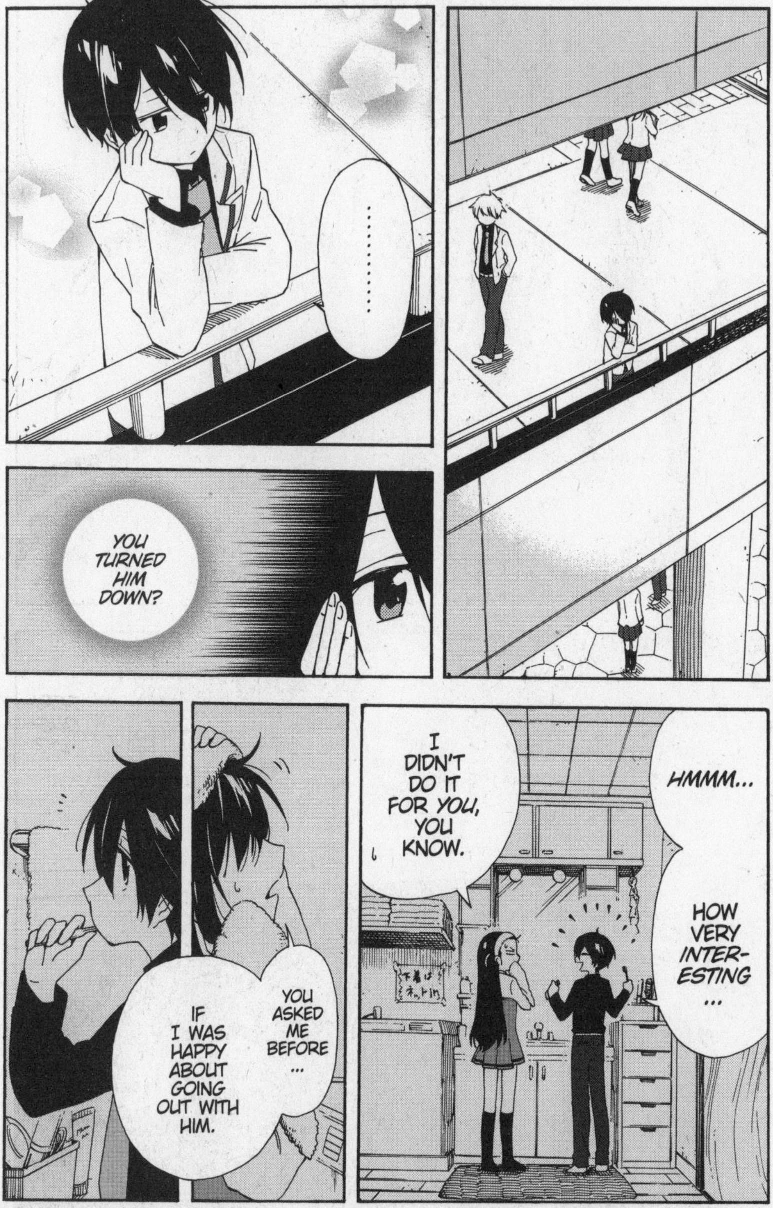
......
YOU TURNED HIM DOWN?
HMMM...
I DIDN'T DO IT FOR YOU, YOU KNOW.
HOW VERY INTER-ESTING ...
YOU ASKED ME BEFORE ...
IF I WAS HAPPY ABOUT GOING OUT WITH HIM.

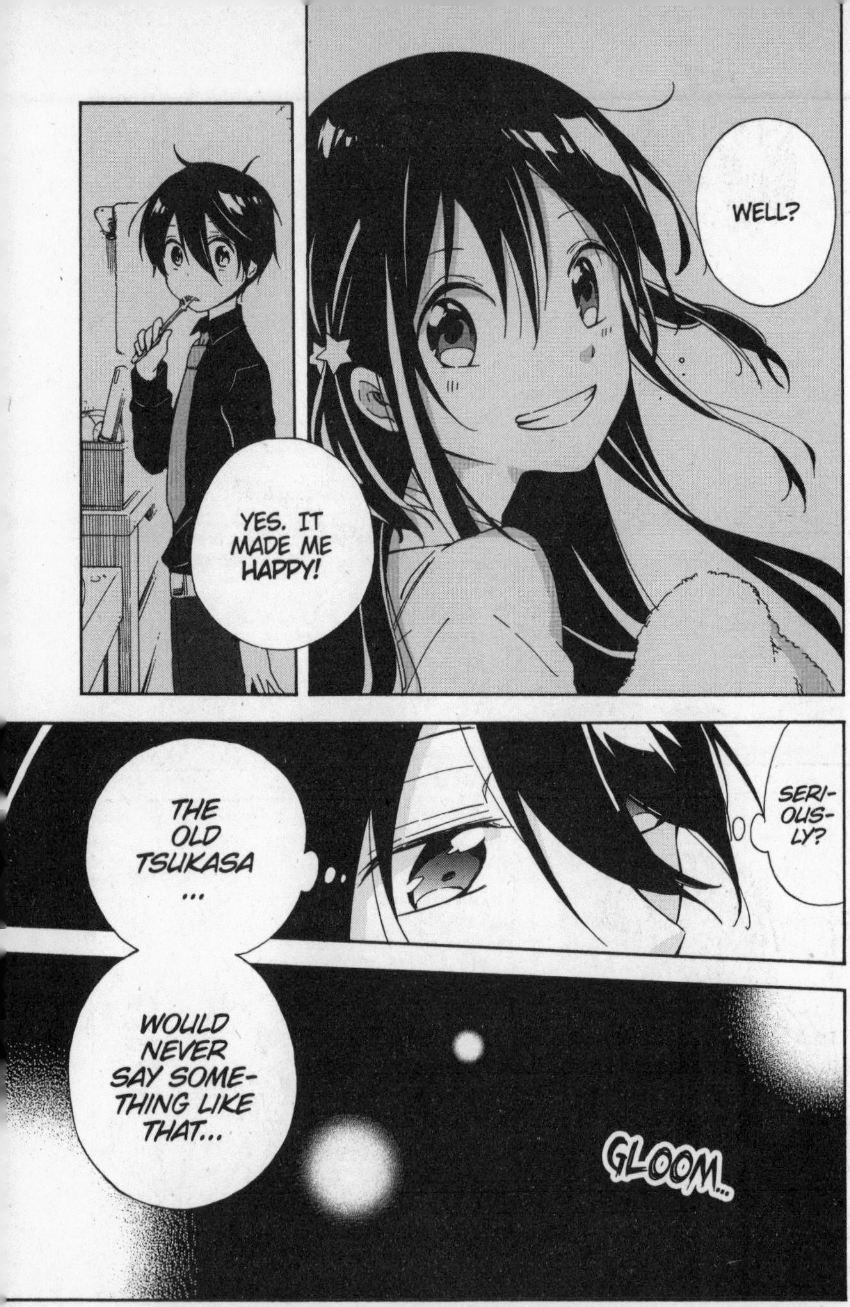
WELL?
YES. IT MADE ME HAPPY!
SERI-OUS-LY?
THE OLD TSUKASA ...
WOULD NEVER SAY SOME-THING LIKE THAT...
GLOOM...

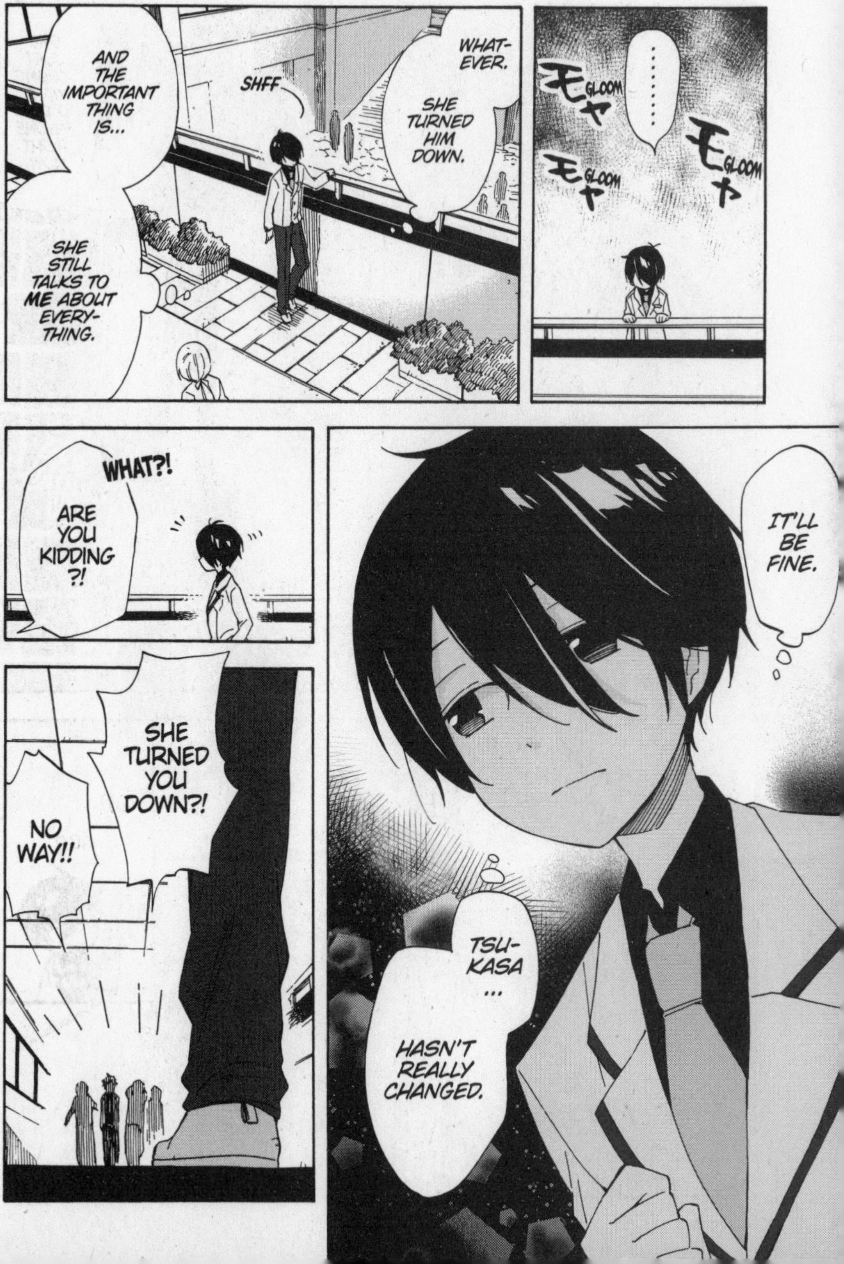
......
モヤ GLOOM
モヤ GLOOM
モヤ GLOOM
WHAT-EVER. SHE TURNED HIM DOWN.
SHFF
AND THE IMPORTANT THING IS... SHE STILL TALKS TO ME ABOUT EVERY-THING.
IT'LL BE FINE.
TSU-KASA... HASN'T REALLY CHANGED.
WHAT?!
ARE YOU KIDDING?!
SHE TURNED YOU DOWN?!
NO WAY!!

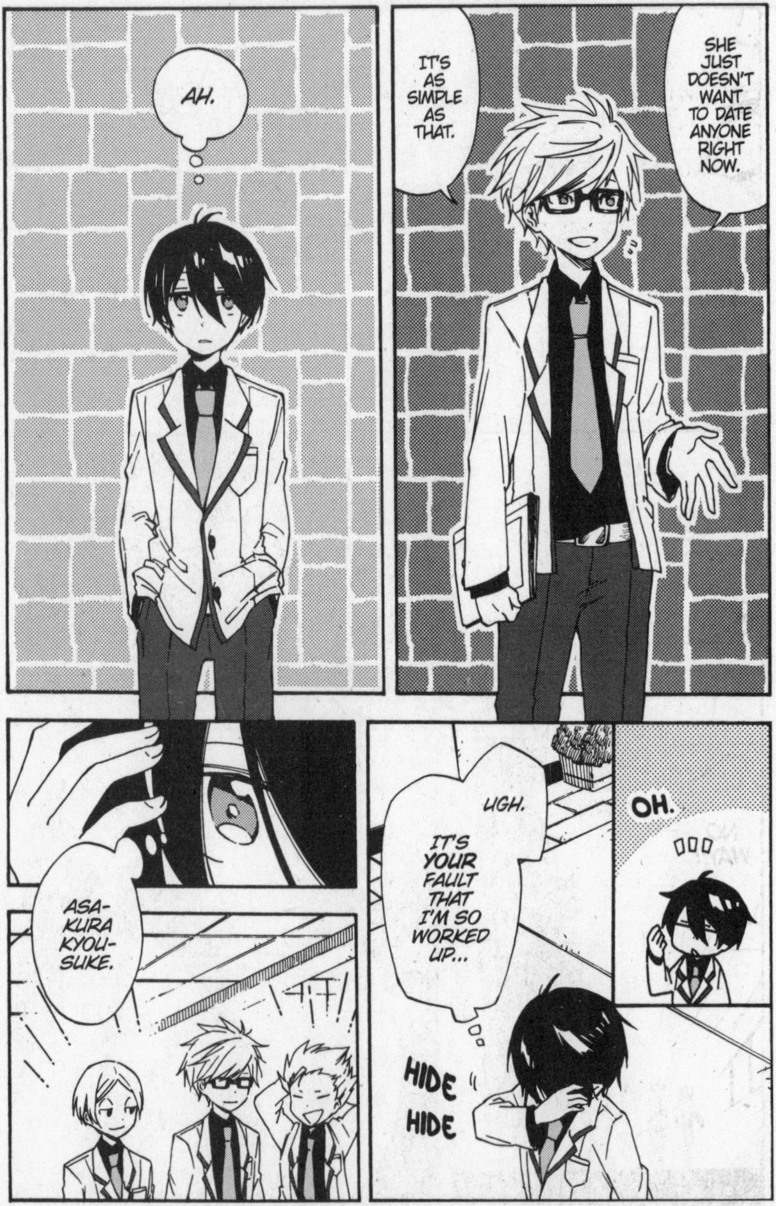
SHE JUST DOESN'T WANT TO DATE ANYONE RIGHT NOW.
IT'S AS SIMPLE AS THAT.
AH.
OH.
UGH.
IT'S YOUR FAULT THAT I'M SO WORKED UP...
HIDE HIDE
ASA-KURA KYOU-SUKE.

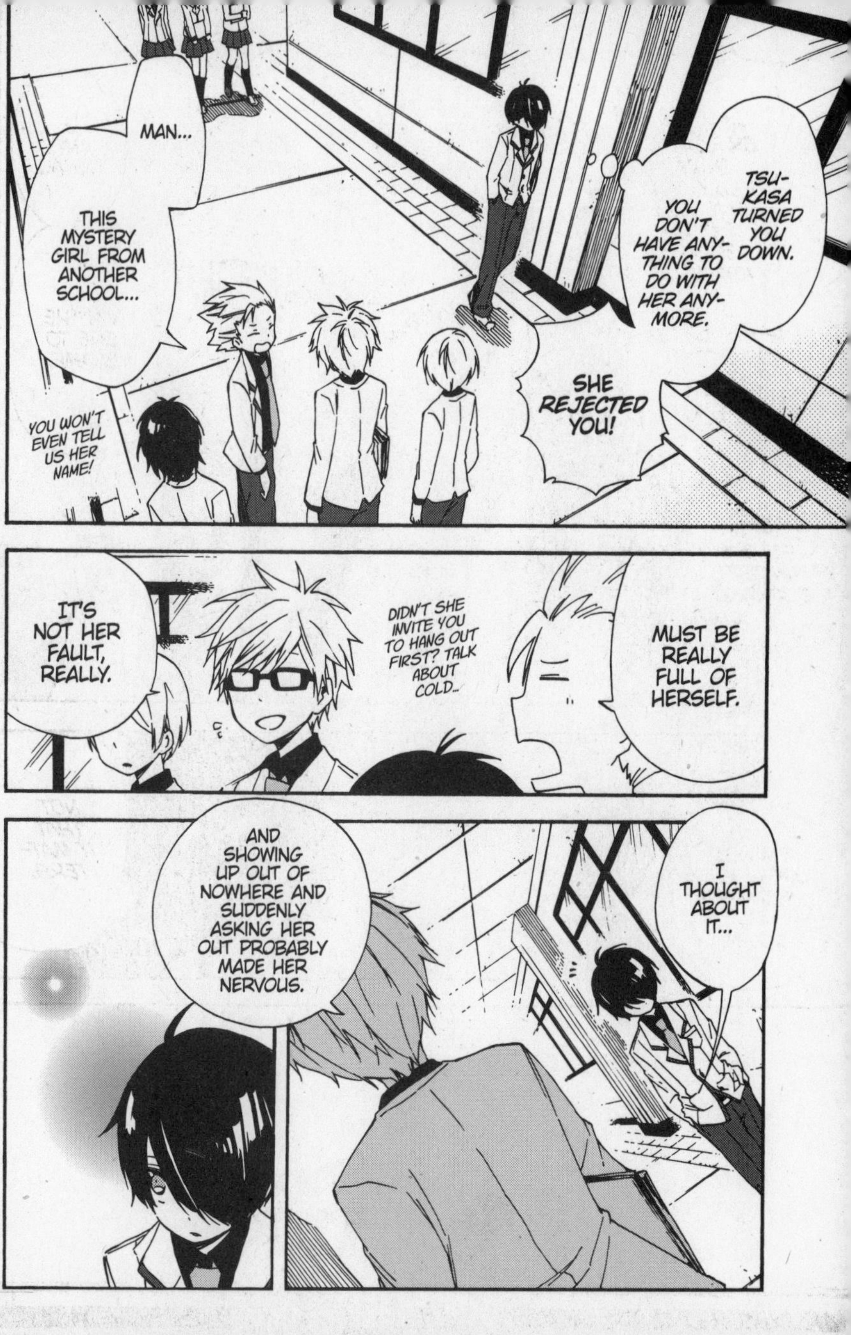
TSU-KASA TURNED YOU DOWN.
YOU DON'T HAVE ANY-THING TO DO WITH HER ANY-MORE.
SHE REJECTED YOU!
MAN...
THIS MYSTERY GIRL FROM ANOTHER SCHOOL...
YOU WON'T EVEN TELL US HER NAME!
MUST BE REALLY FULL OF HERSELF.
DIDN'T SHE INVITE YOU TO HANG OUT FIRST? TALK ABOUT COLD...
IT'S NOT HER FAULT, REALLY.
I THOUGHT ABOUT IT...
AND SHOWING UP OUT OF NOWHERE AND SUDDENLY ASKING HER OUT PROBABLY MADE HER NERVOUS.

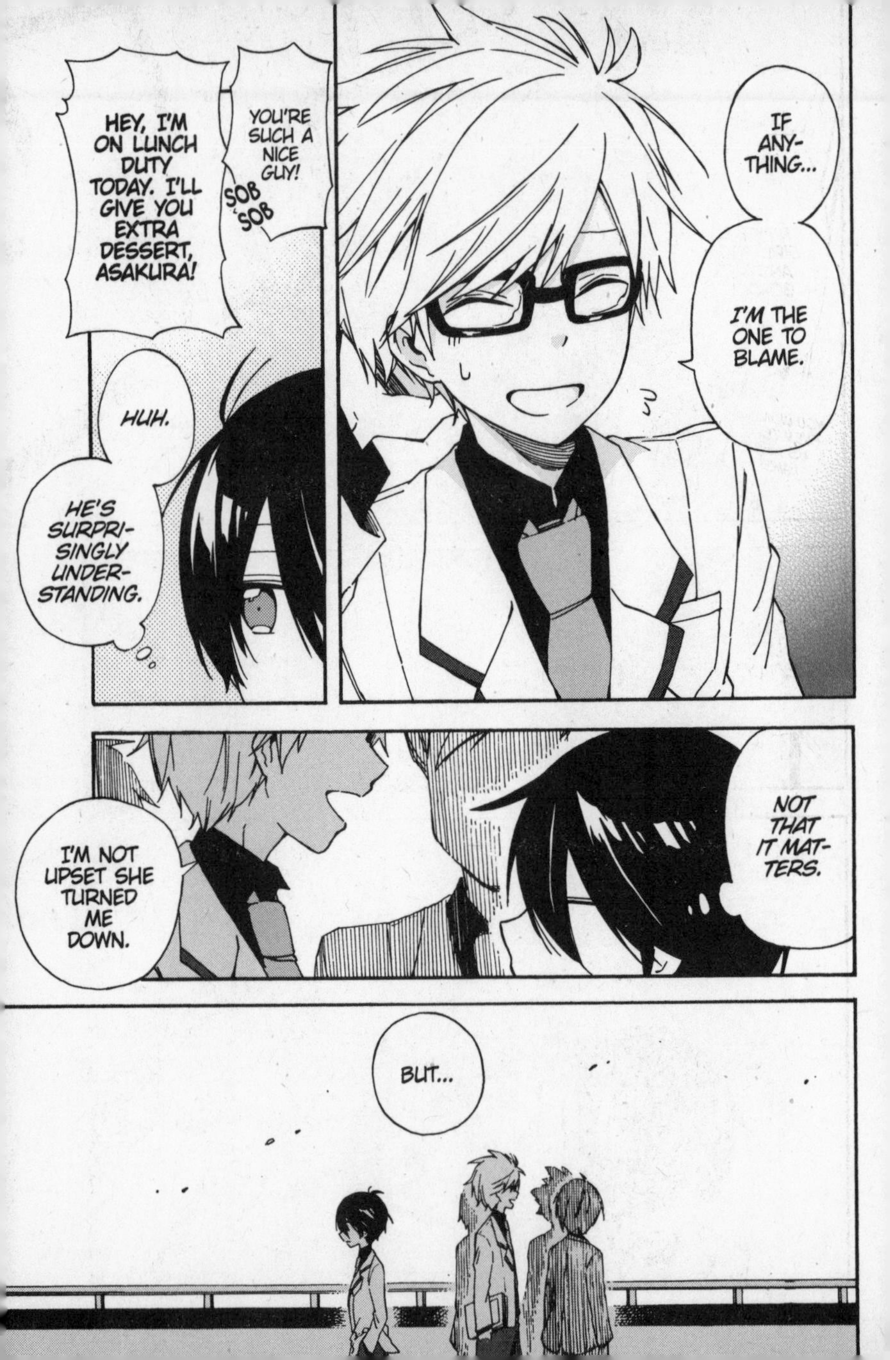
IF ANYTHING...
I'M THE ONE TO BLAME.
YOU'RE SUCH A NICE GUY!
SOB SOB
HEY, I'M ON LUNCH DUTY TODAY. I'LL GIVE YOU EXTRA DESSERT, ASAKURA!
HUH.
HE'S SURPRISINGLY UNDERSTANDING.
NOT THAT IT MATTERS.
I'M NOT UPSET SHE TURNED ME DOWN.
BUT...

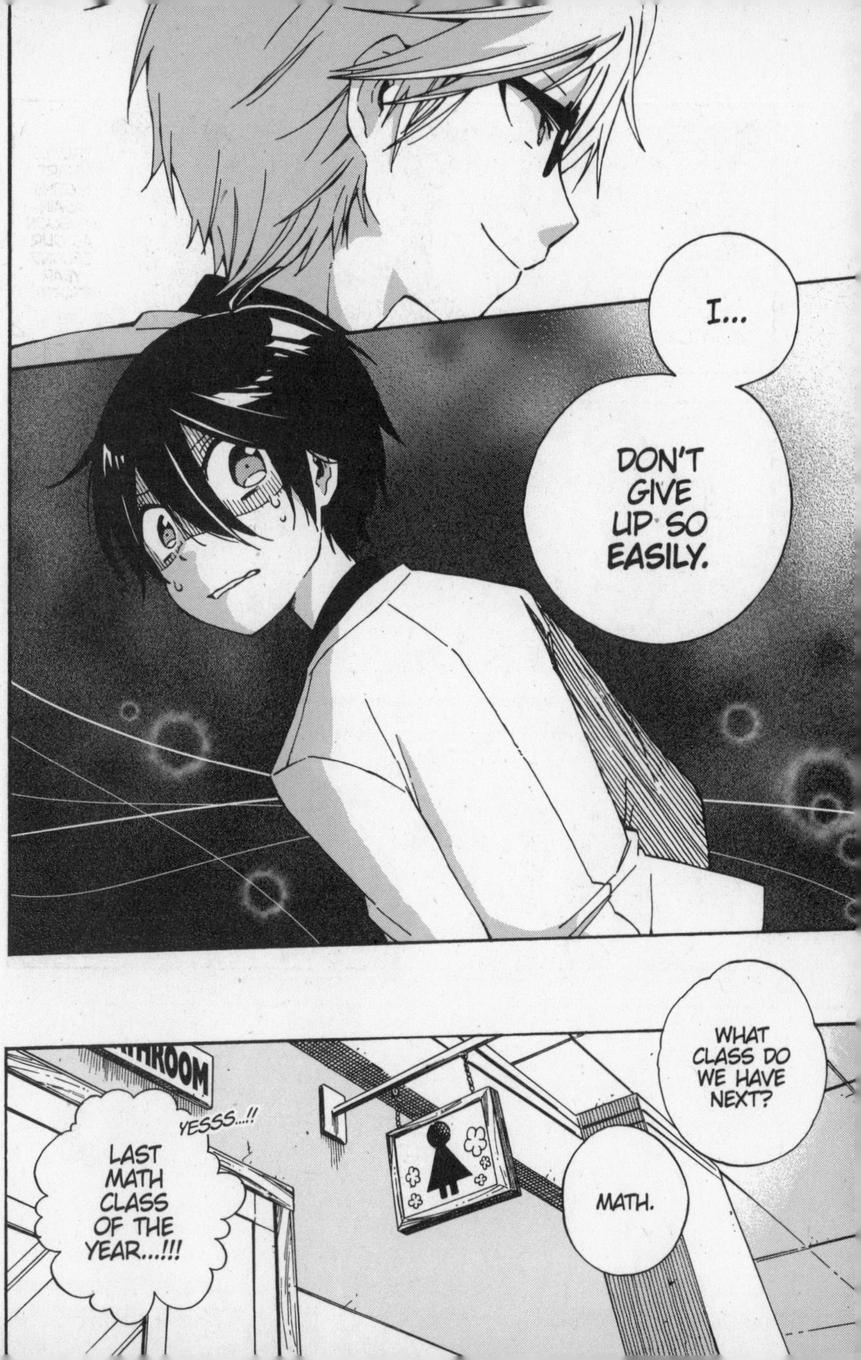
I...
DON'T GIVE UP SO EASILY.
WHAT CLASS DO WE HAVE NEXT?
MATH.
YESSS...!!
LAST MATH CLASS OF THE YEAR...!!!

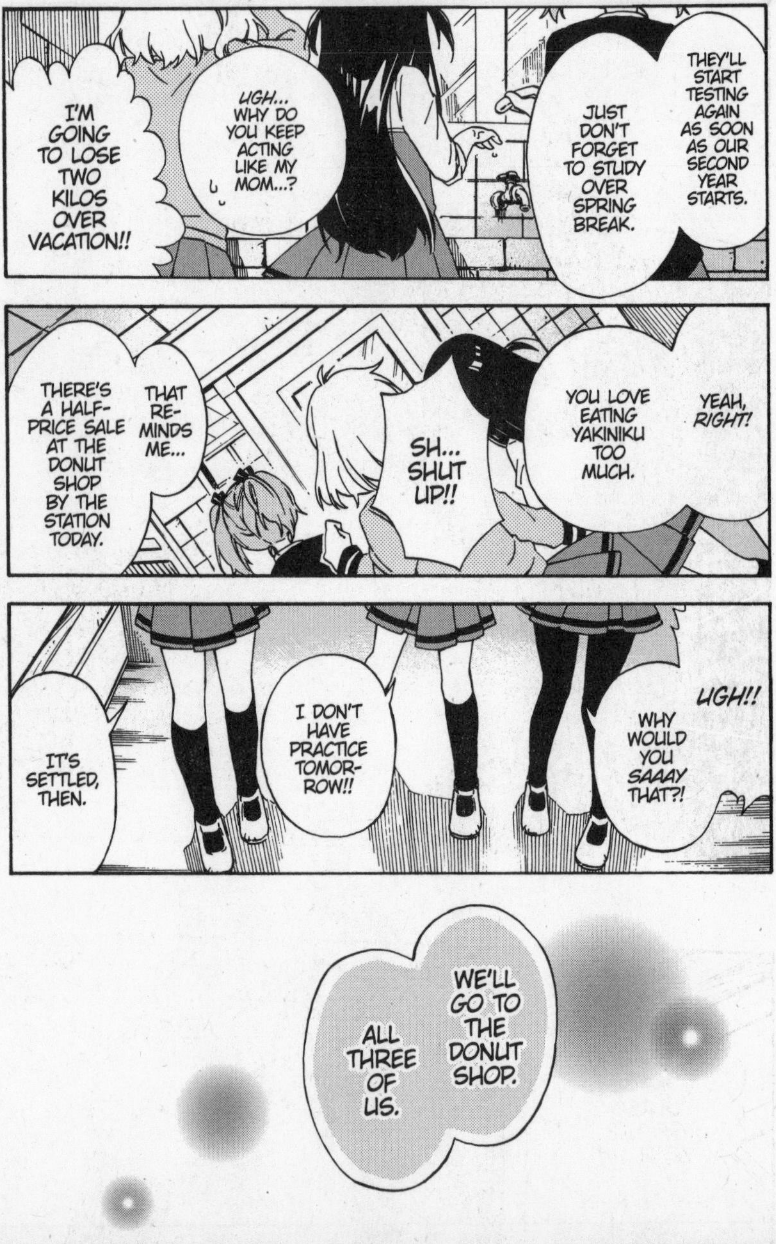
THEY'LL START TESTING AGAIN AS SOON AS OUR SECOND YEAR STARTS.
JUST DON'T FORGET TO STUDY OVER SPRING BREAK.
UGH... WHY DO YOU KEEP ACTING LIKE MY MOM...?
I'M GOING TO LOSE TWO KILOS OVER VACATION!!
YEAH, RIGHT!
YOU LOVE EATING YAKINIKU TOO MUCH.
SH... SHUT UP!!
THAT RE-MINDS ME...
THERE'S A HALF-PRICE SALE AT THE DONUT SHOP BY THE STATION TODAY.
UGH!!
WHY WOULD YOU SAAAY THAT?!
I DON'T HAVE PRACTICE TOMOR-ROW!!
IT'S SETTLED, THEN.
WE'LL GO TO THE DONUT SHOP.
ALL THREE OF US.

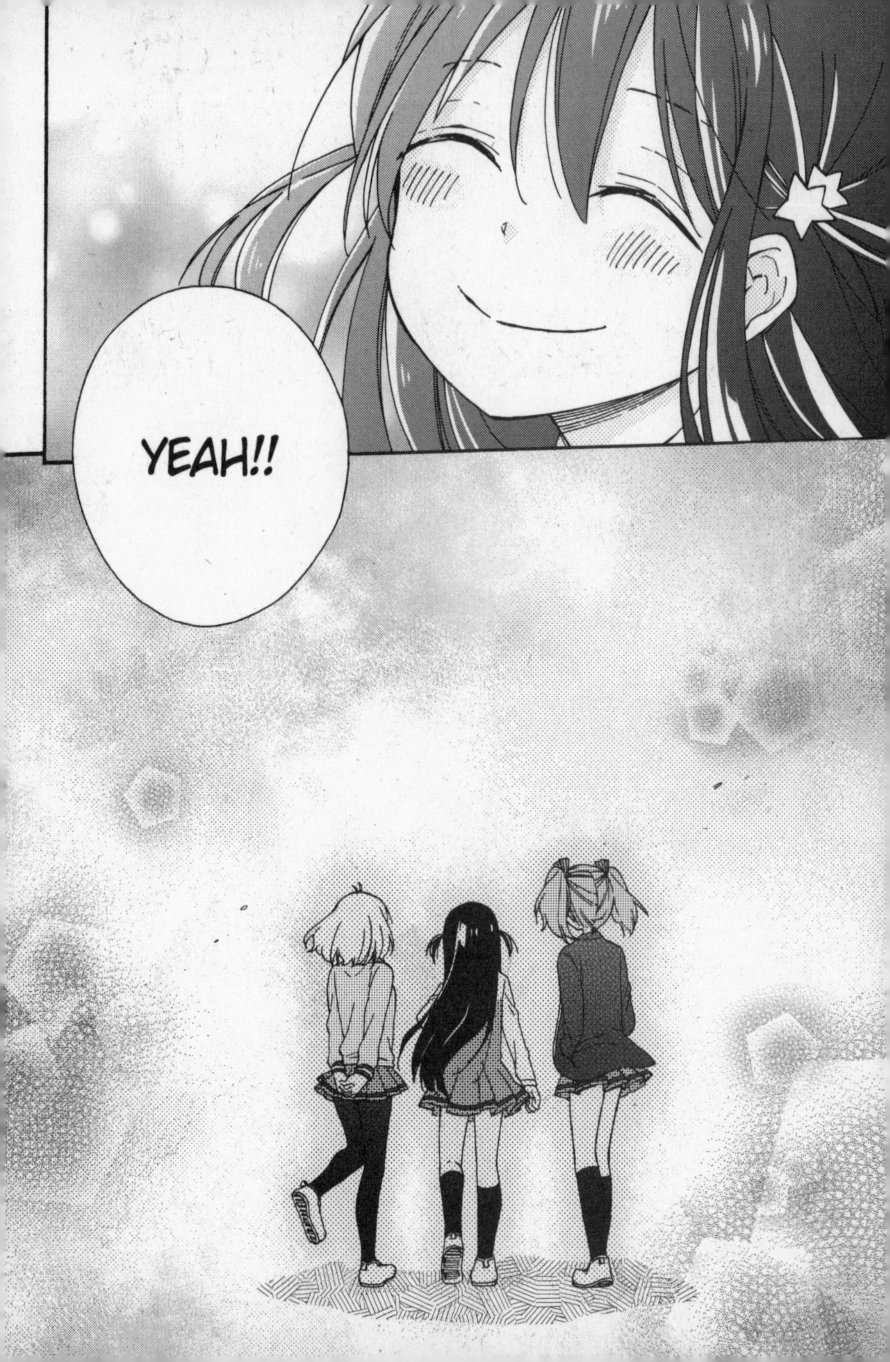
YEAH!!

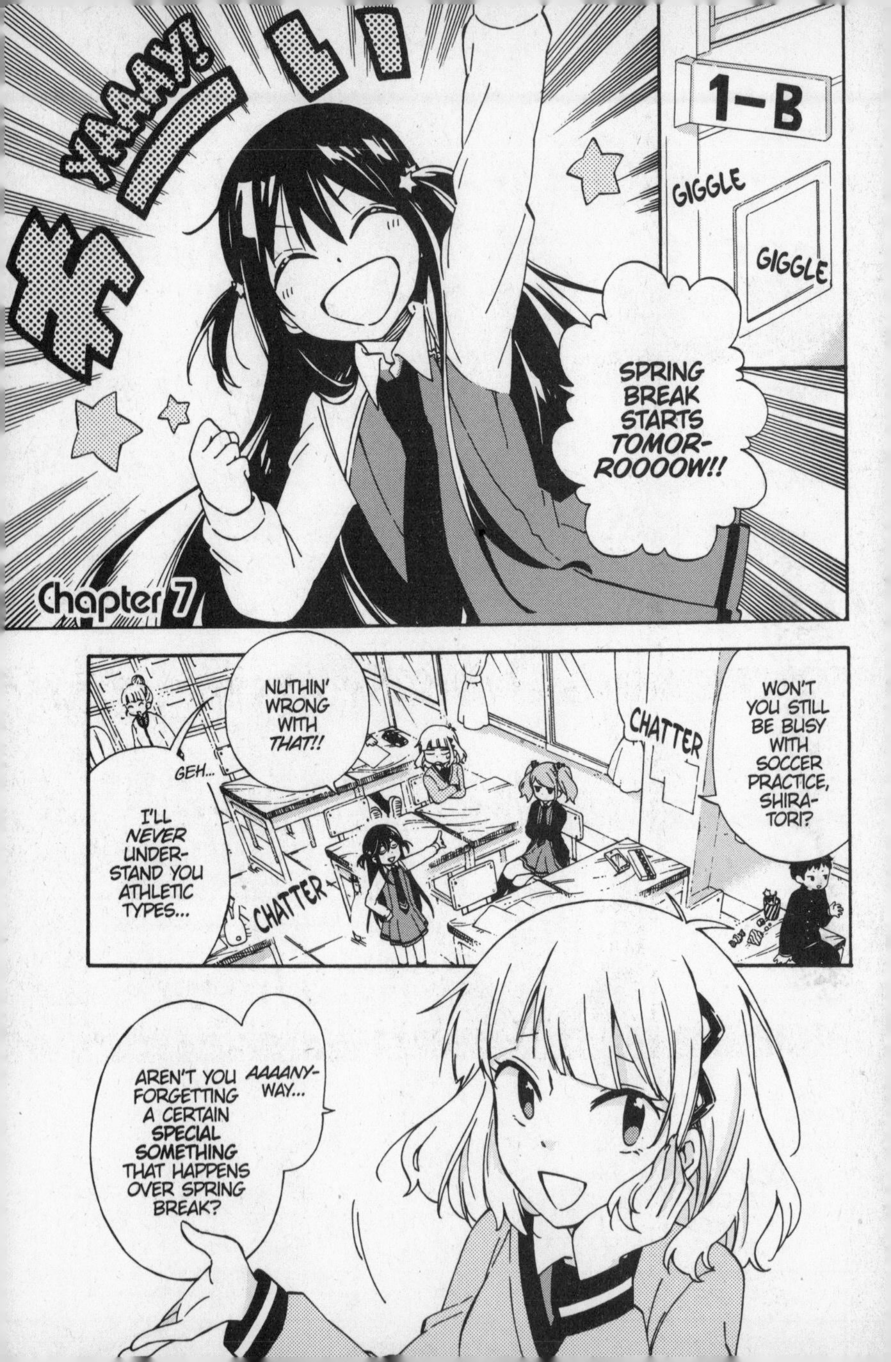

1-B
YAAAY!
GIGGLE
GIGGLE
SPRING BREAK STARTS TOMOR-ROOOOW!!
Chapter 7
WON'T YOU STILL BE BUSY WITH SOCCER PRACTICE, SHIRATORI?
CHATTER
NUTHIN' WRONG WITH *THAT!!*
GEH...
I'LL *NEVER* UNDER-STAND YOU ATHLETIC TYPES...
CHATTER
AAAANY-WAY...
AREN'T YOU FORGETTING A CERTAIN SPECIAL SOMETHING THAT HAPPENS OVER SPRING BREAK?

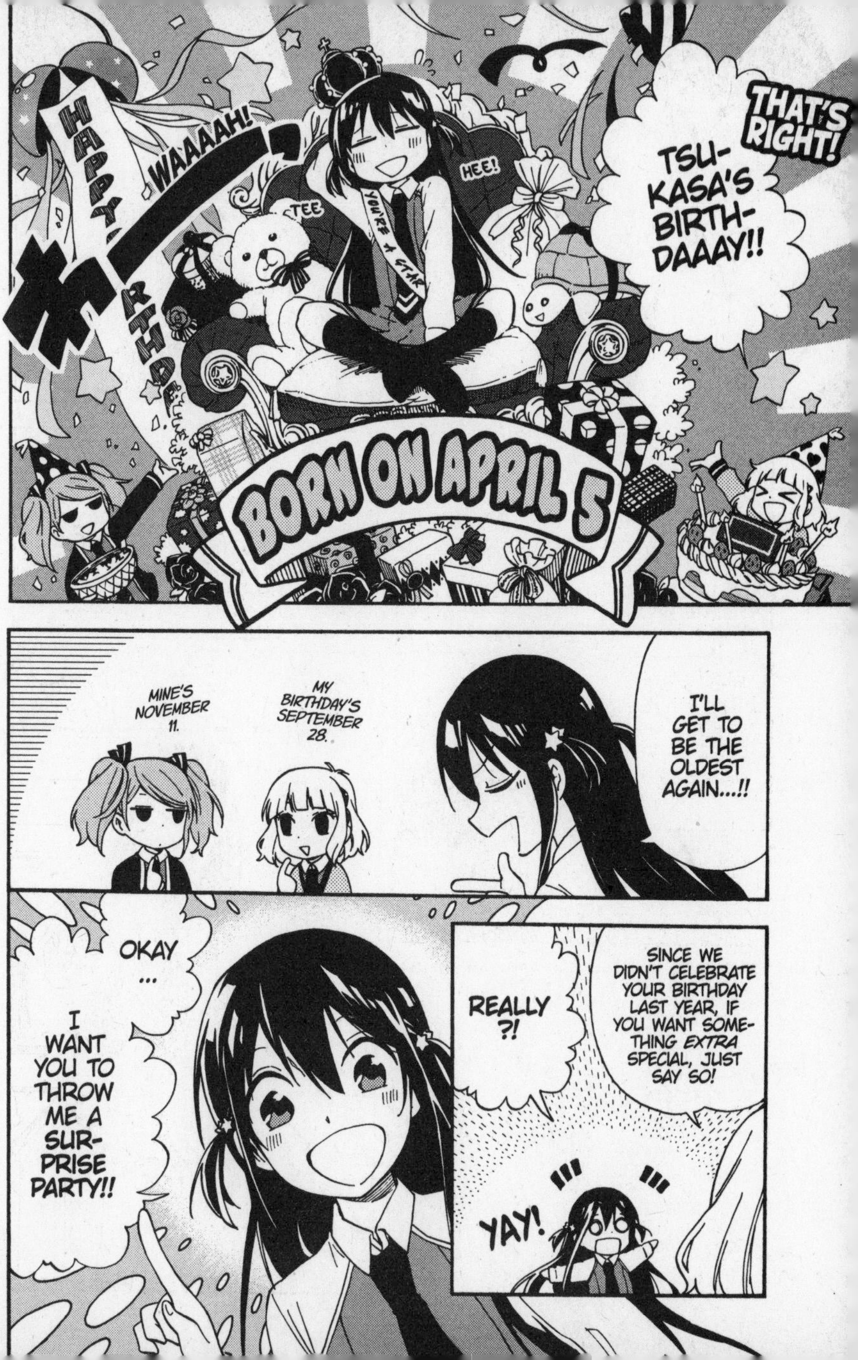
THAT'S RIGHT!
TSU-KASA'S BIRTH-DAAAY!!
HEE!
TEE
WAAAAH!
HAPPY
YOU'RE A STAR
BORN ON APRIL 5
I'LL GET TO BE THE OLDEST AGAIN...!!
MY BIRTHDAY'S SEPTEMBER 28.
MINE'S NOVEMBER 11.
SINCE WE DIDN'T CELEBRATE YOUR BIRTHDAY LAST YEAR, IF YOU WANT SOME-THING *EXTRA* SPECIAL, JUST SAY SO!
REALLY?!
YAY!
OKAY...
I WANT YOU TO THROW ME A SUR-PRISE PARTY!!

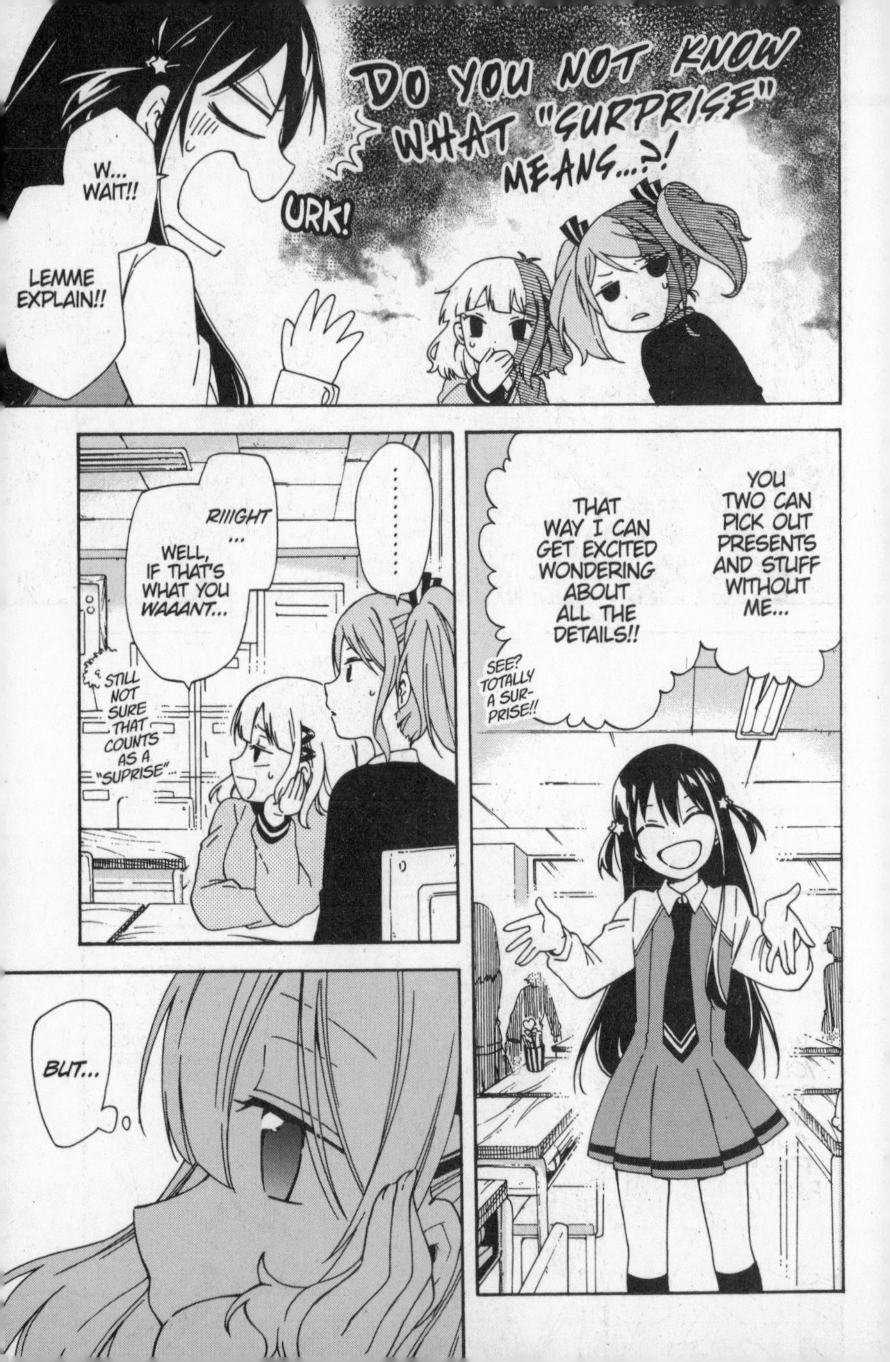
DO YOU NOT KNOW WHAT "SURPRISE" MEANS...?!
URK!
W... WAIT!!
LEMME EXPLAIN!!
YOU TWO CAN PICK OUT PRESENTS AND STUFF WITHOUT ME...
THAT WAY I CAN GET EXCITED WONDERING ABOUT ALL THE DETAILS!!
SEE? TOTALLY A SUR-PRISE!!
......
RIIIGHT... WELL, IF THAT'S WHAT YOU WAAANT...
STILL NOT SURE THAT COUNTS AS A "SUPRISE"...
BUT...

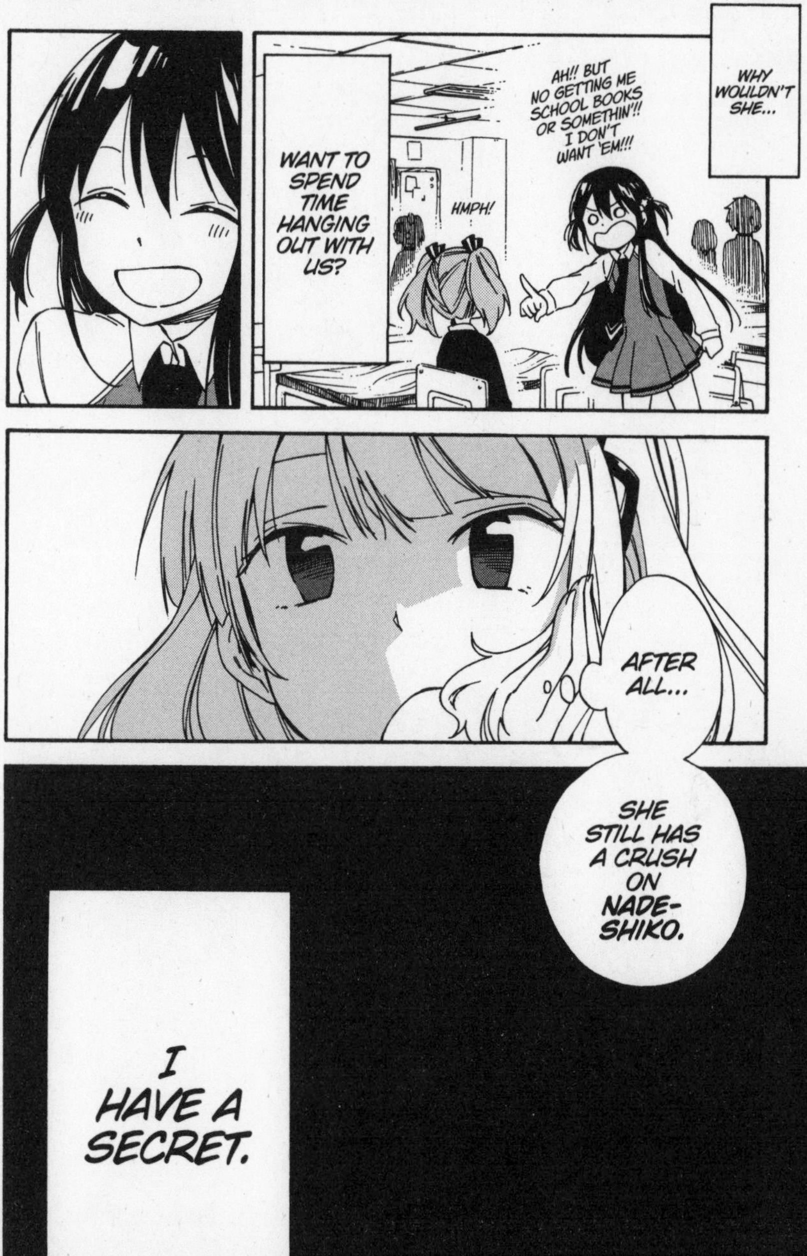
WHY WOULDN'T SHE...
AH!! BUT NO GETTING ME SCHOOL BOOKS OR SOMETHIN'!! I DON'T WANT 'EM!!!
HMPH!
WANT TO SPEND TIME HANGING OUT WITH US?
AFTER ALL...
SHE STILL HAS A CRUSH ON NADE-SHIKO.
I HAVE A SECRET.

Nameless
Asterism

Nameless
Asterism

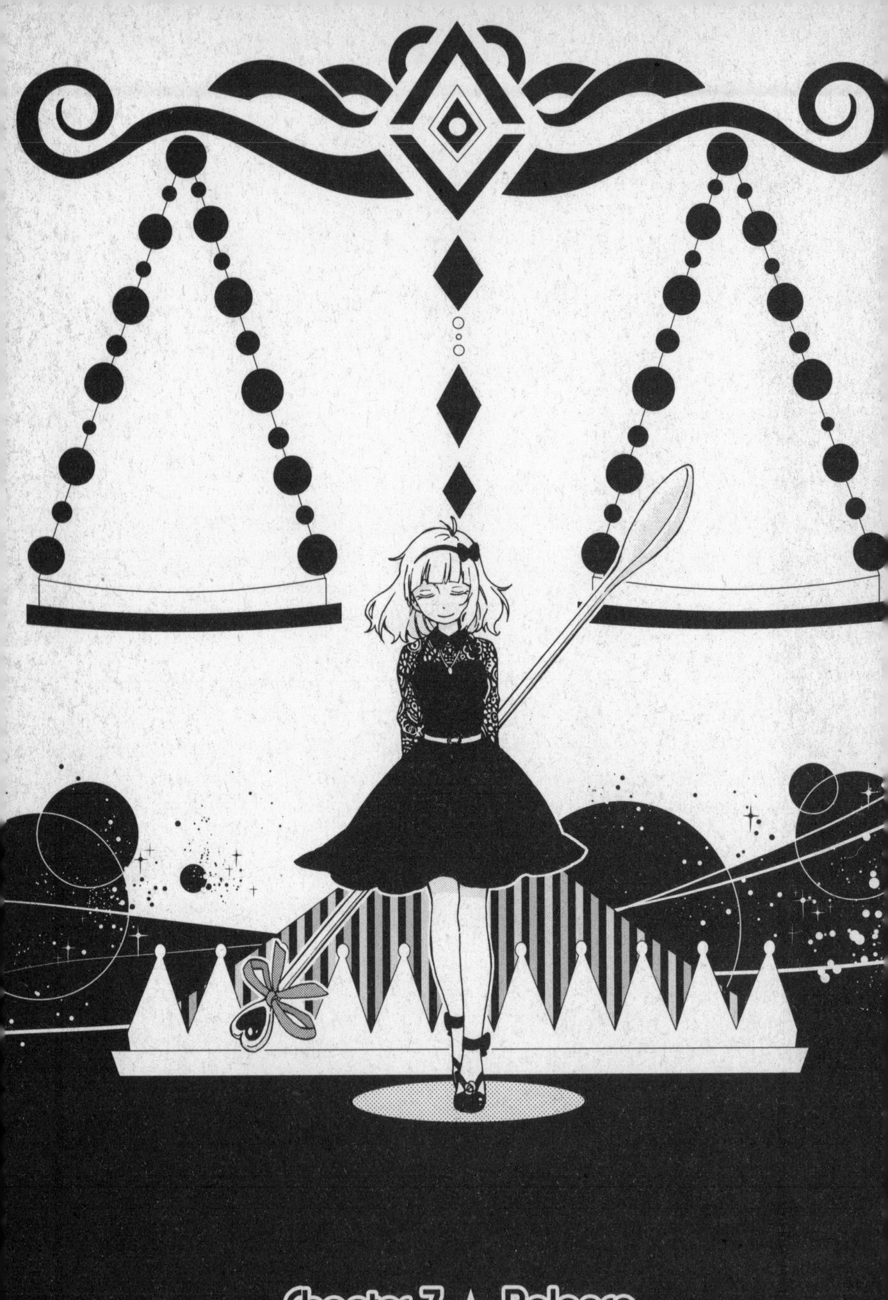

Chapter 7 ★ Balance

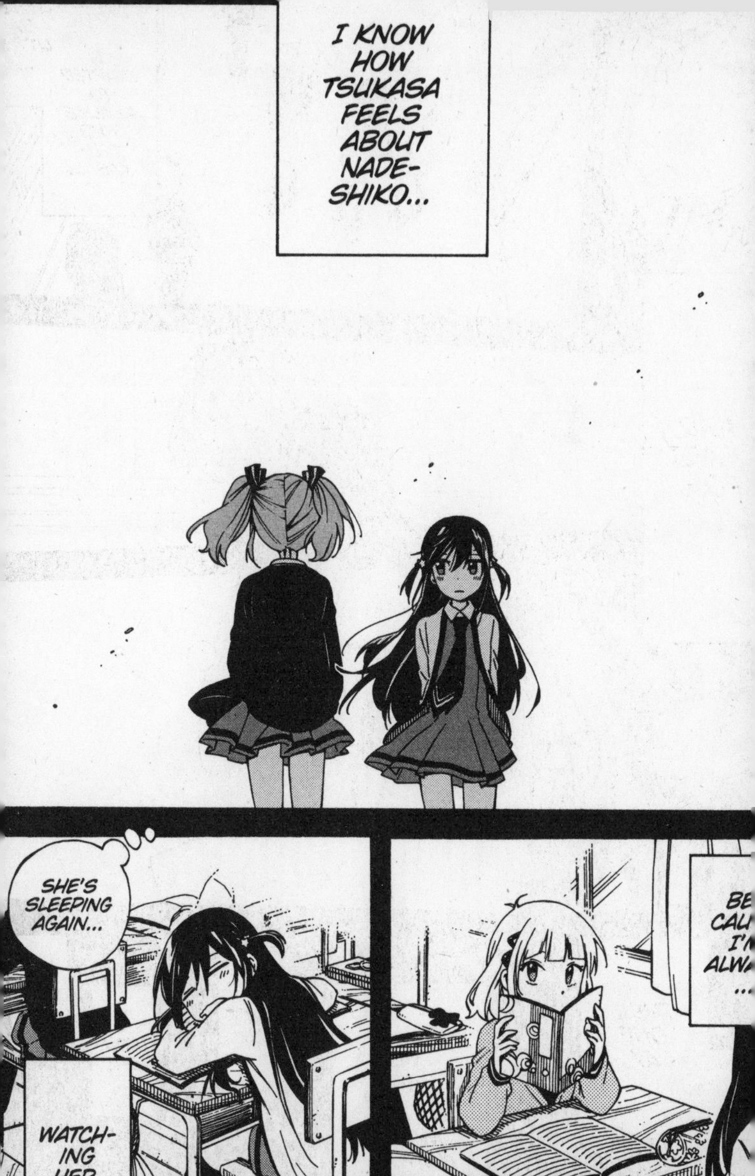
I KNOW HOW TSUKASA FEELS ABOUT NADE-SHIKO...
BE CAU I'M ALWA ...
SHE'S SLEEPING AGAIN...
WATCHING HER.

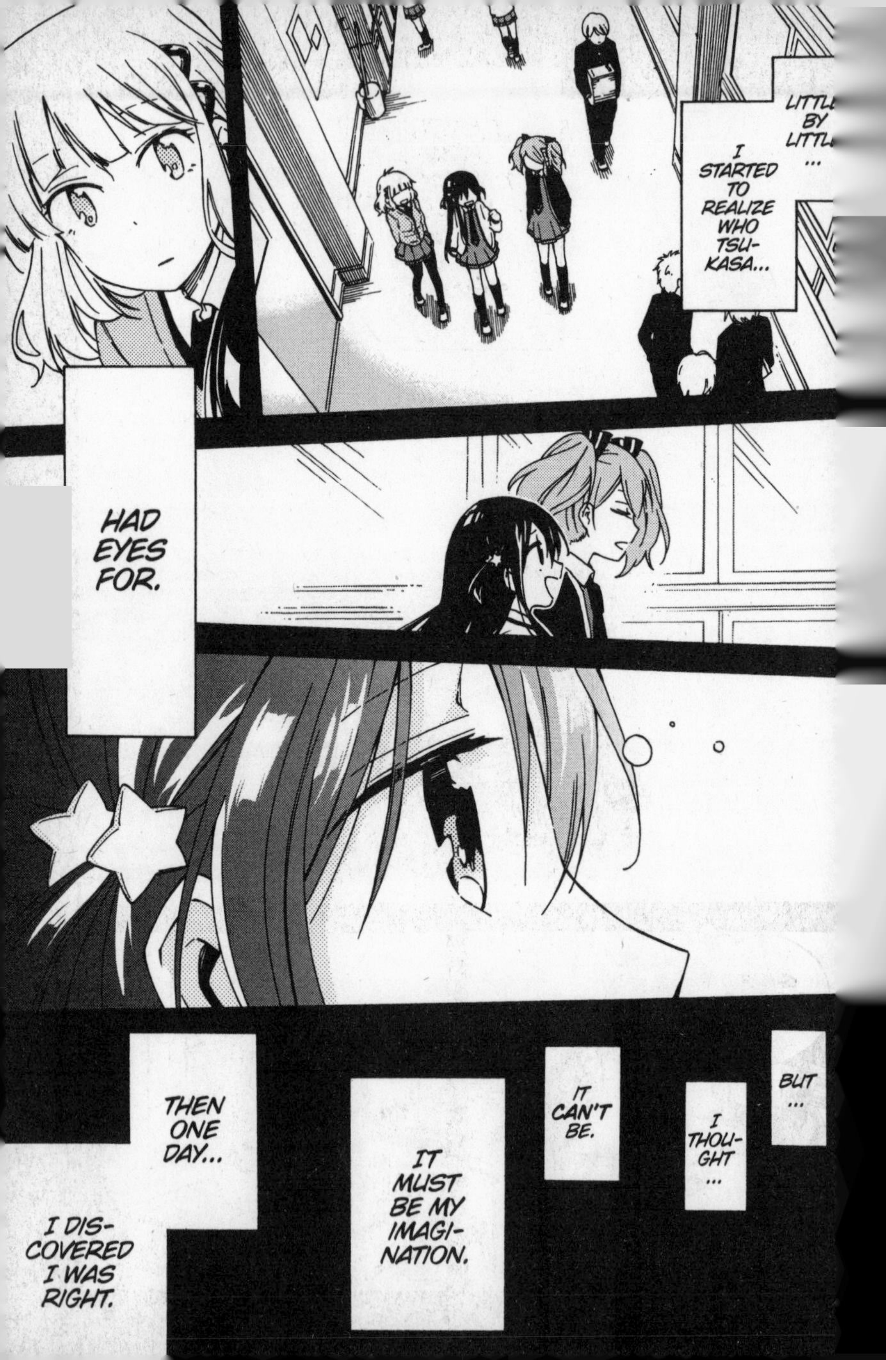
LITTL BY LITTL ...
I STARTED TO REALIZE WHO TSU-KASA...
HAD EYES FOR.
BUT ...
I THOU-GHT ...
IT CAN'T BE.
IT MUST BE MY IMAGI-NATION.
THEN ONE DAY...
I DIS-COVERED I WAS RIGHT.

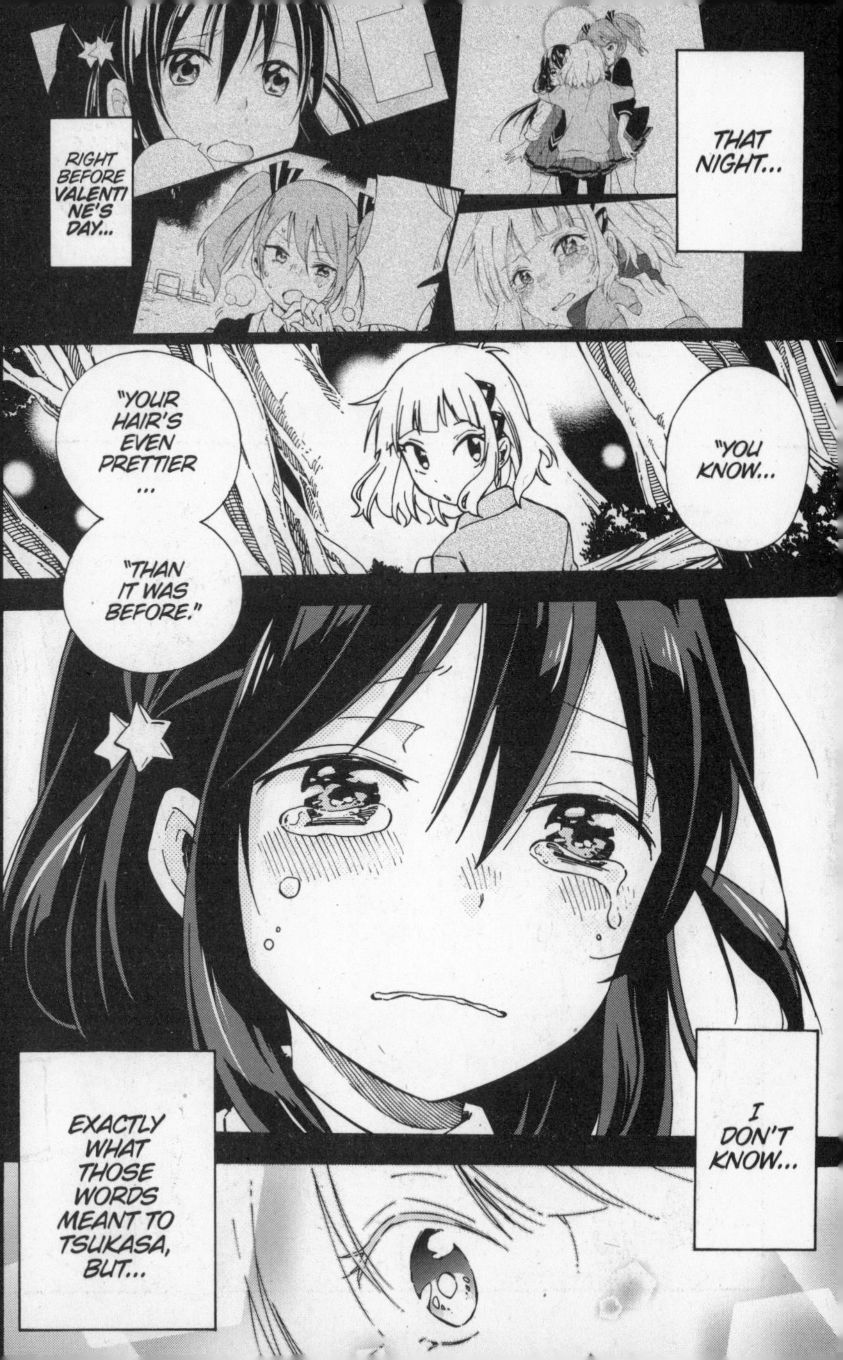
THAT NIGHT...
RIGHT BEFORE VALENTINE'S DAY...
"YOU KNOW...
"YOUR HAIR'S EVEN PRETTIER ...
"THAN IT WAS BEFORE."
I DON'T KNOW...
EXACTLY WHAT THOSE WORDS MEANT TO TSUKASA, BUT...

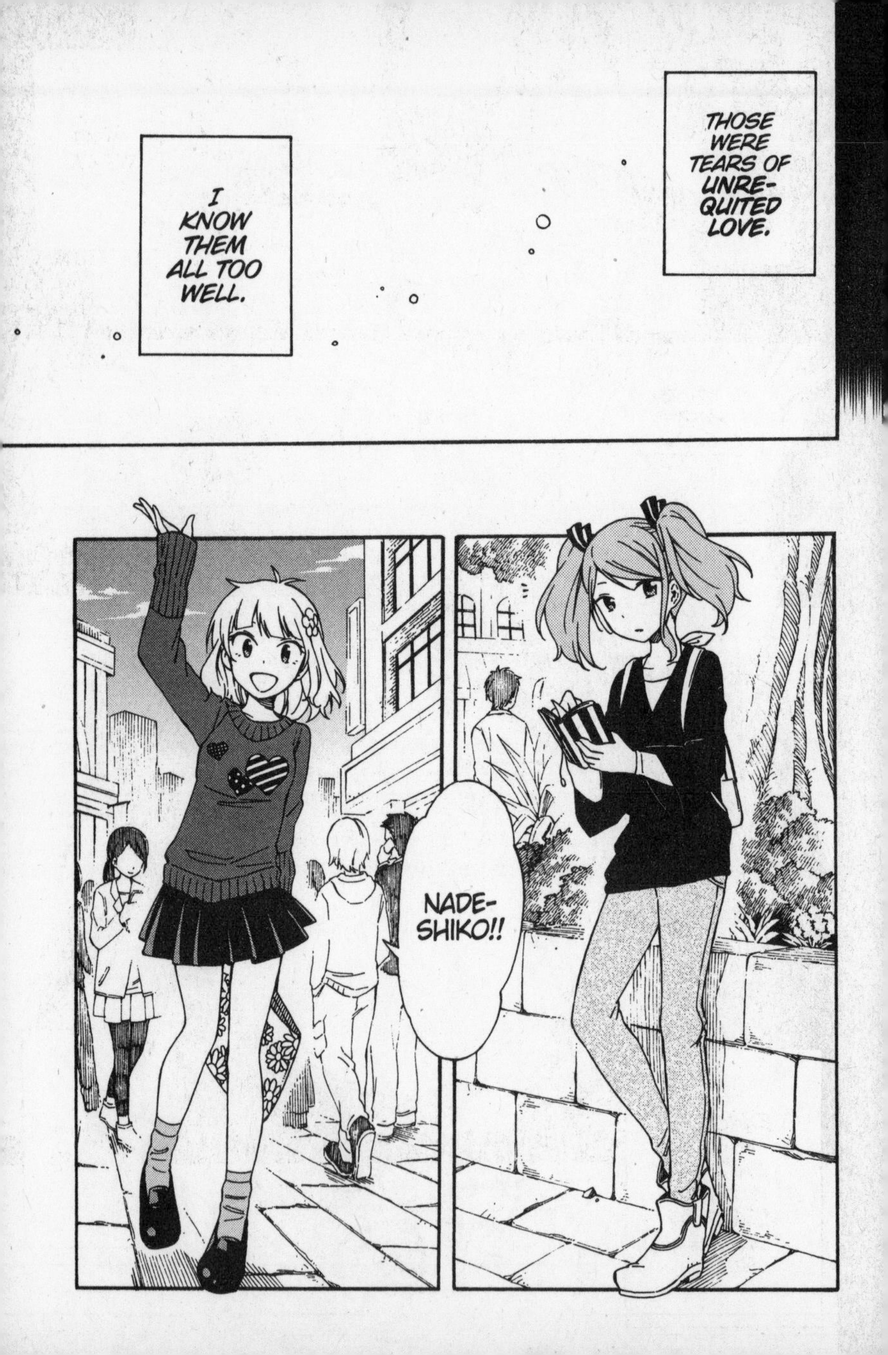
THOSE WERE TEARS OF UNRE-QUITED LOVE.
I KNOW THEM ALL TOO WELL.
NADE-SHIKO!!

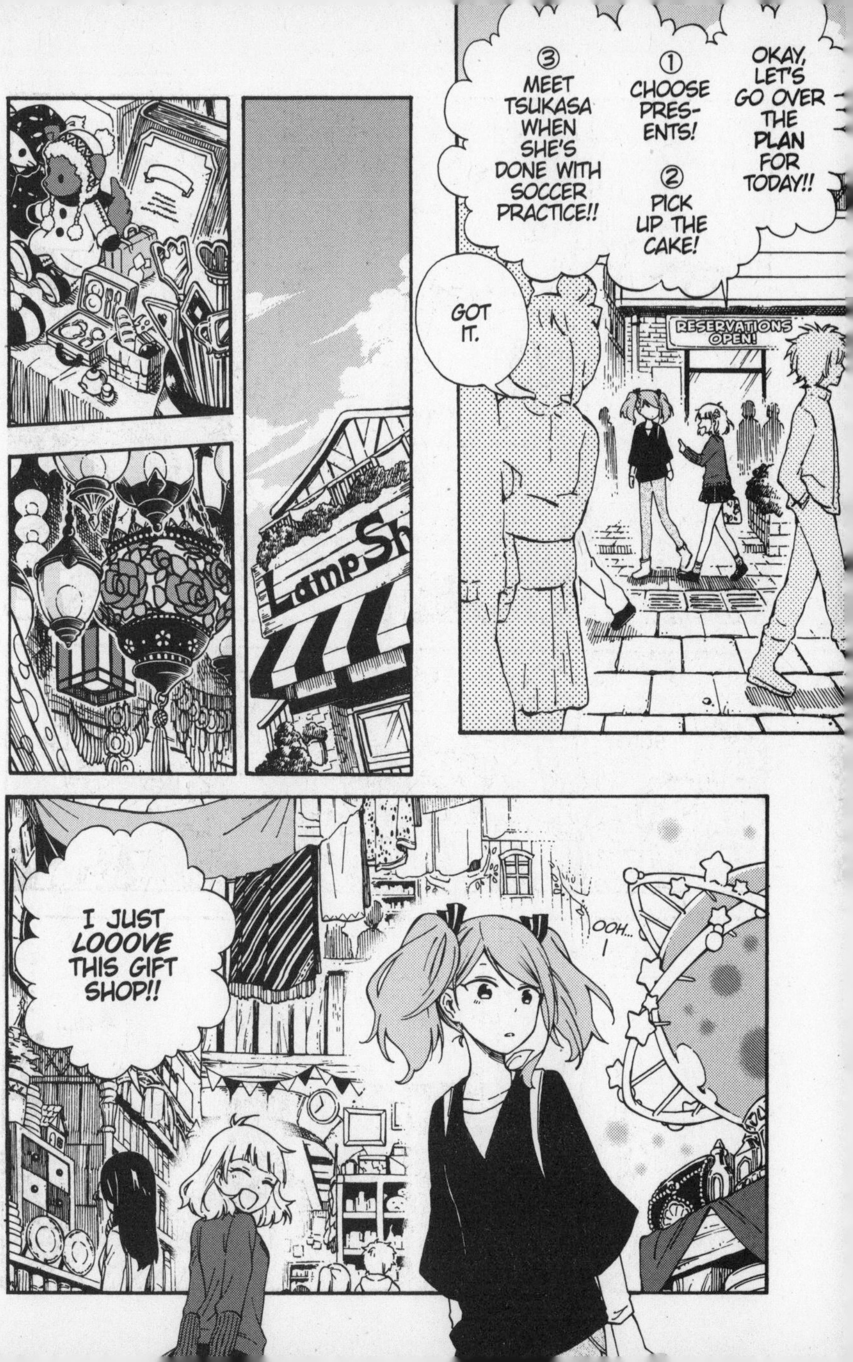

OKAY, LET'S GO OVER THE PLAN FOR TODAY!!
① CHOOSE PRES-ENTS!
② PICK UP THE CAKE!
③ MEET TSUKASA WHEN SHE'S DONE WITH SOCCER PRACTICE!!
GOT IT.
RESERVATIONS OPEN!
Lamp Sh
I JUST LOOOVE THIS GIFT SHOP!!
OOH...

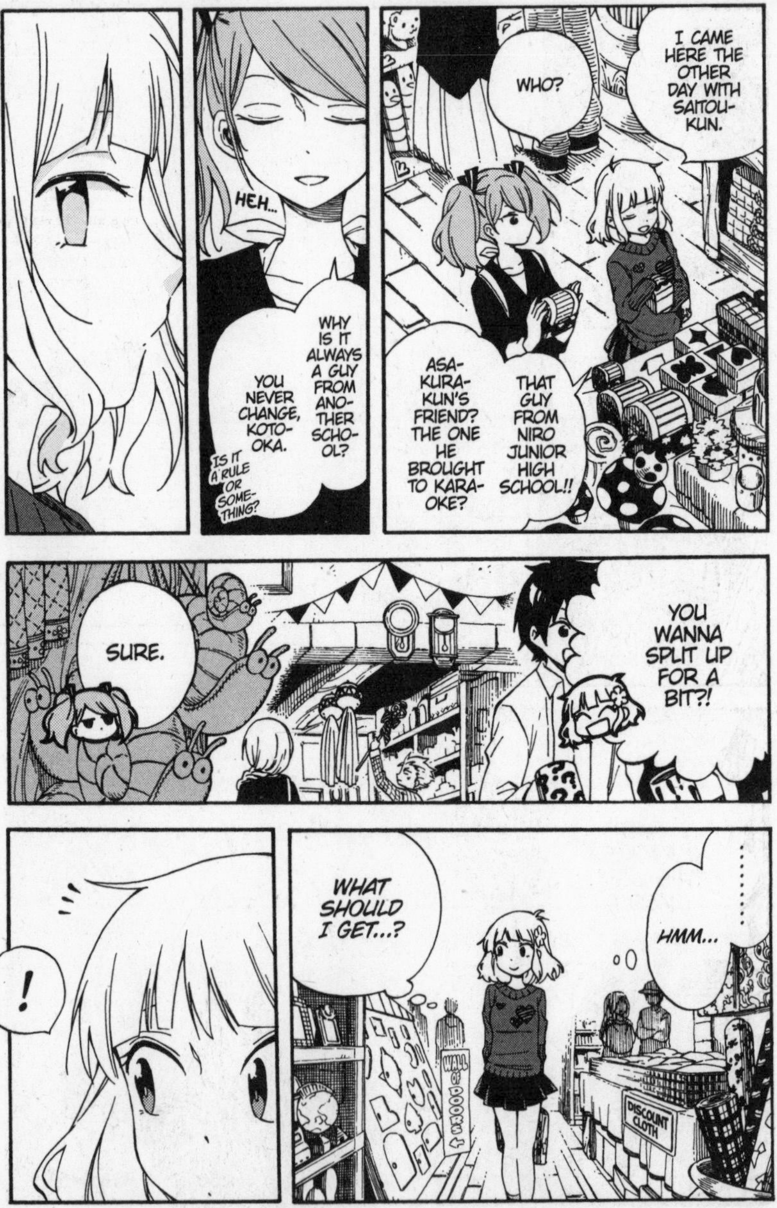
I CAME HERE THE OTHER DAY WITH SAITOU-KUN.
WHO?
THAT GUY FROM NIRO JUNIOR HIGH SCHOOL!!
ASAKURA-KUN'S FRIEND? THE ONE HE BROUGHT TO KARAOKE?
HEH...
WHY IS IT ALWAYS A GUY FROM ANOTHER SCHOOL?
YOU NEVER CHANGE, KOTOOKA.
IS IT A RULE OR SOMETHING?
YOU WANNA SPLIT UP FOR A BIT?!
SURE.
......
HMM...
WHAT SHOULD I GET...?
WALL OF DOORS
DISCOUNT CLOTH
!

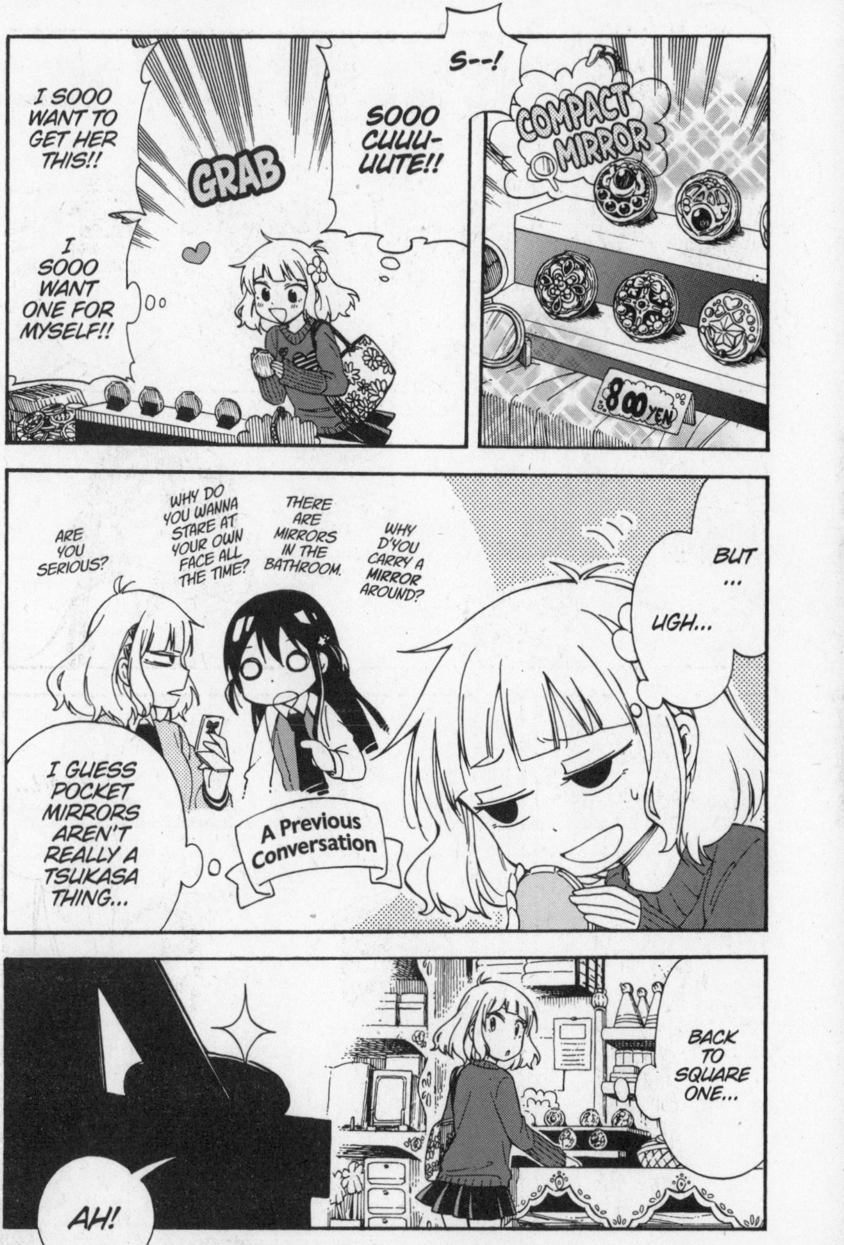
S--!
COMPACT MIRROR
800 YEN
SOOO CUULU-UUTE!!
GRAB
I SOOO WANT TO GET HER THIS!!
I SOOO WANT ONE FOR MYSELF!!
BUT ...
UGH...
WHY D'YOU CARRY A MIRROR AROUND?
THERE ARE MIRRORS IN THE BATHROOM.
WHY DO YOU WANNA STARE AT YOUR OWN FACE ALL THE TIME?
ARE YOU SERIOUS?
A Previous Conversation
I GUESS POCKET MIRRORS AREN'T REALLY A TSUKASA THING...
BACK TO SQUARE ONE...
AH!

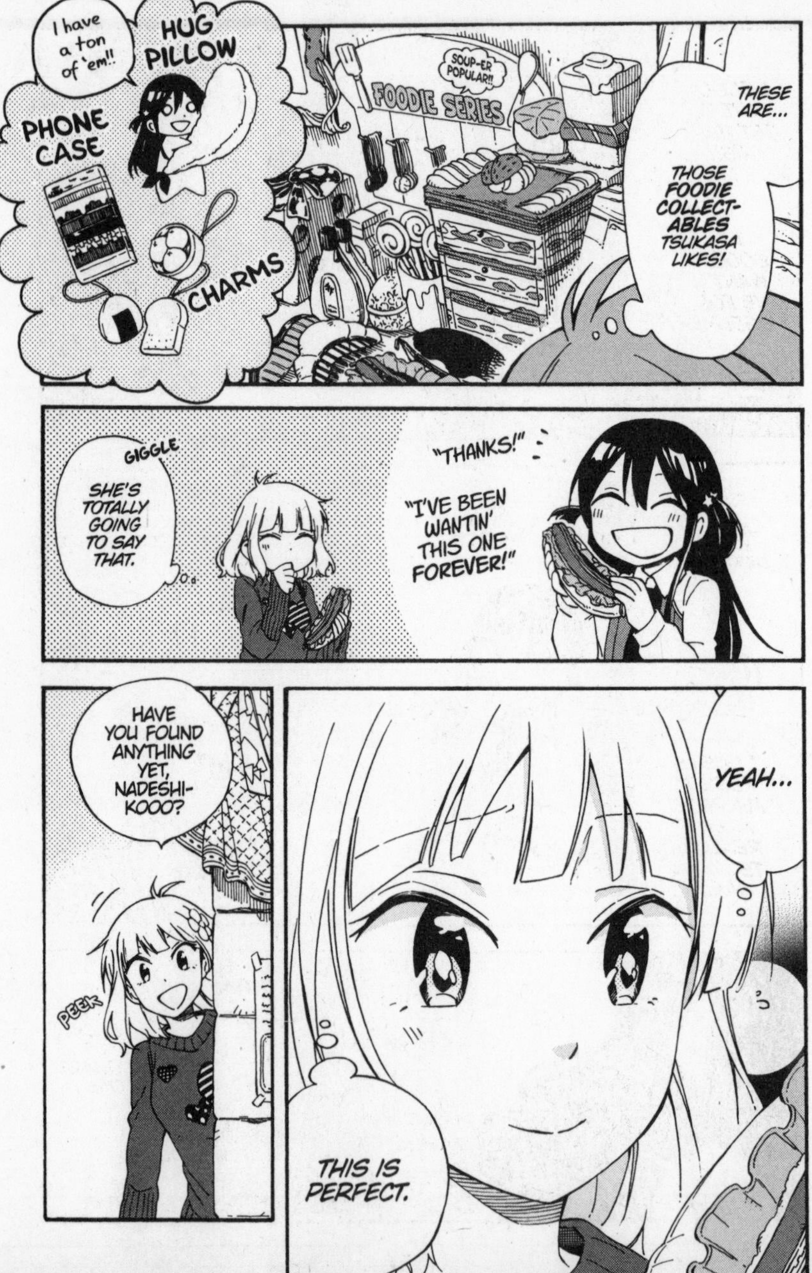
THESE ARE...
THOSE FOODIE COLLECT-ABLES TSUKASA LIKES!
SOUP-ER POPULAR!!
FOODIE SERIES
I have a ton of 'em!!
HUG PILLOW
PHONE CASE
CHARMS
"THANKS!"
"I'VE BEEN WANTIN' THIS ONE FOREVER!"
GIGGLE
SHE'S TOTALLY GOING TO SAY THAT.
YEAH...
THIS IS PERFECT.
HAVE YOU FOUND ANYTHING YET, NADESHI-KOOO?
PEEK

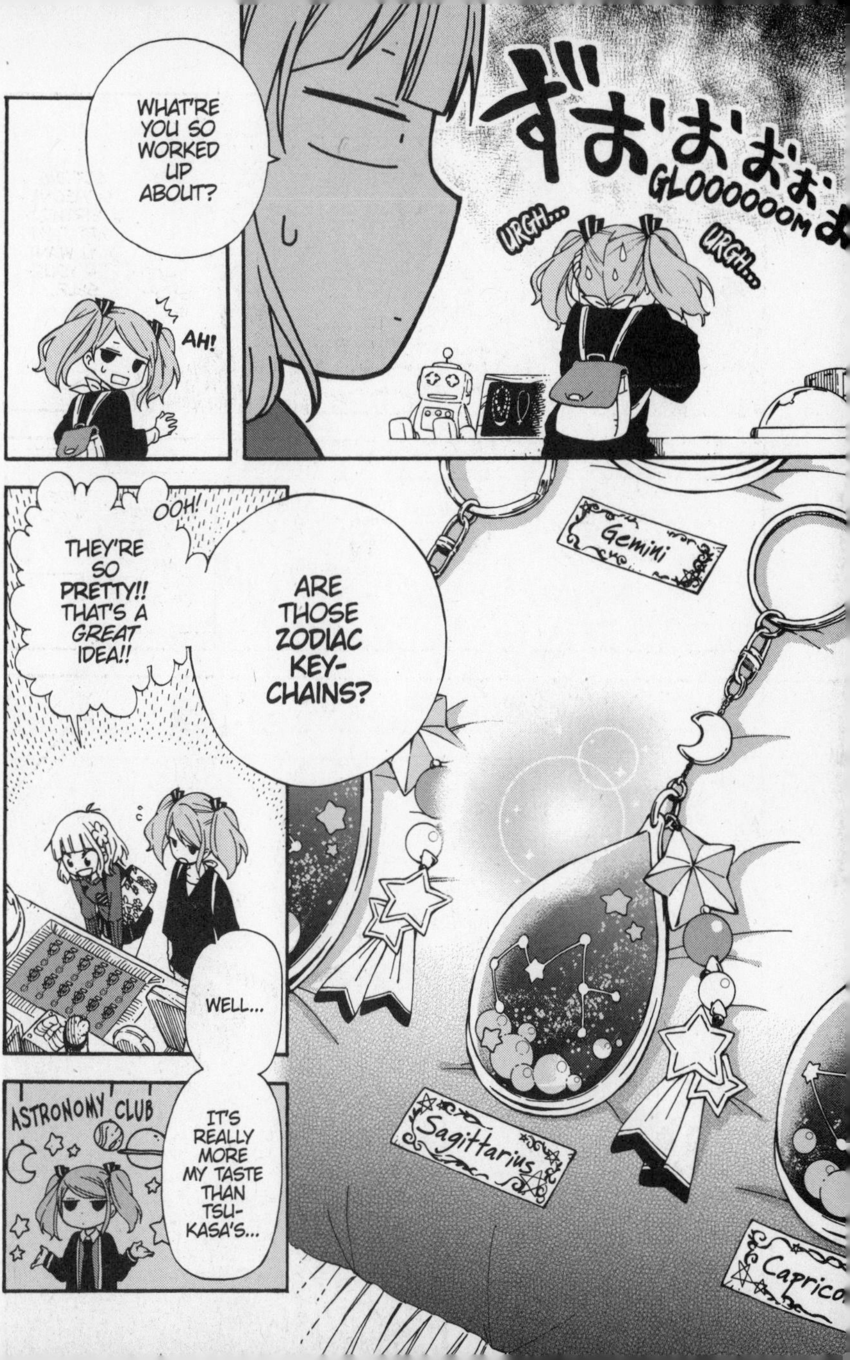
ずおおおおお
GLOOOOOOOM
URGH...
URGH...
WHAT'RE YOU SO WORKED UP ABOUT?
AH!
ARE THOSE ZODIAC KEY-CHAINS?
Gemini
Sagittarius
Caprico
OOH!
THEY'RE SO PRETTY!! THAT'S A GREAT IDEA!!
WELL...
ASTRONOMY CLUB
IT'S REALLY MORE MY TASTE THAN TSU-KASA'S...

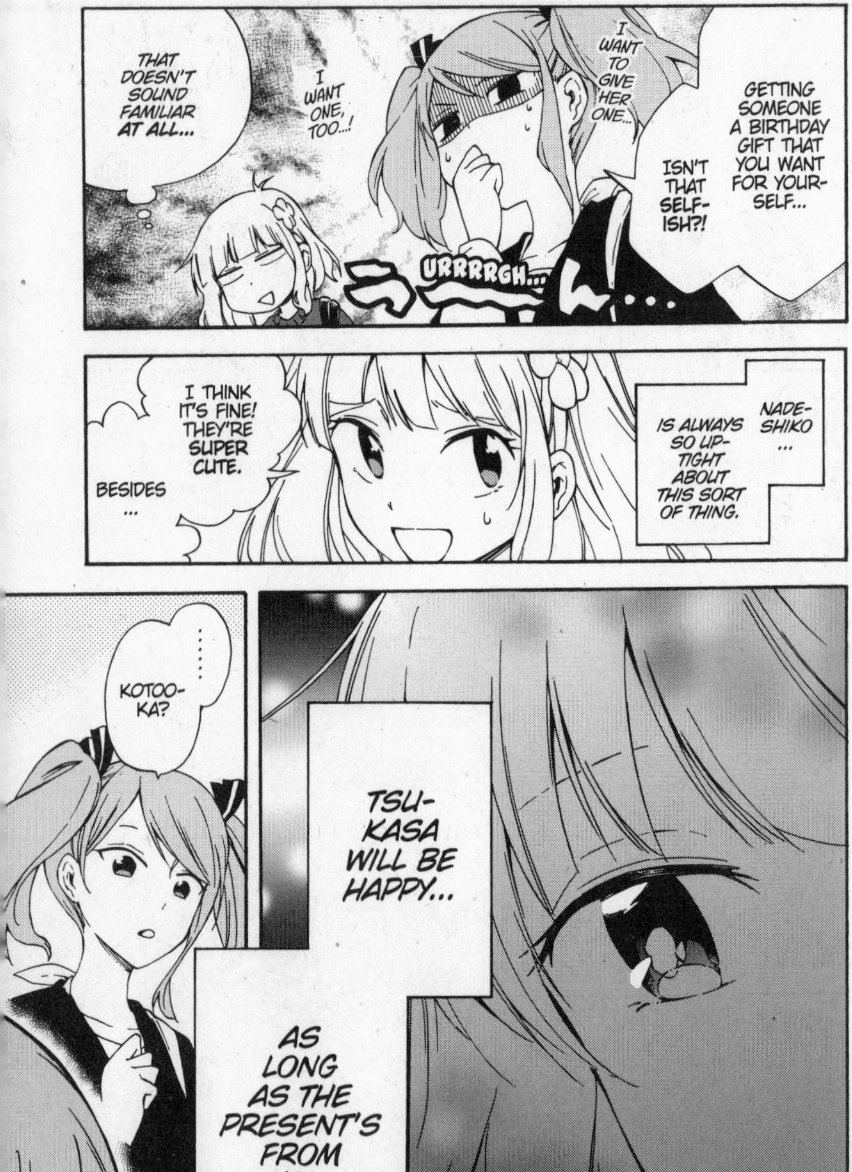
GETTING SOMEONE A BIRTHDAY GIFT THAT YOU WANT FOR YOURSELF...
ISN'T THAT SELFISH?!
I WANT TO GIVE HER ONE...
I WANT ONE, TOO...!
URRRRGH...
THAT DOESN'T SOUND FAMILIAR AT ALL...
NADESHIKO...
IS ALWAYS SO UPTIGHT ABOUT THIS SORT OF THING.
I THINK IT'S FINE! THEY'RE SUPER CUTE.
BESIDES...
TSUKASA WILL BE HAPPY...
AS LONG AS THE PRESENT'S FROM YOU.
......
KOTOOKA?

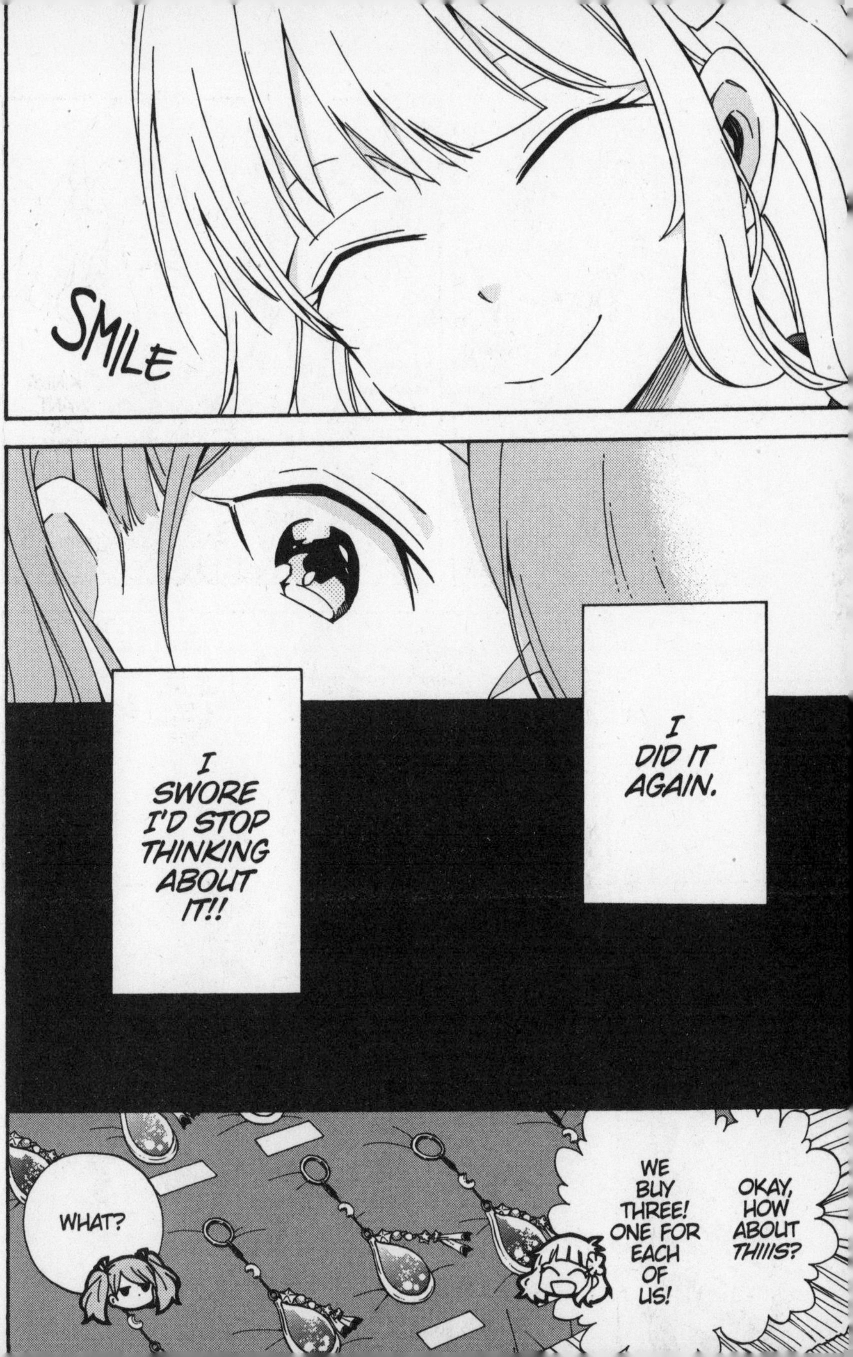
SMILE
I DID IT AGAIN.
I SWORE I'D STOP THINKING ABOUT IT!!
OKAY, HOW ABOUT THIIIS?
WE BUY THREE! ONE FOR EACH OF US!
WHAT?

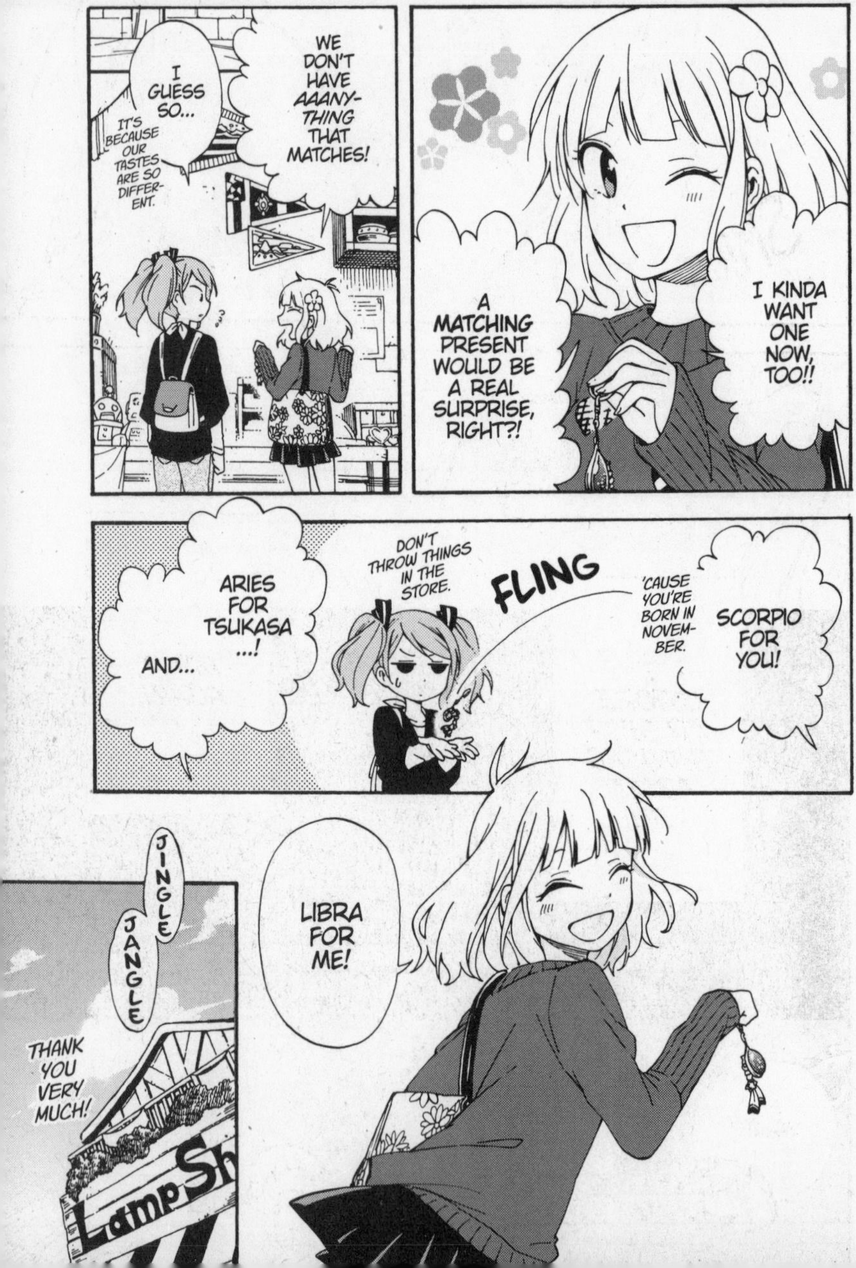
I KINDA WANT ONE NOW, TOO!!
A MATCHING PRESENT WOULD BE A REAL SURPRISE, RIGHT?!
WE DON'T HAVE AAAANY-THING THAT MATCHES!
I GUESS SO...
IT'S BECAUSE OUR TASTES ARE SO DIFFER-ENT.
SCORPIO FOR YOU!
'CAUSE YOU'RE BORN IN NOVEM-BER.
FLING
DON'T THROW THINGS IN THE STORE.
ARIES FOR TSUKASA ...!
AND...
LIBRA FOR ME!
JINGLE
JANGLE
THANK YOU VERY MUCH!
Lamp Sh

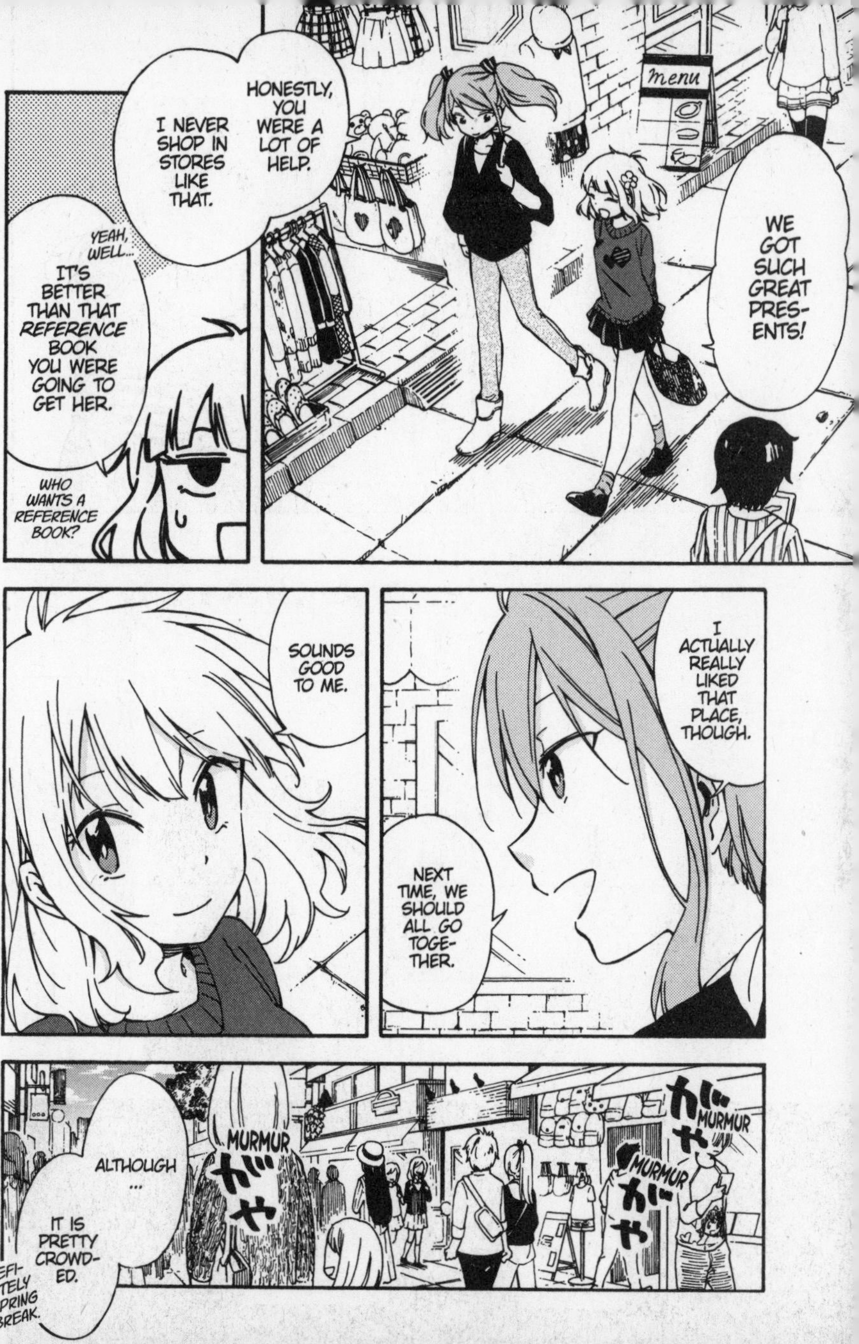
WE GOT SUCH GREAT PRESENTS!
HONESTLY, YOU WERE A LOT OF HELP.
I NEVER SHOP IN STORES LIKE THAT.
YEAH, WELL... IT'S BETTER THAN THAT REFERENCE BOOK YOU WERE GOING TO GET HER.
WHO WANTS A REFERENCE BOOK?
I ACTUALLY REALLY LIKED THAT PLACE, THOUGH.
NEXT TIME, WE SHOULD ALL GO TOGE-THER.
SOUNDS GOOD TO ME.
ガヤ MURMUR
ガヤ MURMUR
MURMUR ガヤ
ALTHOUGH ...
IT IS PRETTY CROWD-ED.
DEFI-NITELY SPRING BREAK.

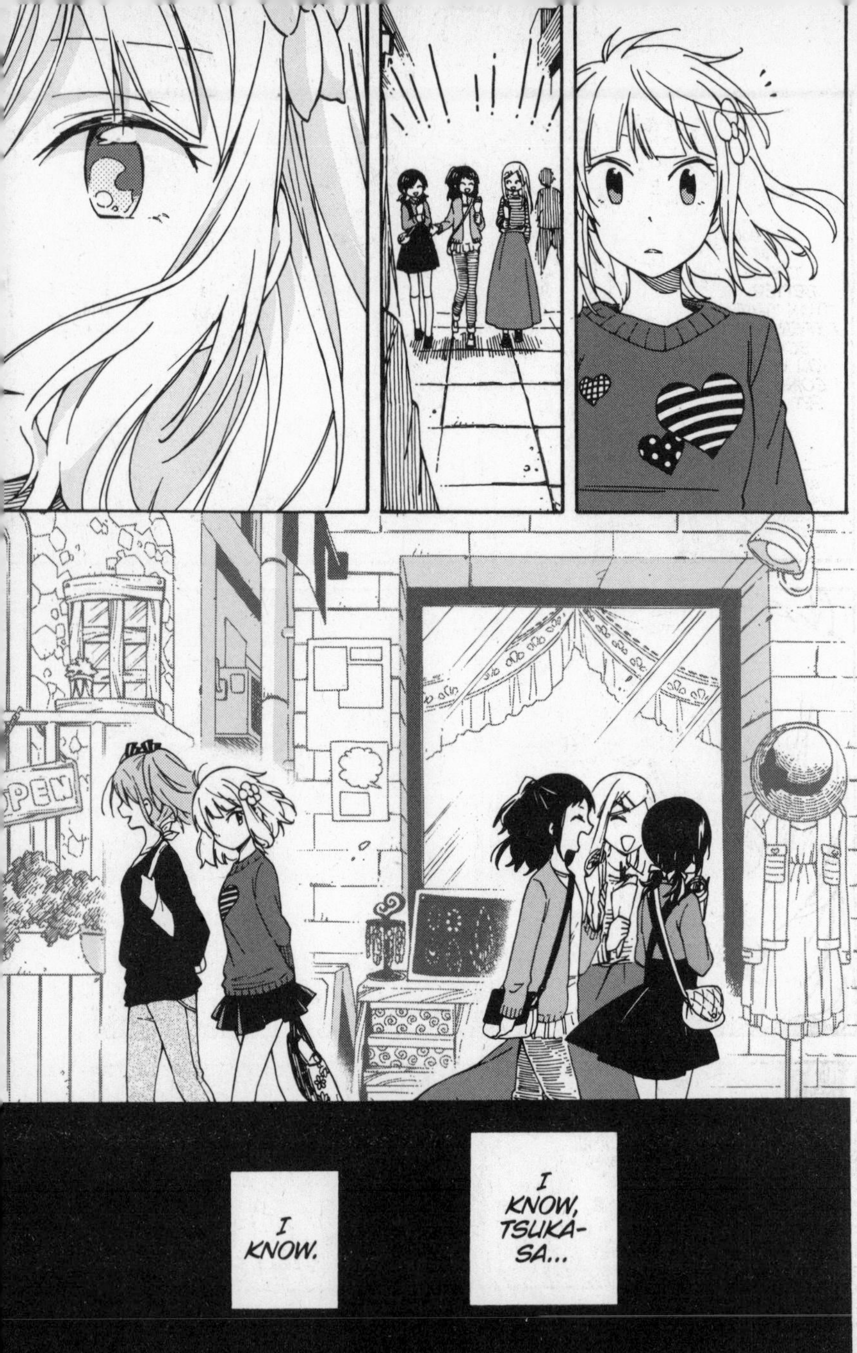
I KNOW, TSUKASA...
I KNOW.

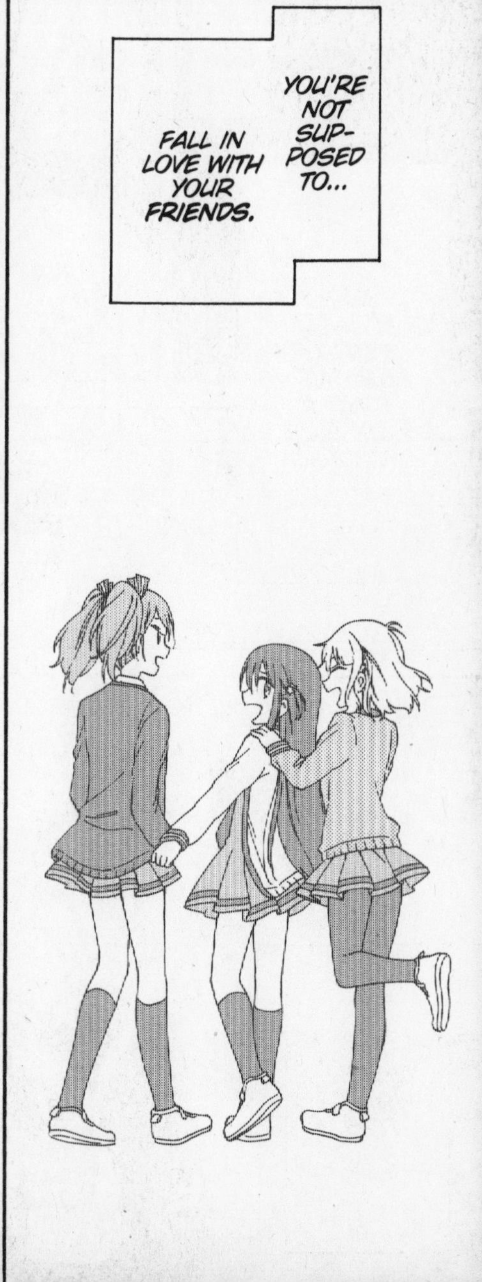
YOU'RE NOT SUP-POSED TO...
FALL IN LOVE WITH YOUR FRIENDS.

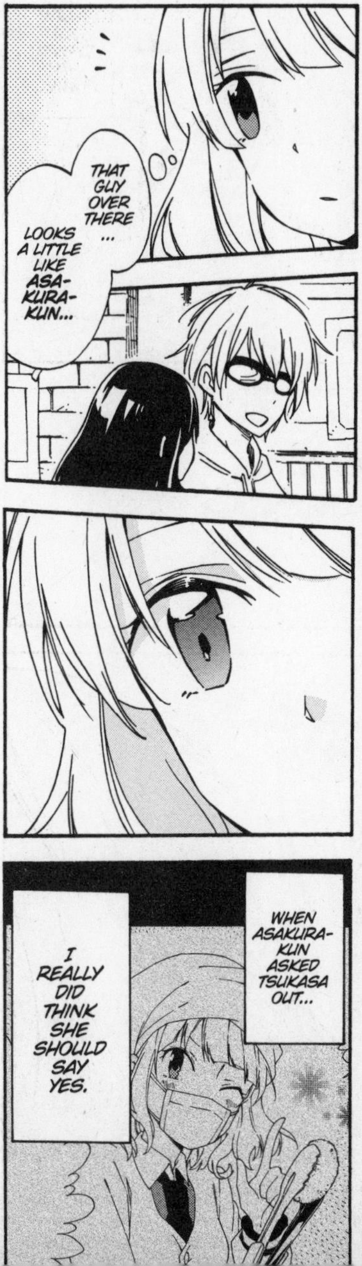
THAT GUY OVER THERE ... LOOKS A LITTLE LIKE ASA-KURA-KUN...
WHEN ASAKURA-KUN ASKED TSUKASA OUT...
I REALLY DID THINK SHE SHOULD SAY YES.

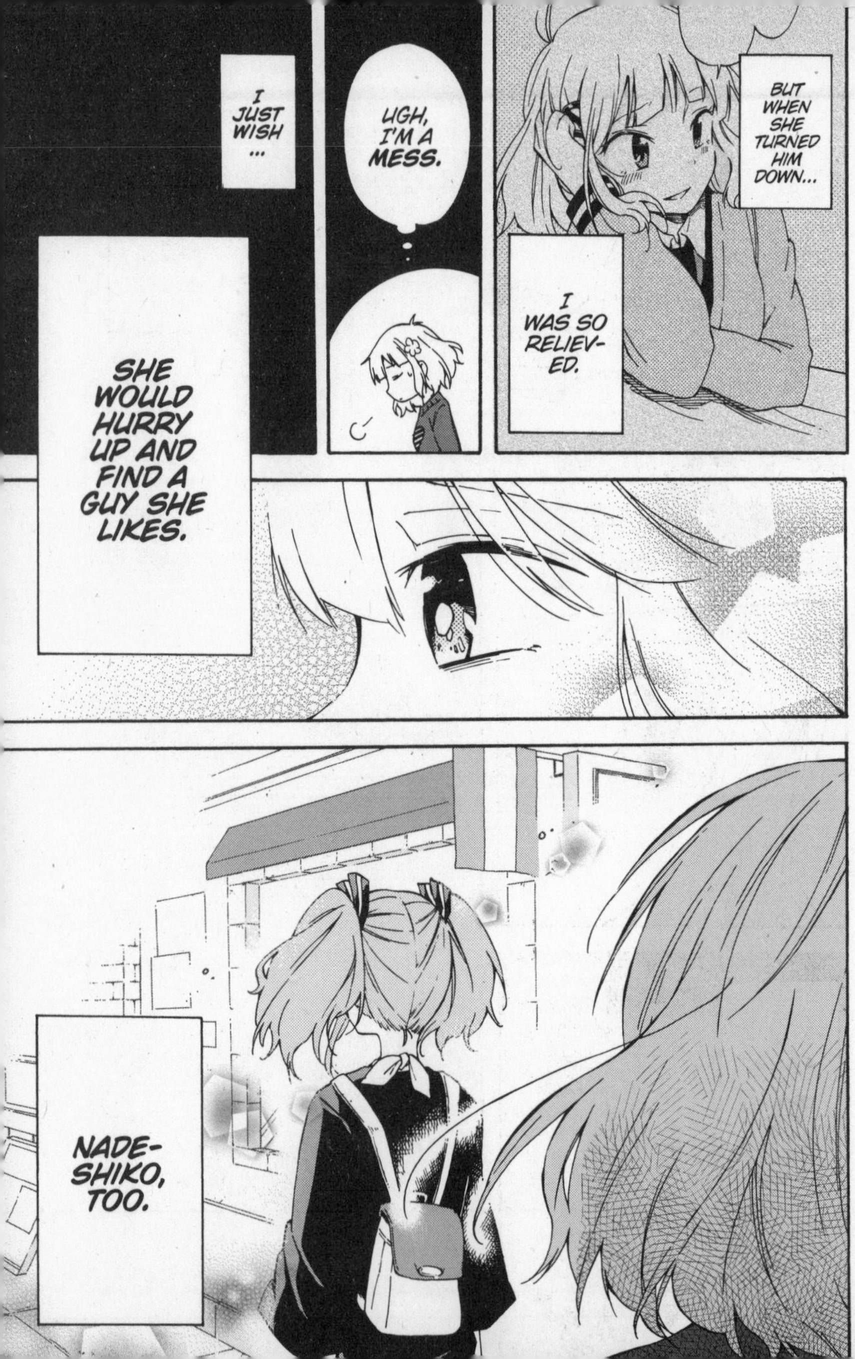
BUT WHEN SHE TURNED HIM DOWN...
I WAS SO RELIEV-ED.
UGH, I'M A MESS.
I JUST WISH ...
SHE WOULD HURRY UP AND FIND A GUY SHE LIKES.
NADE-SHIKO, TOO.

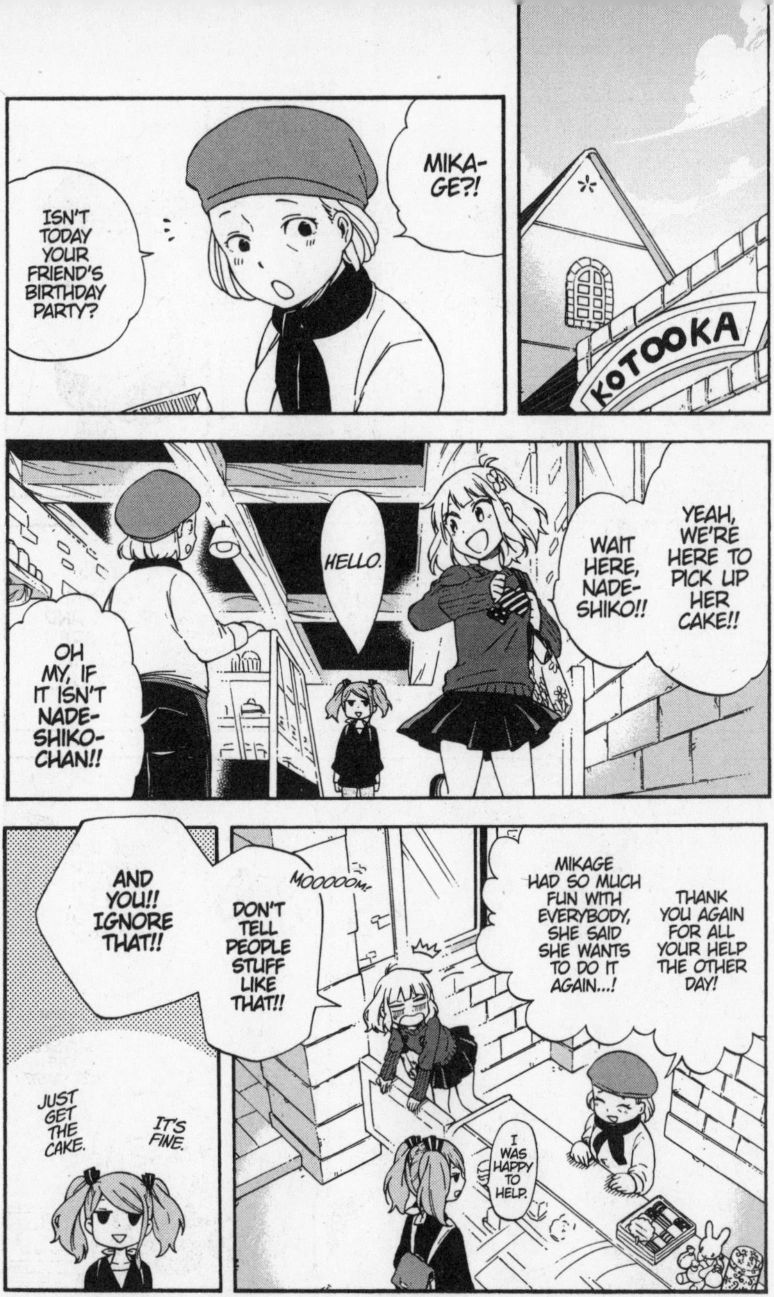
KOTOOKA
MIKA-GE?!
ISN'T TODAY YOUR FRIEND'S BIRTHDAY PARTY?
YEAH, WE'RE HERE TO PICK UP HER CAKE!!
WAIT HERE, NADE-SHIKO!!
HELLO.
OH MY, IF IT ISN'T NADE-SHIKO-CHAN!!
THANK YOU AGAIN FOR ALL YOUR HELP THE OTHER DAY!
MIKAGE HAD SO MUCH FUN WITH EVERYBODY, SHE SAID SHE WANTS TO DO IT AGAIN...!
MOOOOOM!
DON'T TELL PEOPLE STUFF LIKE THAT!!
I WAS HAPPY TO HELP.
AND YOU!! IGNORE THAT!!
IT'S FINE.
JUST GET THE CAKE.

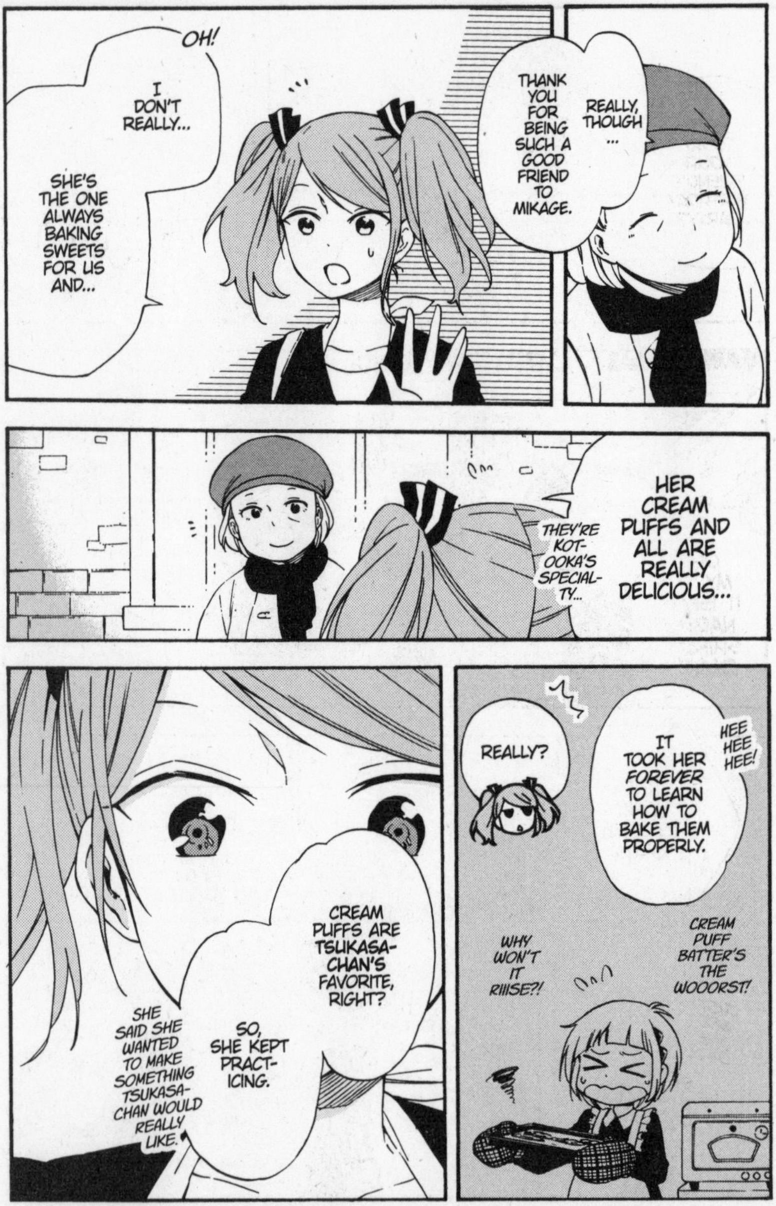
REALLY, THOUGH...
THANK YOU FOR BEING SUCH A GOOD FRIEND TO MIKAGE.
OH!
I DON'T REALLY...
SHE'S THE ONE ALWAYS BAKING SWEETS FOR US AND...
HER CREAM PUFFS AND ALL ARE REALLY DELICIOUS...
THEY'RE KOTOOKA'S SPECIALTY...
HEE HEE HEE!
IT TOOK HER FOREVER TO LEARN HOW TO BAKE THEM PROPERLY.
REALLY?
CREAM PUFF BATTER'S THE WOOORST!
WHY WON'T IT RIIISE?!
CREAM PUFFS ARE TSUKASA-CHAN'S FAVORITE, RIGHT?
SO, SHE KEPT PRACTICING.
SHE SAID SHE WANTED TO MAKE SOMETHING TSUKASA-CHAN WOULD REALLY LIKE.

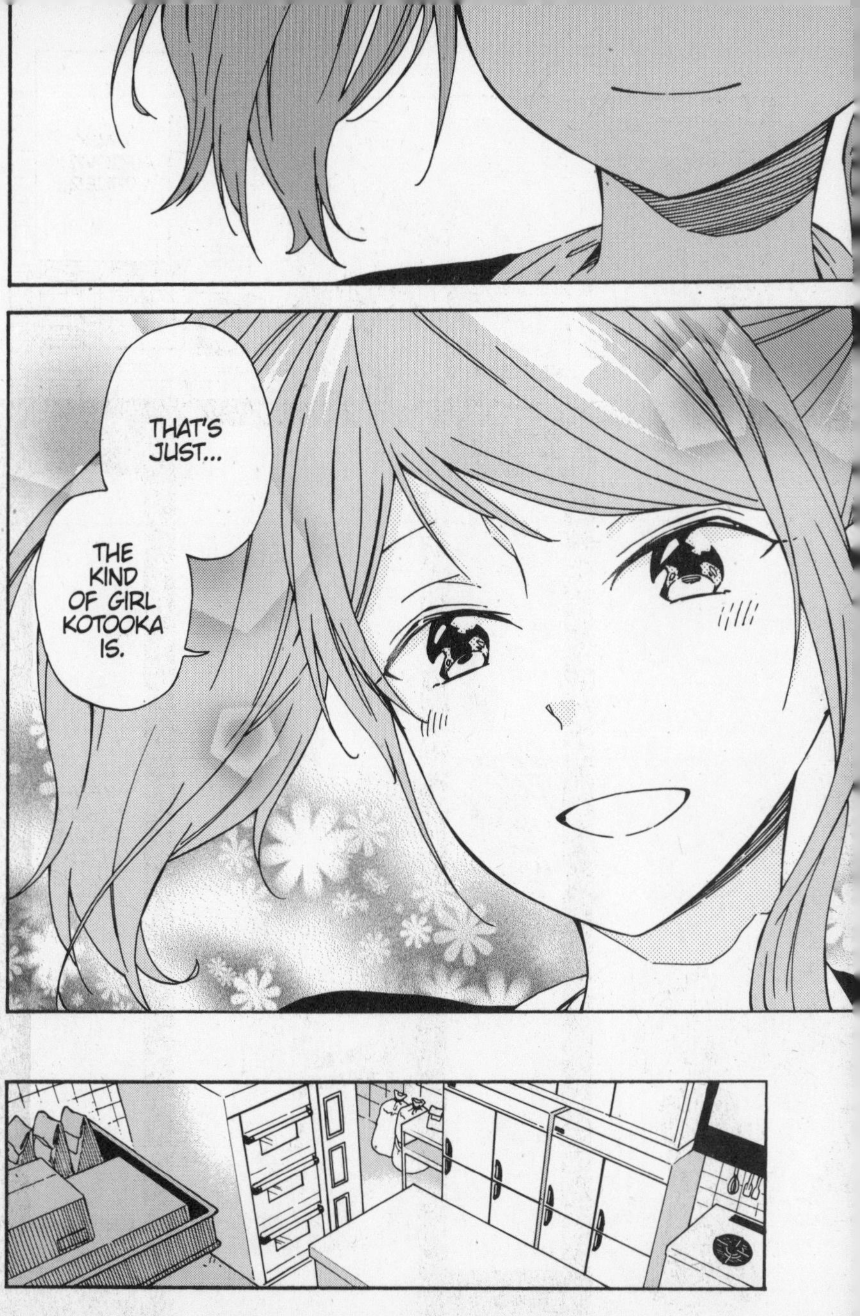
THAT'S JUST...
THE KIND OF GIRL KOTOOKA IS.

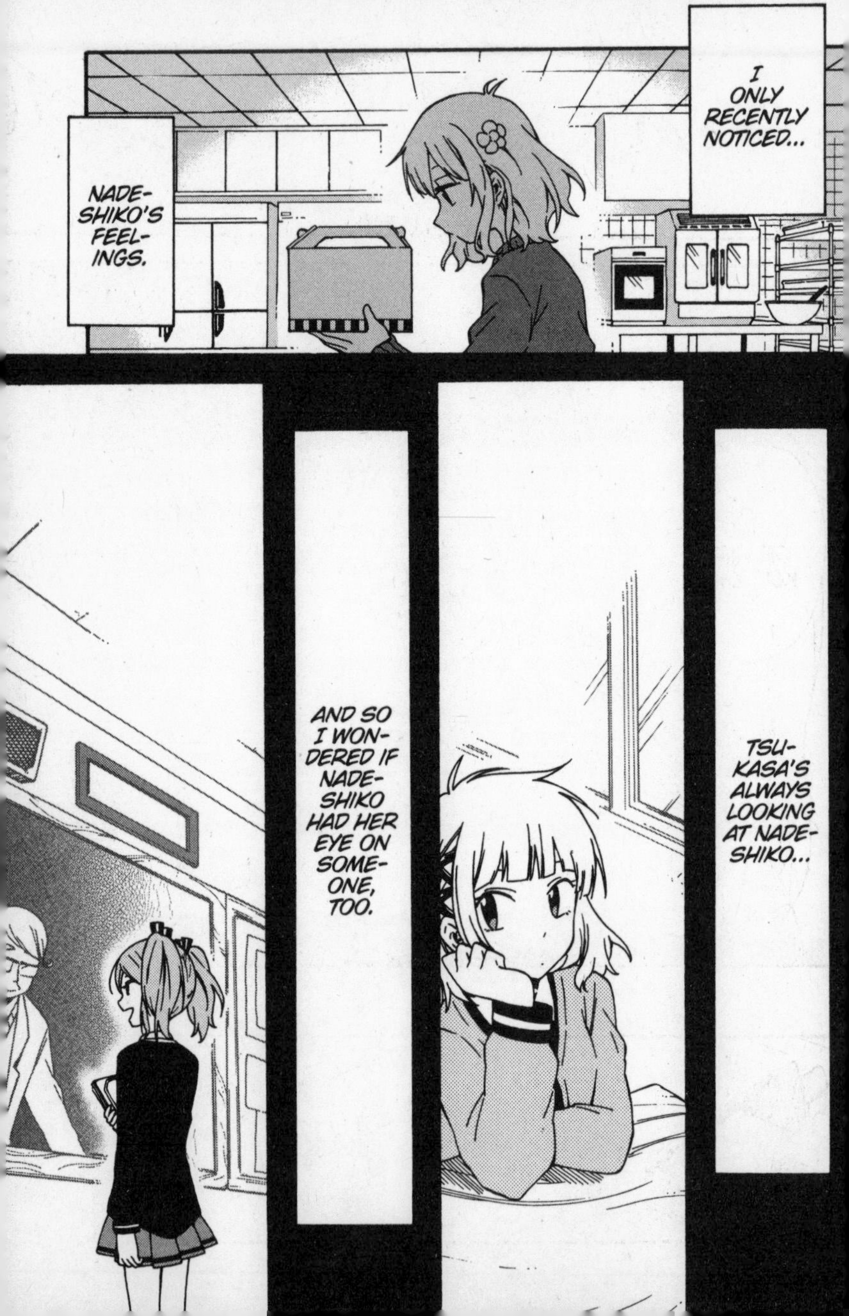
I ONLY RECENTLY NOTICED...
NADE-SHIKO'S FEEL-INGS.
TSU-KASA'S ALWAYS LOOKING AT NADE-SHIKO...
AND SO I WON-DERED IF NADE-SHIKO HAD HER EYE ON SOME-ONE, TOO.

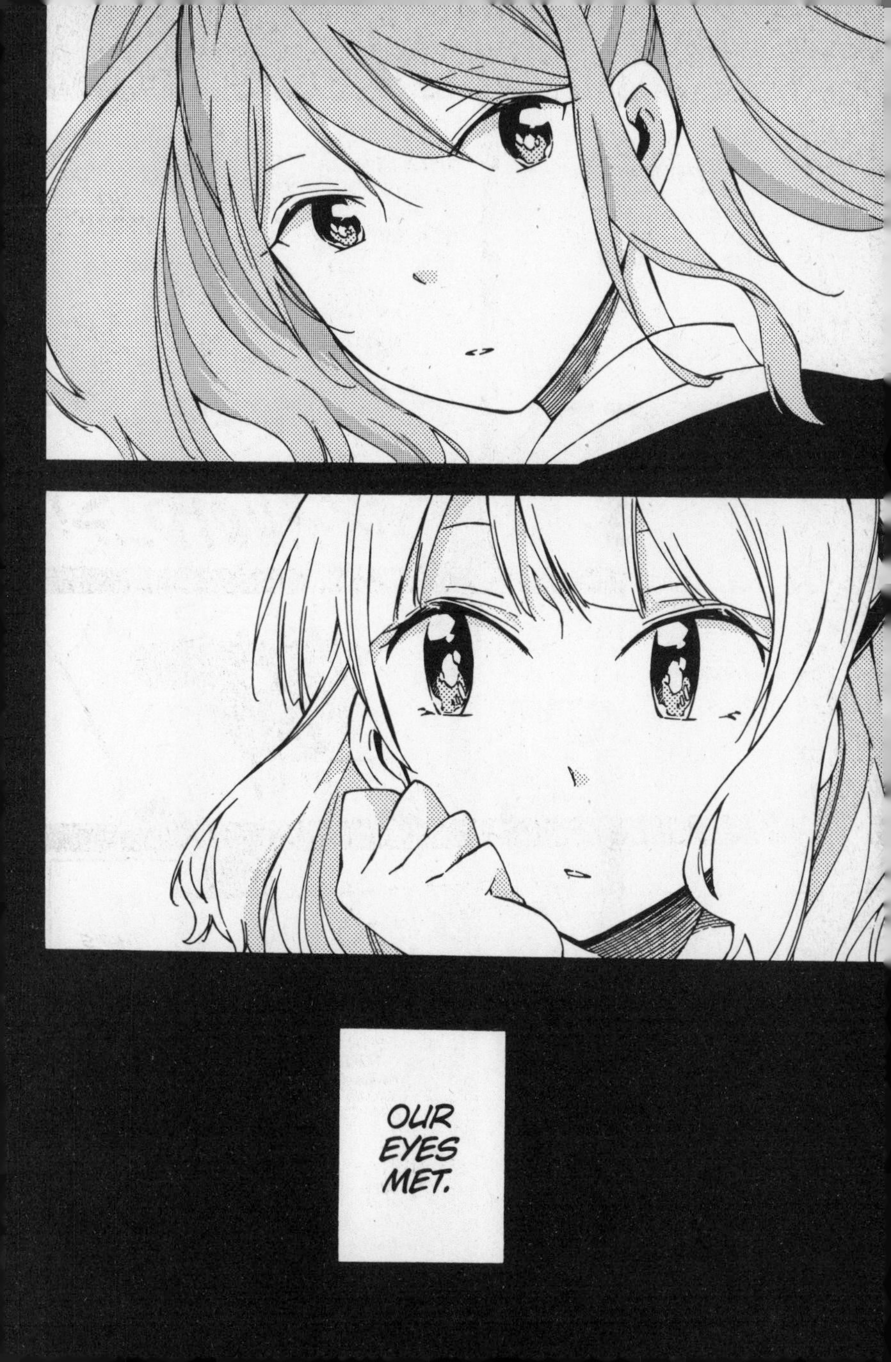
OUR EYES MET.

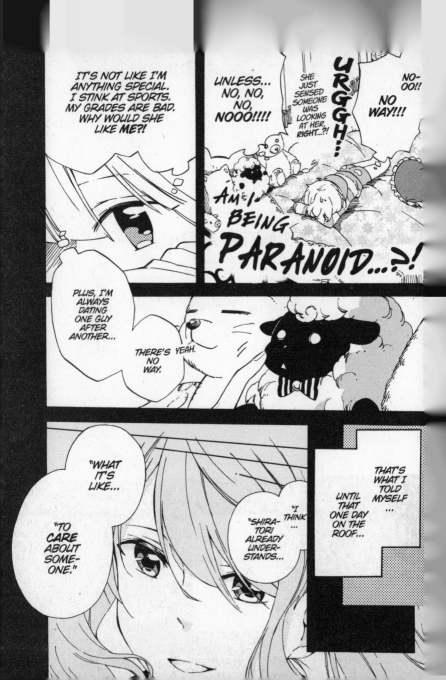

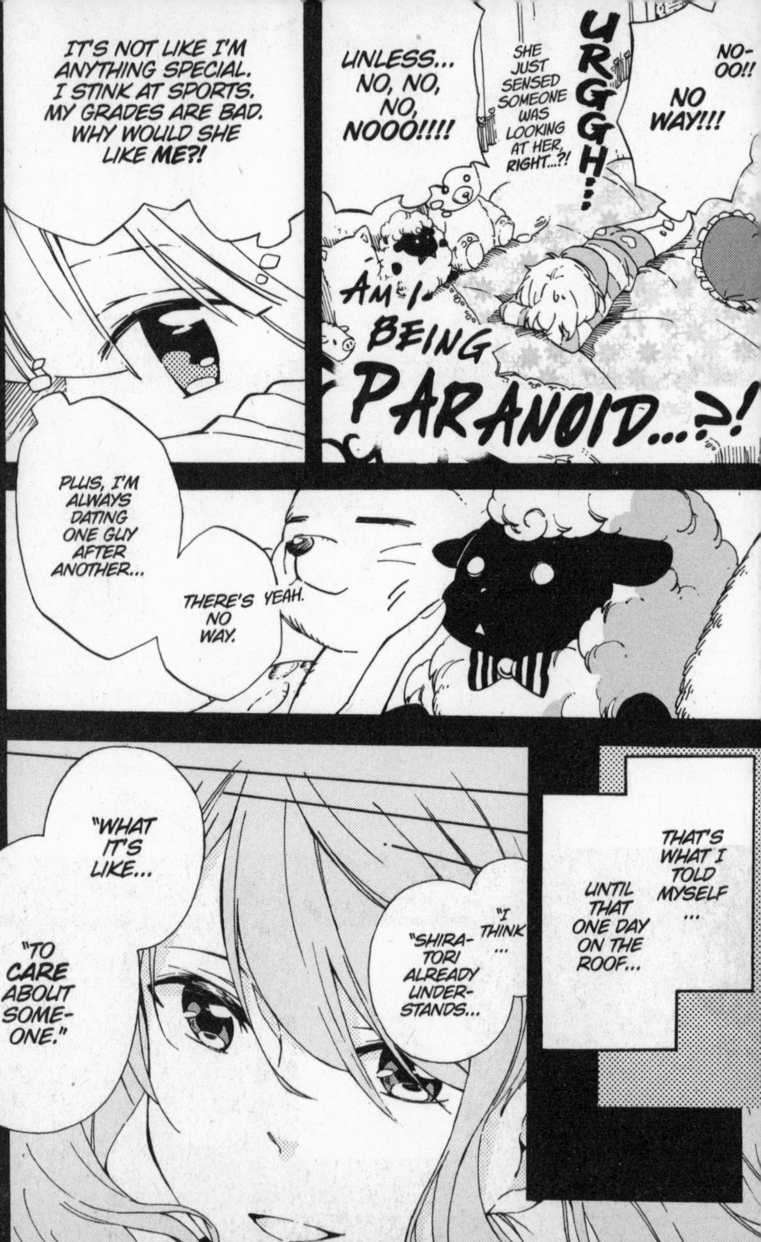
NO-OO!! NO WAY!!!
URGGH!!
SHE JUST SENSED SOMEONE WAS LOOKING AT HER, RIGHT...?!
UNLESS... NO, NO, NO, NOOO!!!!
AM I BEING PARANOID...?!
IT'S NOT LIKE I'M ANYTHING SPECIAL. I STINK AT SPORTS. MY GRADES ARE BAD. WHY WOULD SHE LIKE ME?!
PLUS, I'M ALWAYS DATING ONE GUY AFTER ANOTHER...
YEAH.
THERE'S NO WAY.
THAT'S WHAT I TOLD MYSELF ...
UNTIL THAT ONE DAY ON THE ROOF...
"I THINK ...
"SHIRATORI ALREADY UNDERSTANDS...
"WHAT IT'S LIKE...
"TO CARE ABOUT SOMEONE."

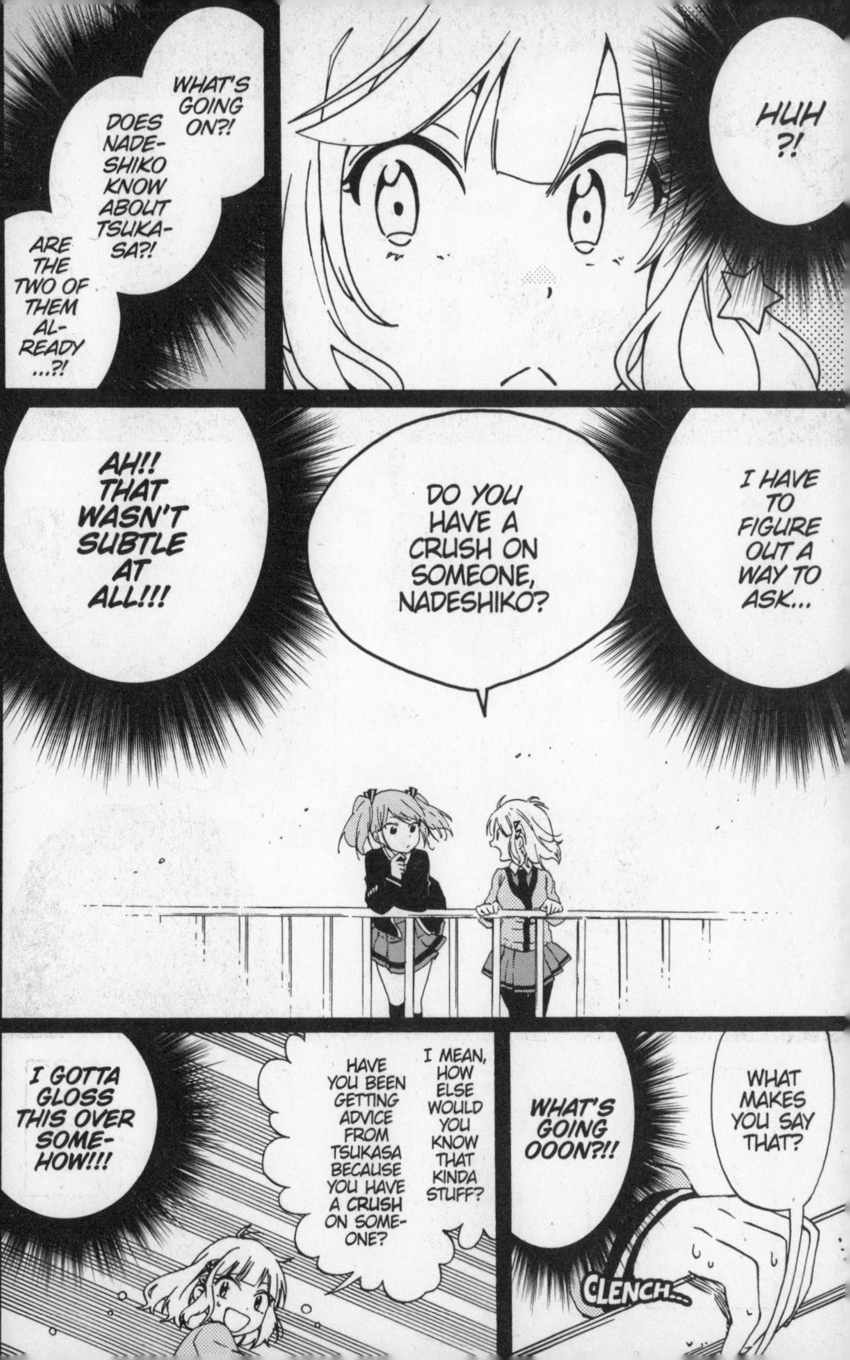
HUH?!
WHAT'S GOING ON?!
DOES NADESHIKO KNOW ABOUT TSUKASA?!
ARE THE TWO OF THEM ALREADY...?!
I HAVE TO FIGURE OUT A WAY TO ASK...
DO YOU HAVE A CRUSH ON SOMEONE, NADESHIKO?
AH!! THAT WASN'T SUBTLE AT ALL!!!
WHAT MAKES YOU SAY THAT?
WHAT'S GOING OOON?!!
CLENCH...
I MEAN, HOW ELSE WOULD YOU KNOW THAT KINDA STUFF?
HAVE YOU BEEN GETTING ADVICE FROM TSUKASA BECAUSE YOU HAVE A CRUSH ON SOMEONE?
I GOTTA GLOSS THIS OVER SOMEHOW!!!

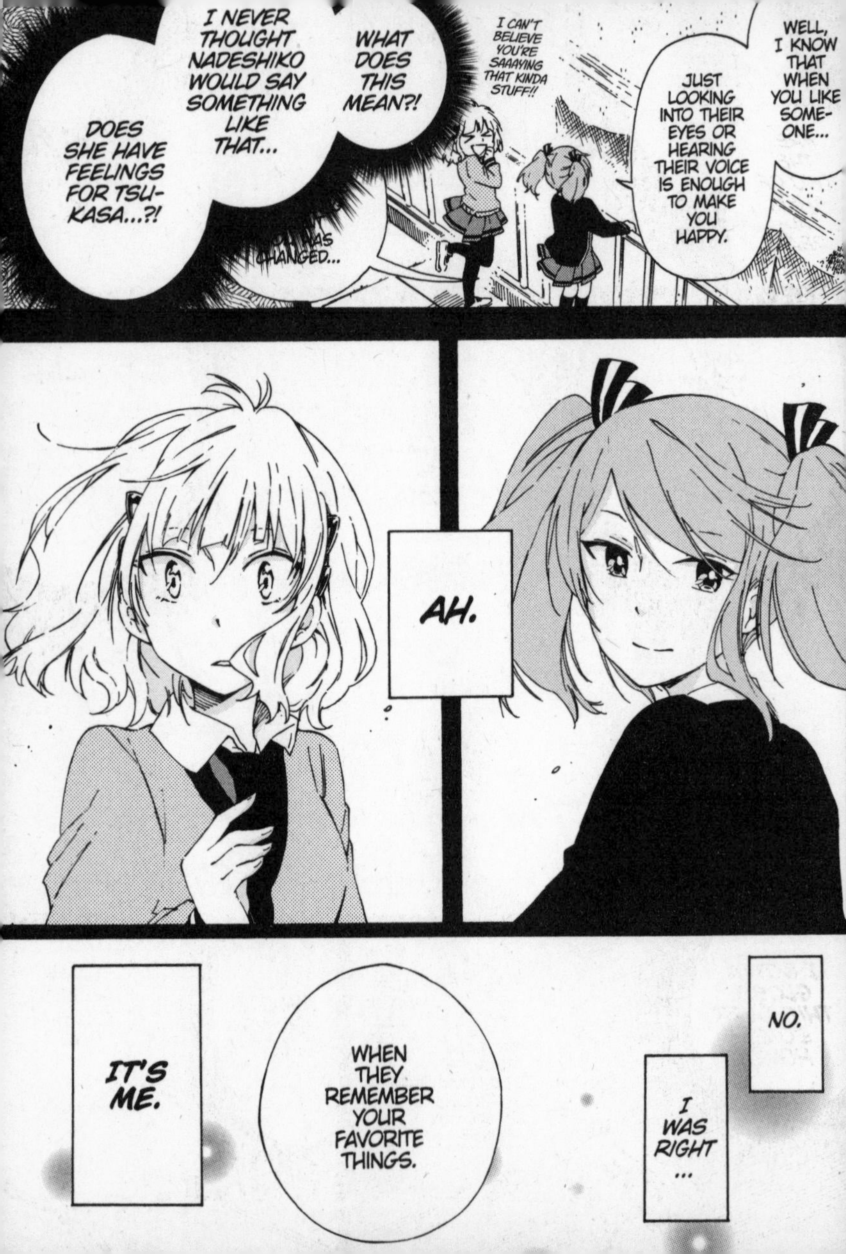

WELL, I KNOW THAT WHEN YOU LIKE SOME-ONE...
JUST LOOKING INTO THEIR EYES OR HEARING THEIR VOICE IS ENOUGH TO MAKE YOU HAPPY.
I CAN'T BELIEVE YOU'RE SAAAYING THAT KINDA STUFF!!
WHAT DOES THIS MEAN?!
I NEVER THOUGHT NADESHIKO WOULD SAY SOMETHING LIKE THAT...
HAS CHANGED...
DOES SHE HAVE FEELINGS FOR TSU-KASA...?!
AH.
NO.
I WAS RIGHT...
WHEN THEY REMEMBER YOUR FAVORITE THINGS.
IT'S ME.

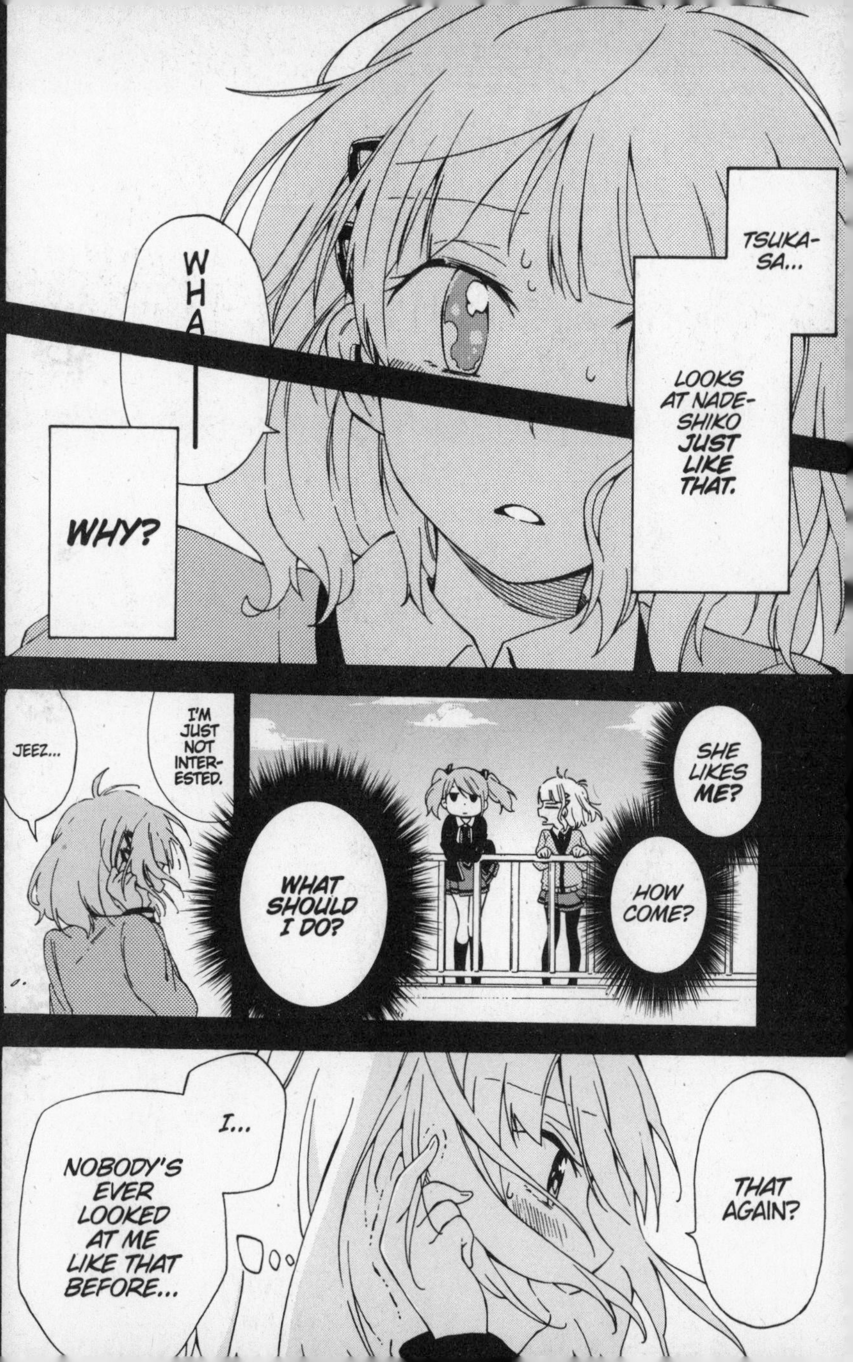
TSUKA-SA... LOOKS AT NADE-SHIKO JUST LIKE THAT.
WHA—
WHY?
SHE LIKES ME?
HOW COME?
WHAT SHOULD I DO?
I'M JUST NOT INTER-ESTED.
JEEZ...
THAT AGAIN?
I... NOBODY'S EVER LOOKED AT ME LIKE THAT BEFORE...

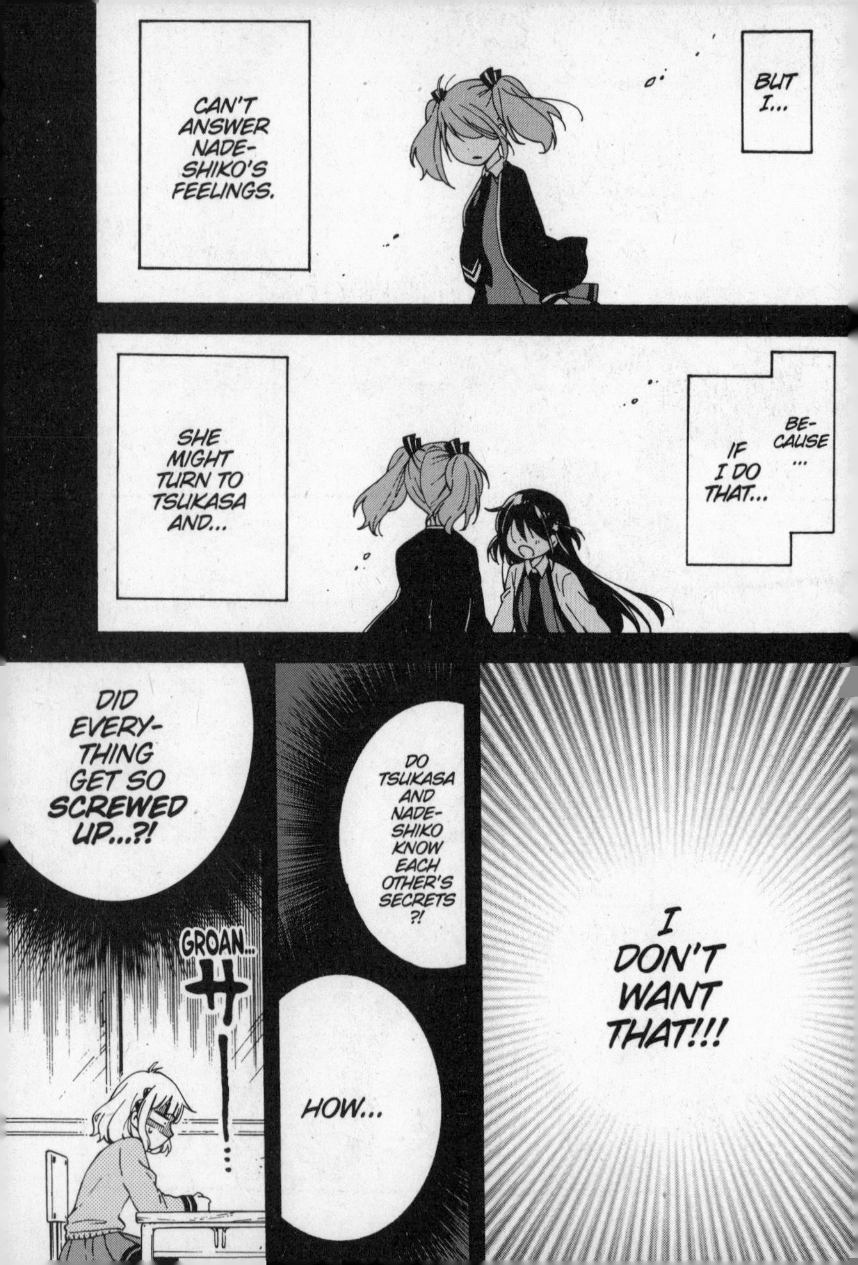
BUT I...
CAN'T ANSWER NADE-SHIKO'S FEELINGS.
BE-CAUSE...
IF I DO THAT...
SHE MIGHT TURN TO TSUKASA AND...
I DON'T WANT THAT!!!
DO TSUKASA AND NADE-SHIKO KNOW EACH OTHER'S SECRETS?!
HOW...
DID EVERY-THING GET SO SCREWED UP...?!
GROAN...

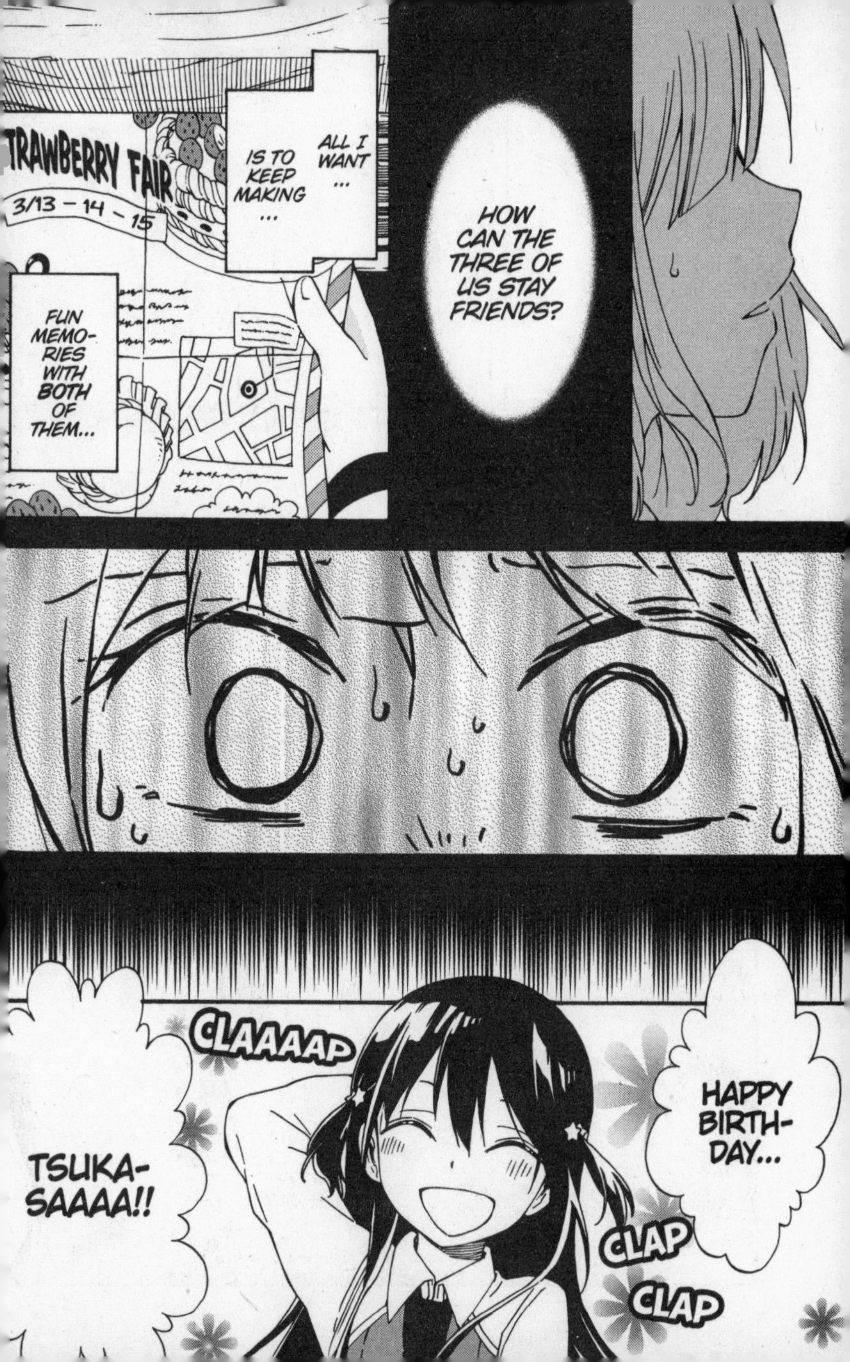
HOW CAN THE THREE OF US STAY FRIENDS?
ALL I WANT ...
IS TO KEEP MAKING ...
FUN MEMO-RIES WITH BOTH OF THEM...
TRAWBERRY FAIR
3/13 – 14 – 15
HAPPY BIRTH-DAY...
CLAAAAP
TSUKA-SAAAAA!!
CLAP
CLAP

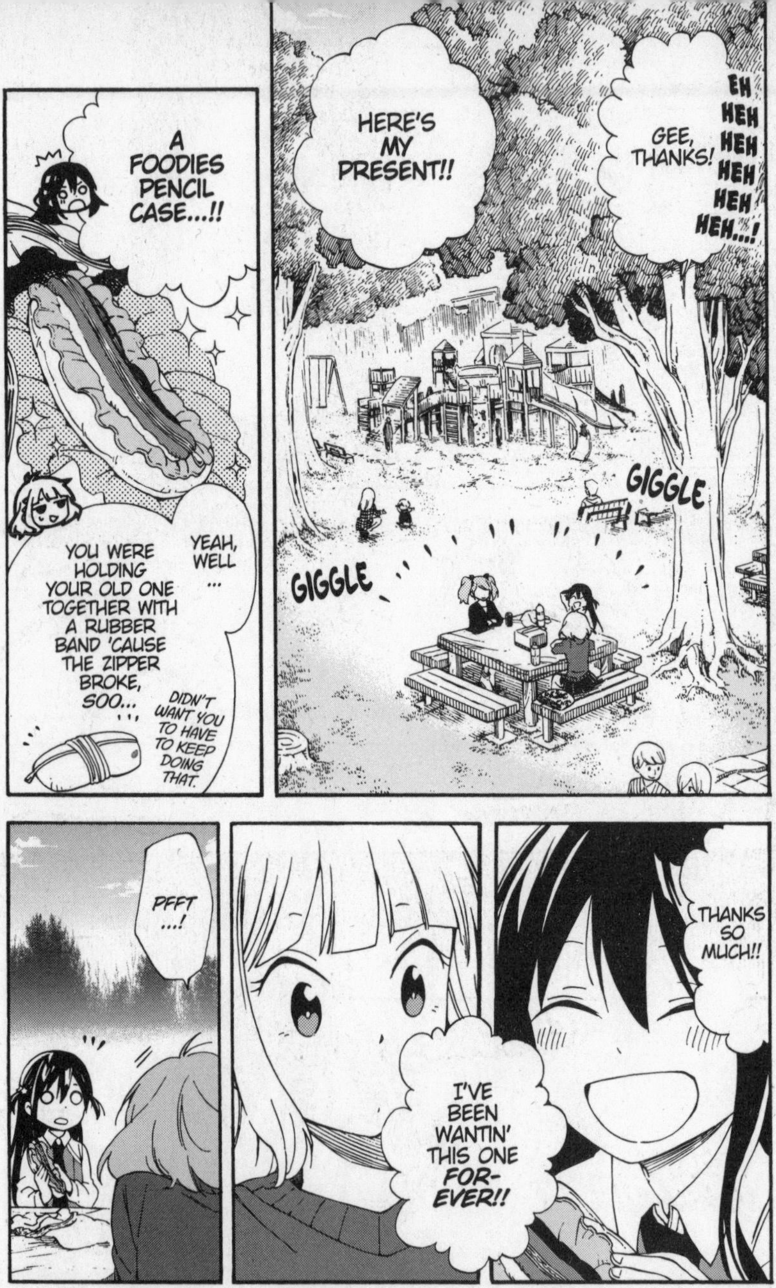
EH HEH HEH HEH HEH HEH...!
GEE, THANKS!
HERE'S MY PRESENT!!
GIGGLE
GIGGLE
A FOODIES PENCIL CASE...!!
YEAH, WELL ...
YOU WERE HOLDING YOUR OLD ONE TOGETHER WITH A RUBBER BAND 'CAUSE THE ZIPPER BROKE, SOO...
DIDN'T WANT YOU TO HAVE TO KEEP DOING THAT.
THANKS SO MUCH!!
I'VE BEEN WANTIN' THIS ONE FOR-EVER!!
PFFT ...!

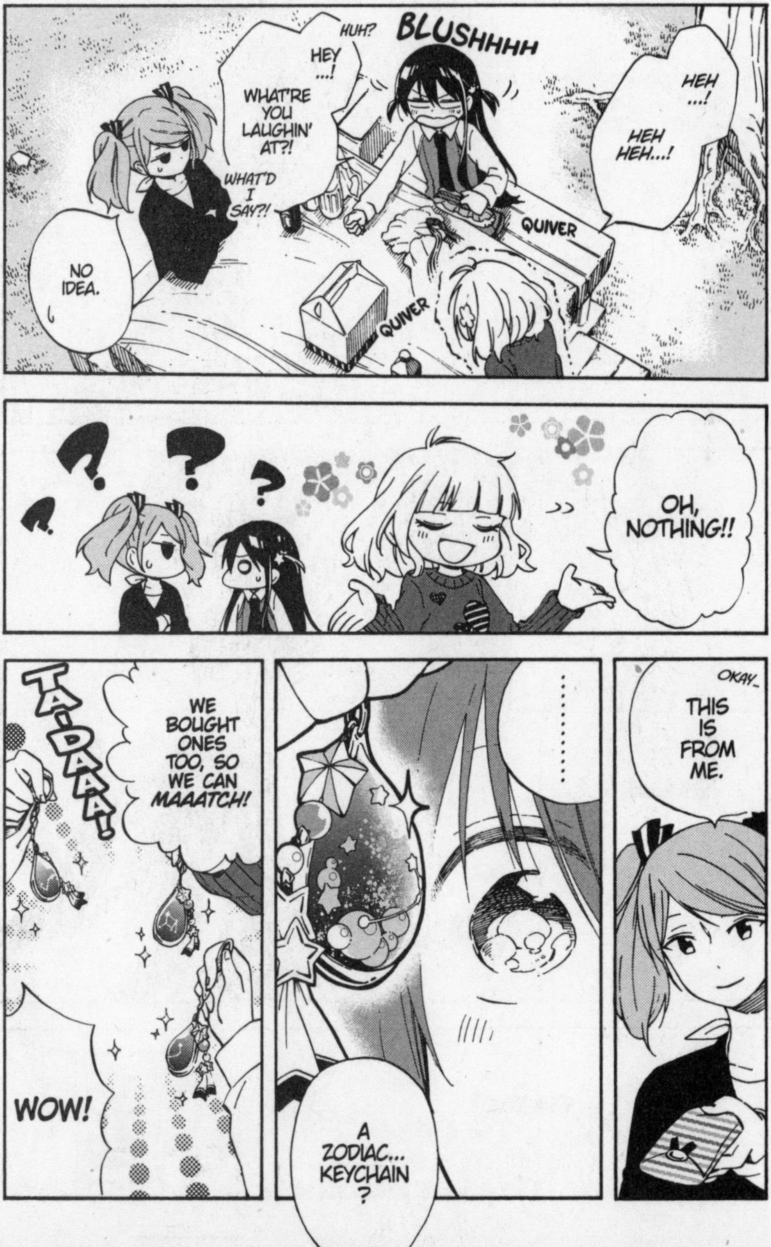
HEH...!
HEH HEH...!
BLUSHHHH
HUH?
HEY...!
WHAT'RE YOU LAUGHIN' AT?!
WHAT'D I SAY?!
QUIVER
QUIVER
NO IDEA.
OH, NOTHING!!
OKAY...
THIS IS FROM ME.
......
A ZODIAC... KEYCHAIN?
TA-DAAAA!
WE BOUGHT ONES TOO, SO WE CAN MAAATCH!
WOW!

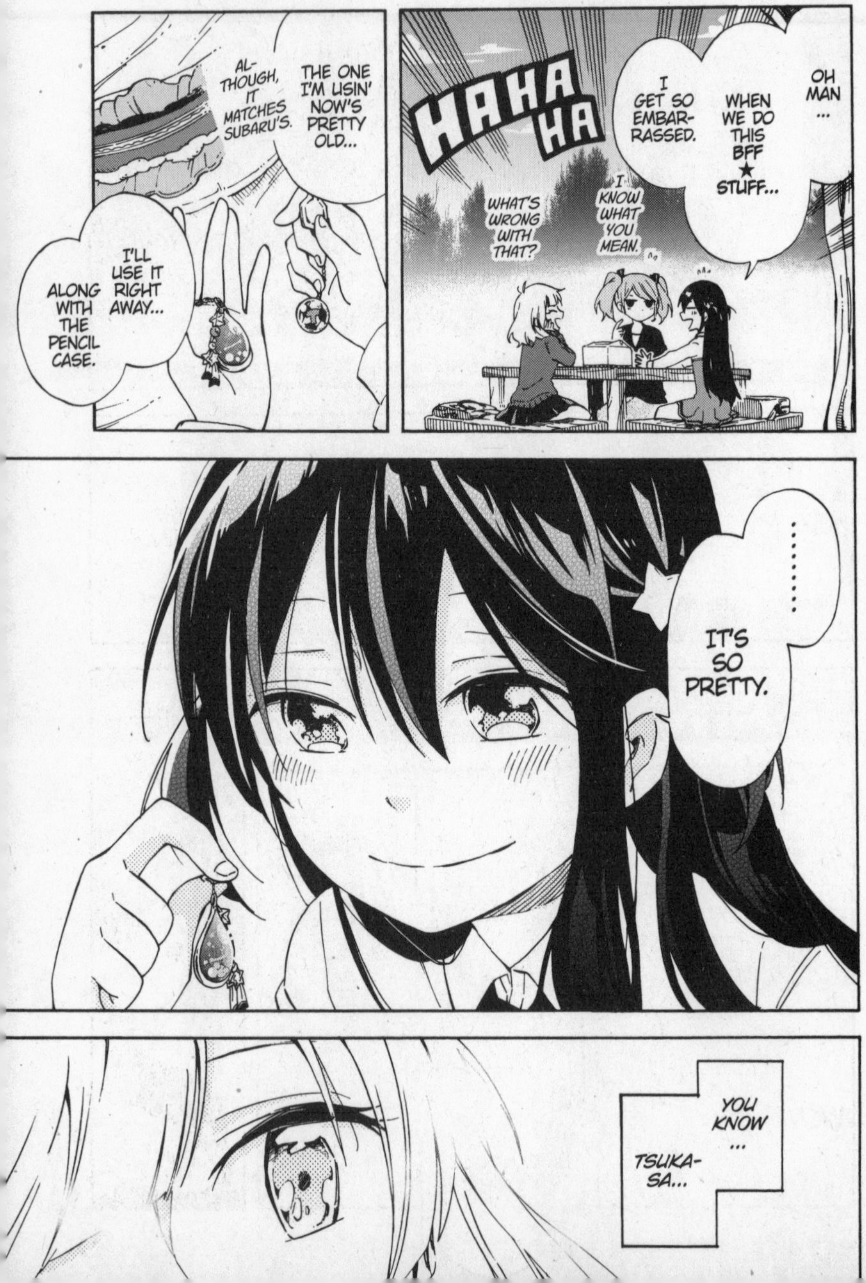
OH MAN...
WHEN WE DO THIS BFF★STUFF...
I GET SO EMBARRASSED.
HAHA HA
I KNOW WHAT YOU MEAN.
WHAT'S WRONG WITH THAT?
THE ONE I'M USIN' NOW'S PRETTY OLD...
ALTHOUGH, IT MATCHES SUBARU'S.
I'LL USE IT RIGHT AWAY...
ALONG WITH THE PENCIL CASE.
......
IT'S SO PRETTY.
YOU KNOW... TSUKASA...

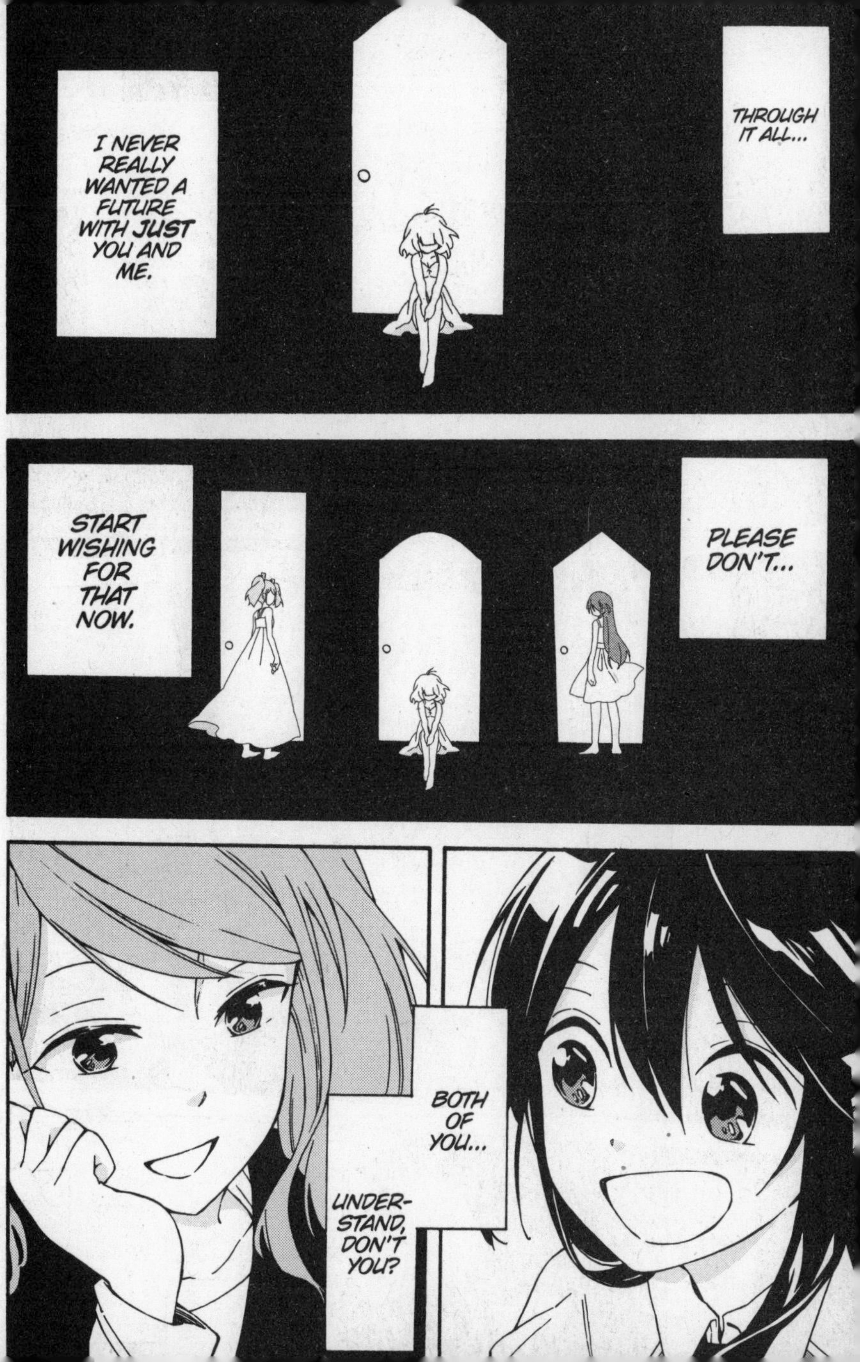
THROUGH IT ALL...
I NEVER REALLY WANTED A FUTURE WITH JUST YOU AND ME.
PLEASE DON'T...
START WISHING FOR THAT NOW.
BOTH OF YOU...
UNDER-STAND, DON'T YOU?

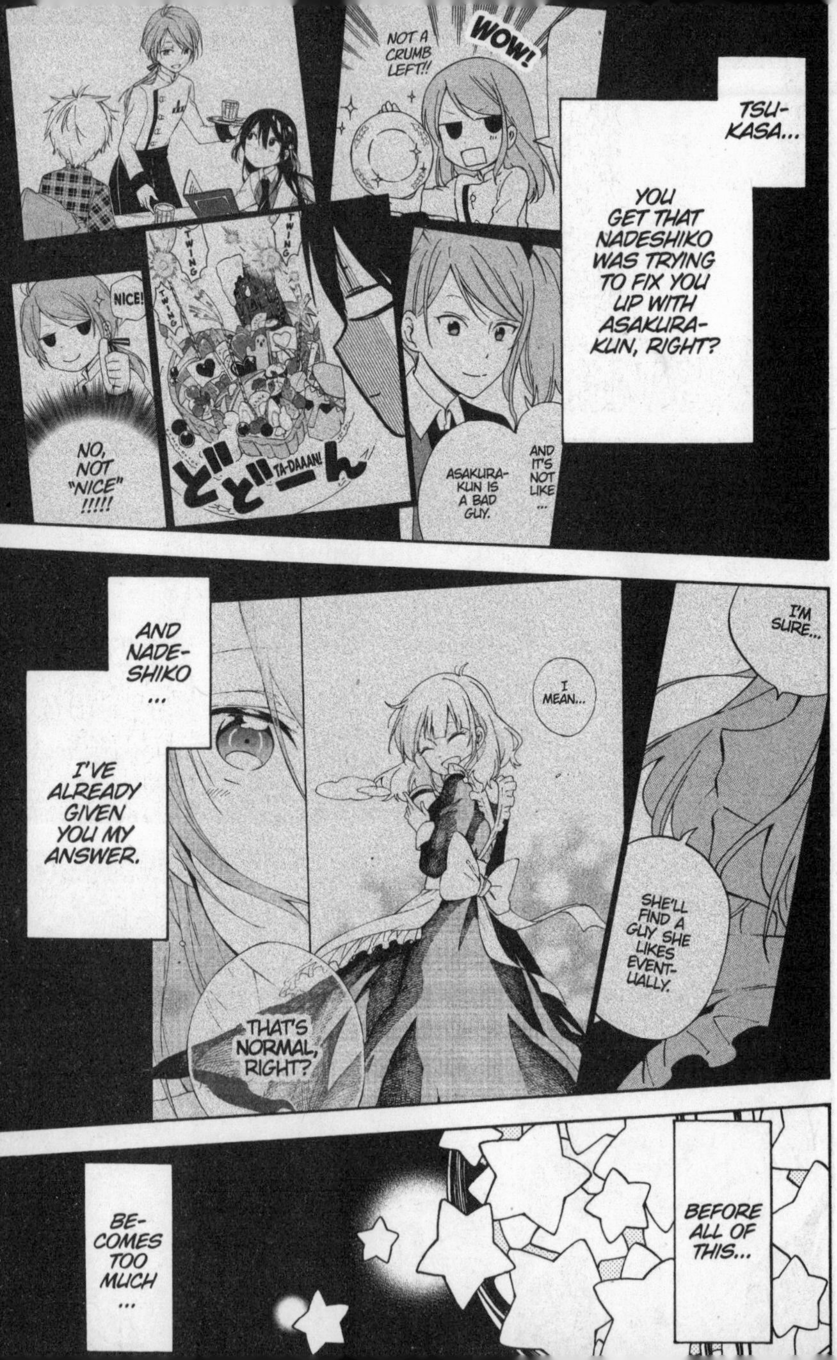
TSU-KASA...
YOU GET THAT NADESHIKO WAS TRYING TO FIX YOU UP WITH ASAKURA-KUN, RIGHT?
WOW!
NOT A CRUMB LEFT!!
AND IT'S NOT LIKE...
ASAKURA-KUN IS A BAD GUY.
TWING
TWING
TWING
どどーん
TA-DAAAN!
NICE!
NO, NOT "NICE"!!!!!
I'M SURE...
SHE'LL FIND A GUY SHE LIKES EVENT-UALLY.
I MEAN...
THAT'S NORMAL, RIGHT?
AND NADE-SHIKO...
I'VE ALREADY GIVEN YOU MY ANSWER.
BEFORE ALL OF THIS...
BE-COMES TOO MUCH...

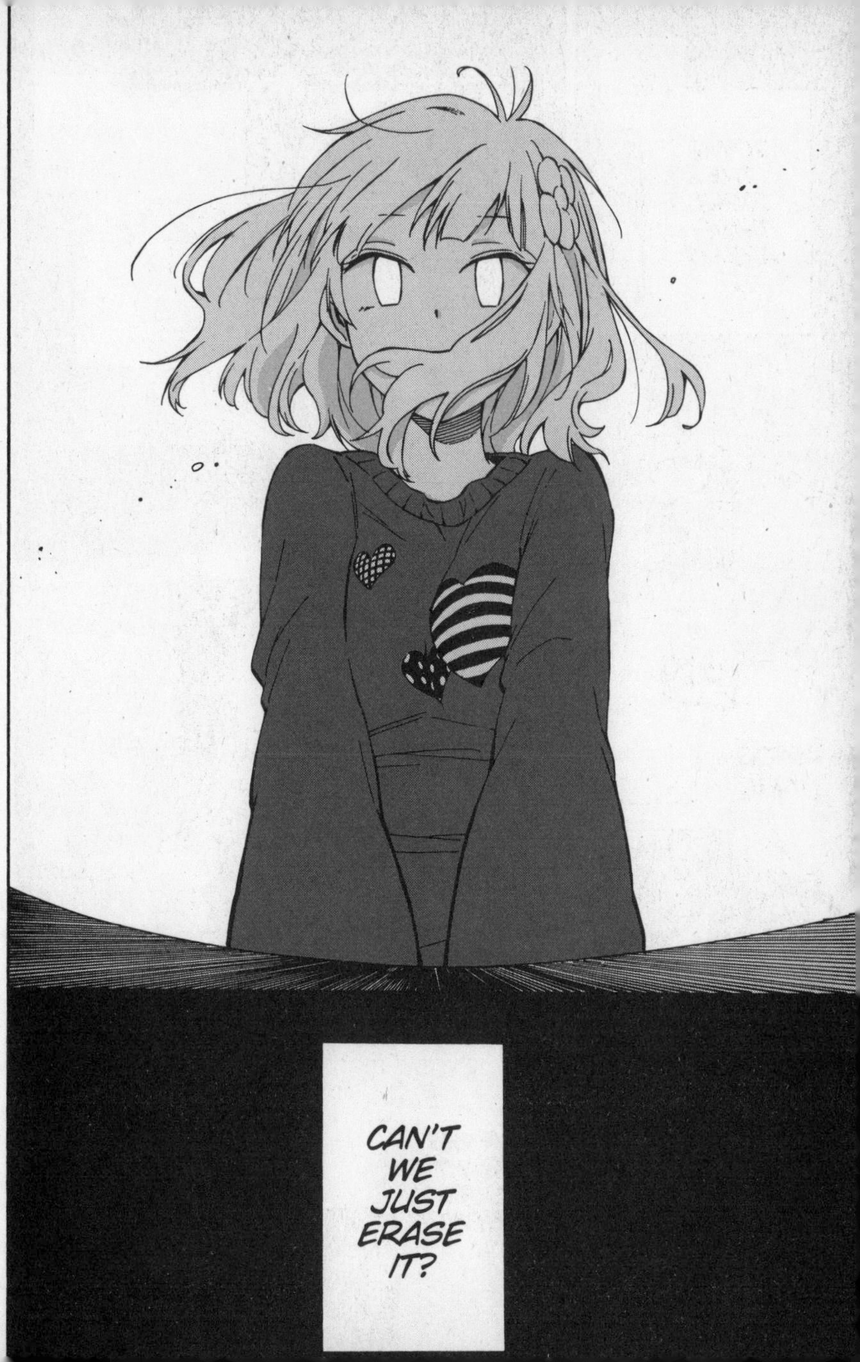
CAN'T WE JUST ERASE IT?

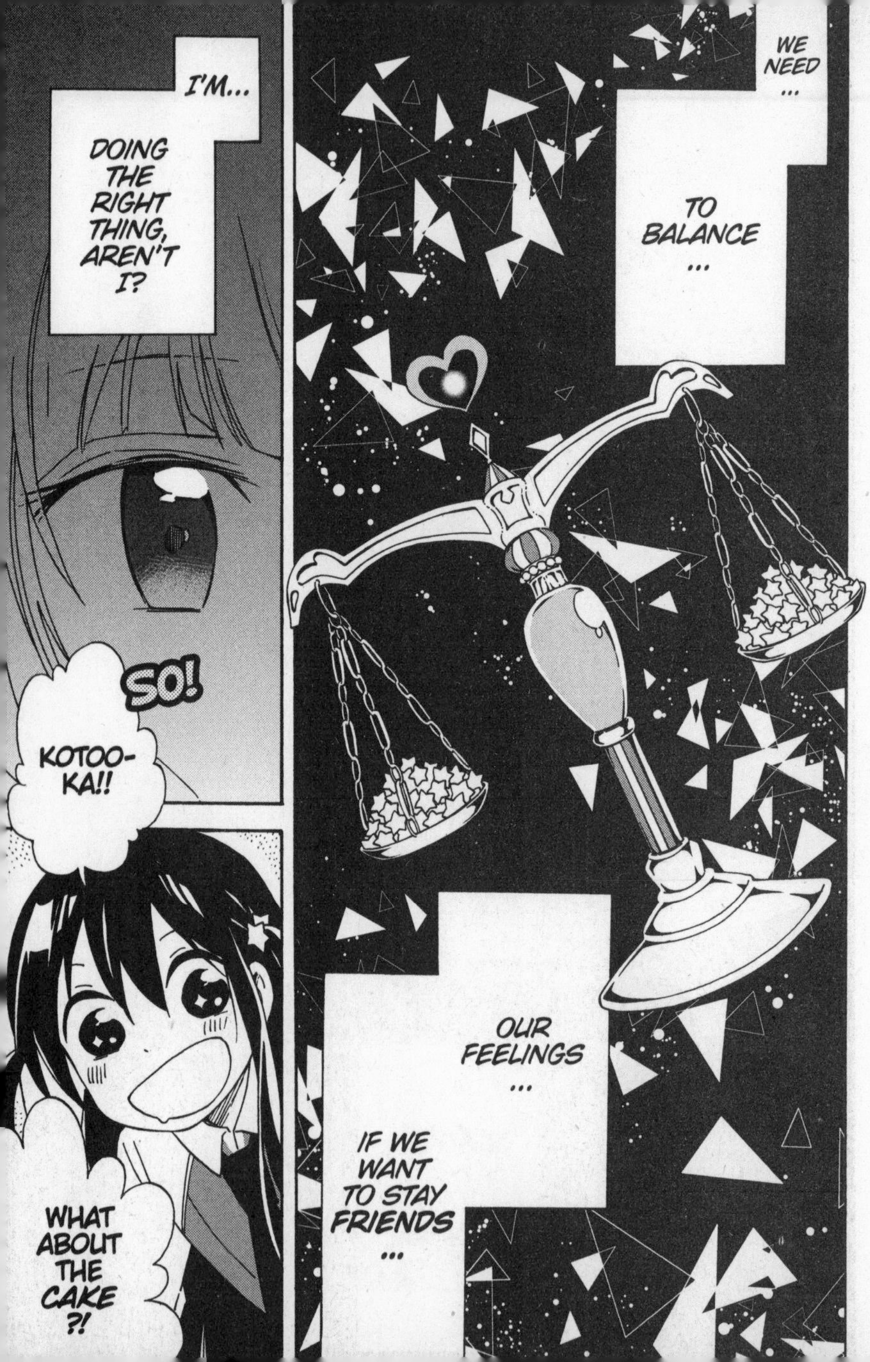
WE NEED ...
TO BALANCE ...
OUR FEELINGS ...
IF WE WANT TO STAY FRIENDS ...
I'M...
DOING THE RIGHT THING, AREN'T I?
SO!
KOTOO-KA!!
WHAT ABOUT THE CAKE ?!

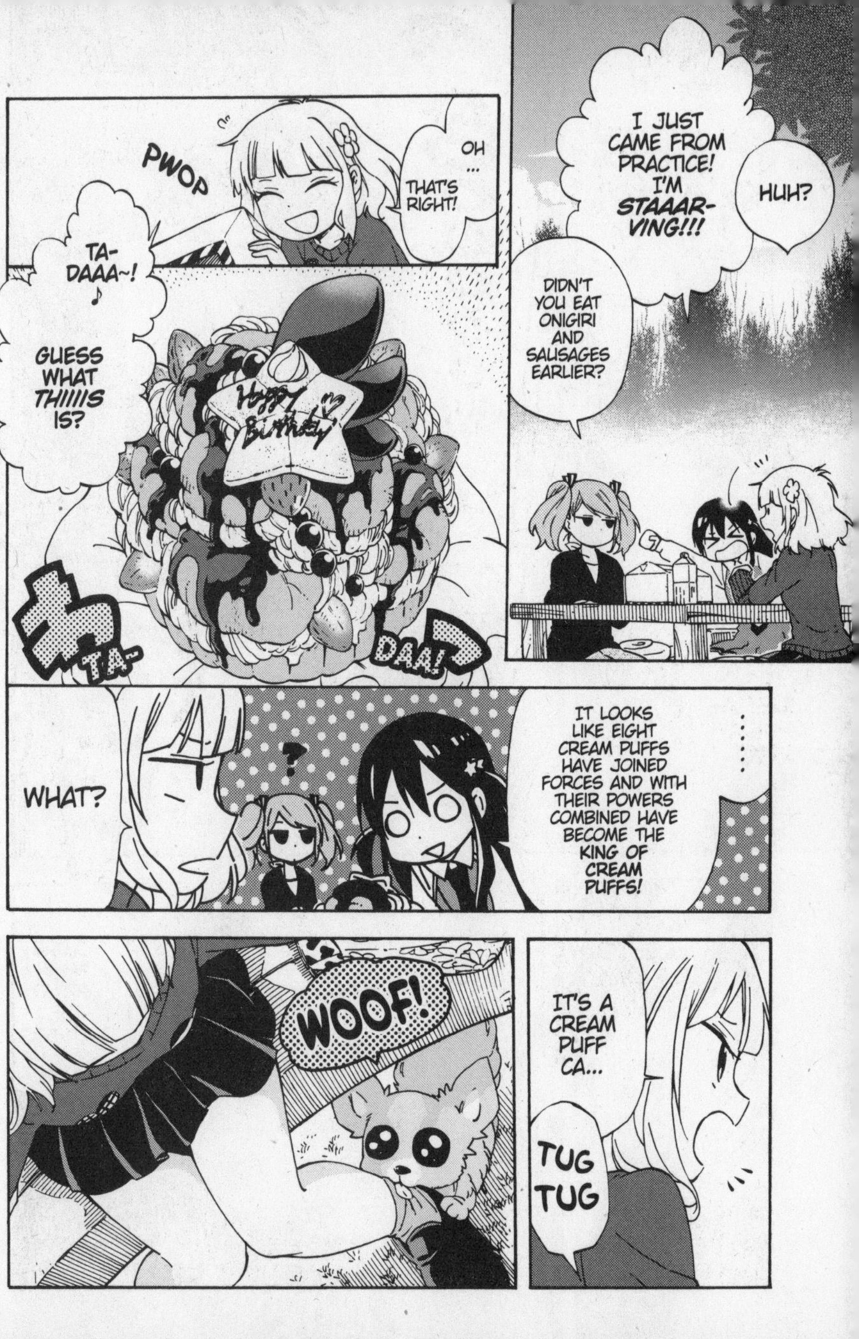
I JUST CAME FROM PRACTICE! I'M STAAAR-VING!!!
HUH?
DIDN'T YOU EAT ONIGIRI AND SAUSAGES EARLIER?
OH ... THAT'S RIGHT!
PWOP
TA-DAAA~! ♪
GUESS WHAT THIIIIS IS?
Happy Birthday
TA-DAA!
......
IT LOOKS LIKE EIGHT CREAM PUFFS HAVE JOINED FORCES AND WITH THEIR POWERS COMBINED HAVE BECOME THE KING OF CREAM PUFFS!
WHAT?
IT'S A CREAM PUFF CA...
TUG TUG
WOOF!

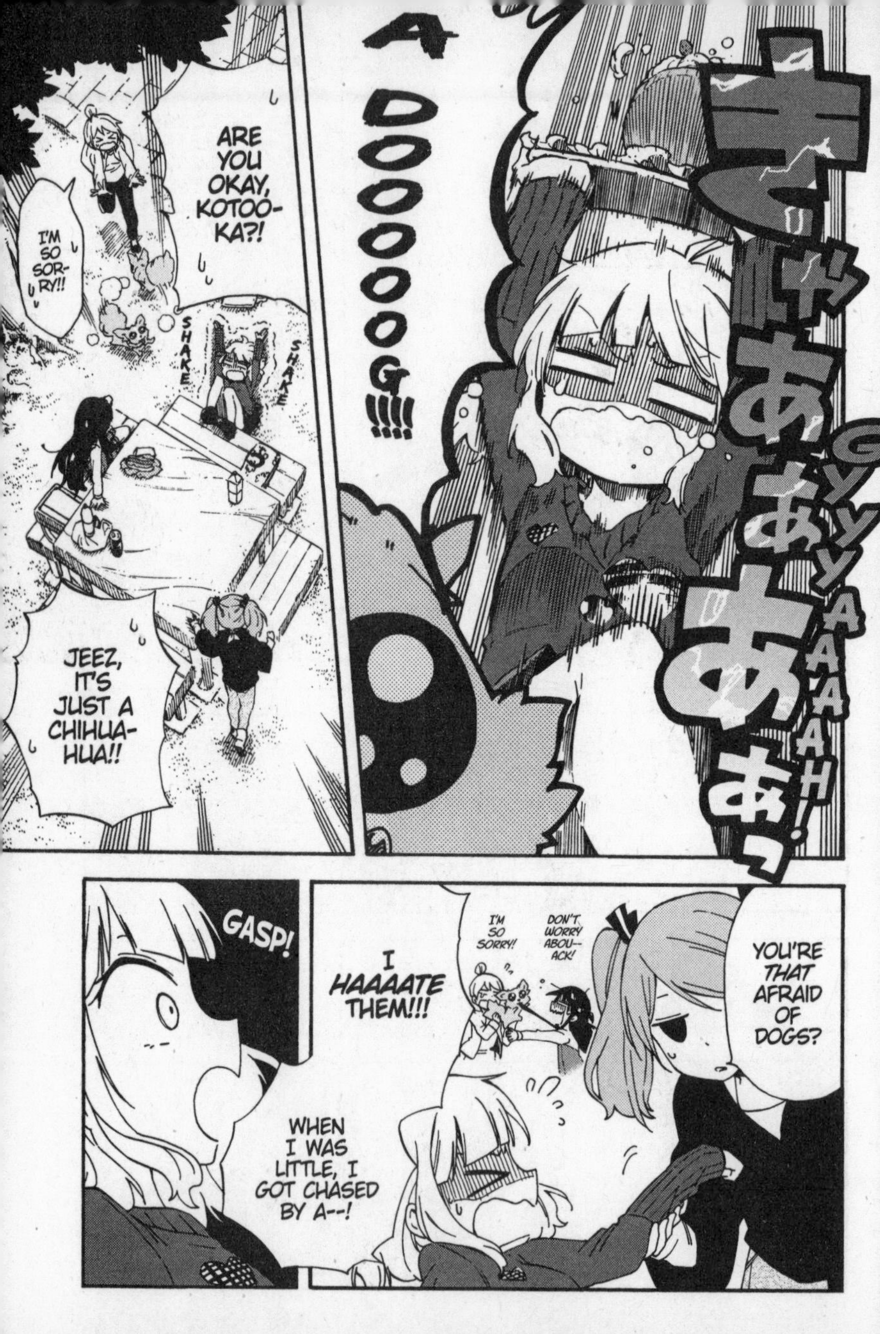

GYYAAAAH!
きゃああああぁっ
A DOOOOOOOG!!!!
ARE YOU OKAY, KOTOO-KA?!
I'M SO SOR-RY!!
SHAKE
SHAKE
JEEZ, IT'S JUST A CHIHUA-HUA!!
YOU'RE THAT AFRAID OF DOGS?
DON'T WORRY ABOU--ACK!
I'M SO SORRY!
I HAAAATE THEM!!!
WHEN I WAS LITTLE, I GOT CHASED BY A--!
GASP!

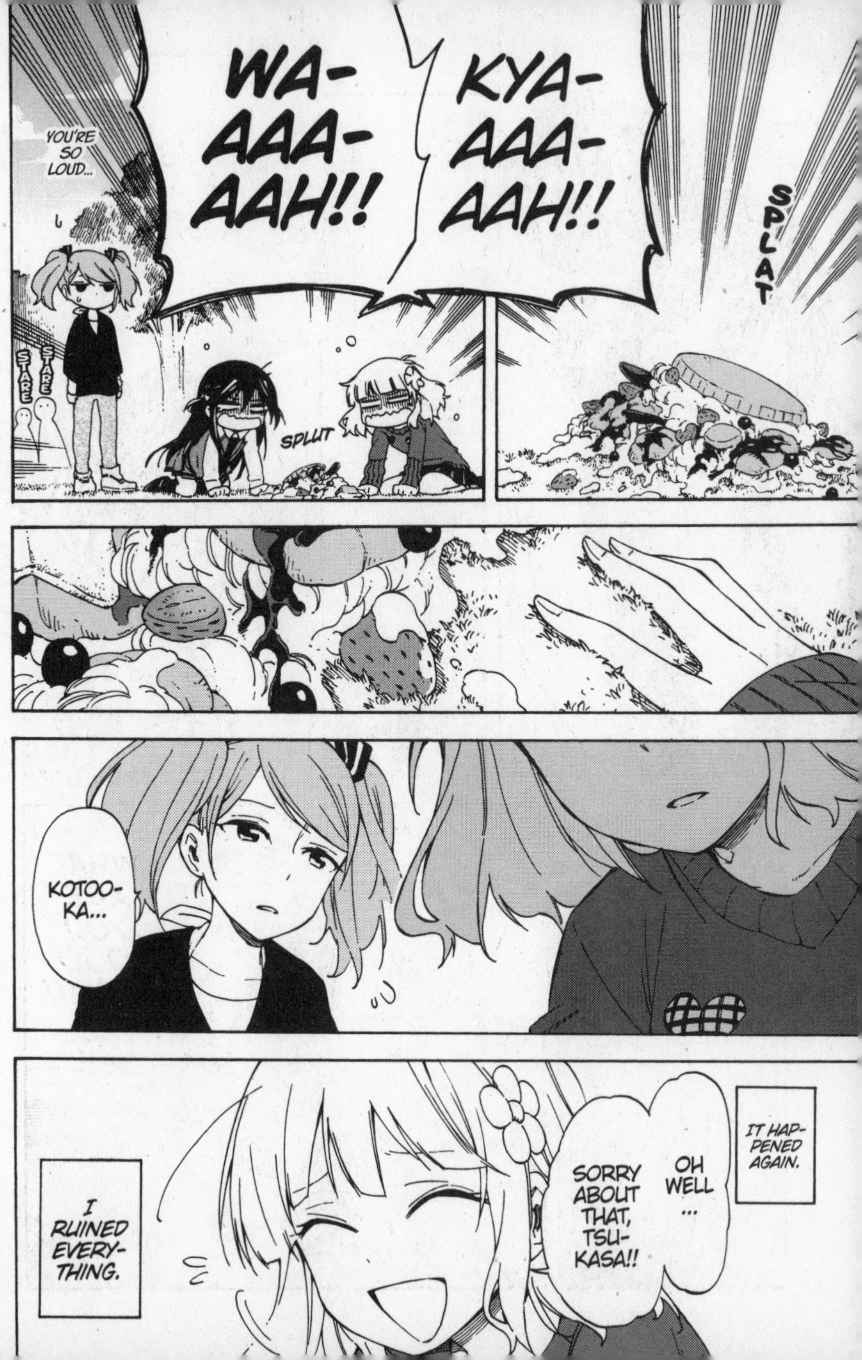
SPLAT
KYA-AAA-AAH!!
WA-AAA-AAH!!
YOU'RE SO LOUD...
STARE
STARE
SPLUT
KOTOO-KA...
IT HAP-PENED AGAIN.
OH WELL ...
SORRY ABOUT THAT, TSU-KASA!!
I RUINED EVERY-THING.

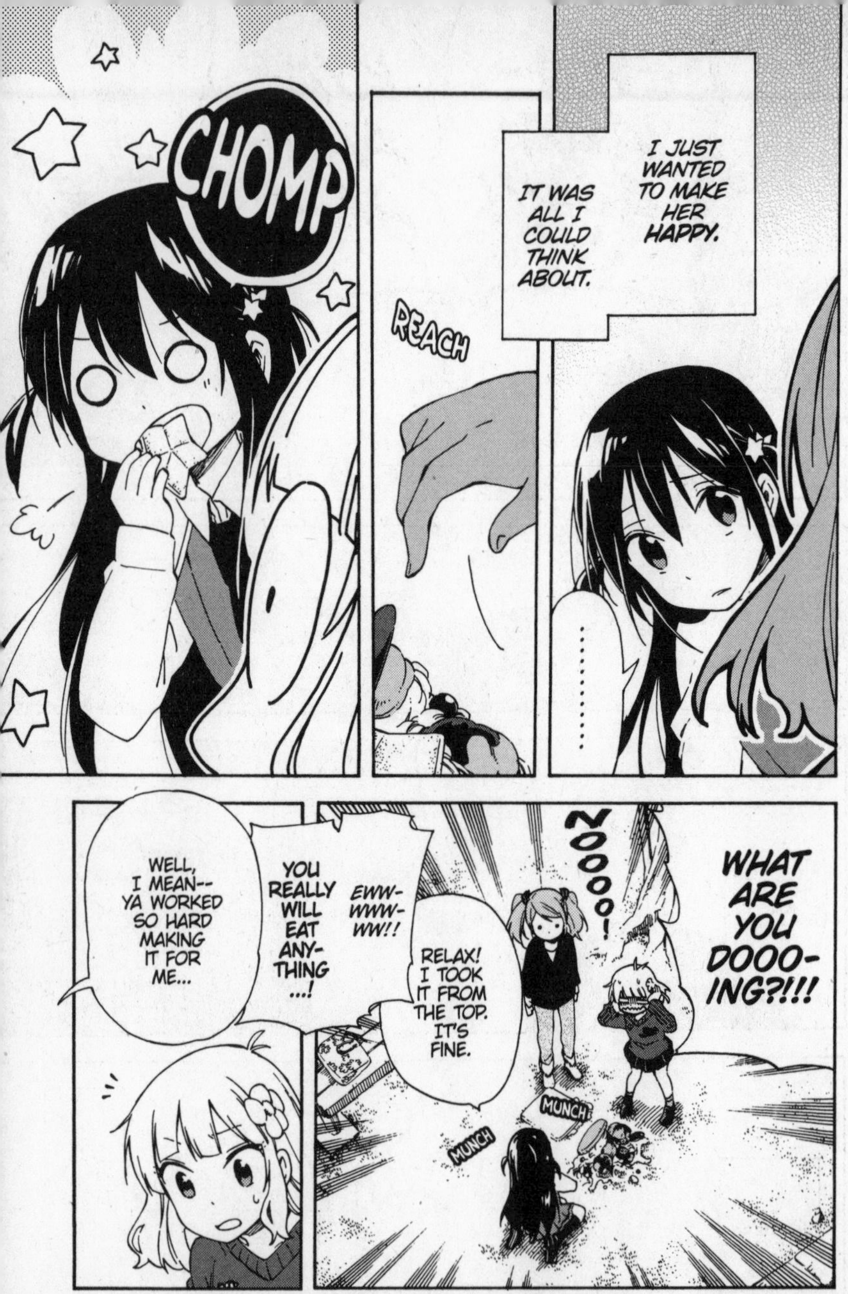
I JUST WANTED TO MAKE HER HAPPY.
IT WAS ALL I COULD THINK ABOUT.
......
REACH
CHOMP
Ew
WHAT ARE YOU DOOOO-ING?!!!
NOOOOO!
RELAX! I TOOK IT FROM THE TOP. IT'S FINE.
EWW-WWW-WW!!
YOU REALLY WILL EAT ANY-THING ...!
MUNCH
MUNCH
WELL, I MEAN-- YA WORKED SO HARD MAKING IT FOR ME...

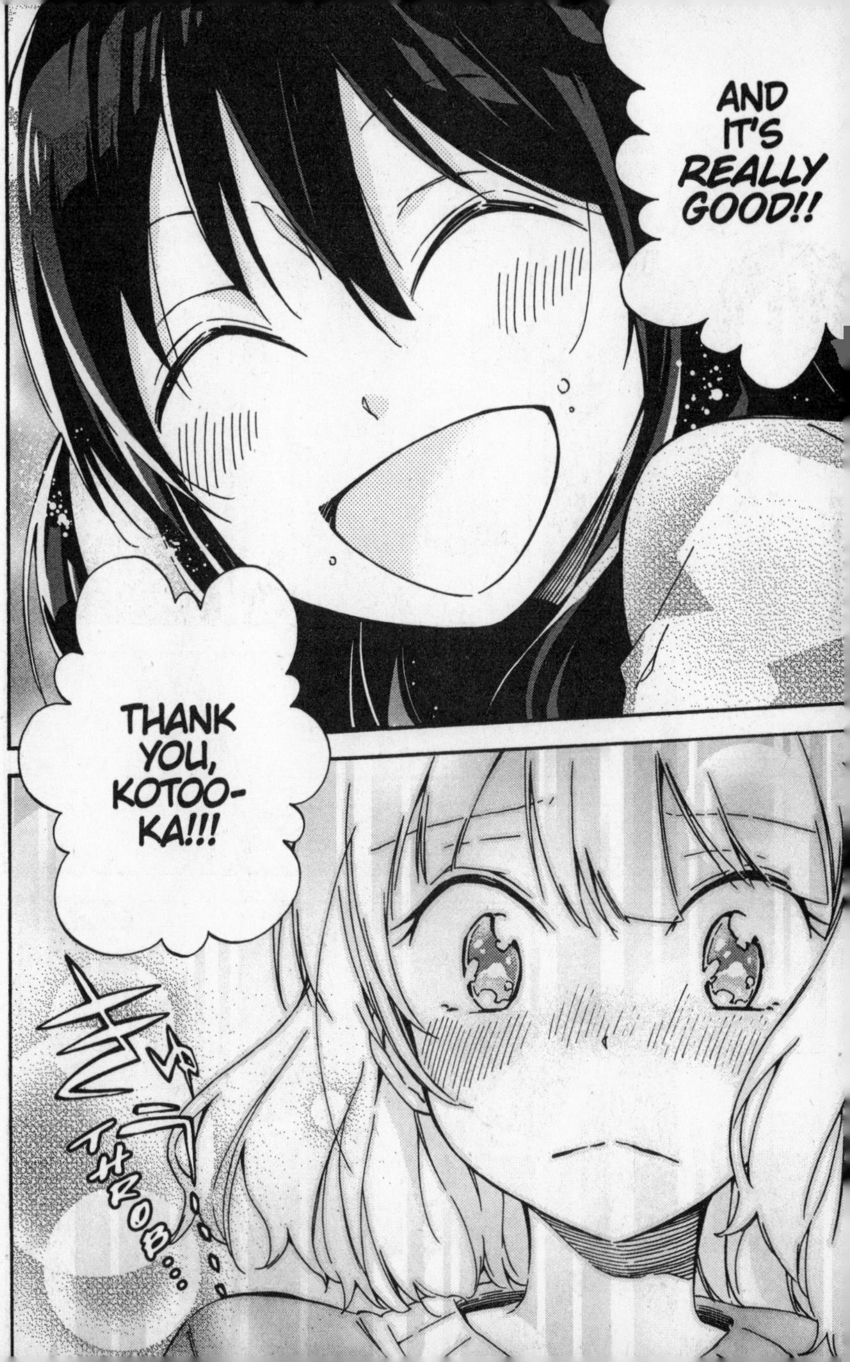
AND IT'S REALLY GOOD!!
THANK YOU, KOTOO-KA!!!
THROB...

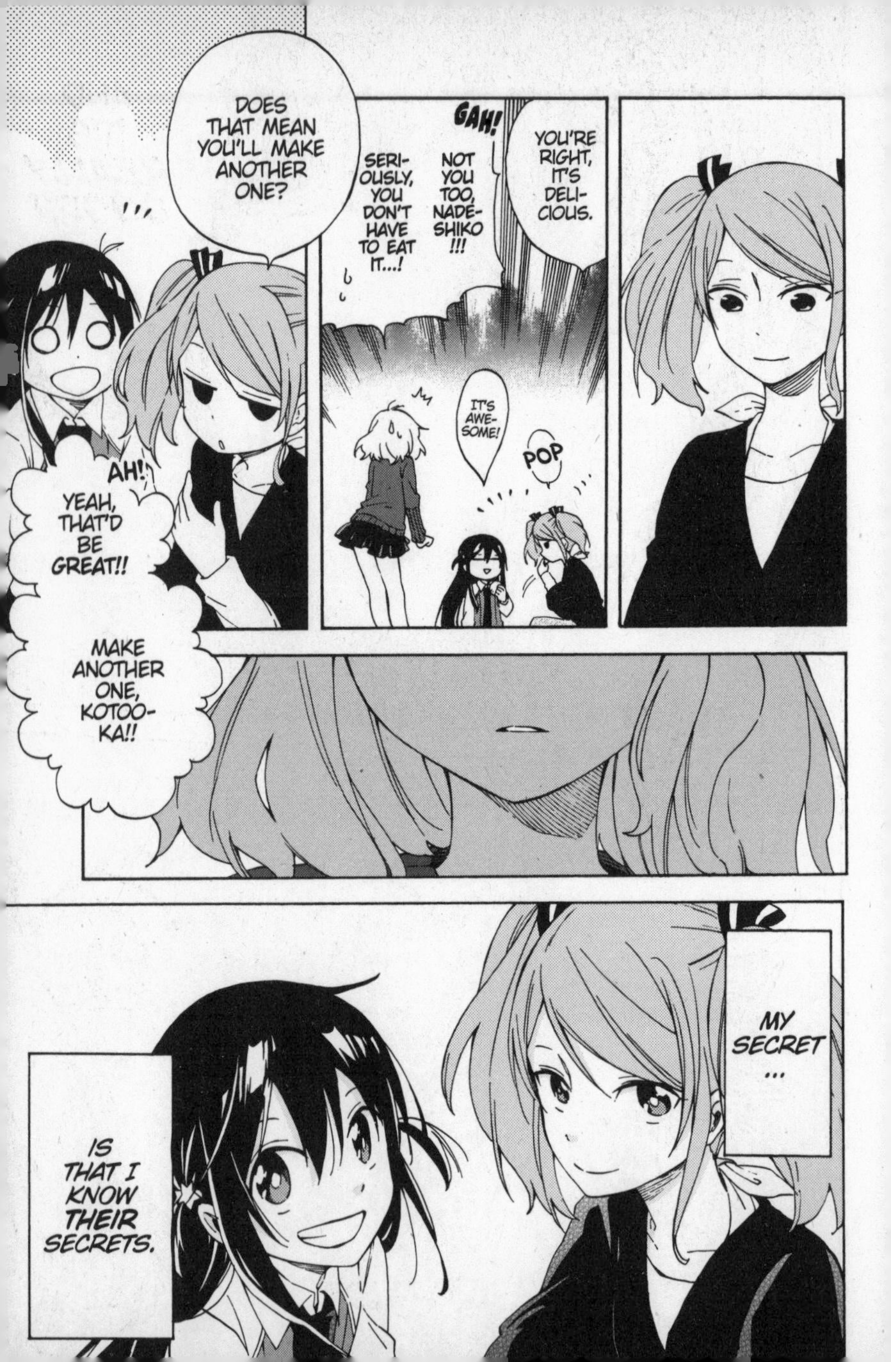

YOU'RE RIGHT, IT'S DELICIOUS.
GAH!
NOT YOU TOO, NADESHIKO!!!
SERIOUSLY, YOU DON'T HAVE TO EAT IT...!
IT'S AWESOME!
POP
DOES THAT MEAN YOU'LL MAKE ANOTHER ONE?
AH!
YEAH, THAT'D BE GREAT!!
MAKE ANOTHER ONE, KOTOOKA!!
MY SECRET ...
IS THAT I KNOW THEIR SECRETS.

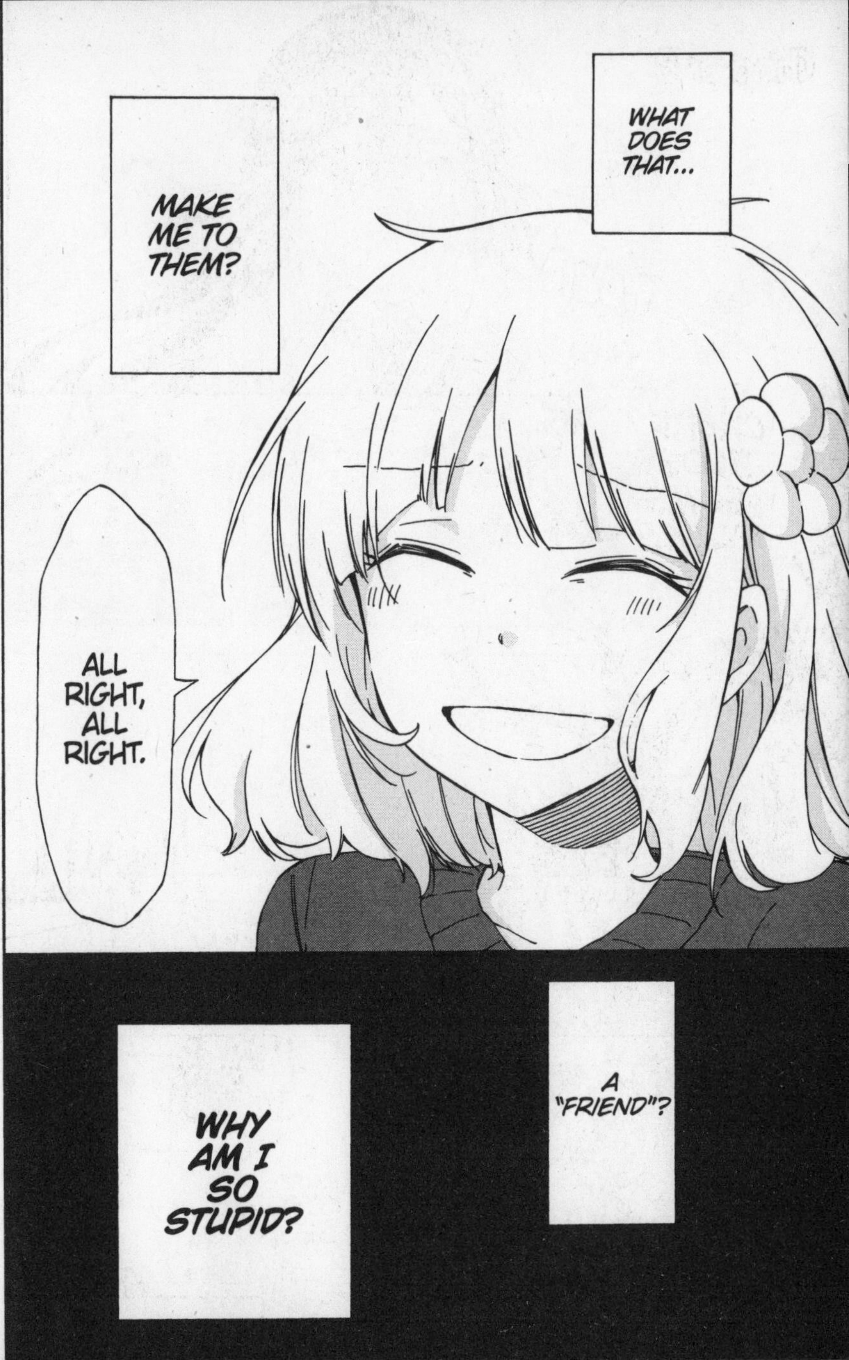
WHAT DOES THAT...
MAKE ME TO THEM?
ALL RIGHT, ALL RIGHT.
A "FRIEND"?
WHY AM I SO STUPID?

Chapter 8

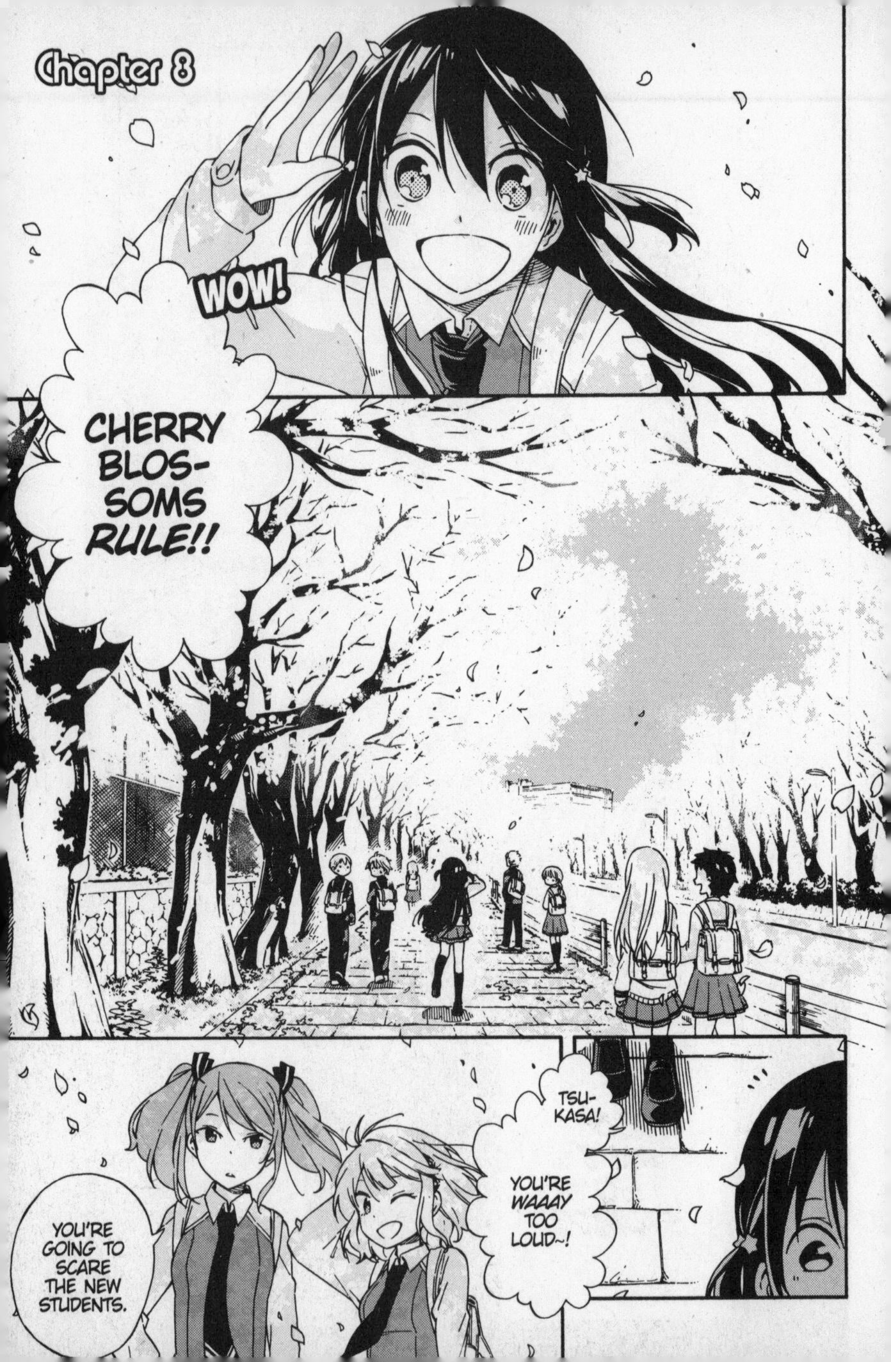
WOW!
CHERRY BLOS-SOMS RULE!!
TSU-KASA!
YOU'RE WAAAY TOO LOUD~!
YOU'RE GOING TO SCARE THE NEW STUDENTS.

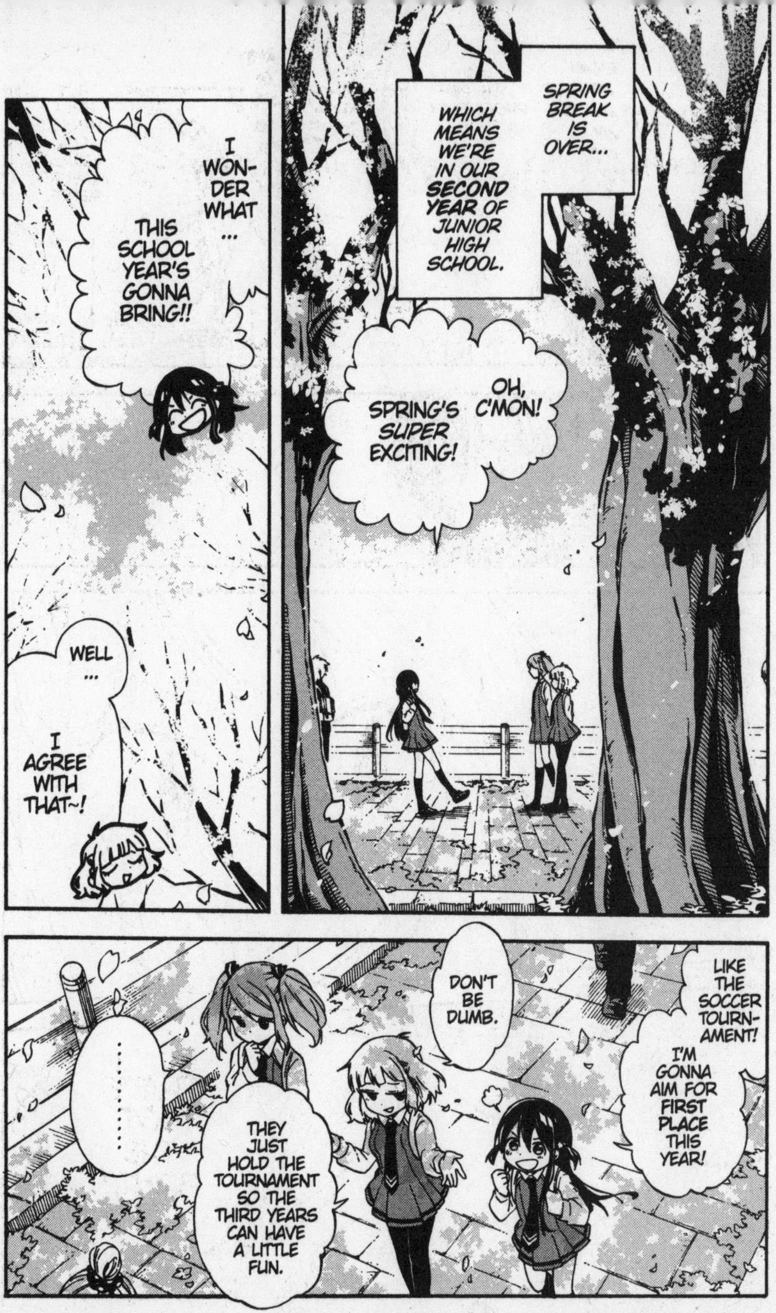
SPRING BREAK IS OVER...
WHICH MEANS WE'RE IN OUR SECOND YEAR OF JUNIOR HIGH SCHOOL.
OH, C'MON!
SPRING'S SUPER EXCITING!
I WONDER WHAT...
THIS SCHOOL YEAR'S GONNA BRING!!
WELL...
I AGREE WITH THAT~!
LIKE THE SOCCER TOURNAMENT!
I'M GONNA AIM FOR FIRST PLACE THIS YEAR!
DON'T BE DUMB.
THEY JUST HOLD THE TOURNAMENT SO THE THIRD YEARS CAN HAVE A LITTLE FUN.
......

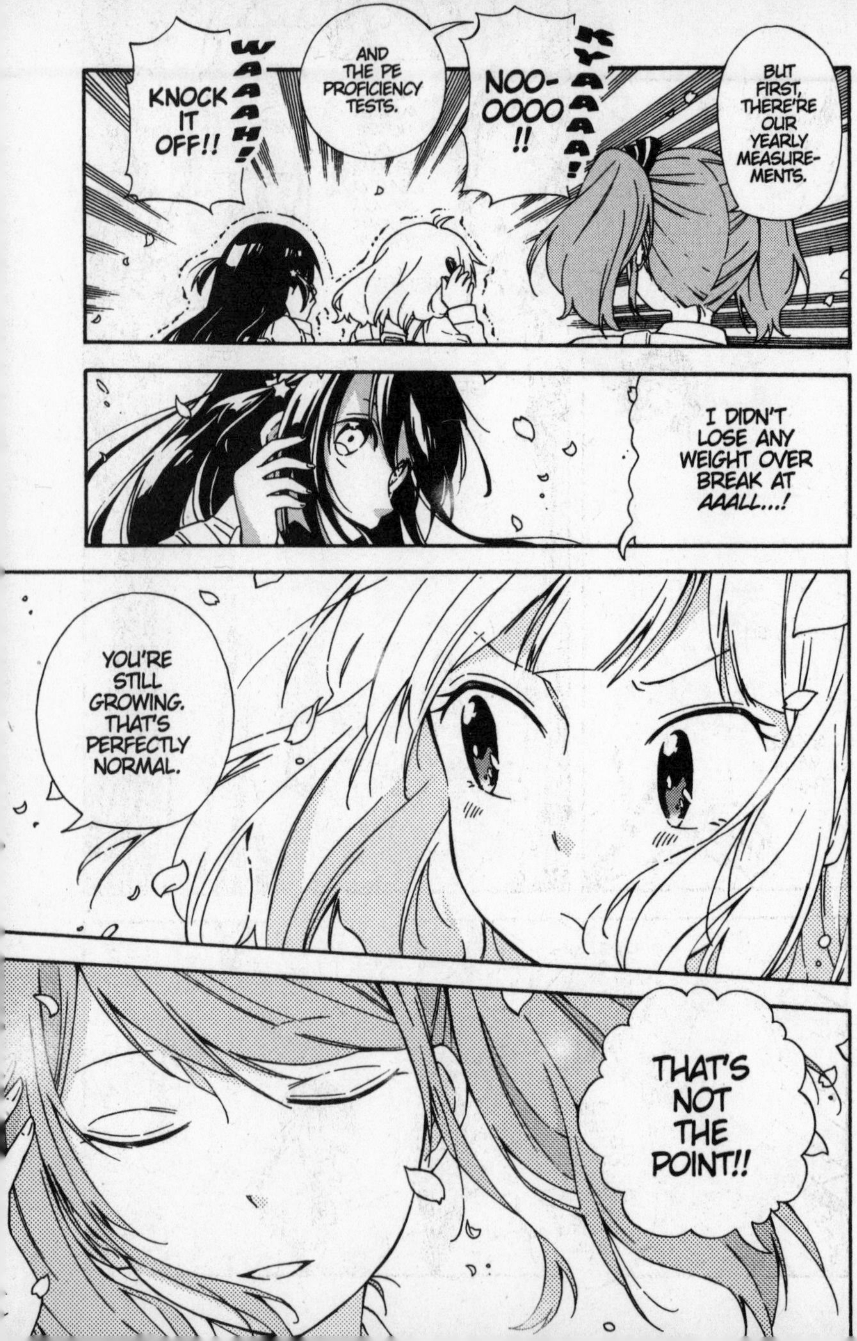
BUT FIRST, THERE'RE OUR YEARLY MEASUREMENTS.
KYAAAAA!
NOO-OOOO!!
AND THE PE PROFICIENCY TESTS.
WAAAAH!
KNOCK IT OFF!!
I DIDN'T LOSE ANY WEIGHT OVER BREAK AT *AAALL...!*
YOU'RE STILL GROWING. THAT'S PERFECTLY NORMAL.
THAT'S NOT THE POINT!!

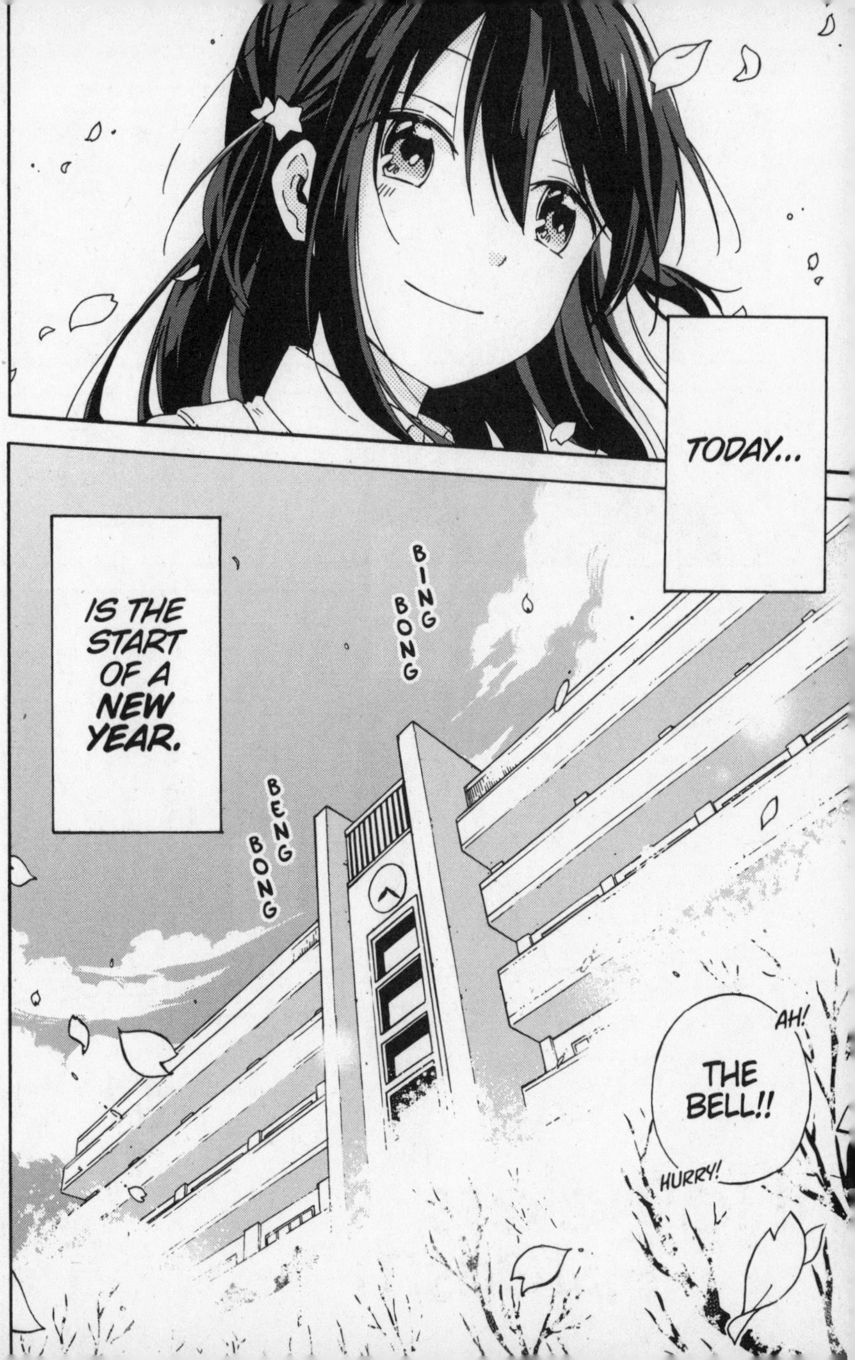
TODAY...
BING BONG
IS THE START OF A NEW YEAR.
BENG BONG
AH!
THE BELL!!
HURRY!

Nameless
Asterism

Nameless
Asterism

Chapter 8 ★ Committee

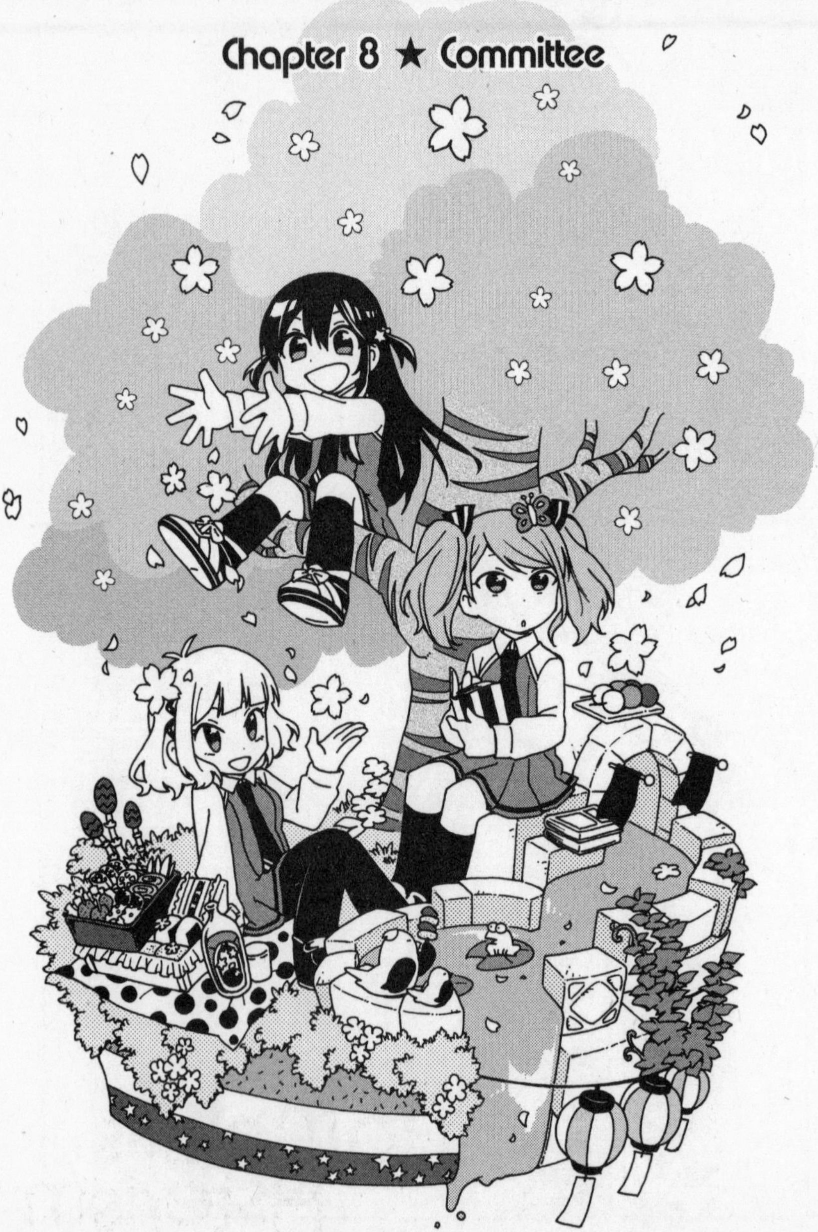

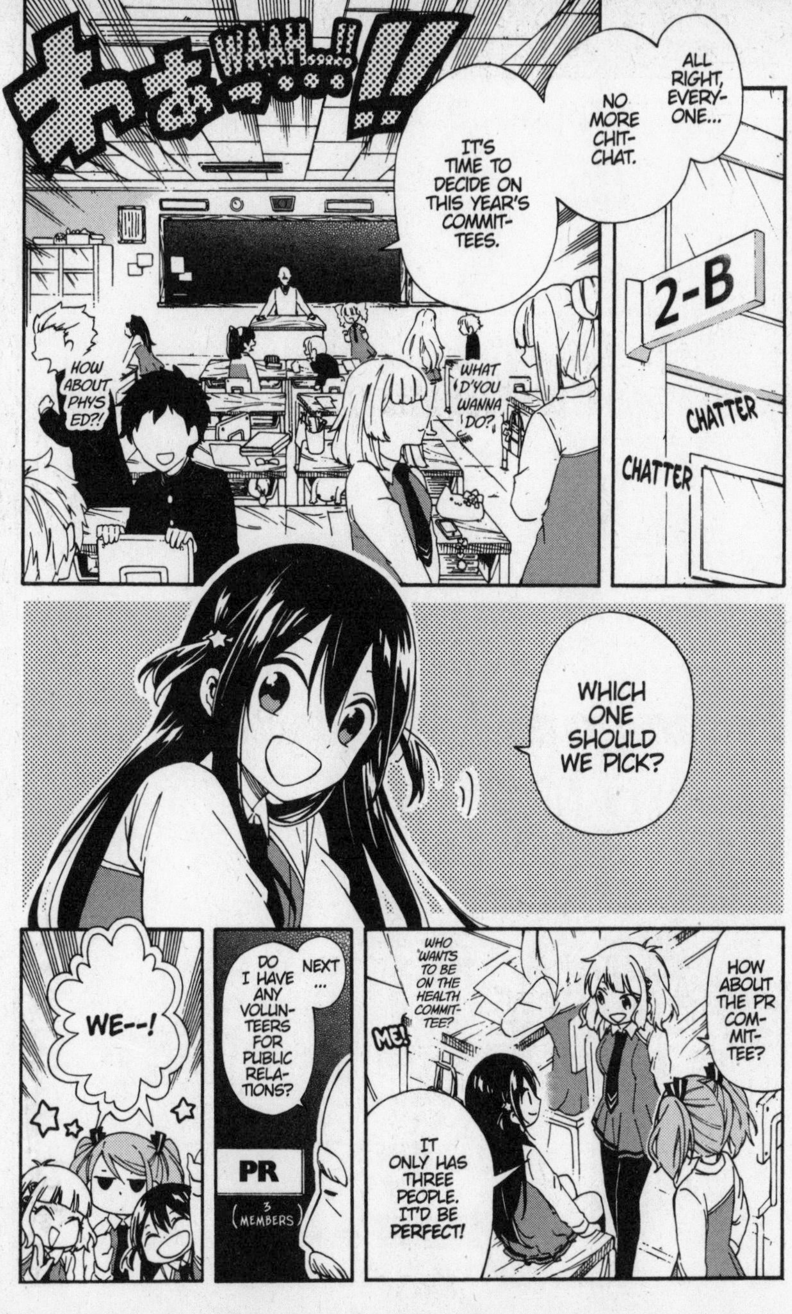
2-B
CHATTER
CHATTER
ALL RIGHT, EVERY-ONE...
NO MORE CHIT-CHAT.
IT'S TIME TO DECIDE ON THIS YEAR'S COMMIT-TEES.
WAAH!!
WHAT D'YOU WANNA DO?
HOW ABOUT PHYS ED?!
WHICH ONE SHOULD WE PICK?
HOW ABOUT THE PR COM-MIT-TEE?
IT ONLY HAS THREE PEOPLE. IT'D BE PERFECT!
WHO WANTS TO BE ON THE HEALTH COMMIT-TEE?
ME!
NEXT...
DO I HAVE ANY VOLUN-TEERS FOR PUBLIC RELA-TIONS?
PR
(3 MEMBERS)
WE--!

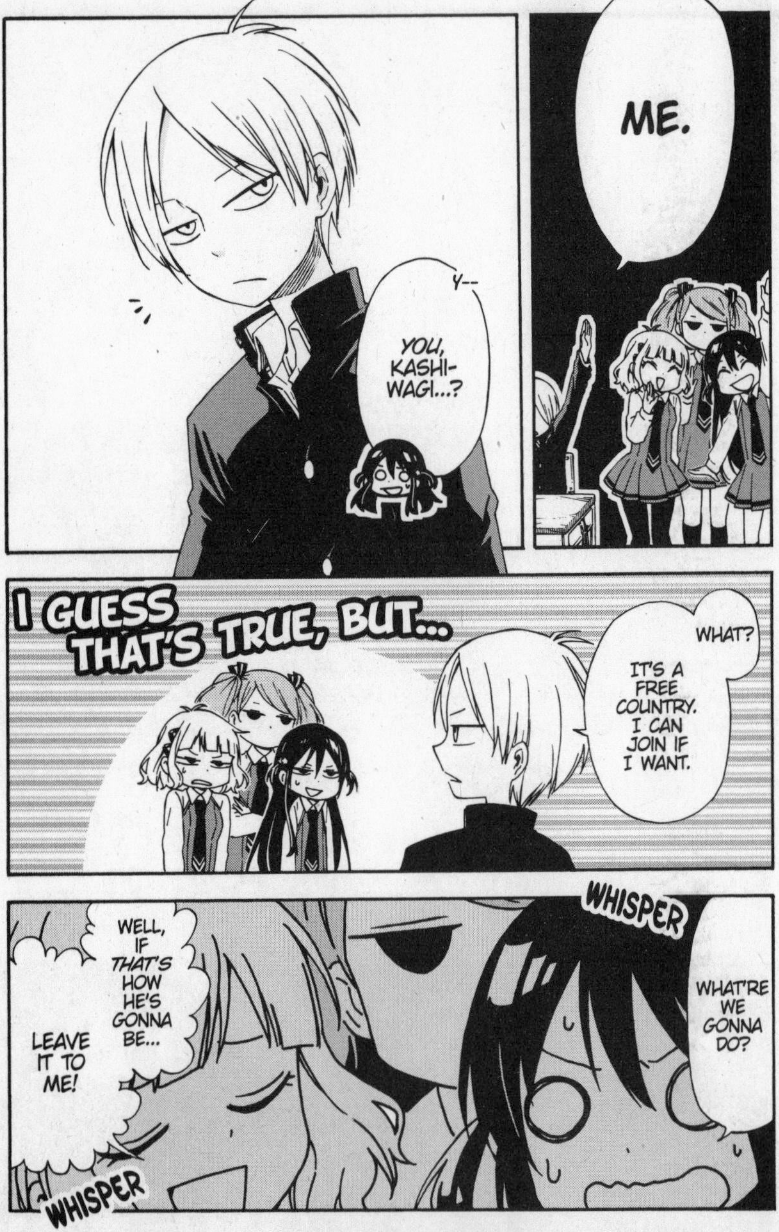
ME.
Y--
YOU, KASHI-WAGI...?
WHAT?
IT'S A FREE COUNTRY. I CAN JOIN IF I WANT.
I GUESS THAT'S TRUE, BUT...
WHISPER
WHAT'RE WE GONNA DO?
WELL, IF THAT'S HOW HE'S GONNA BE...
LEAVE IT TO ME!
WHISPER

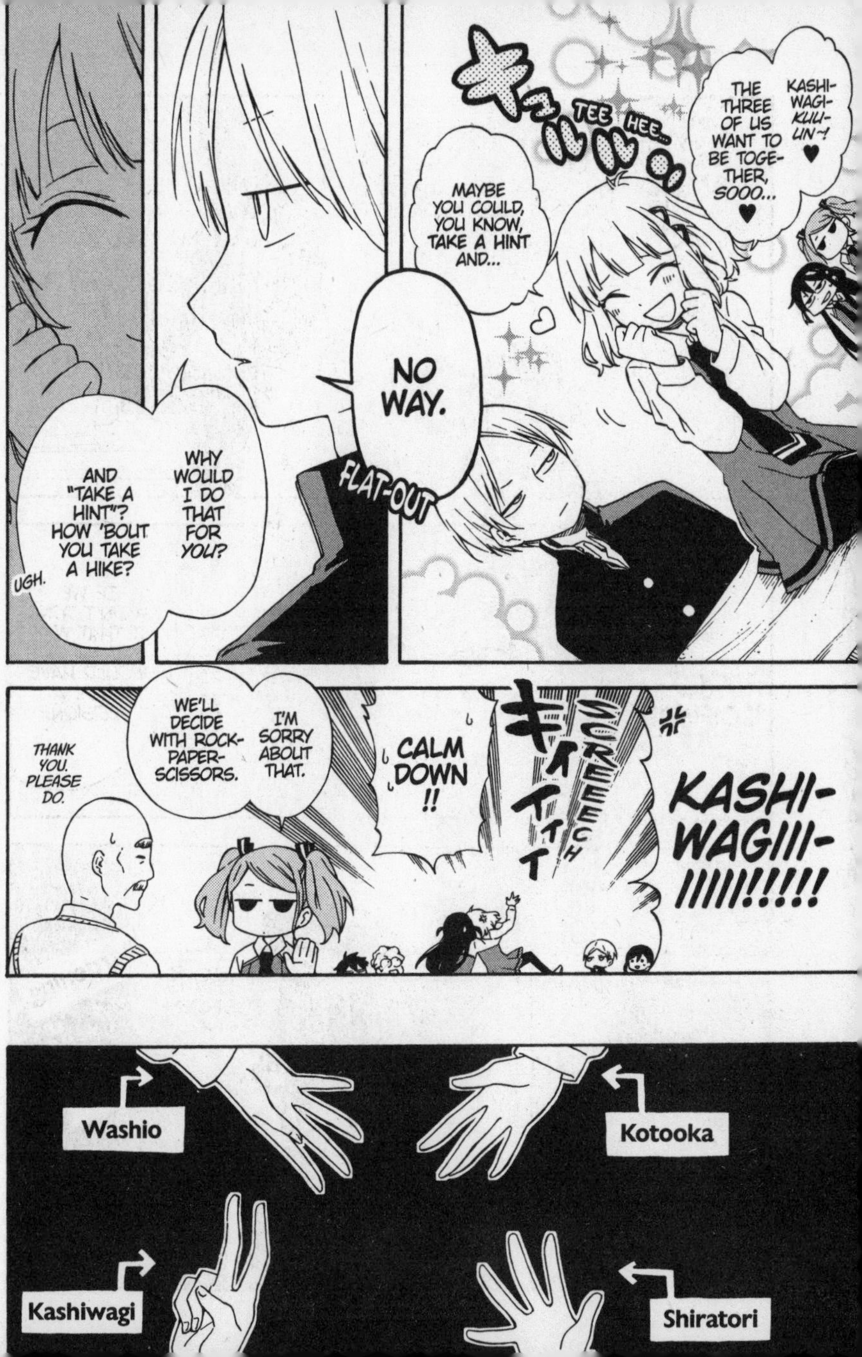

KASHI-WAGI-KUU-UN~! ♥
THE THREE OF US WANT TO BE TOGE-THER, SOOO... ♥
TEE HEE...
MAYBE YOU COULD, YOU KNOW, TAKE A HINT AND...
NO WAY.
FLAT-OUT
WHY WOULD I DO THAT FOR *YOU*?
AND "TAKE A HINT"? HOW 'BOUT YOU TAKE A HIKE?
UGH.
KASHI-WAGIIII-IIIIII!!!!!
SCREEEECH
CALM DOWN!!
I'M SORRY ABOUT THAT.
WE'LL DECIDE WITH ROCK-PAPER-SCISSORS.
THANK YOU. PLEASE DO.
Kotooka
Washio
Shiratori
Kashiwagi

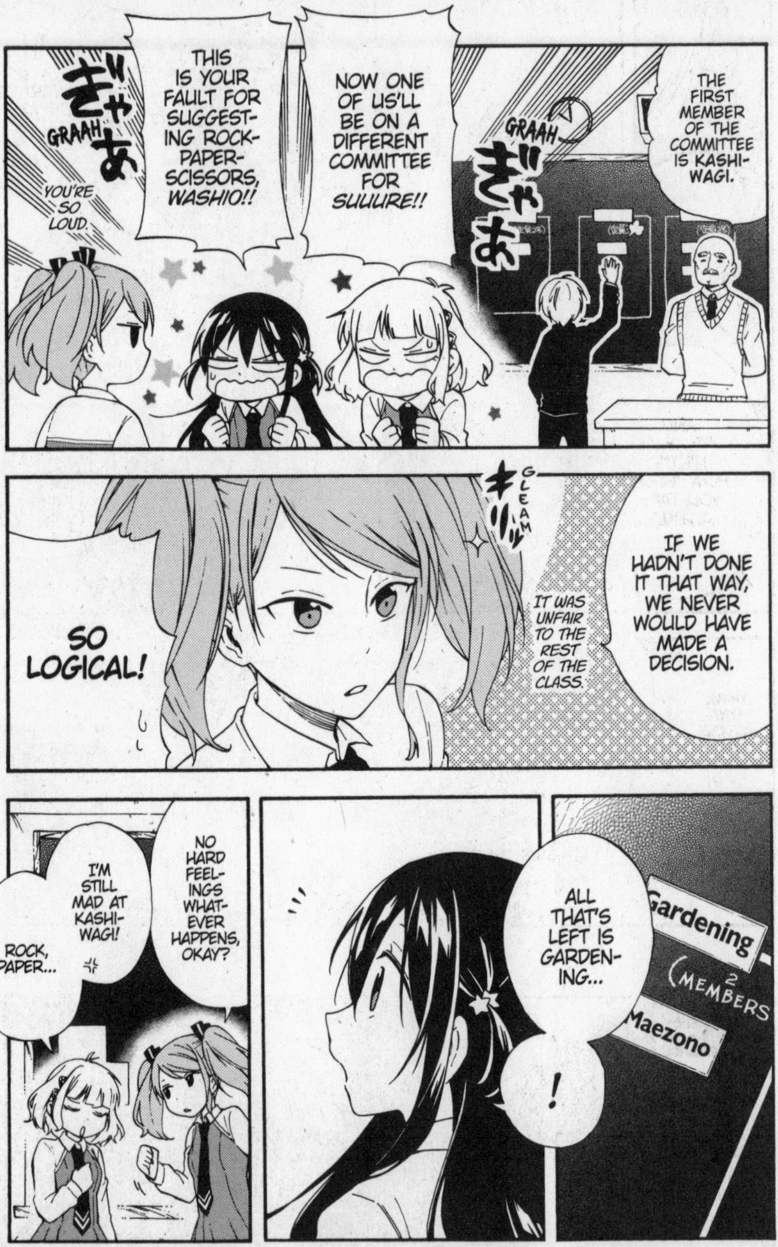
THE FIRST MEMBER OF THE COMMITTEE IS KASHIWAGI.
ぎゃあ GRAAH
NOW ONE OF US'LL BE ON A DIFFERENT COMMITTEE FOR SUUURE!!
THIS IS YOUR FAULT FOR SUGGESTING ROCK-PAPER-SCISSORS, WASHIO!!
ぎゃあ GRAAH
YOU'RE SO LOUD.
IF WE HADN'T DONE IT THAT WAY, WE NEVER WOULD HAVE MADE A DECISION.
キリッ GLEAM
IT WAS UNFAIR TO THE REST OF THE CLASS.
SO LOGICAL!
Gardening
(2 MEMBERS
Maezono
ALL THAT'S LEFT IS GARDENING...
!
NO HARD FEELINGS WHATEVER HAPPENS, OKAY?
I'M STILL MAD AT KASHIWAGI!
ROCK, PAPER...

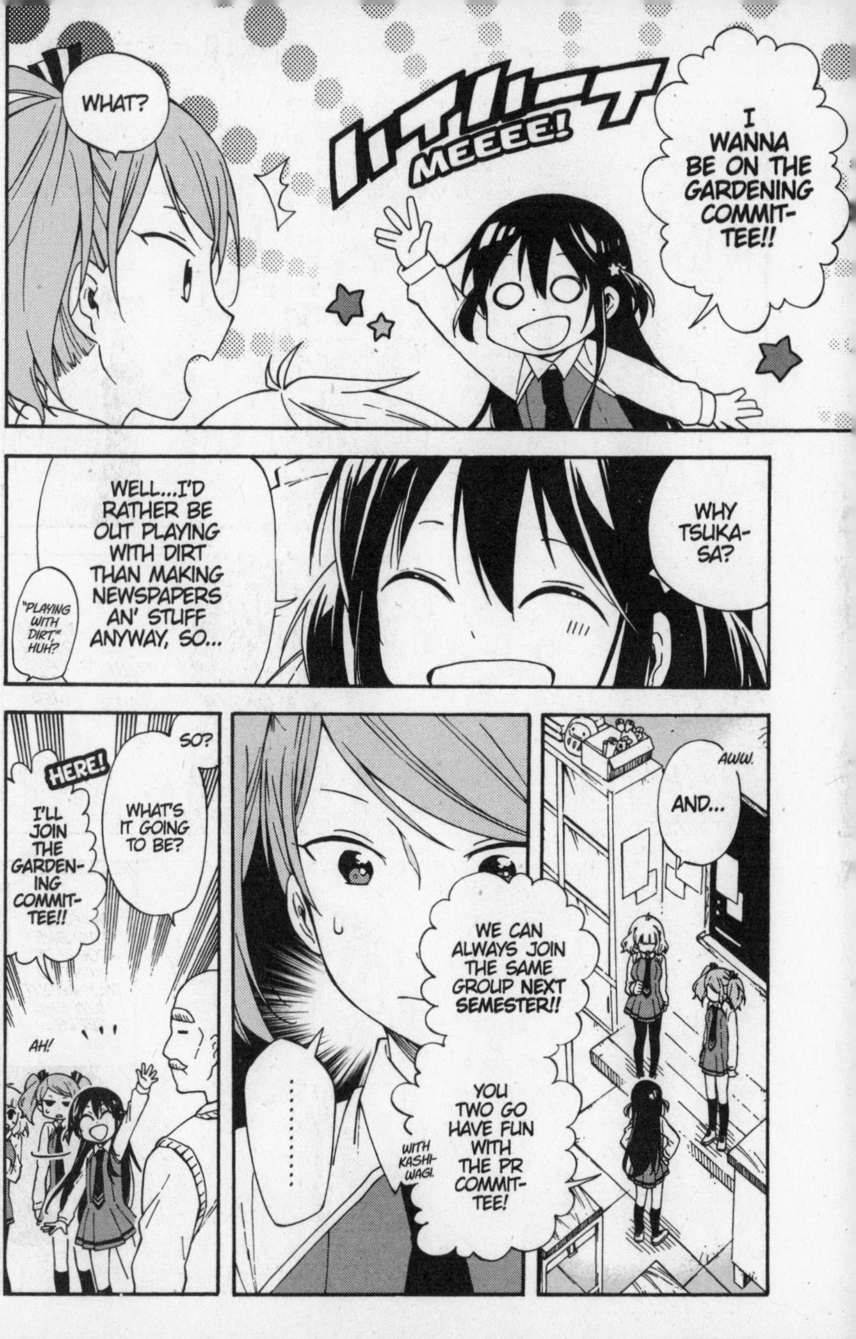
I WANNA BE ON THE GARDENING COMMIT-TEE!!
MEEEEE!
WHAT?
WHY TSUKA-SA?
WELL...I'D RATHER BE OUT PLAYING WITH DIRT THAN MAKING NEWSPAPERS AN' STUFF ANYWAY, SO...
"PLAYING WITH DIRT," HUH?
AWW.
AND...
WE CAN ALWAYS JOIN THE SAME GROUP NEXT SEMESTER!!
YOU TWO GO HAVE FUN WITH THE PR COMMIT-TEE!
WITH KASHI-WAGI.
......
SO?
WHAT'S IT GOING TO BE?
HERE!
I'LL JOIN THE GARDEN-ING COMMIT-TEE!!
...
AH!

DURING THE WHOLE ASAKURA-KUN THING...

iening		PR	
(MEMBERS)		(MEMBE	
Maezono		Kashiwagi	
Shiratori		Washio	
		Kotooka	

WASHIO DID LOTS OF THOUGHTFUL STUFF FOR ME.

LIKE SHE DID FOR ME.

I WANT TO CHEER HER ON...

I WANNA DO THE SAME FOR HER.

BUT I'M SURE SHE'LL LIKE SPENDING EXTRA TIME WITH HER CRUSH.

PLEASE DISTRIBUTE THESE FLYERS.

PR COMMITTEE...

WASHIO SAID SHE DOESN'T WANT TO TALK ABOUT HOW SHE FEELS...

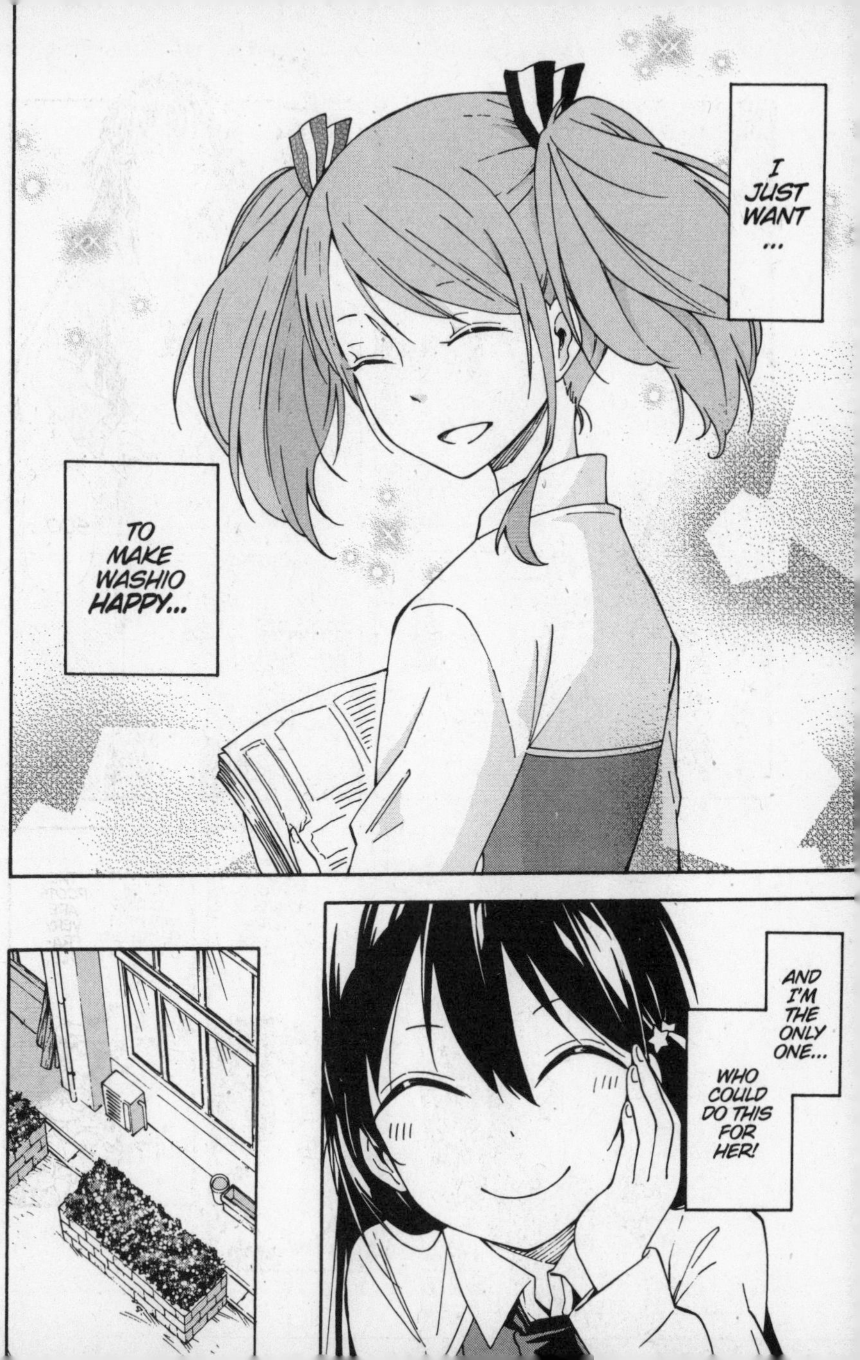
I JUST WANT ...
TO MAKE WASHIO HAPPY...
AND I'M THE ONLY ONE... WHO COULD DO THIS FOR HER!

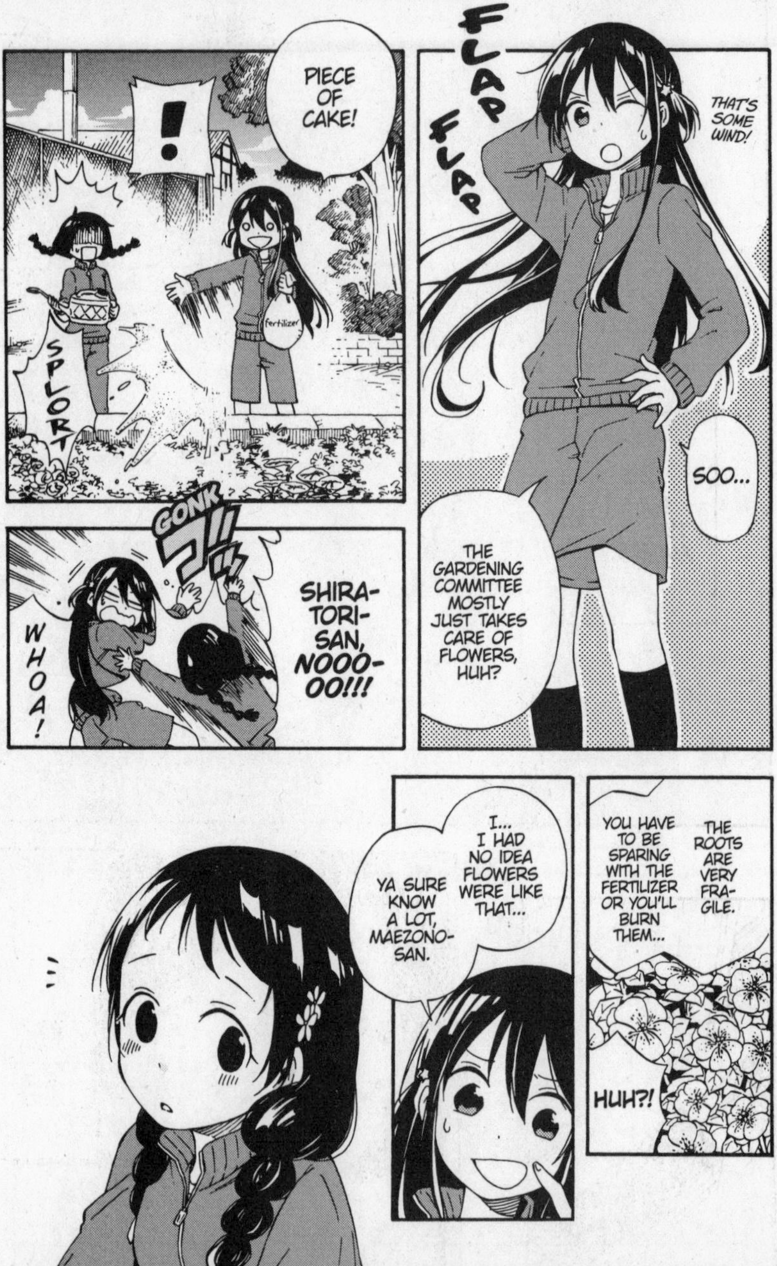
FLAP FLAP
FLAP FLAP
THAT'S SOME WIND!
SOO...
THE GARDENING COMMITTEE MOSTLY JUST TAKES CARE OF FLOWERS, HUH?
PIECE OF CAKE!
!
SPLORT
GONK
SHIRA-TORI-SAN, NOOO-OO!!!
WHOA!
THE ROOTS ARE VERY FRA-GILE.
YOU HAVE TO BE SPARING WITH THE FERTILIZER OR YOU'LL BURN THEM...
HUH?!
I... I HAD NO IDEA FLOWERS WERE LIKE THAT...
YA SURE KNOW A LOT, MAEZONO-SAN.

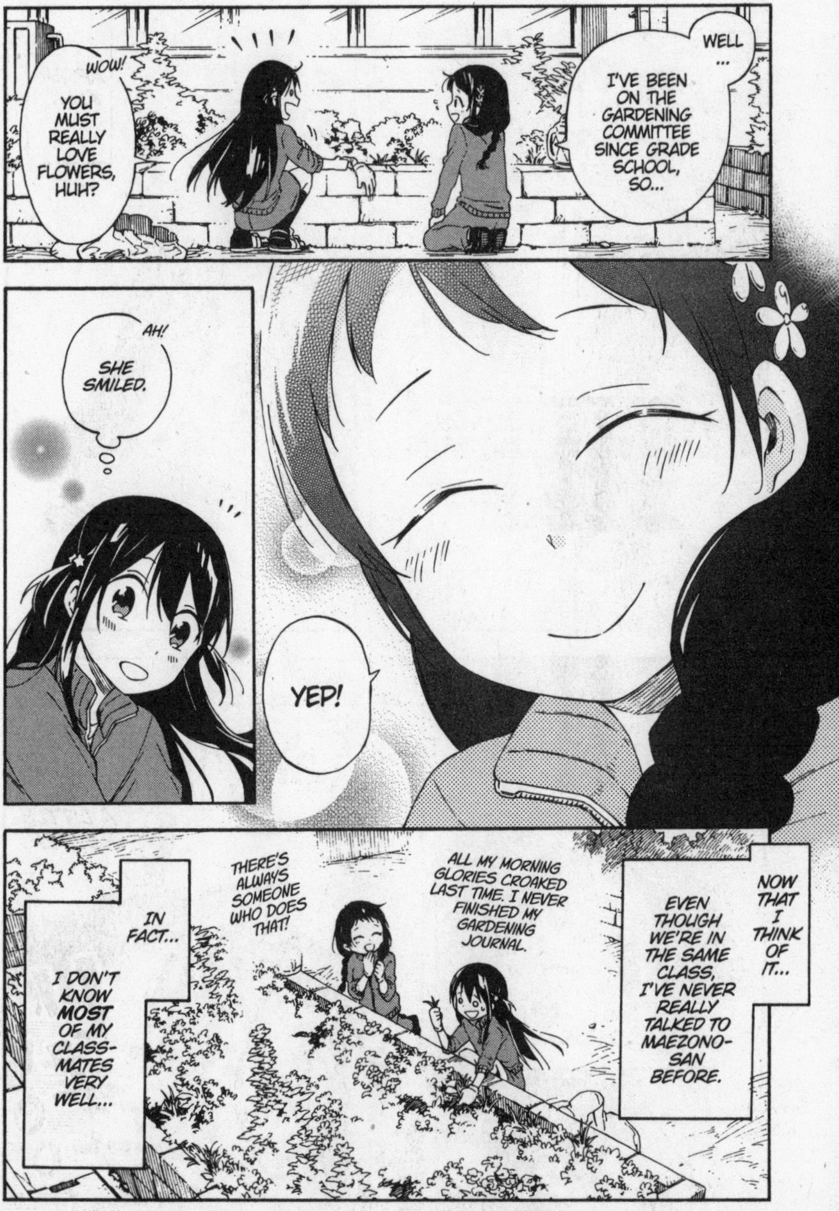
WELL ...
I'VE BEEN ON THE GARDENING COMMITTEE SINCE GRADE SCHOOL, SO...
WOW!
YOU MUST REALLY LOVE FLOWERS, HUH?
YEP!
AH!
SHE SMILED.
NOW THAT I THINK OF IT...
EVEN THOUGH WE'RE IN THE SAME CLASS, I'VE NEVER REALLY TALKED TO MAEZONO-SAN BEFORE.
ALL MY MORNING GLORIES CROAKED LAST TIME. I NEVER FINISHED MY GARDENING JOURNAL.
THERE'S ALWAYS SOMEONE WHO DOES THAT!
IN FACT...
I DON'T KNOW MOST OF MY CLASSMATES VERY WELL...

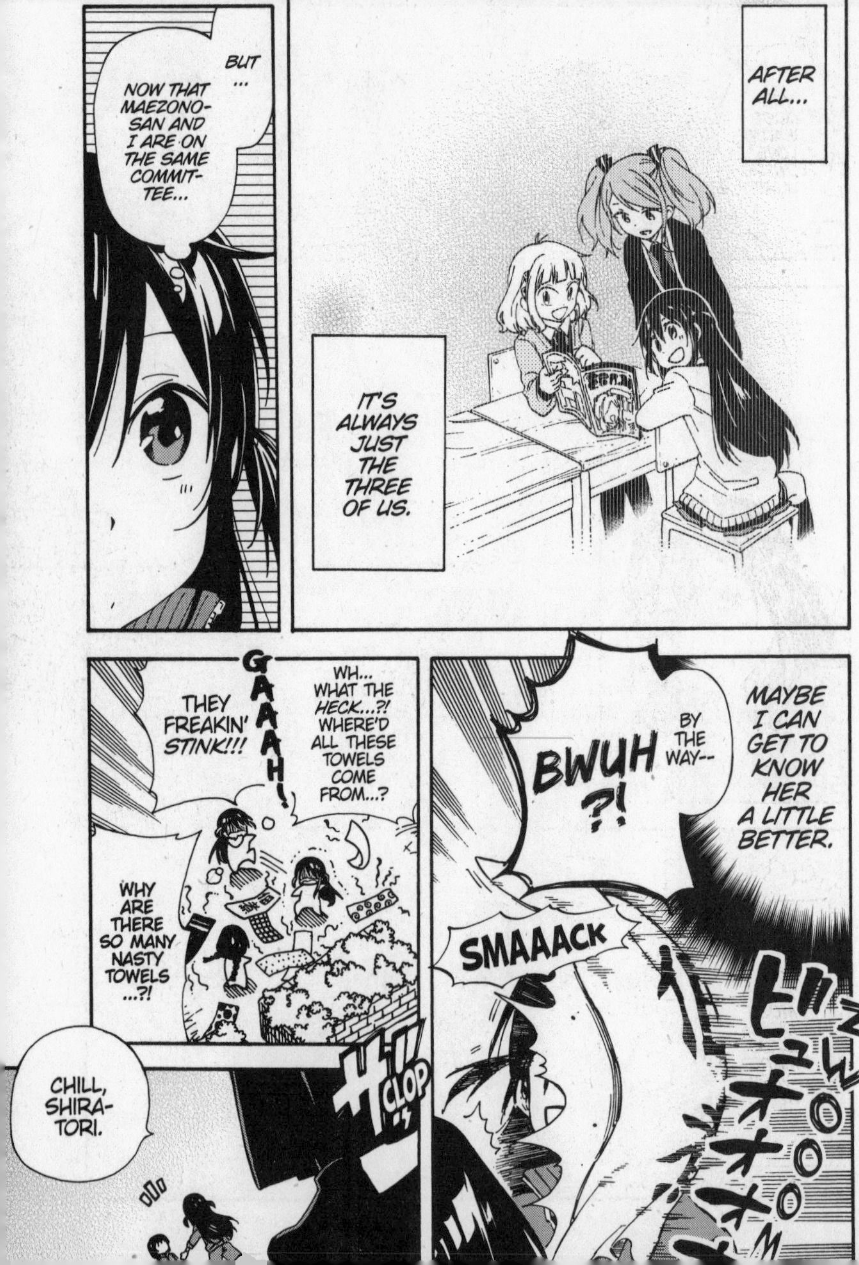
AFTER ALL...
IT'S ALWAYS JUST THE THREE OF US.
BUT ...
NOW THAT MAEZONO-SAN AND I ARE ON THE SAME COMMITTEE...
MAYBE I CAN GET TO KNOW HER A LITTLE BETTER.
BY THE WAY--
BWUH ?!
SMAAACK
WH... WHAT THE HECK...?! WHERE'D ALL THESE TOWELS COME FROM...?
GAAAAH!
THEY FREAKIN' STINK!!!
WHY ARE THERE SO MANY NASTY TOWELS ...?!
CLOP
CHILL, SHIRATORI.

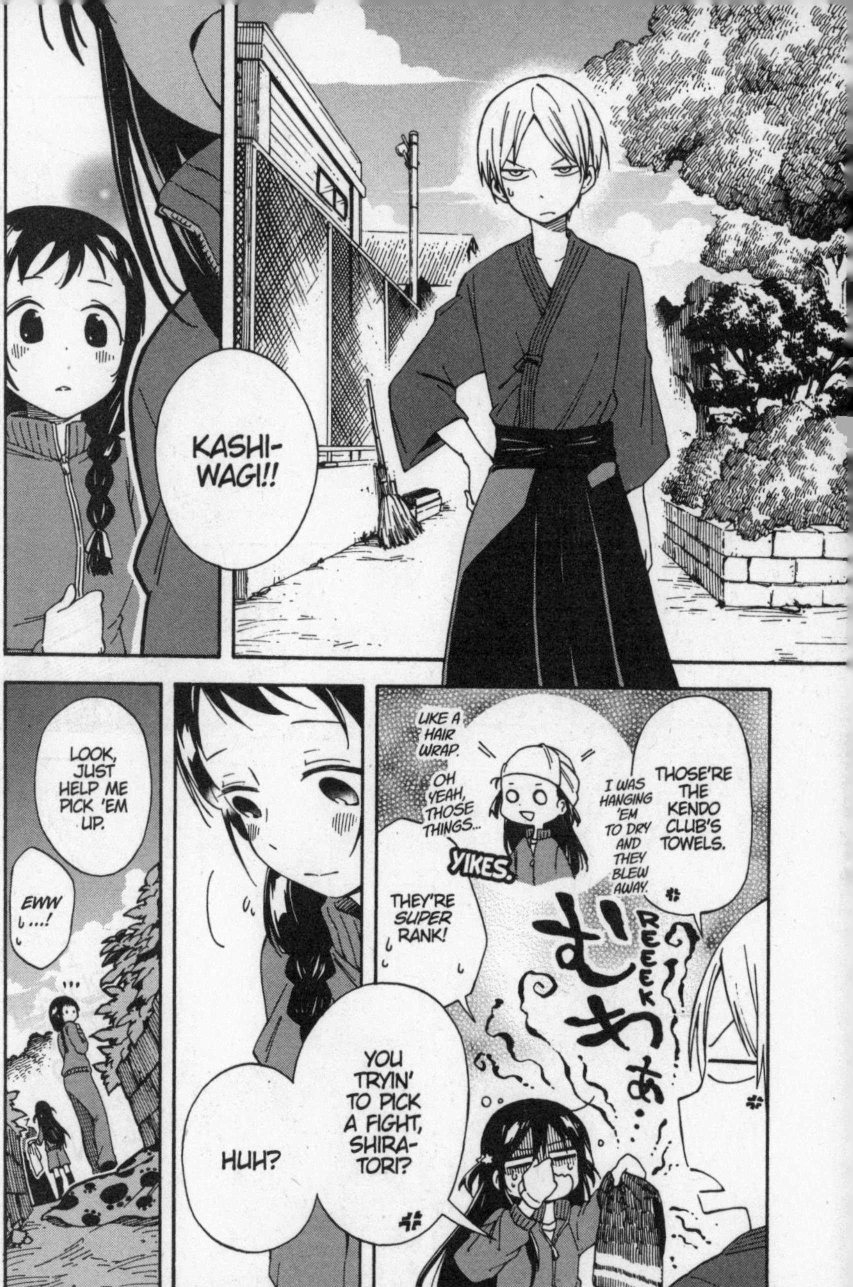
KASHI-WAGI!!
THOSE'RE THE KENDO CLUB'S TOWELS.
I WAS HANGING 'EM TO DRY AND THEY BLEW AWAY.
REEEK
むわぁ…
LIKE A HAIR WRAP.
OH YEAH, THOSE THINGS...
YIKES.
THEY'RE SUPER RANK!
YOU TRYIN' TO PICK A FIGHT, SHIRATORI?
HUH?
LOOK, JUST HELP ME PICK 'EM UP.
EWW ......!

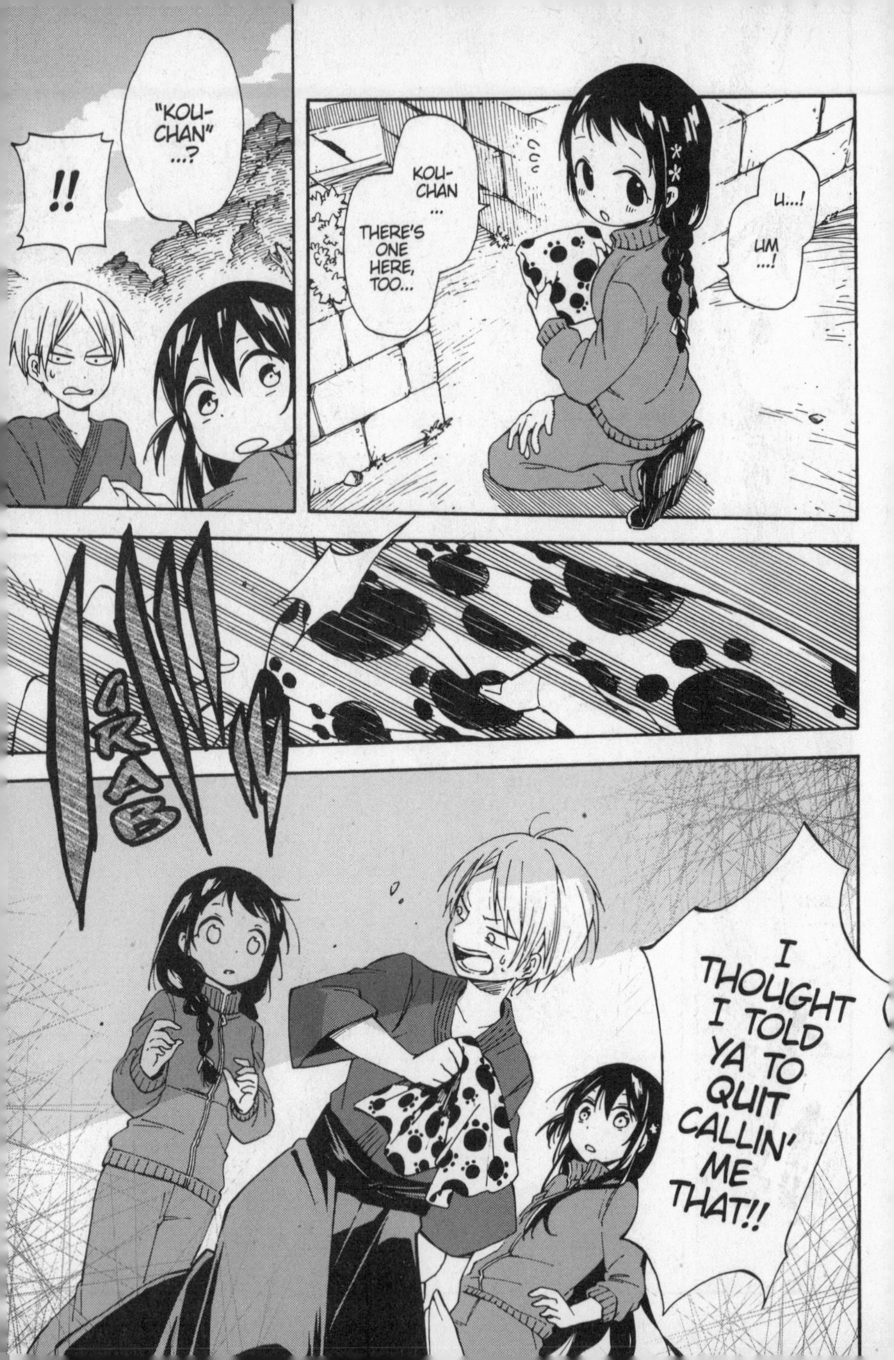
U...!
UM ...!
KOU-CHAN ...
THERE'S ONE HERE, TOO...
"KOU-CHAN" ...?
!!
GRAB
I THOUGHT I TOLD YA TO QUIT CALLIN' ME THAT!!

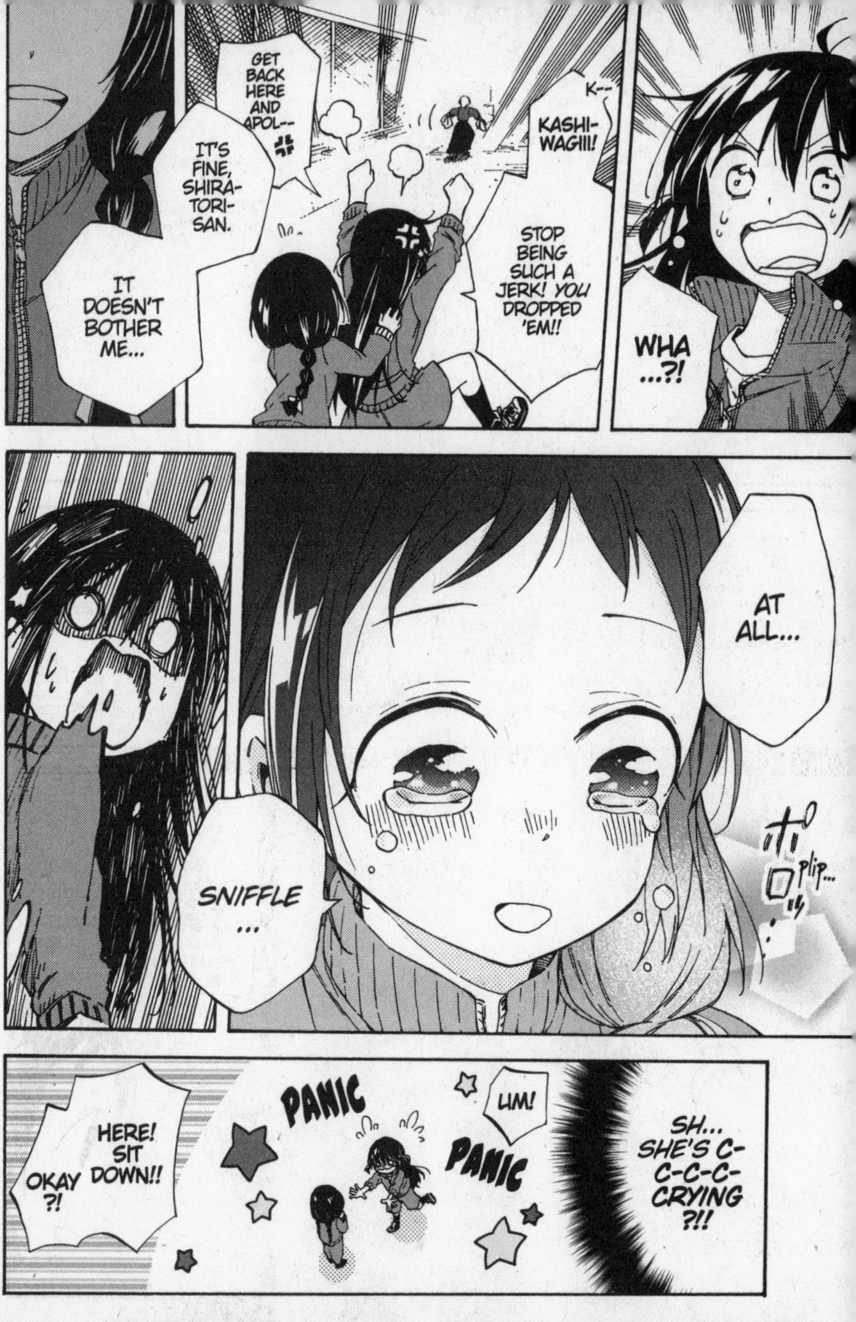
WHA ...?!
K-- KASHIWAGIII!
STOP BEING SUCH A JERK! YOU DROPPED 'EM!!
GET BACK HERE AND APOL--
IT'S FINE, SHIRATORI-SAN.
IT DOESN'T BOTHER ME...
AT ALL...
plip...
SNIFFLE ...
SH... SHE'S C-C-C-C-CRYING ?!!
UM!
PANIC
PANIC
HERE! SIT DOWN!!
OKAY ?!

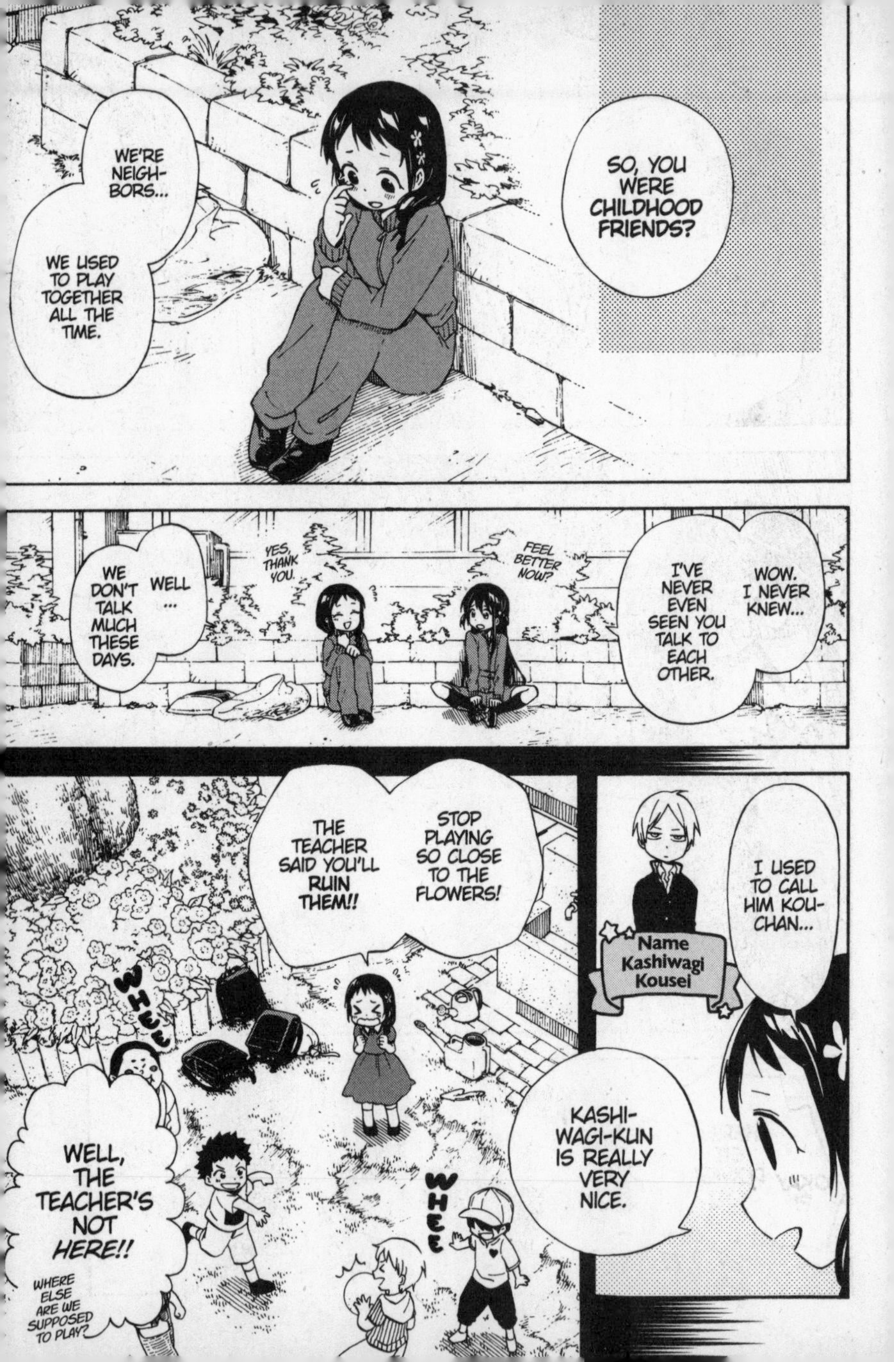
SO, YOU WERE CHILDHOOD FRIENDS?
WE'RE NEIGHBORS...
WE USED TO PLAY TOGETHER ALL THE TIME.
WOW. I NEVER KNEW...
I'VE NEVER EVEN SEEN YOU TALK TO EACH OTHER.
FEEL BETTER NOW?
YES, THANK YOU.
WELL...
WE DON'T TALK MUCH THESE DAYS.
I USED TO CALL HIM KOU-CHAN...
Name Kashiwagi Kousei
KASHIWAGI-KUN IS REALLY VERY NICE.
STOP PLAYING SO CLOSE TO THE FLOWERS!
THE TEACHER SAID YOU'LL RUIN THEM!!
WHEE
WHEE
WELL, THE TEACHER'S NOT HERE!!
WHERE ELSE ARE WE SUPPOSED TO PLAY?

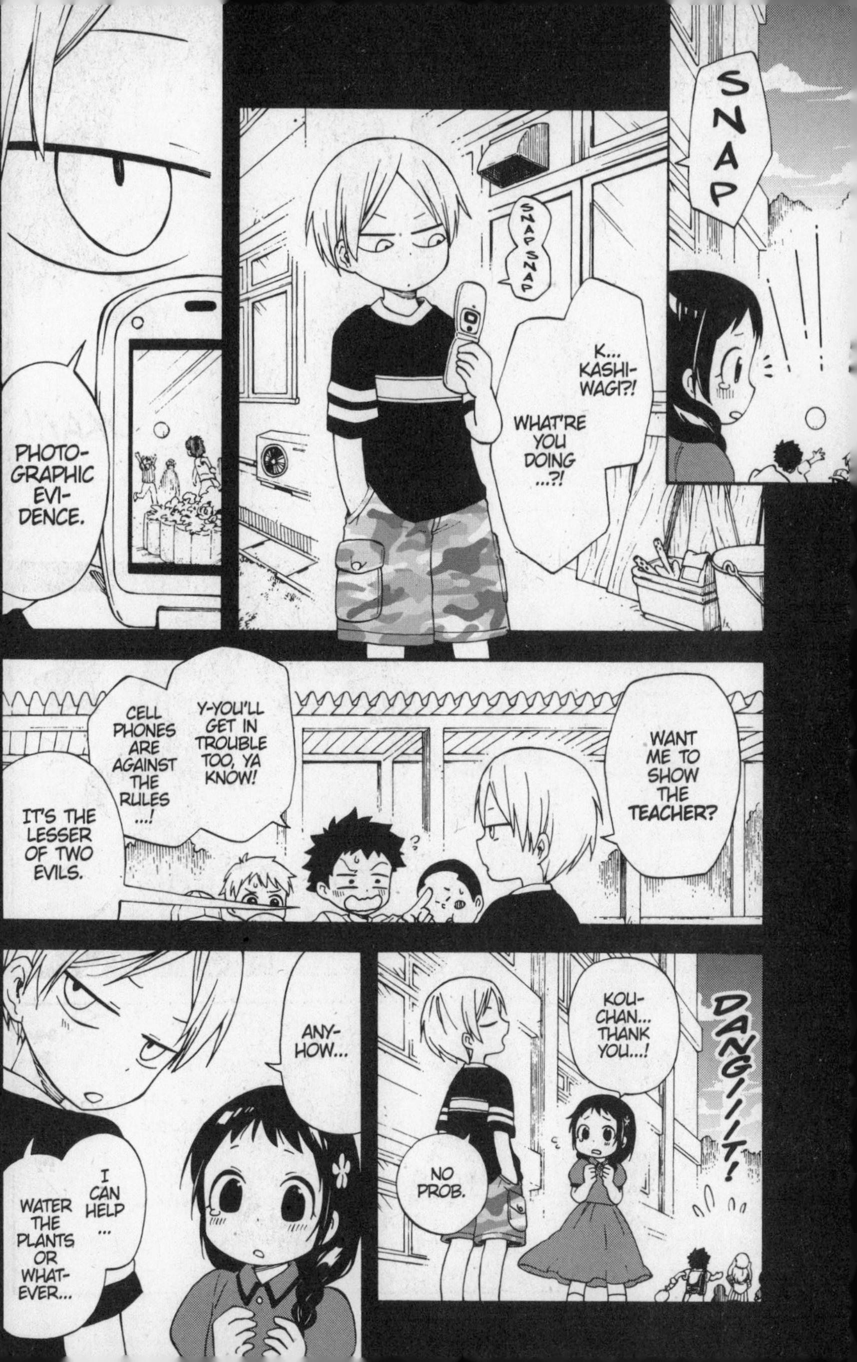
SNAP
SNAP SNAP
K... KASHIWAGI?!
WHAT'RE YOU DOING ...?!
PHOTO-GRAPHIC EVI-DENCE.
WANT ME TO SHOW THE TEACHER?
Y-YOU'LL GET IN TROUBLE TOO, YA KNOW!
CELL PHONES ARE AGAINST THE RULES ...!
IT'S THE LESSER OF TWO EVILS.
DANGIIIIT!
KOU-CHAN... THANK YOU...!
NO PROB.
ANY-HOW...
I CAN HELP ...
WATER THE PLANTS OR WHAT-EVER...

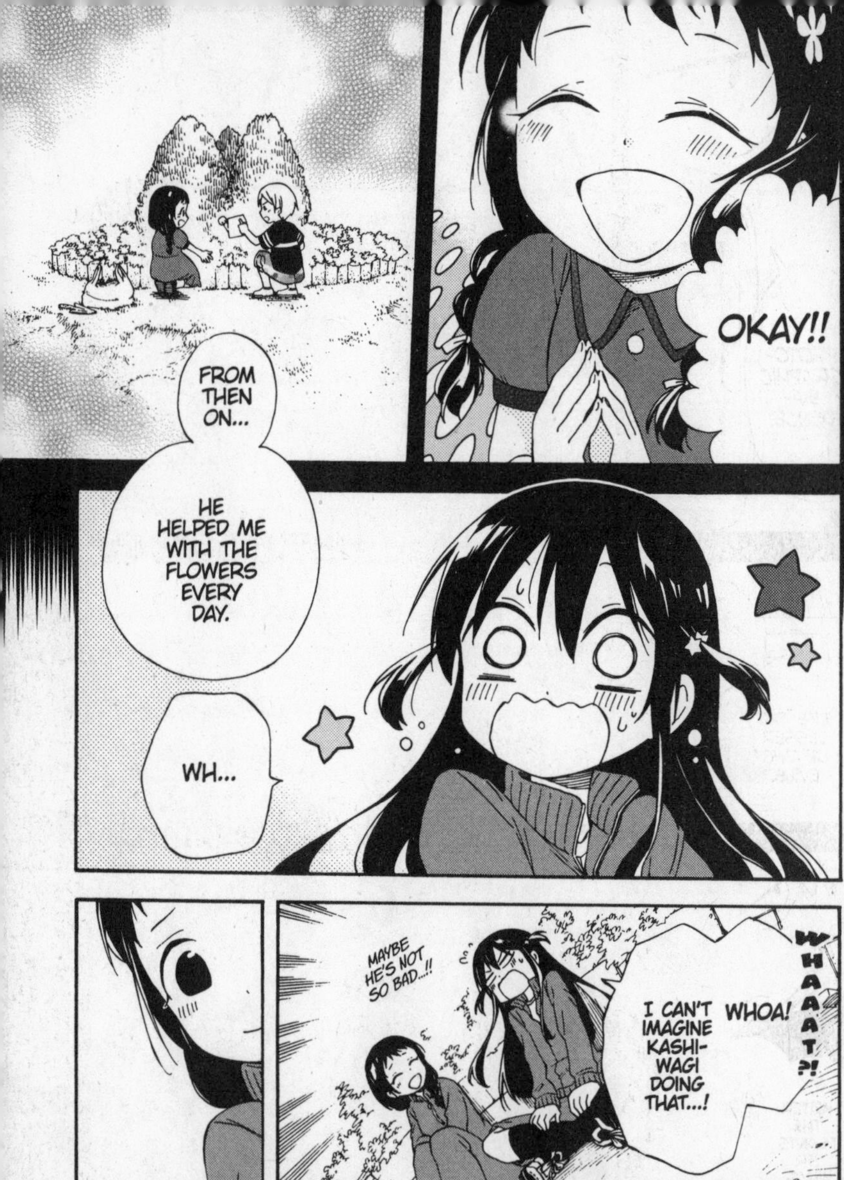
OKAY!!
FROM THEN ON...
HE HELPED ME WITH THE FLOWERS EVERY DAY.
WH...
WHAAAAT?!
WHOA!
I CAN'T IMAGINE KASHI-WAGI DOING THAT...!
MAYBE HE'S NOT SO BAD...!!

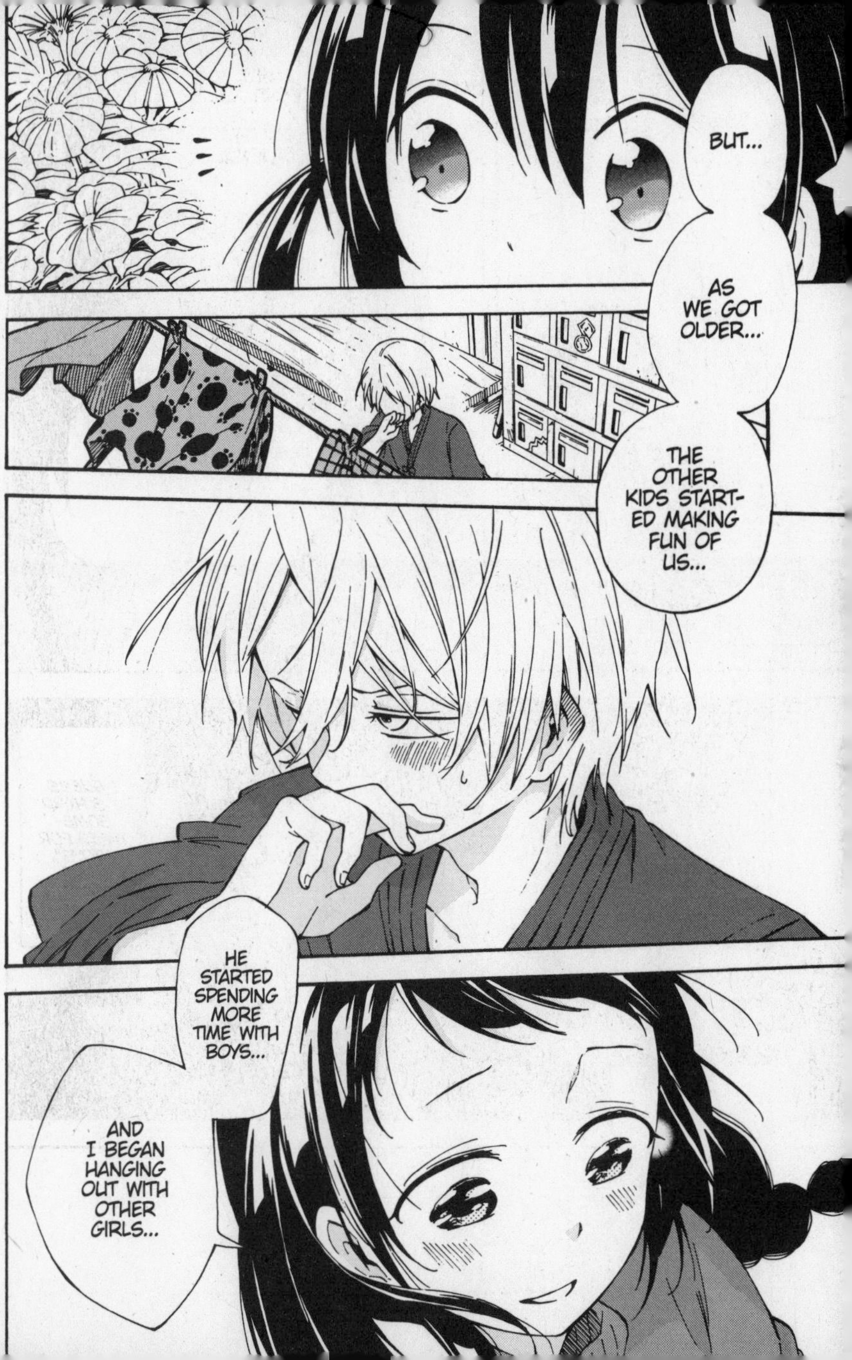
BUT...
AS WE GOT OLDER...
THE OTHER KIDS START-ED MAKING FUN OF US...
HE STARTED SPENDING MORE TIME WITH BOYS...
AND I BEGAN HANGING OUT WITH OTHER GIRLS...

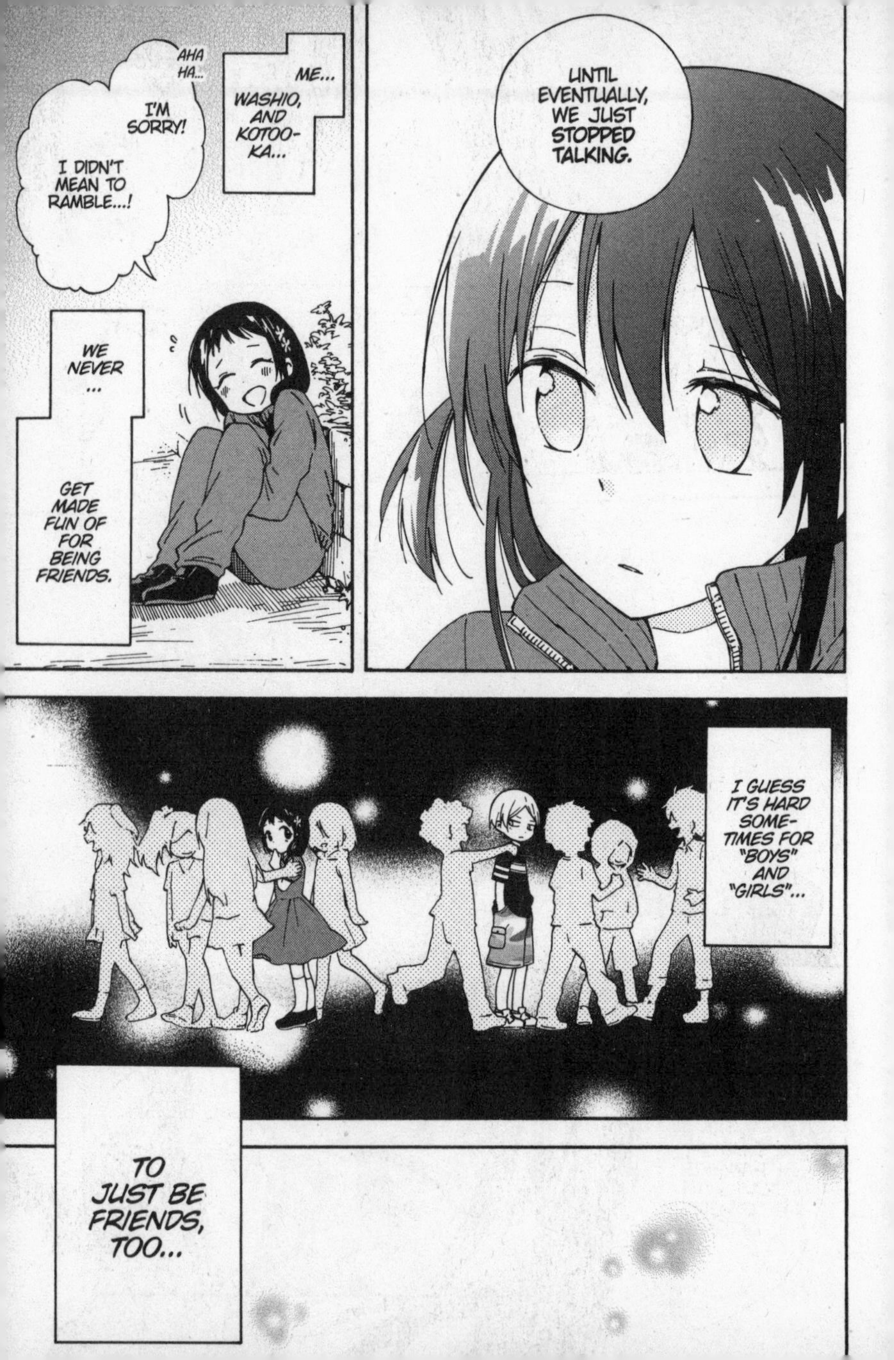
UNTIL EVENTUALLY, WE JUST STOPPED TALKING.
ME... WASHIO, AND KOTOO-KA...
AHA HA...
I'M SORRY!
I DIDN'T MEAN TO RAMBLE...!
WE NEVER ...
GET MADE FUN OF FOR BEING FRIENDS.
I GUESS IT'S HARD SOME-TIMES FOR "BOYS" AND "GIRLS"...
TO JUST BE FRIENDS, TOO...

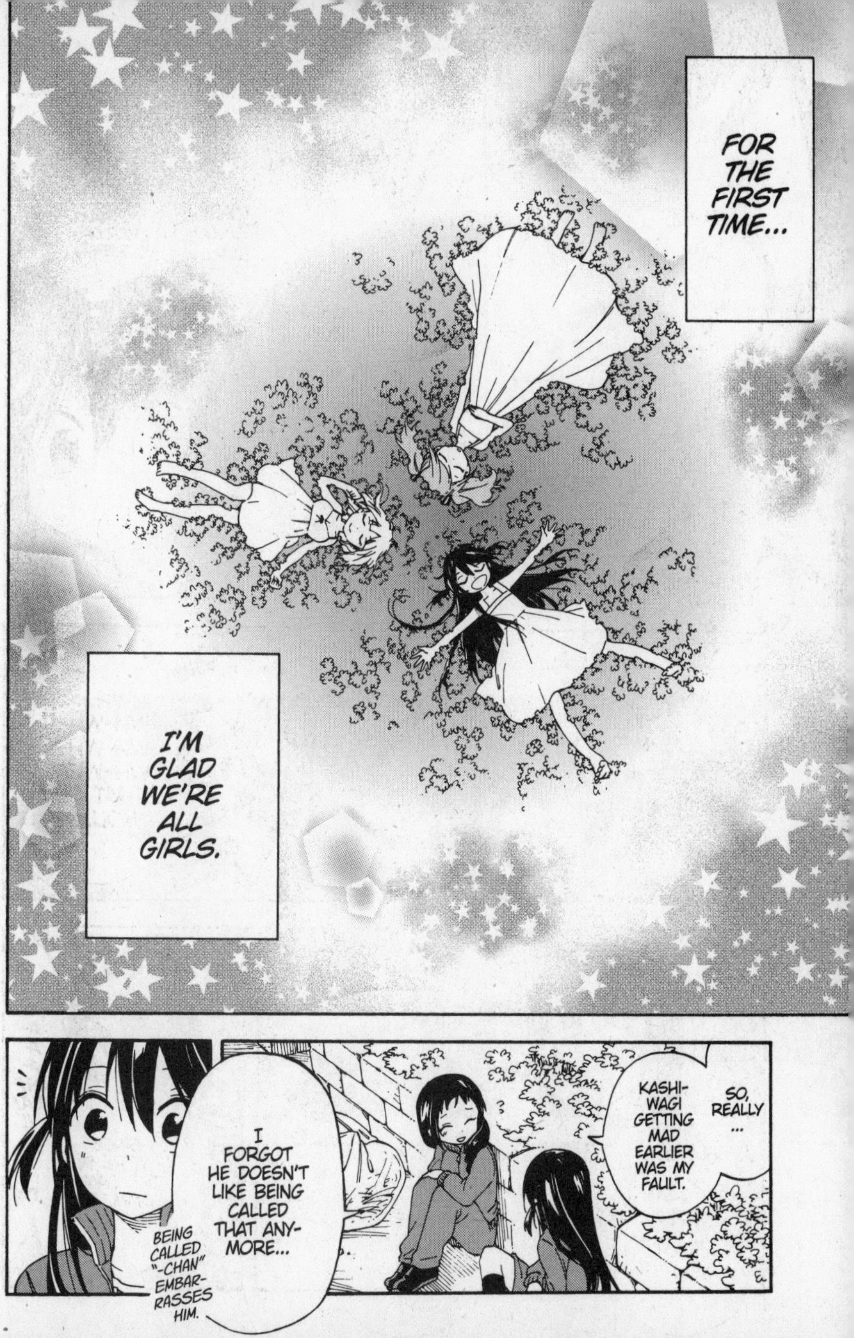
FOR THE FIRST TIME...
I'M GLAD WE'RE ALL GIRLS.
SO, REALLY...
KASHI-WAGI GETTING MAD EARLIER WAS MY FAULT.
I FORGOT HE DOESN'T LIKE BEING CALLED THAT ANY-MORE...
BEING CALLED "-CHAN" EMBAR-RASSES HIM.

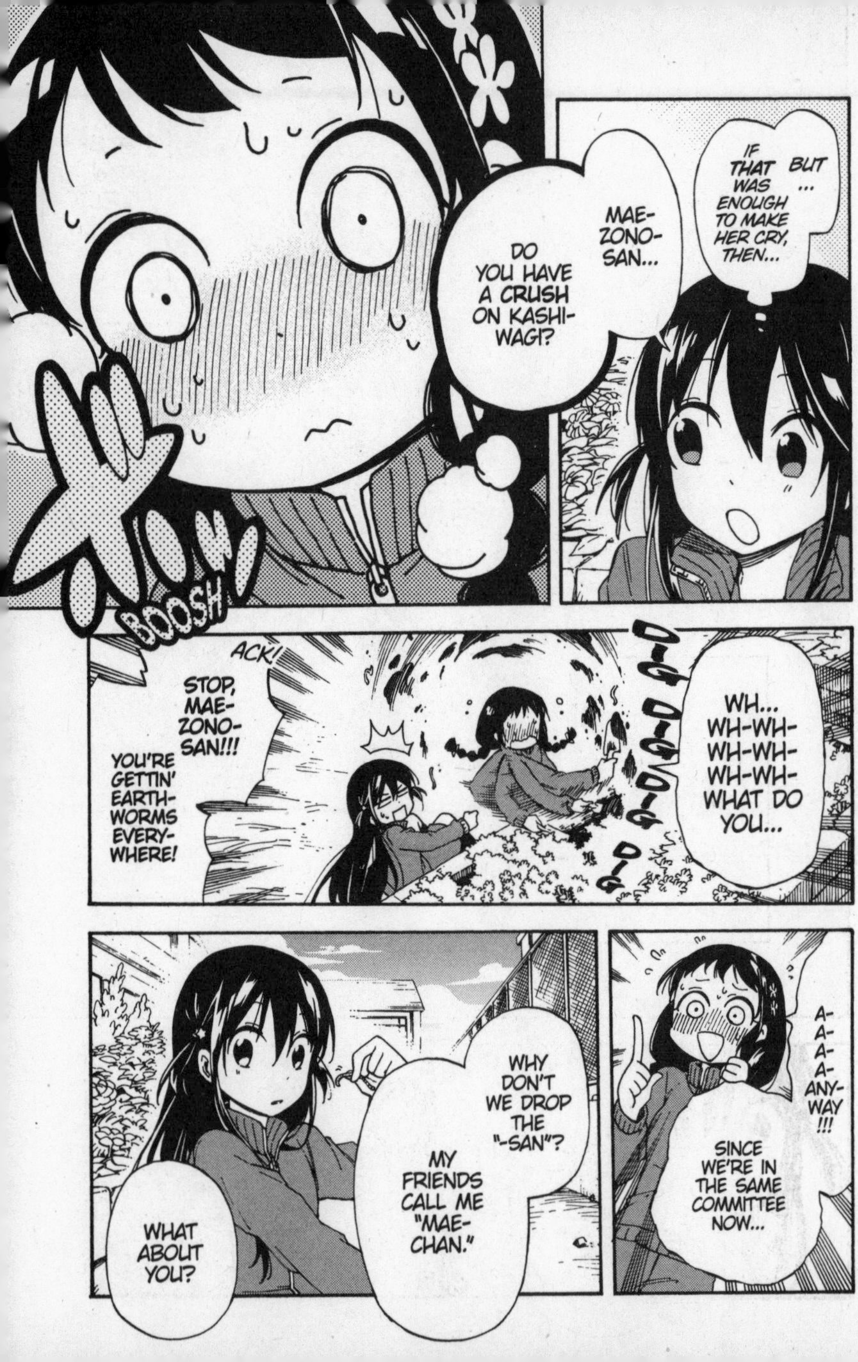
BUT...
IF THAT WAS ENOUGH TO MAKE HER CRY, THEN...
MAE-ZONO-SAN...
DO YOU HAVE A CRUSH ON KASHI-WAGI?
BOOSH
WH... WH-WH-WH-WH-WH-WH-WHAT DO YOU...
DIG DIG DIG DIG DIG
ACK!
STOP, MAE-ZONO-SAN!!!
YOU'RE GETTIN' EARTH-WORMS EVERY-WHERE!
A-A-A-A-ANY-WAY!!!
SINCE WE'RE IN THE SAME COMMITTEE NOW...
WHY DON'T WE DROP THE "-SAN"?
MY FRIENDS CALL ME "MAE-CHAN."
WHAT ABOUT YOU?

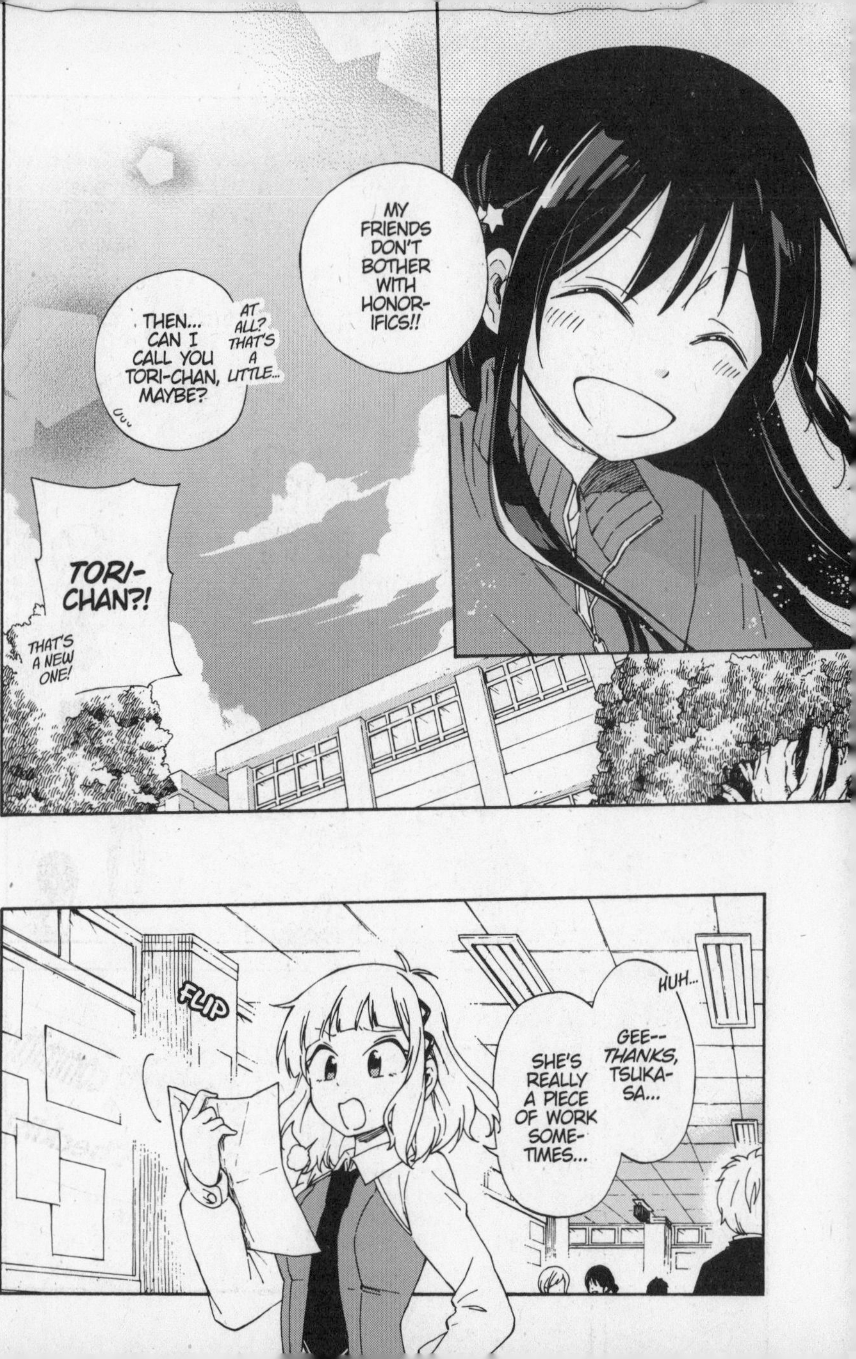
MY FRIENDS DON'T BOTHER WITH HONORIFICS!!
AT ALL? THAT'S A LITTLE...
THEN... CAN I CALL YOU TORI-CHAN, MAYBE?
TORI-CHAN?!
THAT'S A NEW ONE!
HUH...
GEE--THANKS, TSUKASA...
SHE'S REALLY A PIECE OF WORK SOME-TIMES...
FLIP

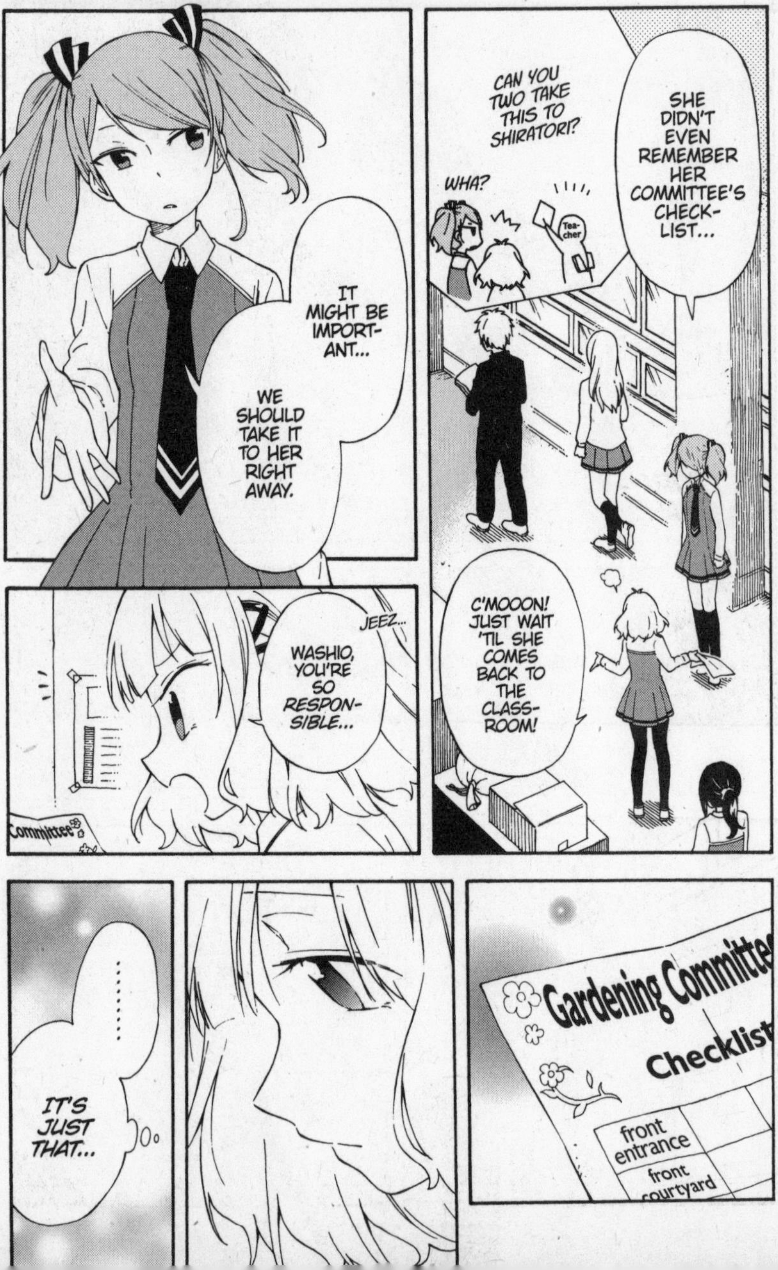
SHE DIDN'T EVEN REMEMBER HER COMMITTEE'S CHECK-LIST...
CAN YOU TWO TAKE THIS TO SHIRATORI?
Teacher
WHA?
C'MOOON! JUST WAIT 'TIL SHE COMES BACK TO THE CLASS-ROOM!
IT MIGHT BE IMPORT-ANT...
WE SHOULD TAKE IT TO HER RIGHT AWAY.
JEEZ...
WASHIO, YOU'RE SO RESPON-SIBLE...
Committee
Gardening Committe
Checklist
front entrance
front courtyard
......
IT'S JUST THAT...

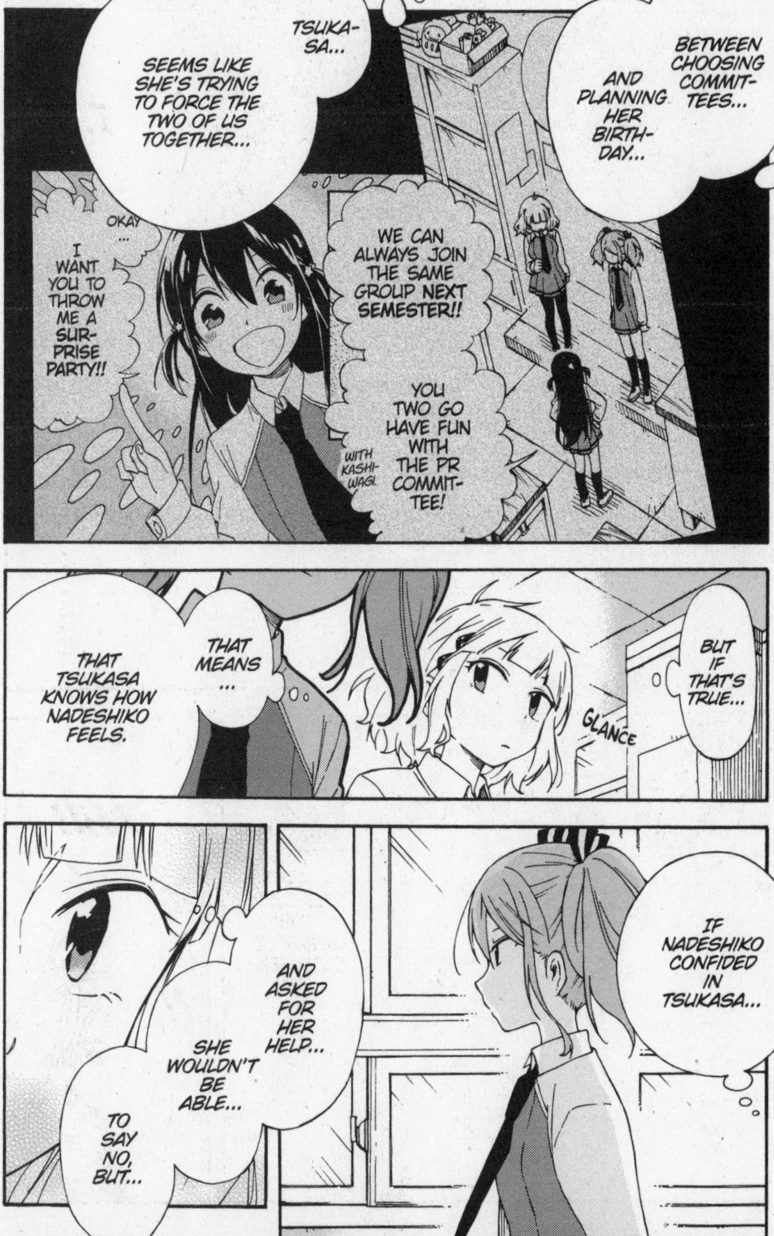
BETWEEN CHOOSING COMMIT-TEES...
AND PLANNING HER BIRTH-DAY...
TSUKA-SA...
SEEMS LIKE SHE'S TRYING TO FORCE THE TWO OF US TOGETHER...
WE CAN ALWAYS JOIN THE SAME GROUP NEXT SEMESTER!!
YOU TWO GO HAVE FUN WITH THE PR COMMIT-TEE!
WITH KASHI-WAGI.
OKAY...
I WANT YOU TO THROW ME A SUR-PRISE PARTY!!
BUT IF THAT'S TRUE...
GLANCE
THAT MEANS...
THAT TSUKASA KNOWS HOW NADESHIKO FEELS.
IF NADESHIKO CONFIDED IN TSUKASA...
AND ASKED FOR HER HELP...
SHE WOULDN'T BE ABLE...
TO SAY NO, BUT...

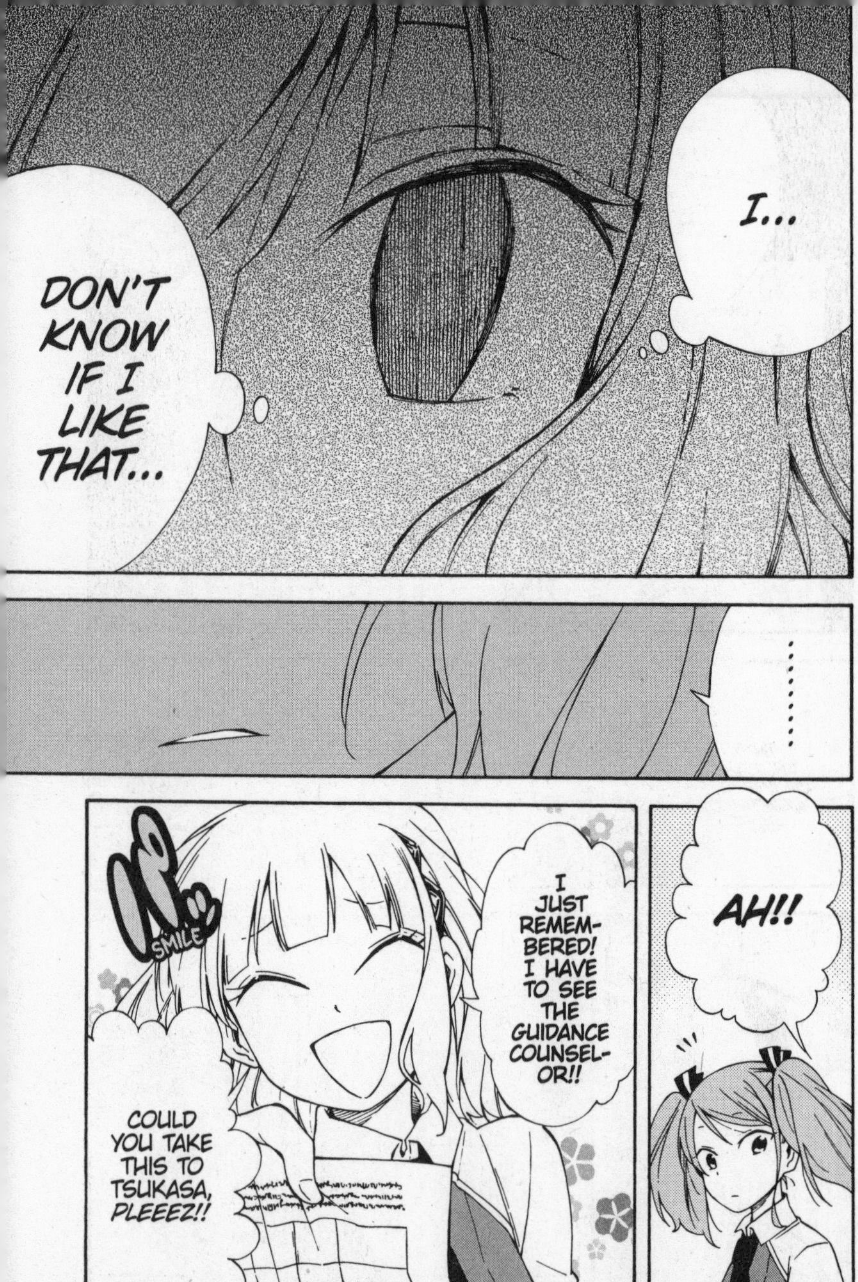
I...
DON'T KNOW IF I LIKE THAT...
......
AH!!
I JUST REMEMBERED! I HAVE TO SEE THE GUIDANCE COUNSELOR!!
SMILE
COULD YOU TAKE THIS TO TSUKASA, PLEEEZ!!

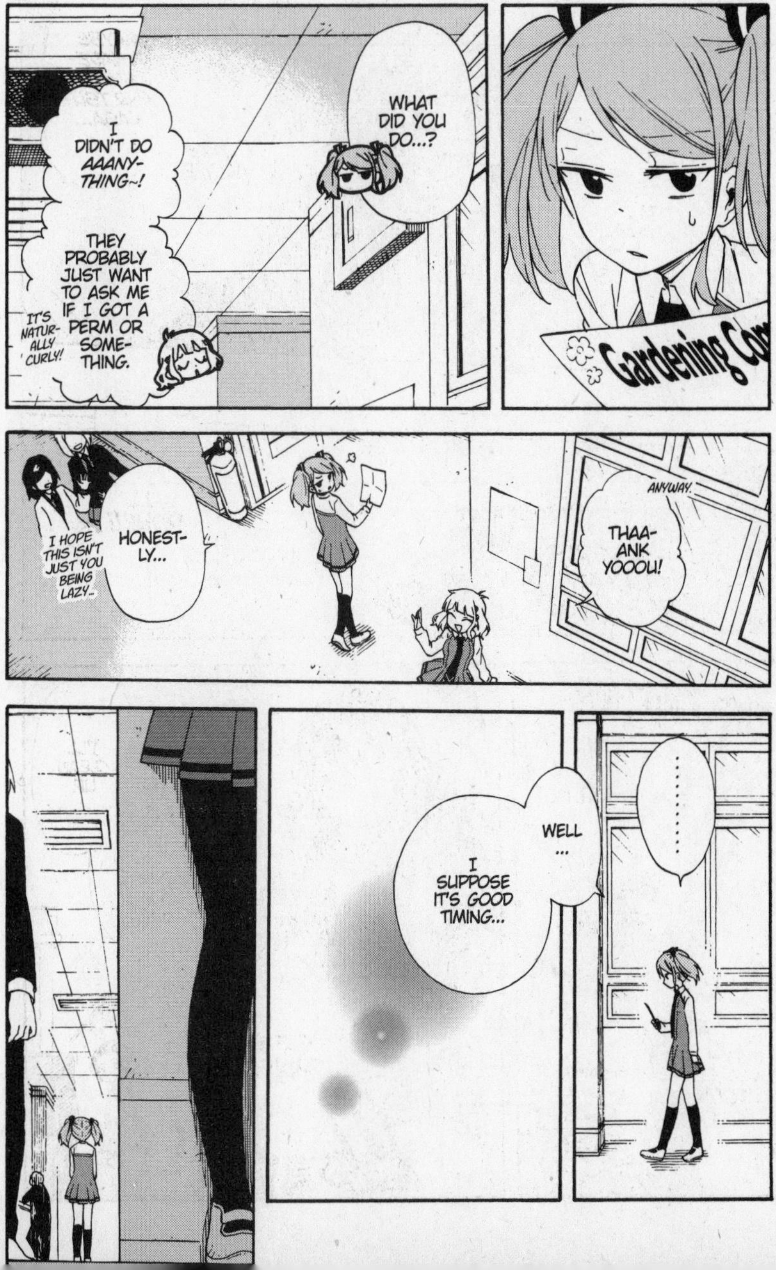
Gardening Co
WHAT DID YOU DO...?
I DIDN'T DO AAANY-THING~!
THEY PROBABLY JUST WANT TO ASK ME IF I GOT A PERM OR SOME-THING.
IT'S NATUR-ALLY CURLY!
ANYWAY.
THAA-ANK YOOOU!
HONEST-LY...
I HOPE THIS ISN'T JUST YOU BEING LAZY...
......
WELL ...
I SUPPOSE IT'S GOOD TIMING...

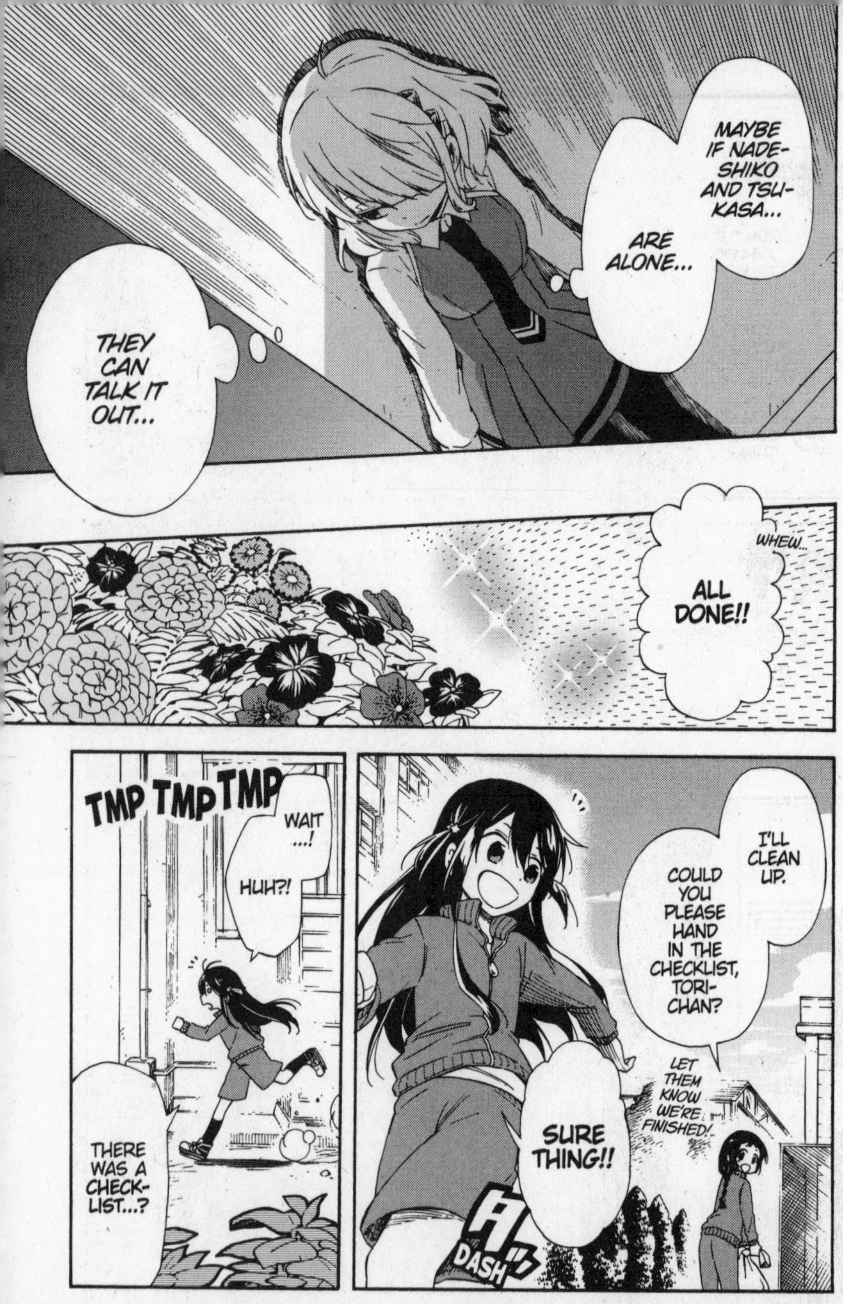
MAYBE IF NADE-SHIKO AND TSU-KASA...
ARE ALONE...
THEY CAN TALK IT OUT...
WHEW...
ALL DONE!!
I'LL CLEAN UP.
COULD YOU PLEASE HAND IN THE CHECKLIST, TORI-CHAN?
LET THEM KNOW WE'RE FINISHED!
SURE THING!!
DASH
TMP TMP TMP
WAIT ...!
HUH?!
THERE WAS A CHECK-LIST...?

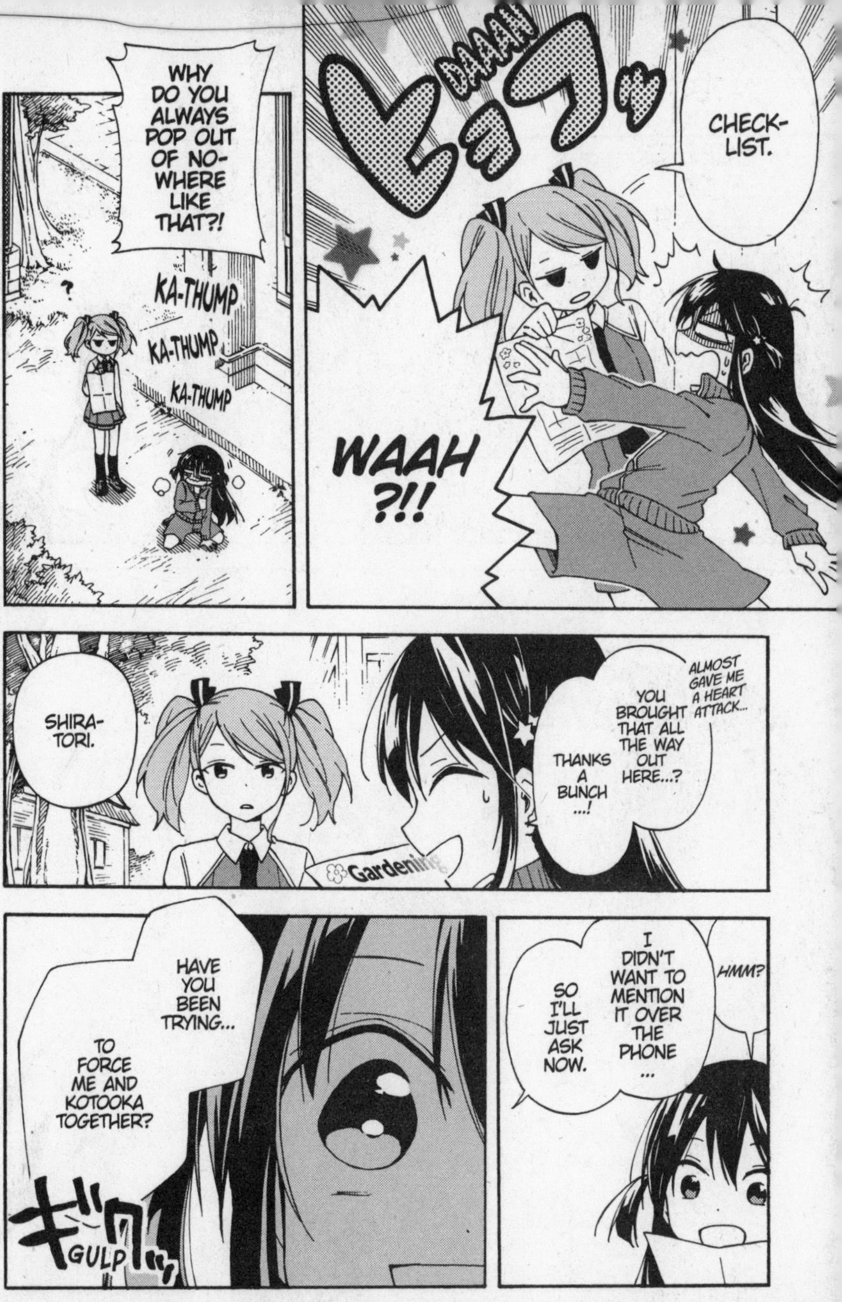
DAAAN
CHECK-LIST.
WAAH ?!!
WHY DO YOU ALWAYS POP OUT OF NO-WHERE LIKE THAT?!
?
KA-THUMP
KA-THUMP
KA-THUMP
ALMOST GAVE ME A HEART ATTACK...
YOU BROUGHT THAT ALL THE WAY OUT HERE...?
THANKS A BUNCH ...!
SHIRA-TORI.
Gardening
HMM?
I DIDN'T WANT TO MENTION IT OVER THE PHONE ...
SO I'LL JUST ASK NOW.
HAVE YOU BEEN TRYING...
TO FORCE ME AND KOTOOKA TOGETHER?
GULP

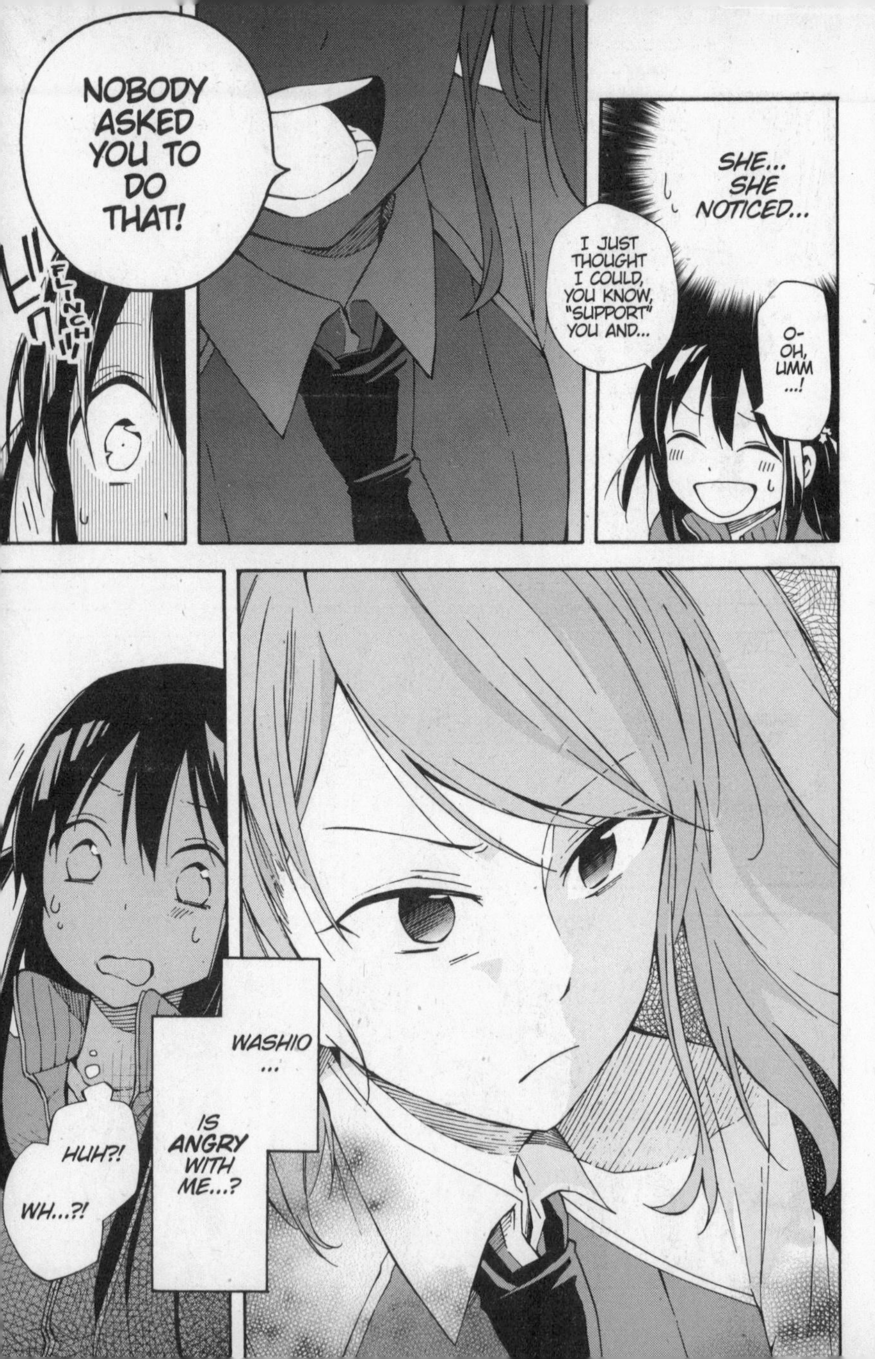
SHE... SHE NOTICED...
O-OH, UMM ...!
I JUST THOUGHT I COULD, YOU KNOW, "SUPPORT" YOU AND...
NOBODY ASKED YOU TO DO THAT!
FLINCH
WASHIO ...
IS ANGRY WITH ME...?
HUH?!
WH...?!

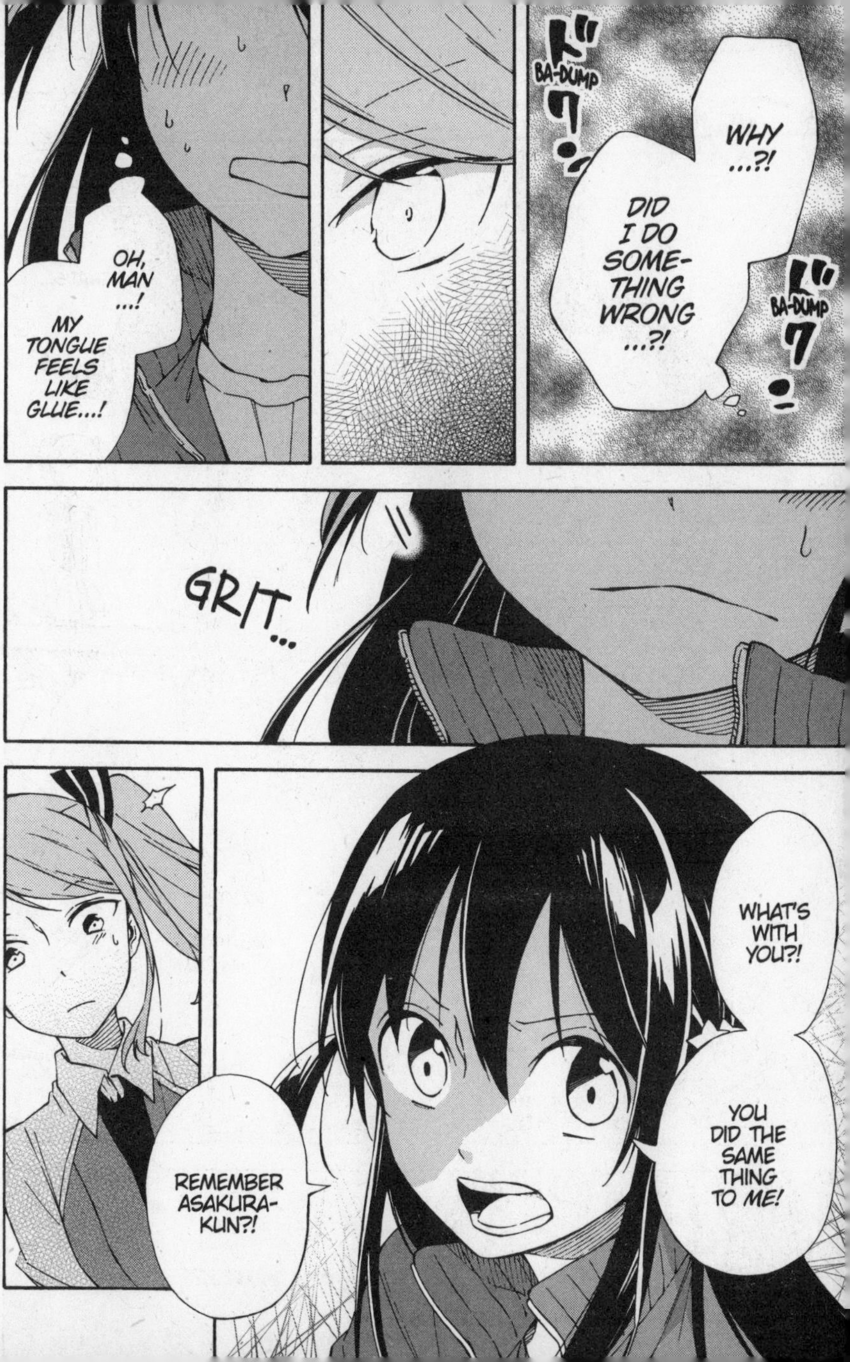
BA-DUMP
WHY ...?!
DID I DO SOME-THING WRONG ...?!
BA-DUMP
OH, MAN ...!
MY TONGUE FEELS LIKE GLUE...!
GRIT...
WHAT'S WITH YOU?!
YOU DID THE SAME THING TO ME!
REMEMBER ASAKURA-KUN?!

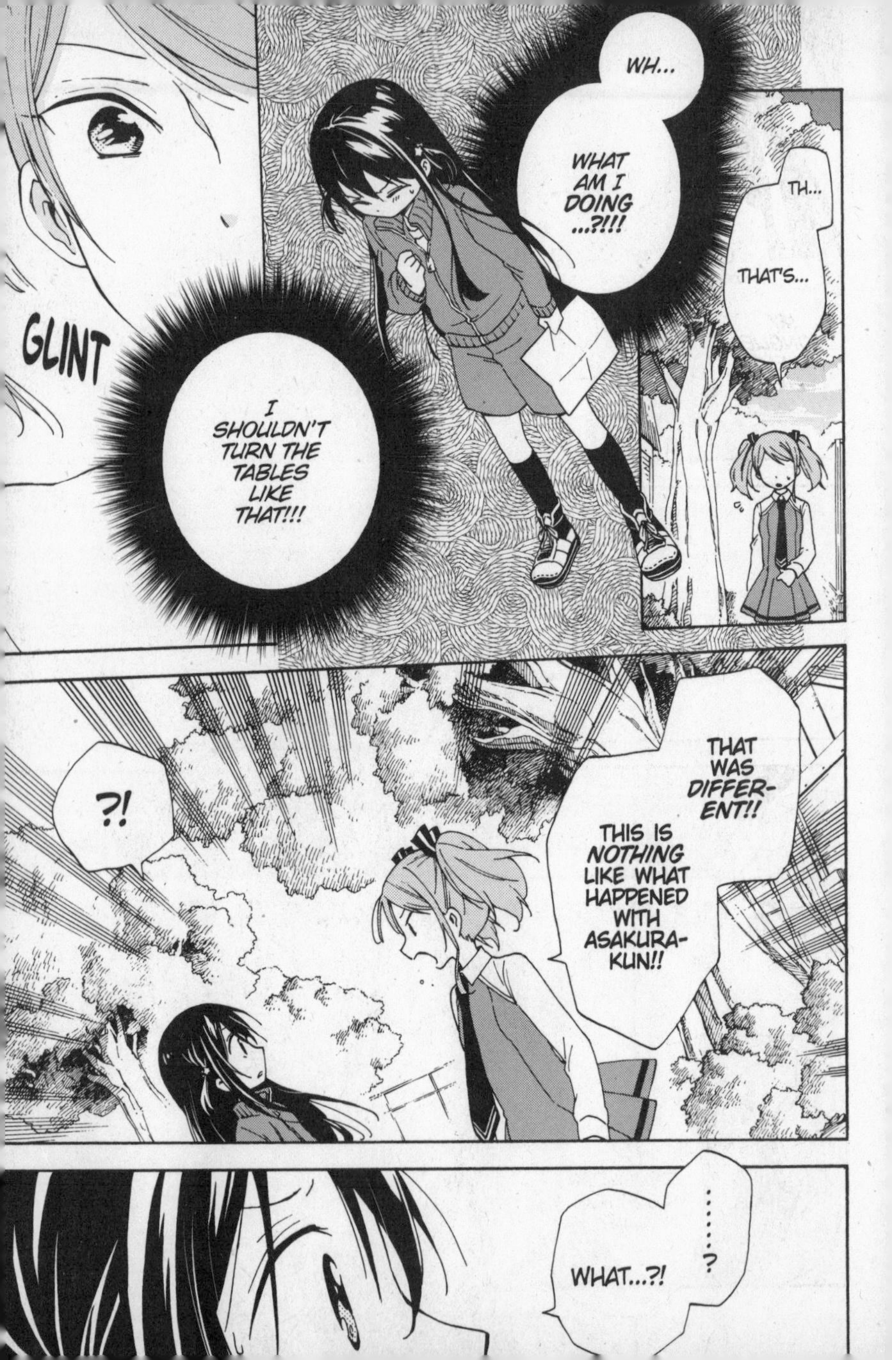
TH...
THAT'S...
WH...
WHAT AM I DOING ...?!!!
I SHOULDN'T TURN THE TABLES LIKE THAT!!!
GLINT
THAT WAS DIFFER-ENT!!
THIS IS NOTHING LIKE WHAT HAPPENED WITH ASAKURA-KUN!!
?!
.....?
WHAT...?!

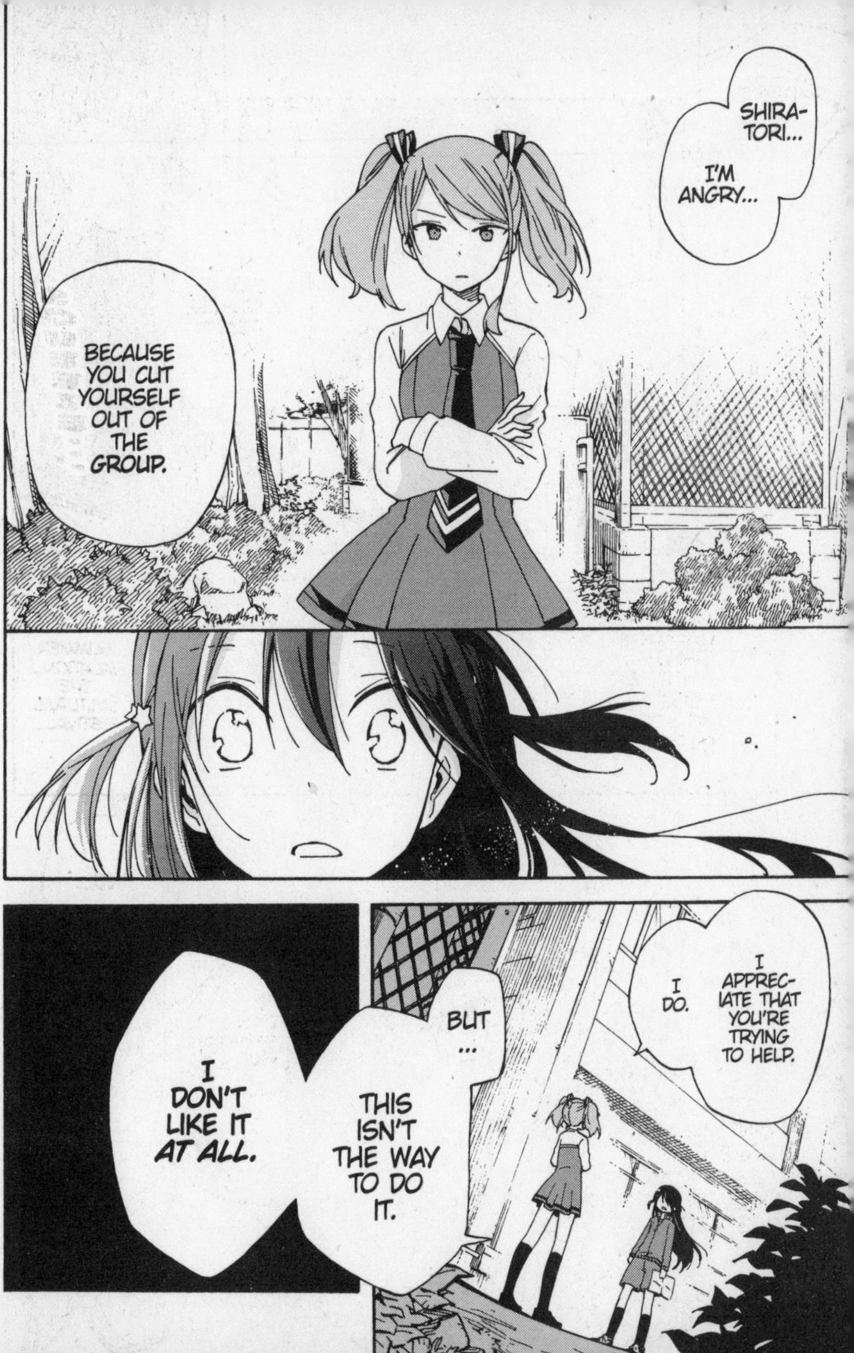
SHIRA-TORI...
I'M ANGRY...
BECAUSE YOU CUT YOURSELF OUT OF THE GROUP.
I APPREC-IATE THAT YOU'RE TRYING TO HELP.
I DO.
BUT ...
THIS ISN'T THE WAY TO DO IT.
I DON'T LIKE IT *AT ALL.*

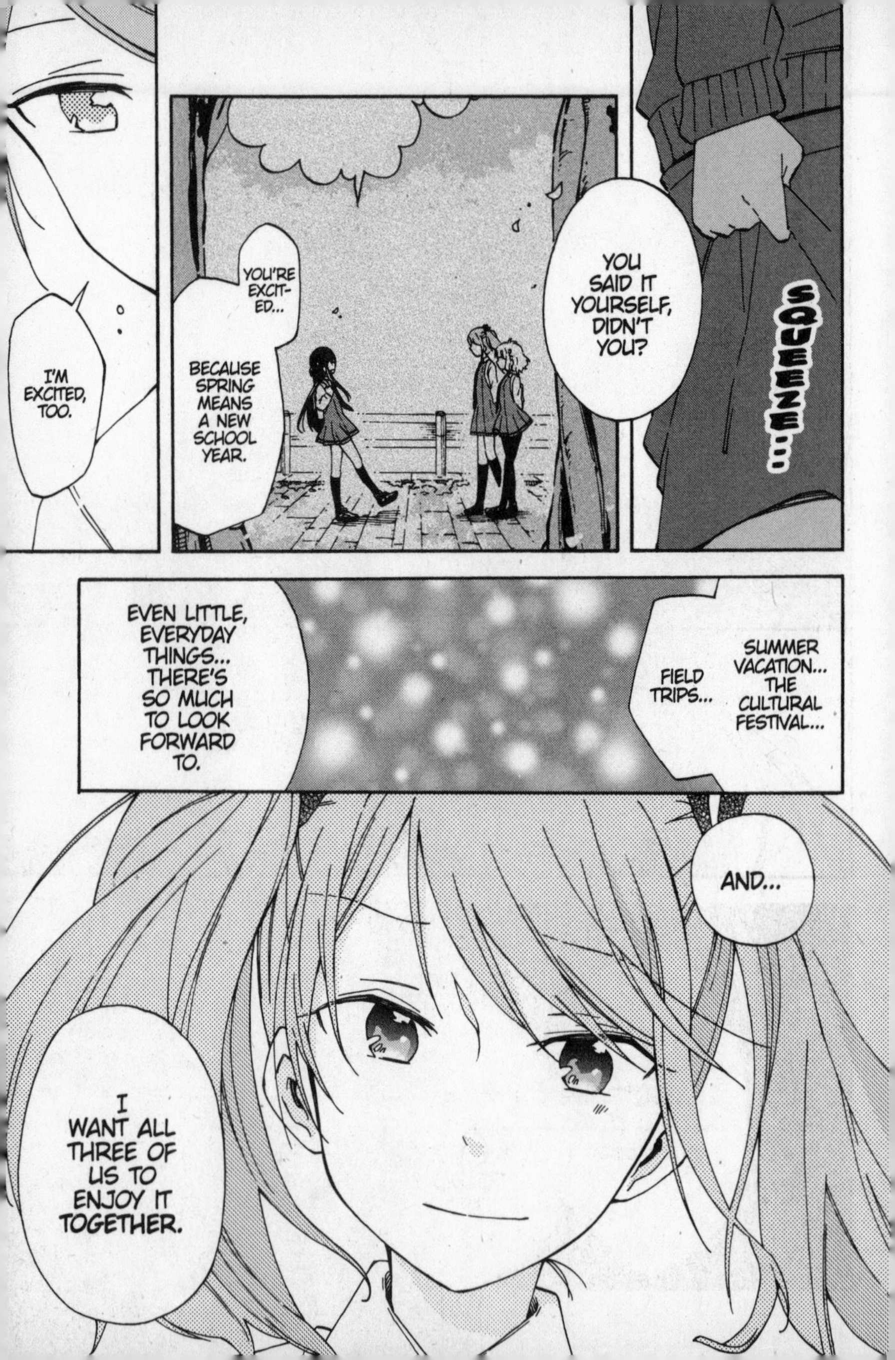
YOU SAID IT YOURSELF, DIDN'T YOU?
SQUEEZE...
YOU'RE EXCIT-ED...
BECAUSE SPRING MEANS A NEW SCHOOL YEAR.
I'M EXCITED, TOO.
SUMMER VACATION... THE CULTURAL FESTIVAL...
FIELD TRIPS...
EVEN LITTLE, EVERYDAY THINGS... THERE'S SO MUCH TO LOOK FORWARD TO.
AND...
I WANT ALL THREE OF US TO ENJOY IT TOGETHER.

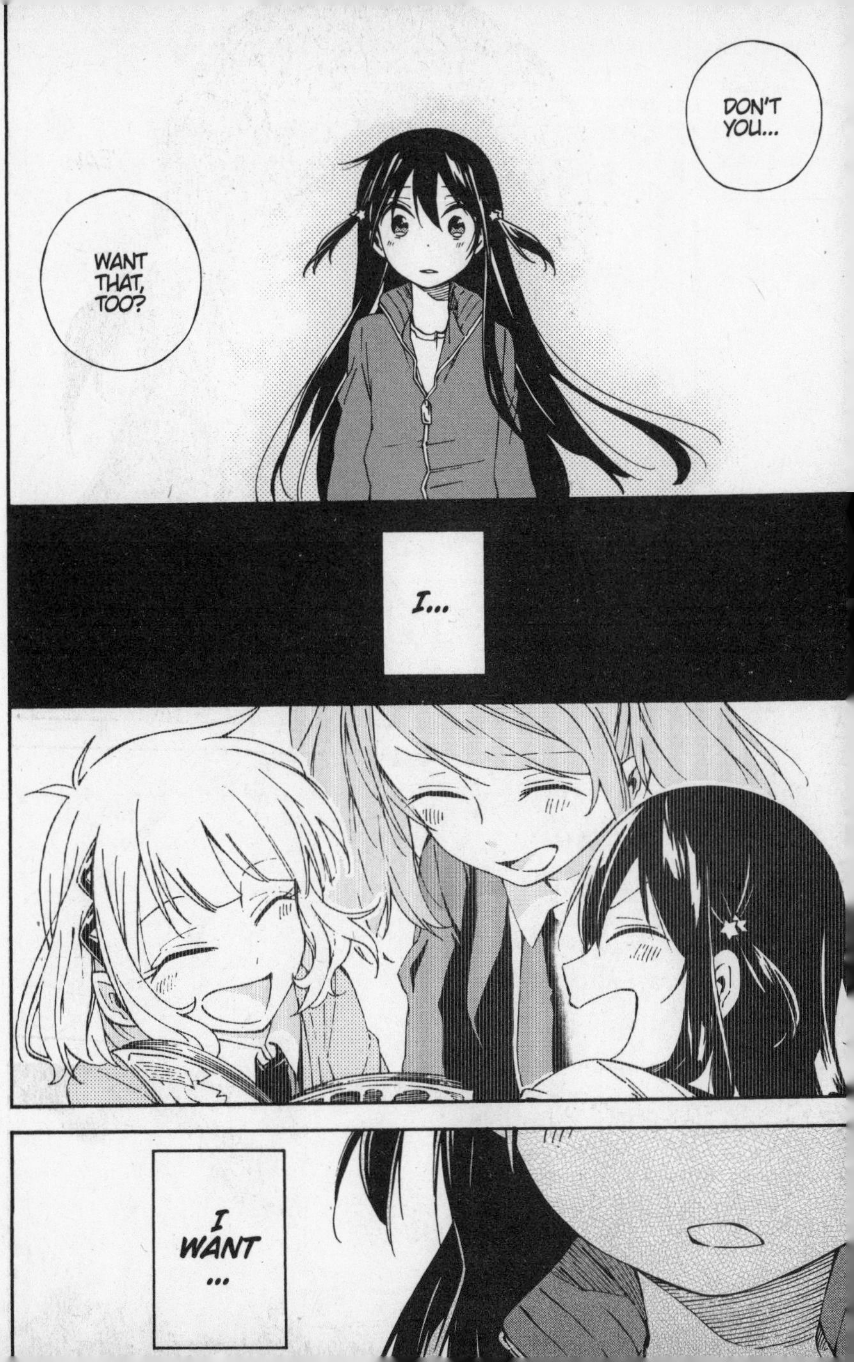
DON'T YOU...
WANT THAT, TOO?
I...
I WANT ...

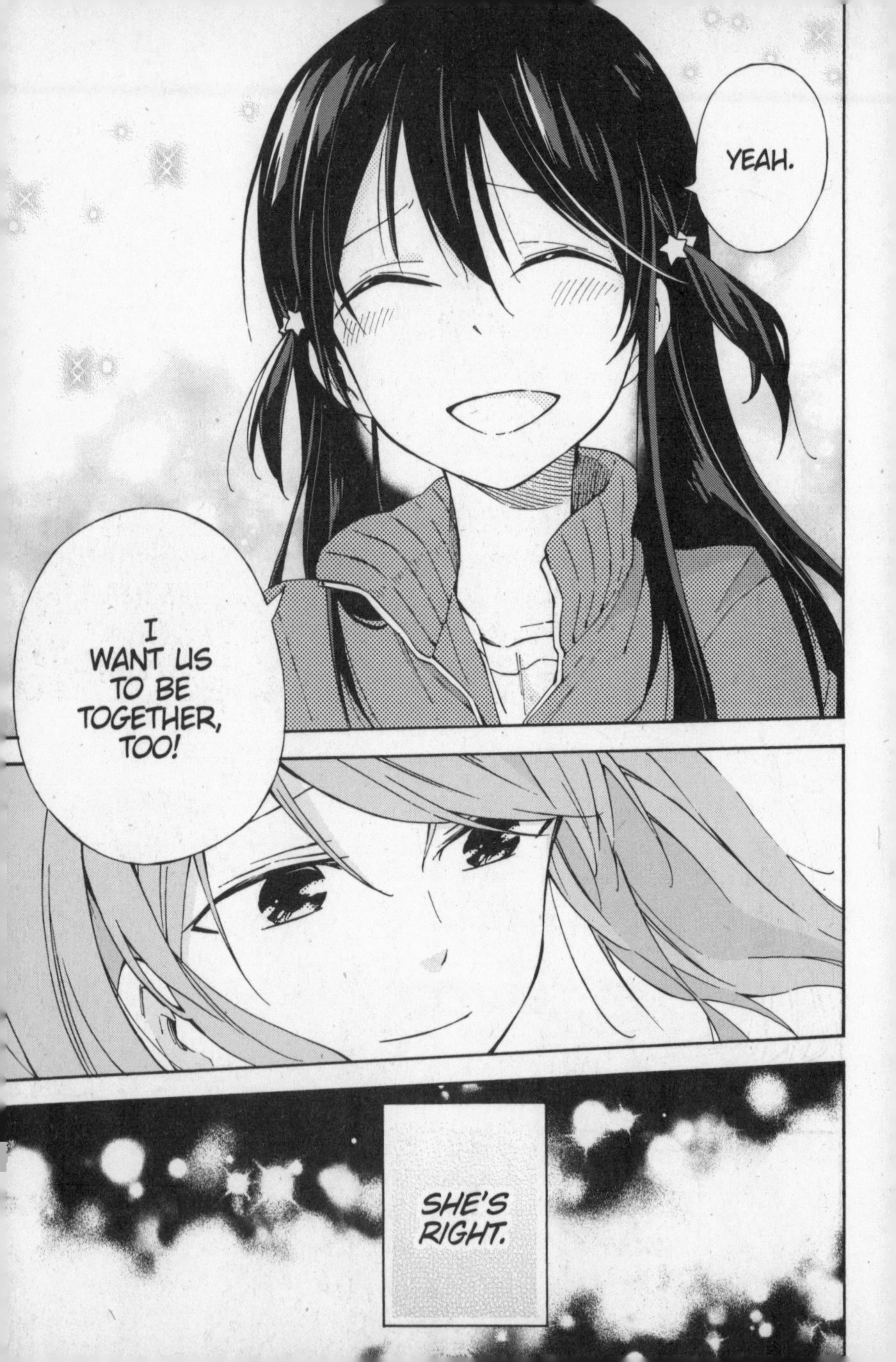
YEAH.
I WANT US TO BE TOGETHER, TOO!
SHE'S RIGHT.

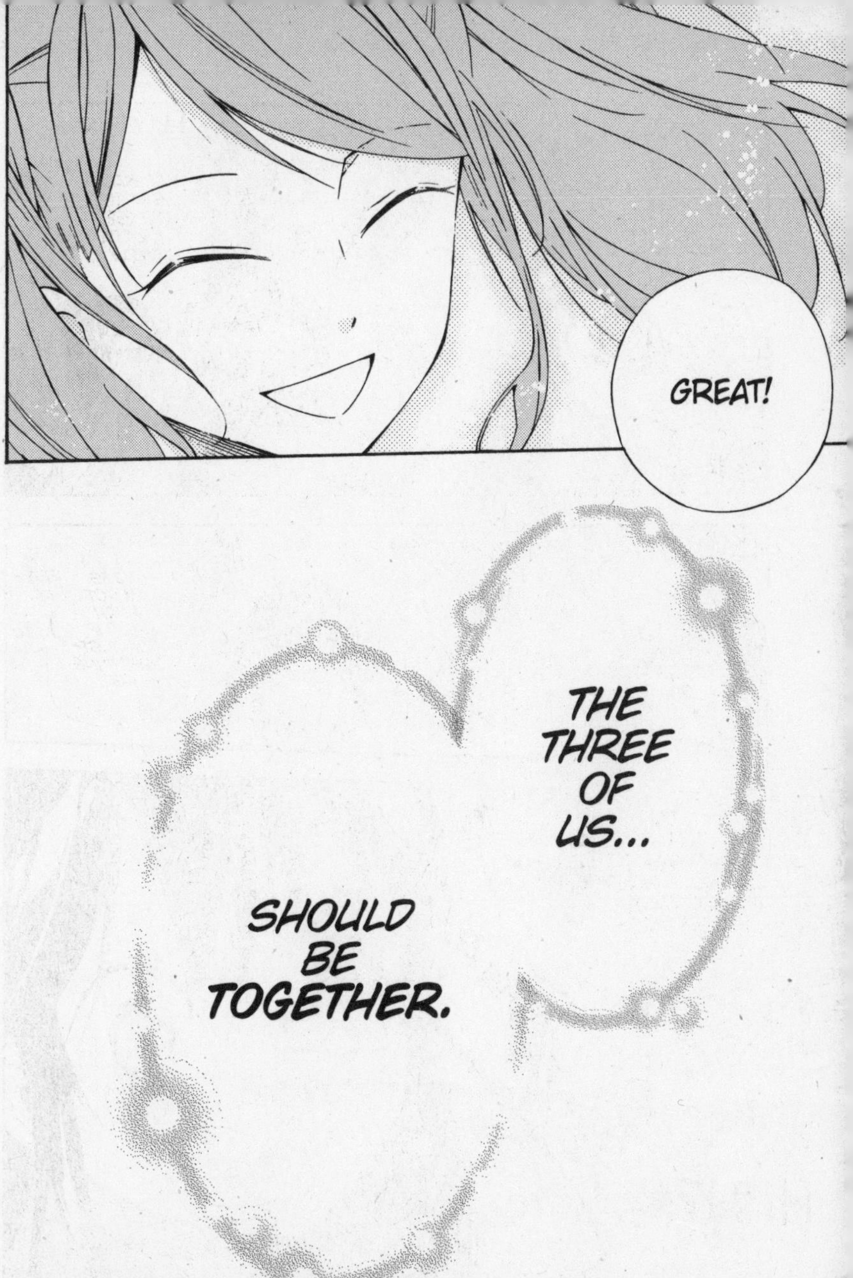
GREAT!
THE THREE OF US...
SHOULD BE TOGETHER.

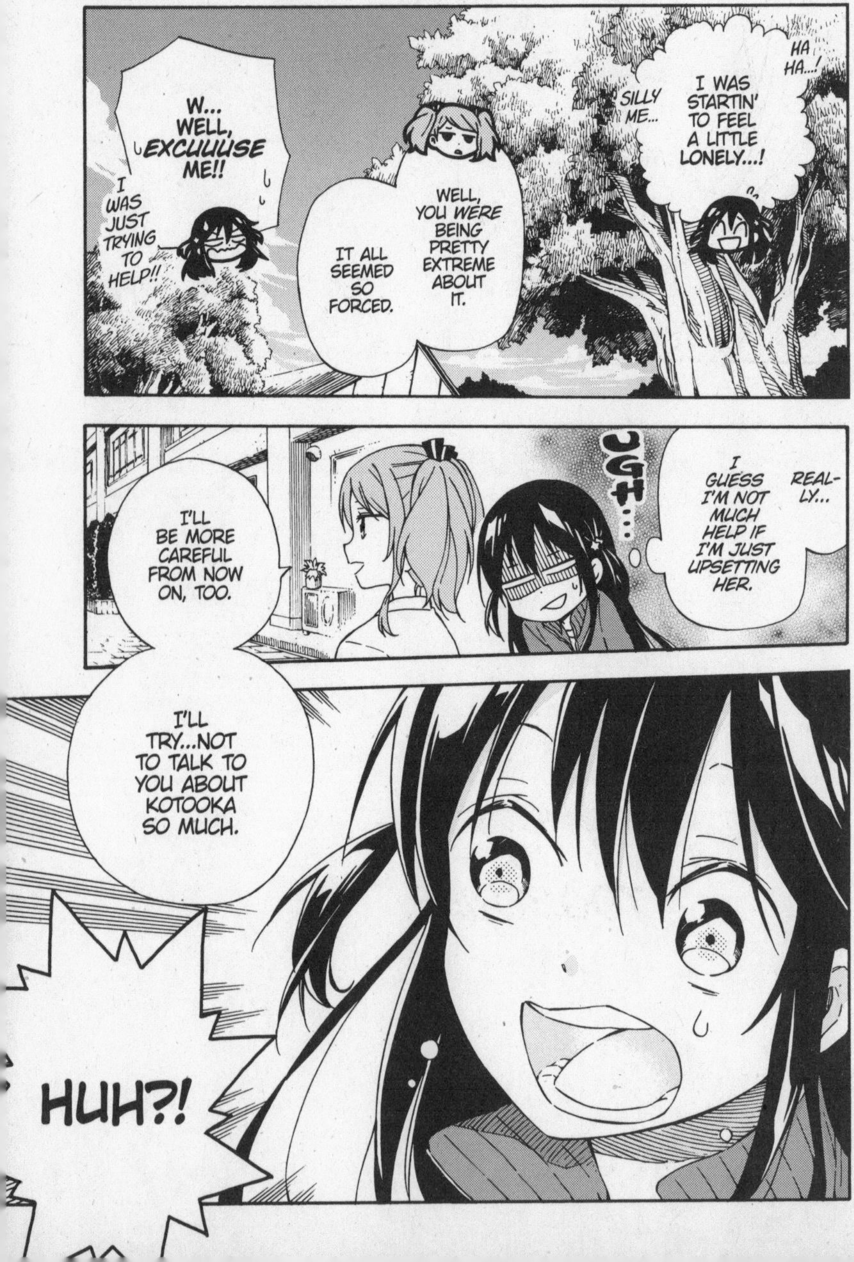
HA HA...!
I WAS STARTIN' TO FEEL A LITTLE LONELY...!
SILLY ME...
WELL, YOU WERE BEING PRETTY EXTREME ABOUT IT.
IT ALL SEEMED SO FORCED.
W... WELL, EXCUUUSE ME!!
I WAS JUST TRYING TO HELP!!
REAL-LY...
I GUESS I'M NOT MUCH HELP IF I'M JUST UPSETTING HER.
UGH...
I'LL BE MORE CAREFUL FROM NOW ON, TOO.
I'LL TRY...NOT TO TALK TO YOU ABOUT KOTOOKA SO MUCH.
HUH?!

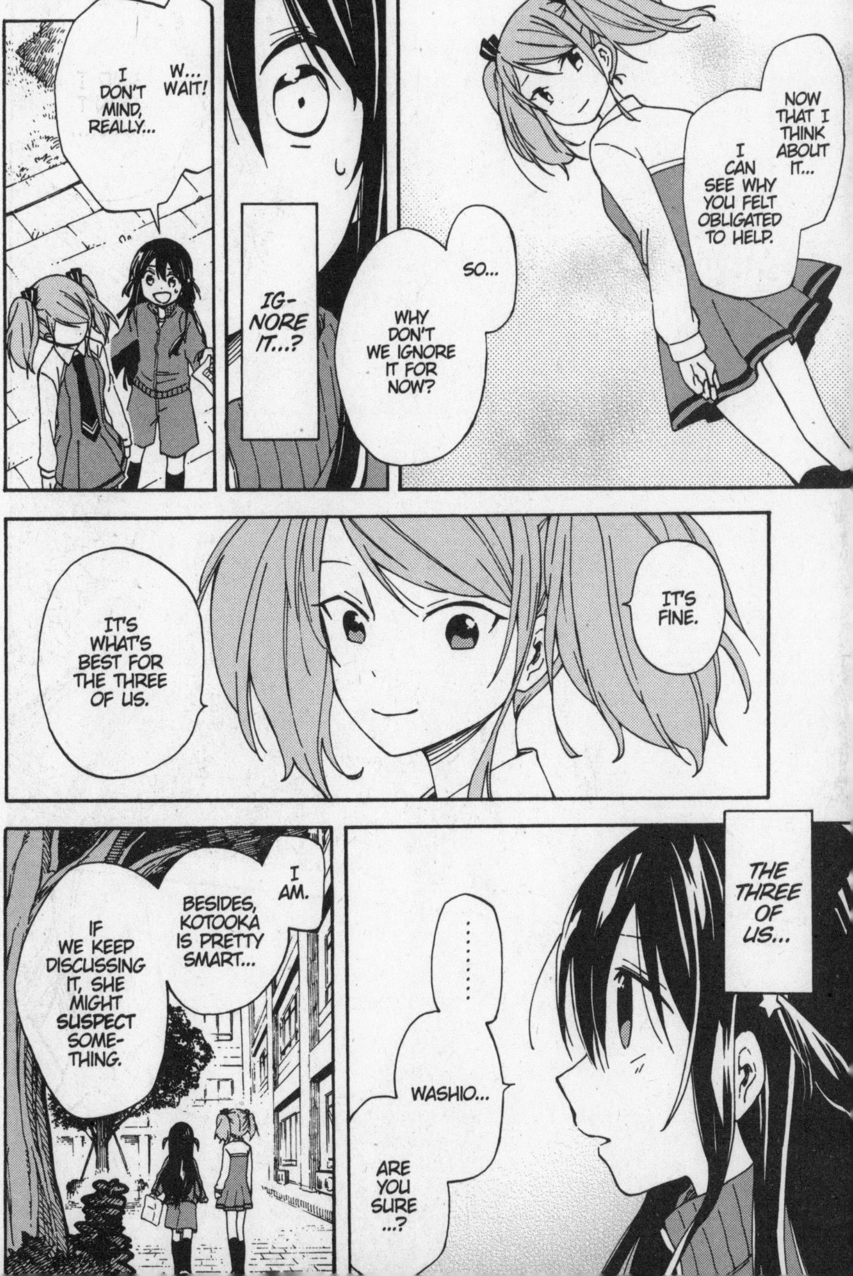
NOW THAT I THINK ABOUT IT... I CAN SEE WHY YOU FELT OBLIGATED TO HELP.
SO... WHY DON'T WE IGNORE IT FOR NOW?
IG-NORE IT...?
W... WAIT! I DON'T MIND, REALLY...
IT'S FINE.
IT'S WHAT'S BEST FOR THE THREE OF US.
THE THREE OF US...
......
WASHIO... ARE YOU SURE ...?
I AM.
BESIDES, KOTOOKA IS PRETTY SMART...
IF WE KEEP DISCUSSING IT, SHE MIGHT SUSPECT SOME-THING.

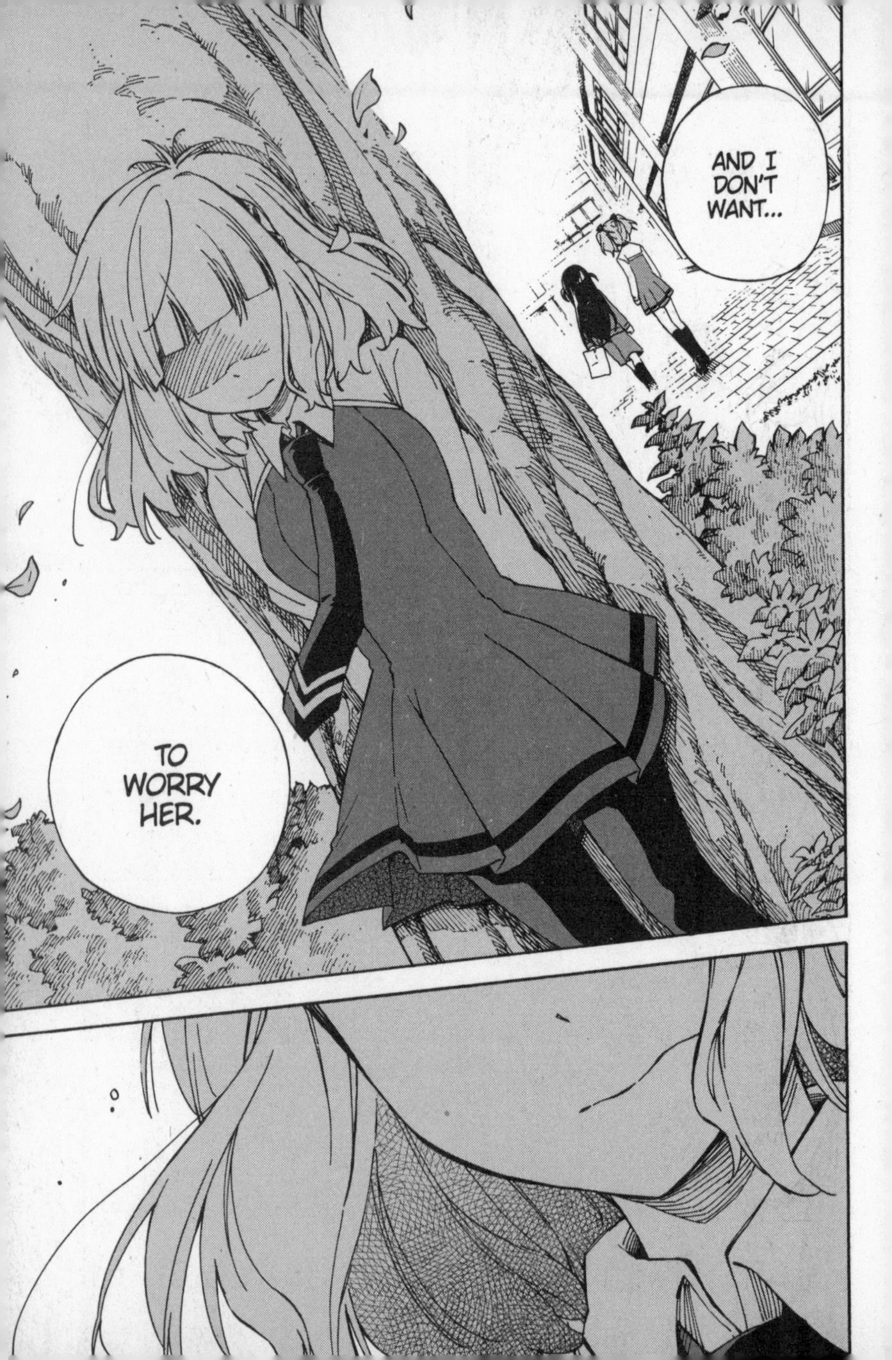
AND I DON'T WANT...
TO WORRY HER.

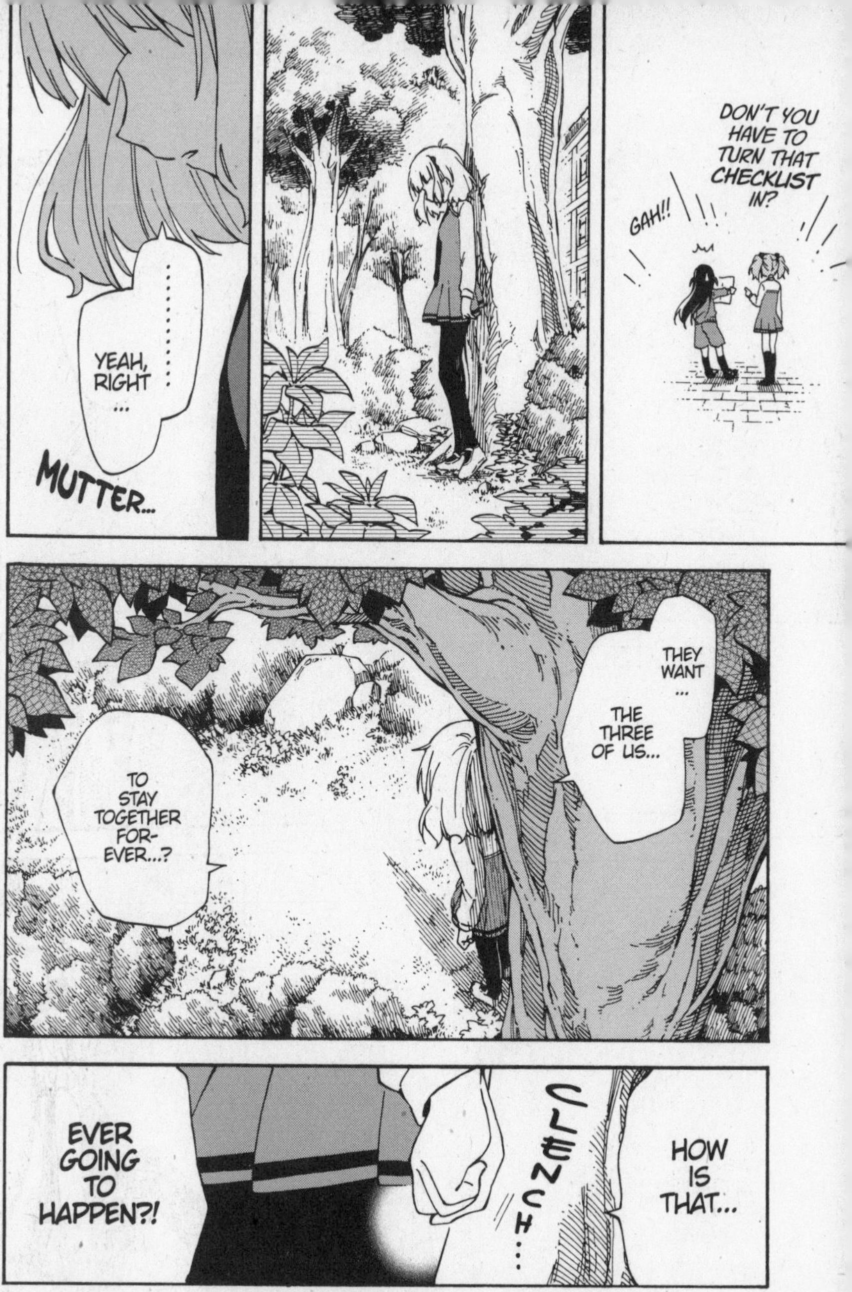
DON'T YOU HAVE TO TURN THAT CHECKLIST IN?
GAH!!
......
YEAH, RIGHT...
MUTTER...
THEY WANT... THE THREE OF US...
TO STAY TOGETHER FOR-EVER...?
HOW IS THAT...
CLENCH...
EVER GOING TO HAPPEN?!

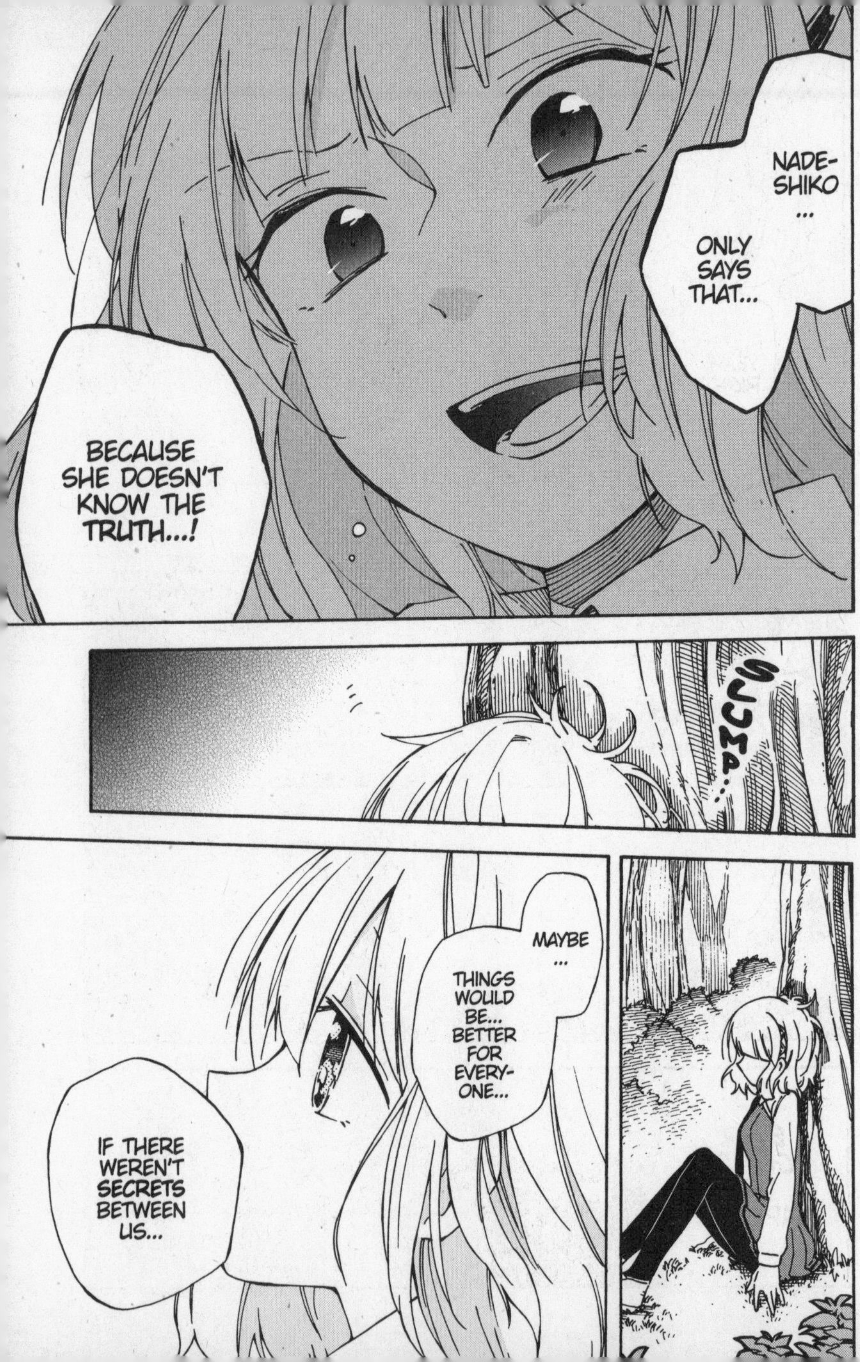
NADE-SHIKO... ONLY SAYS THAT...
BECAUSE SHE DOESN'T KNOW THE TRUTH...!
SLUMP...
MAYBE... THINGS WOULD BE... BETTER FOR EVERYONE...
IF THERE WEREN'T SECRETS BETWEEN US...

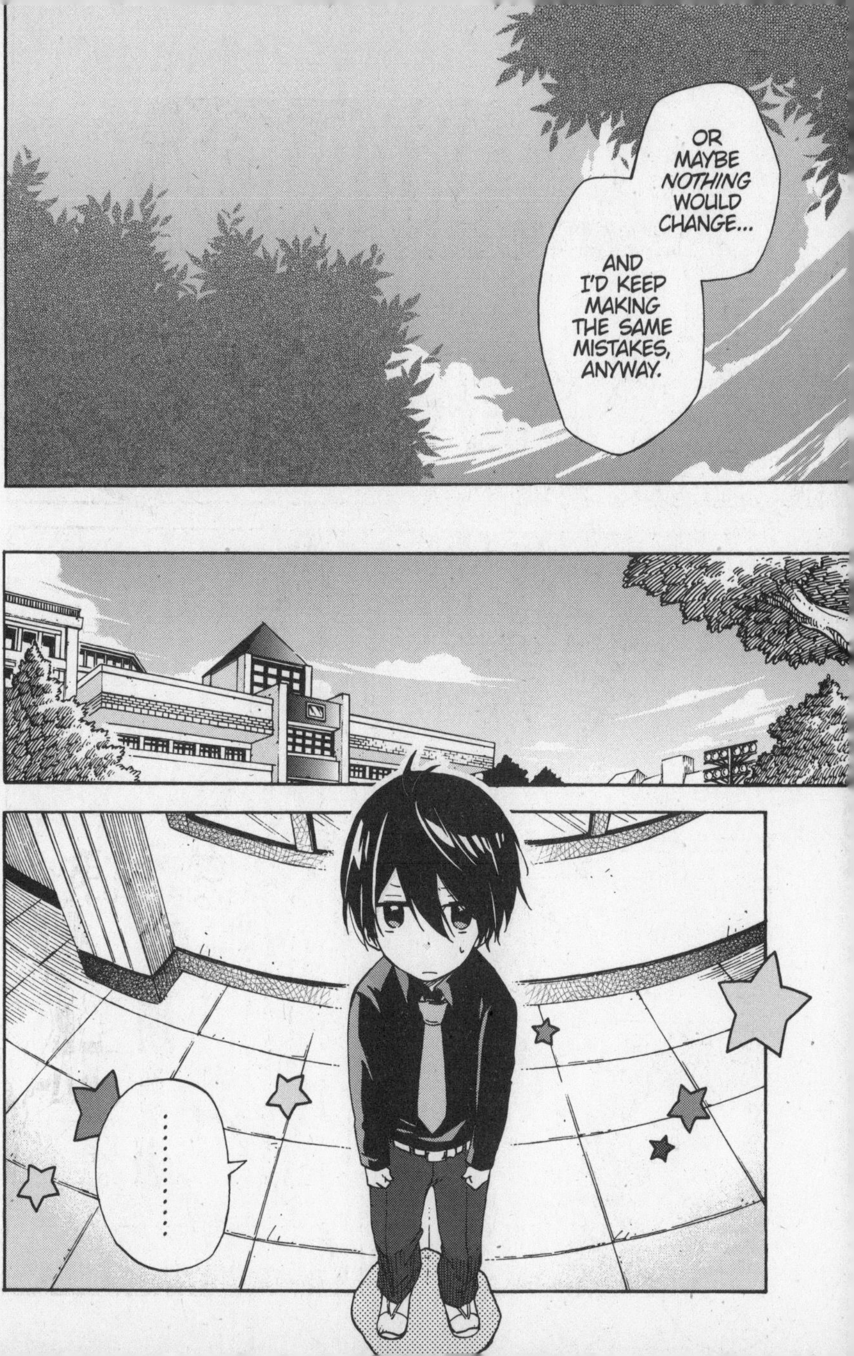
OR MAYBE *NOTHING* WOULD CHANGE...
AND I'D KEEP MAKING THE SAME MISTAKES, ANYWAY.
......

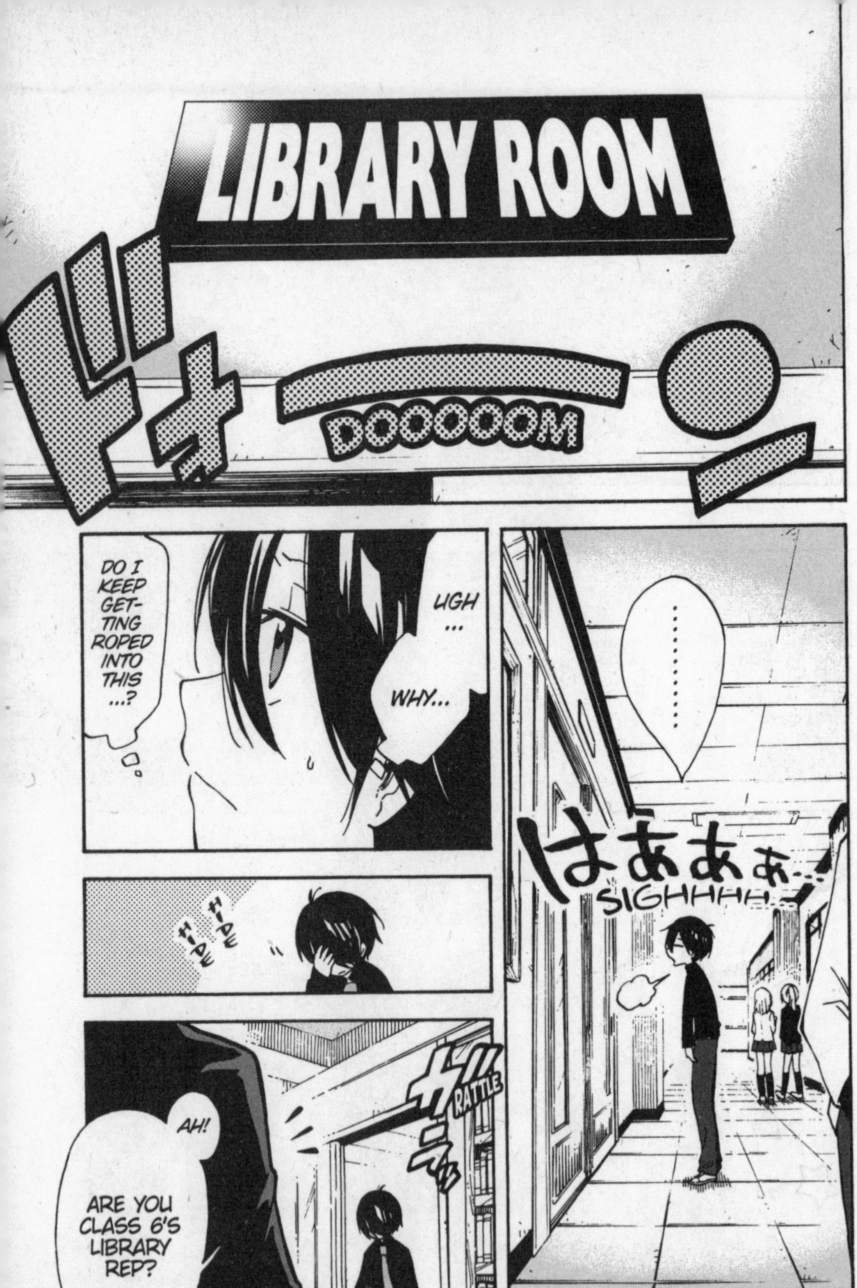
LIBRARY ROOM
DOOOOOM
......
SIGHHHH
UGH ...
WHY...
DO I KEEP GETTING ROPED INTO THIS ...?
HIDE HIDE
RATTLE
AH!
ARE YOU CLASS 6'S LIBRARY REP?

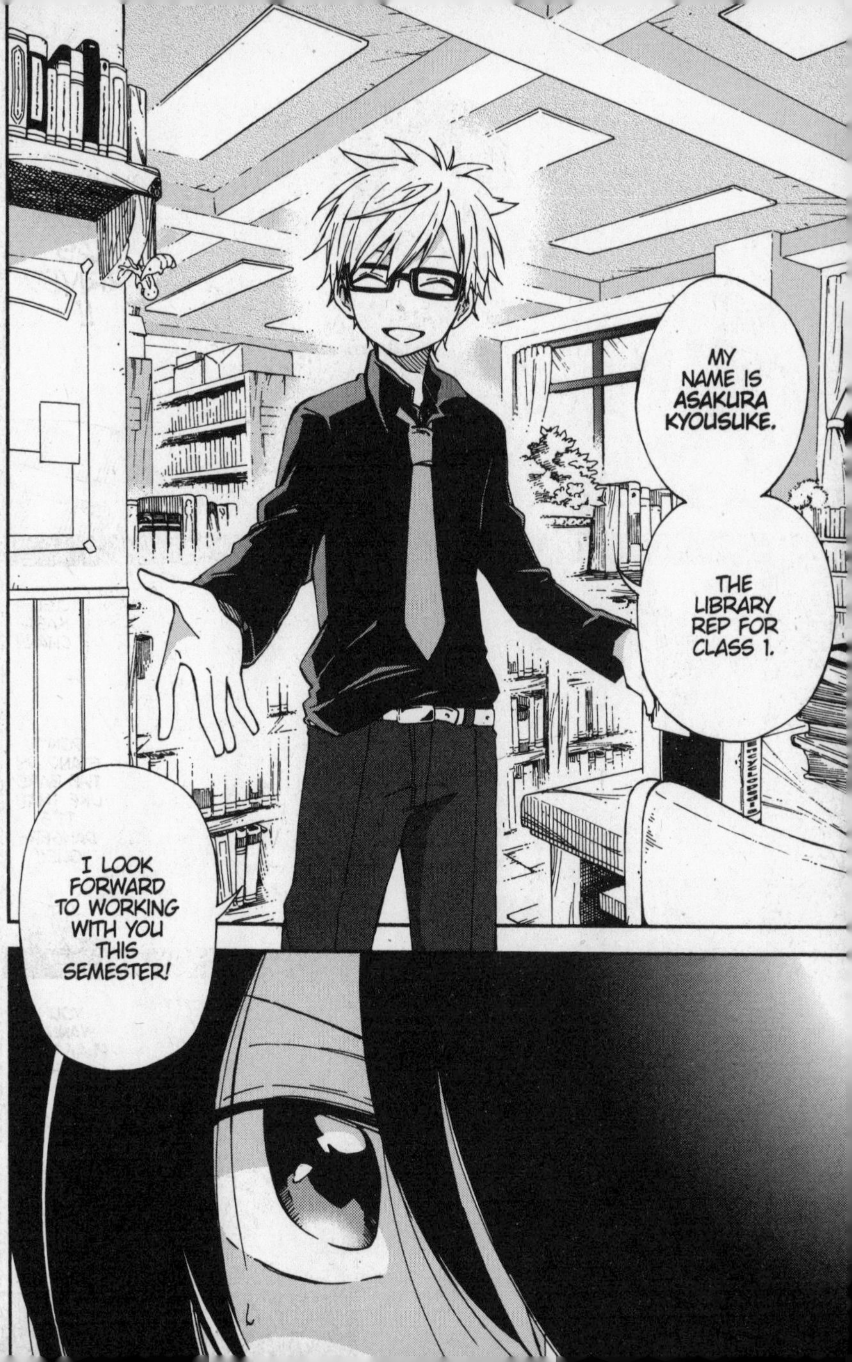
MY NAME IS ASAKURA KYOUSUKE.
THE LIBRARY REP FOR CLASS 1.
I LOOK FORWARD TO WORKING WITH YOU THIS SEMESTER!

Chapter 9

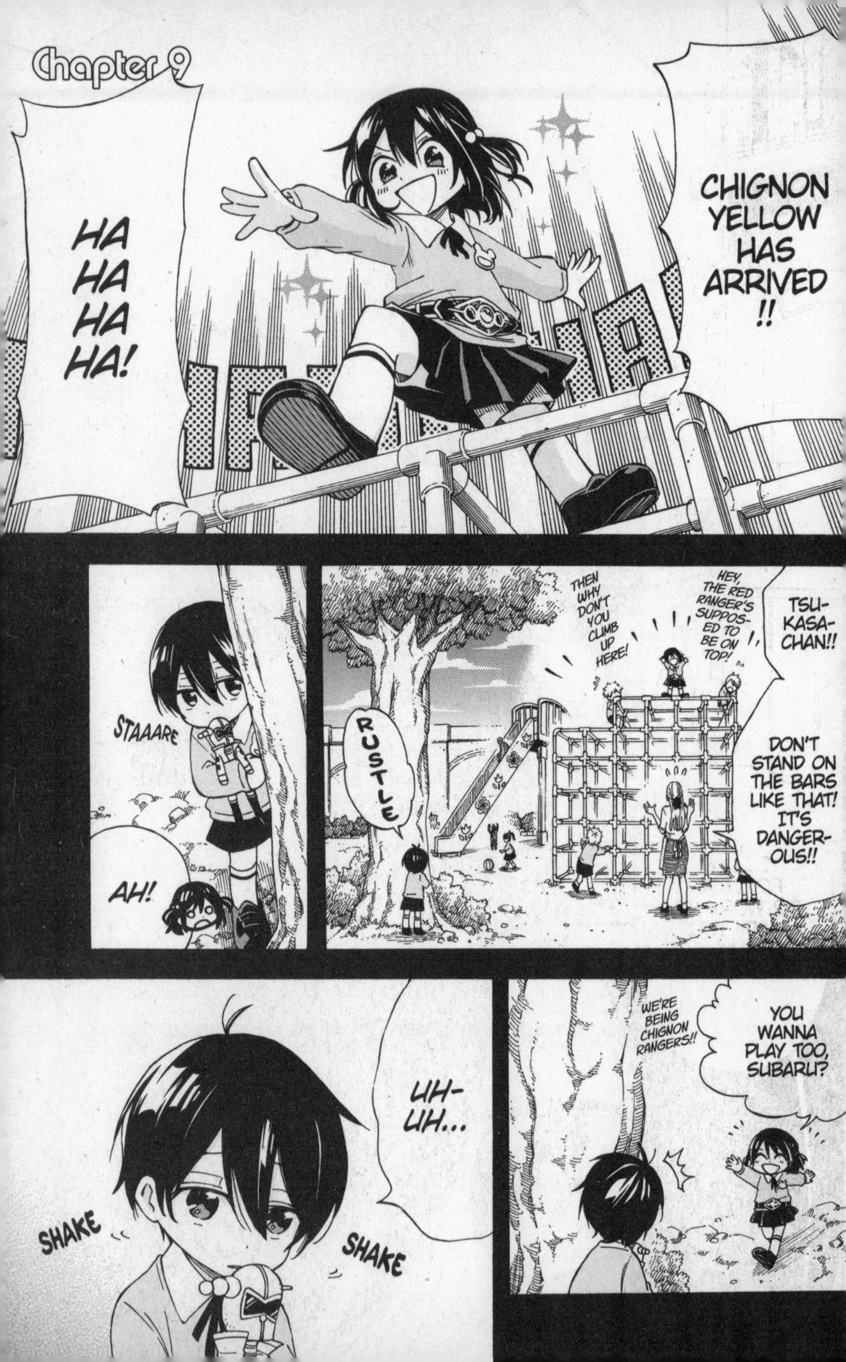
CHIGNON YELLOW HAS ARRIVED!!
HA HA HA HA!
TSU-KASA-CHAN!!
DON'T STAND ON THE BARS LIKE THAT! IT'S DANGER-OUS!!
HEY, THE RED RANGER'S SUPPOS-ED TO BE ON TOP!
THEN WHY DON'T YOU CLIMB UP HERE!
RUSTLE
STAAARE
AH!
YOU WANNA PLAY TOO, SUBARU?
WE'RE BEING CHIGNON RANGERS!!
UH-UH...
SHAKE
SHAKE

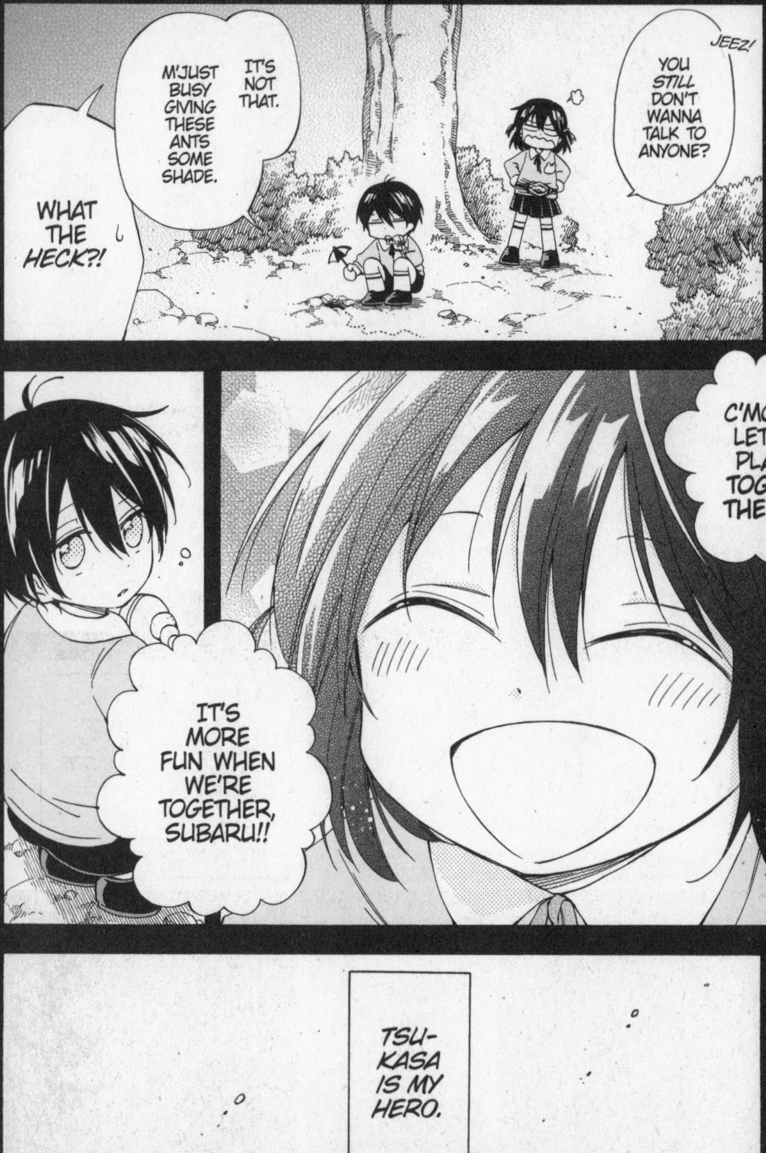
JEEZ!
YOU STILL DON'T WANNA TALK TO ANYONE?
IT'S NOT THAT.
M'JUST BUSY GIVING THESE ANTS SOME SHADE.
WHAT THE HECK?!
C'MON, LET'S PLAY TOGE-THER!!
IT'S MORE FUN WHEN WE'RE TOGETHER, SUBARU!!
TSU-KASA IS MY HERO.

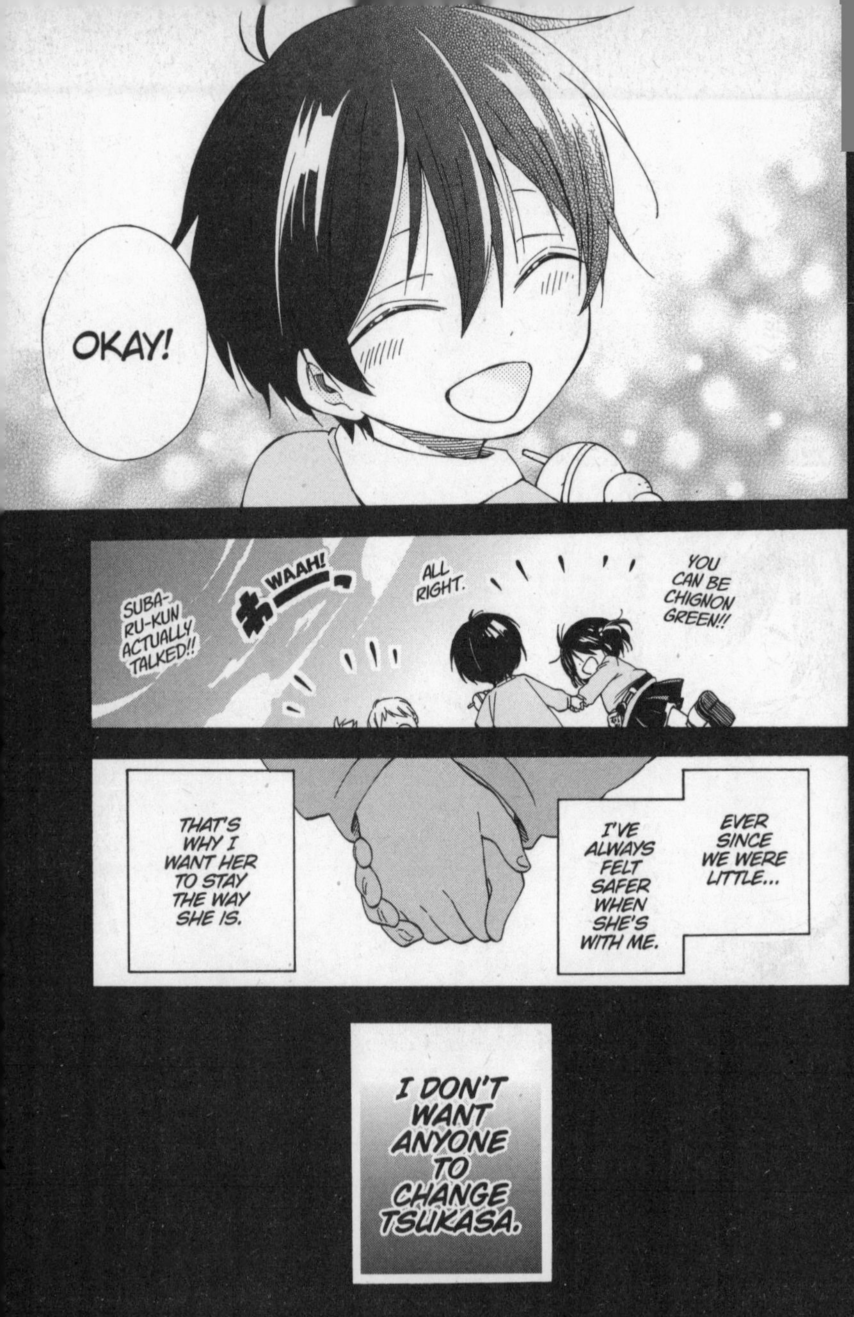
OKAY!
YOU CAN BE CHIGNON GREEN!!
ALL RIGHT.
WAAH!
SUBA-RU-KUN ACTUALLY TALKED!!
EVER SINCE WE WERE LITTLE...
I'VE ALWAYS FELT SAFER WHEN SHE'S WITH ME.
THAT'S WHY I WANT HER TO STAY THE WAY SHE IS.
I DON'T WANT ANYONE TO CHANGE TSUKASA.

Nameless
Asterism

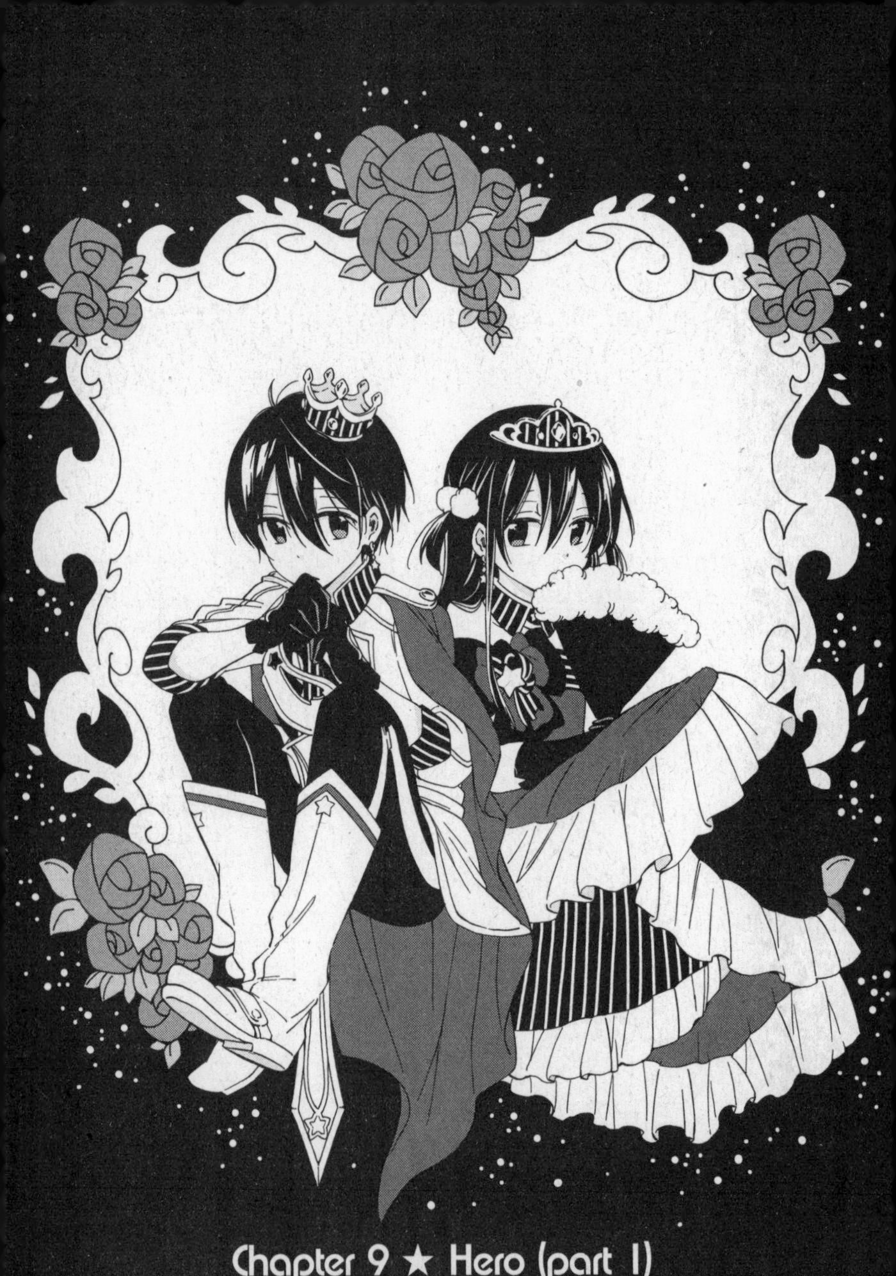

Chapter 9 ★ Hero (part 1)

Nameless
Asterism

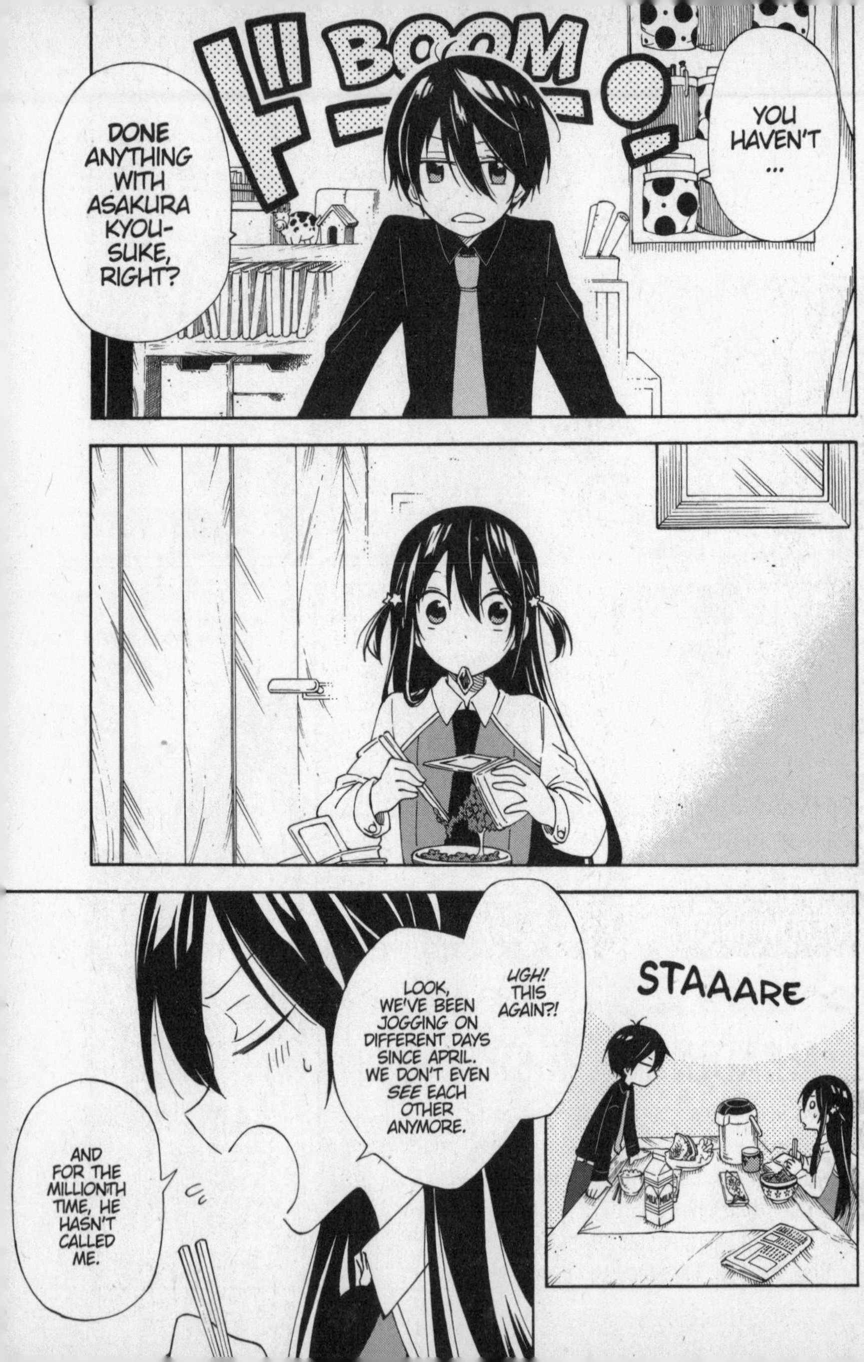
YOU HAVEN'T ...
BOOM
DONE ANYTHING WITH ASAKURA KYOU-SUKE, RIGHT?
STAAARE
UGH! THIS AGAIN?!
LOOK, WE'VE BEEN JOGGING ON DIFFERENT DAYS SINCE APRIL. WE DON'T EVEN *SEE* EACH OTHER ANYMORE.
AND FOR THE MILLIONTH TIME, HE HASN'T CALLED ME.

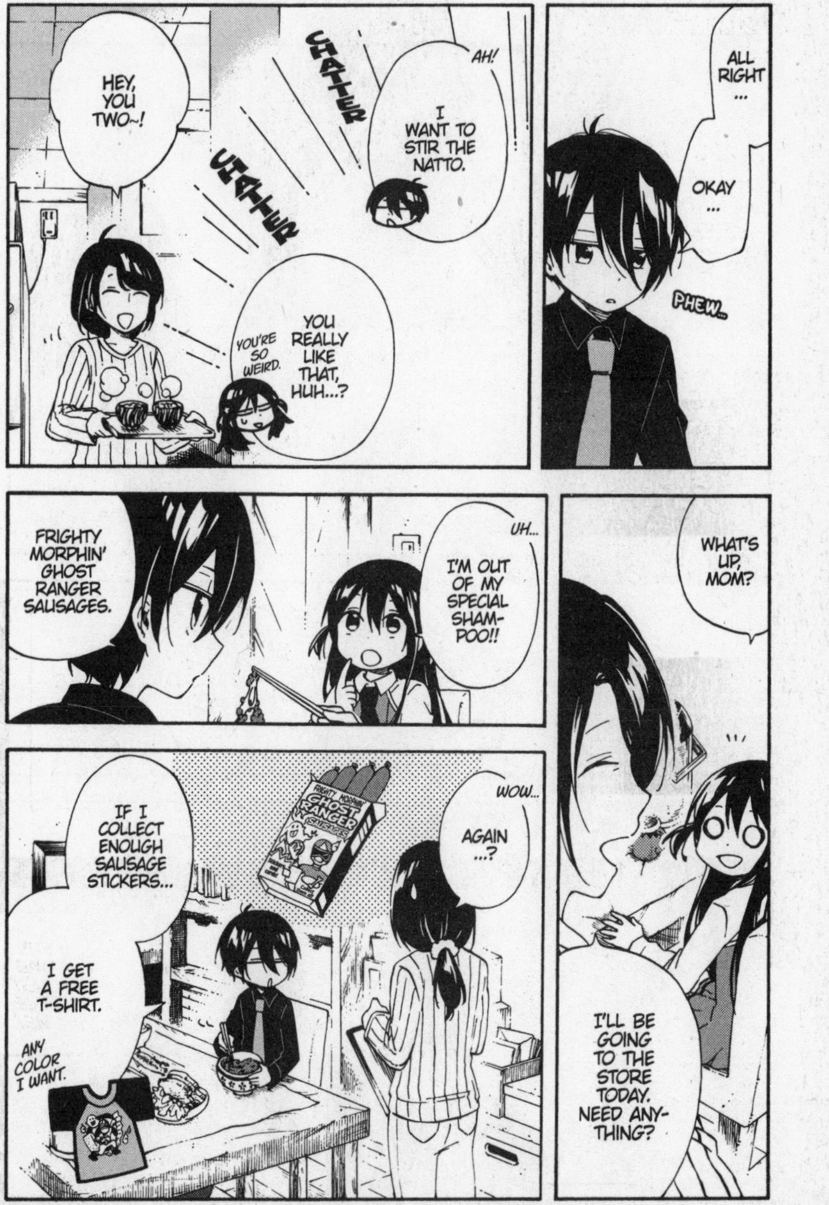
ALL RIGHT...
OKAY...
PHEW...
AH!
I WANT TO STIR THE NATTO.
CHATTER
HEY, YOU TWO~!
CHATTER
YOU REALLY LIKE THAT, HUH...?
YOU'RE SO WEIRD.
WHAT'S UP, MOM?
I'LL BE GOING TO THE STORE TODAY. NEED ANYTHING?
UH...
I'M OUT OF MY SPECIAL SHAMPOO!!
FRIGHTY MORPHIN' GHOST RANGER SAUSAGES.
WOW...
AGAIN...?
FRIGHTY MORPHIN GHOST RANGER SAUSAGES
IF I COLLECT ENOUGH SAUSAGE STICKERS...
I GET A FREE T-SHIRT.
ANY COLOR I WANT.

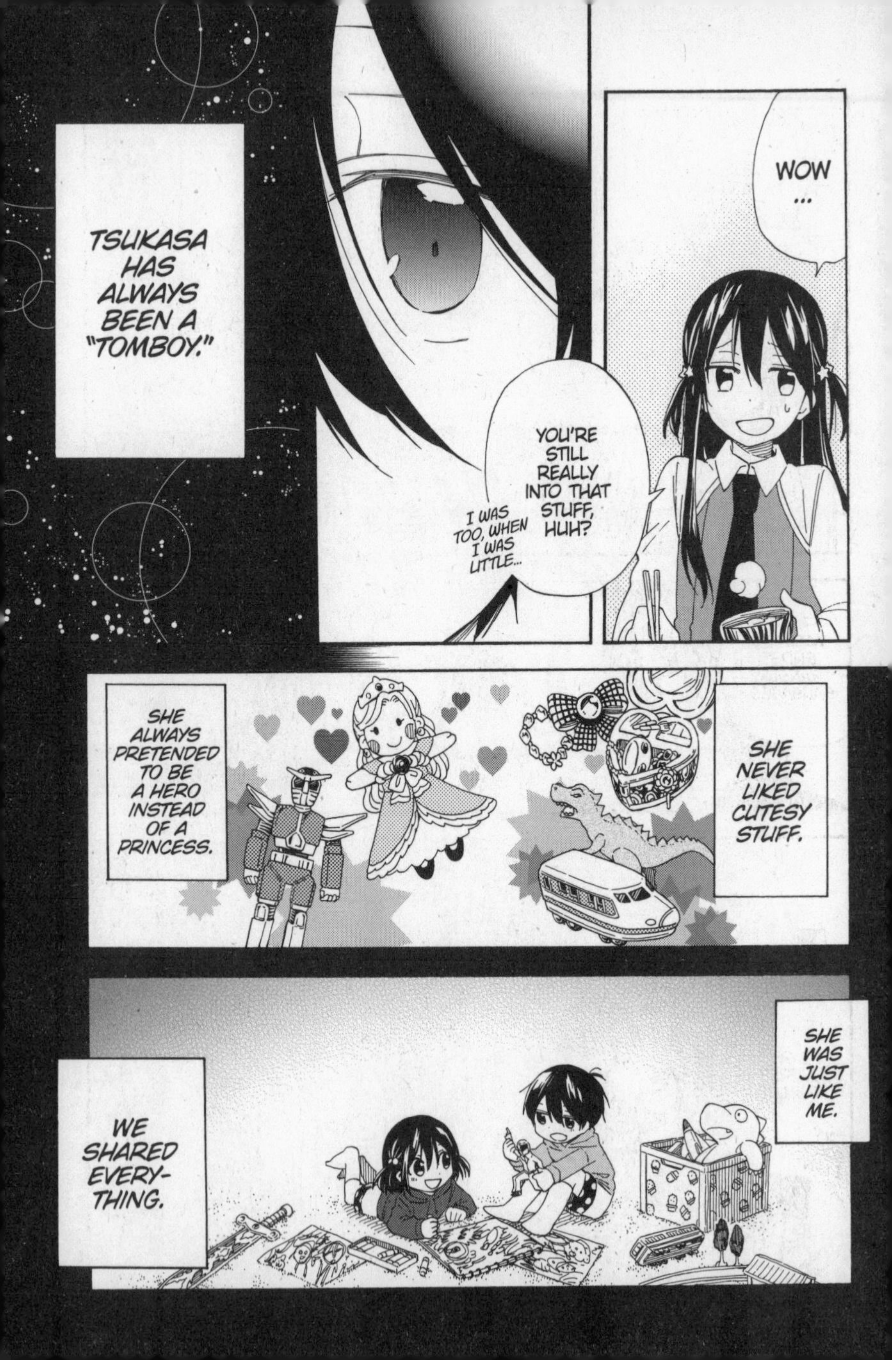
WOW ...
YOU'RE STILL REALLY INTO THAT STUFF, HUH?
I WAS TOO, WHEN I WAS LITTLE...
TSUKASA HAS ALWAYS BEEN A "TOMBOY."
SHE NEVER LIKED CUTESY STUFF.
SHE ALWAYS PRETENDED TO BE A HERO INSTEAD OF A PRINCESS.
SHE WAS JUST LIKE ME.
WE SHARED EVERY-THING.

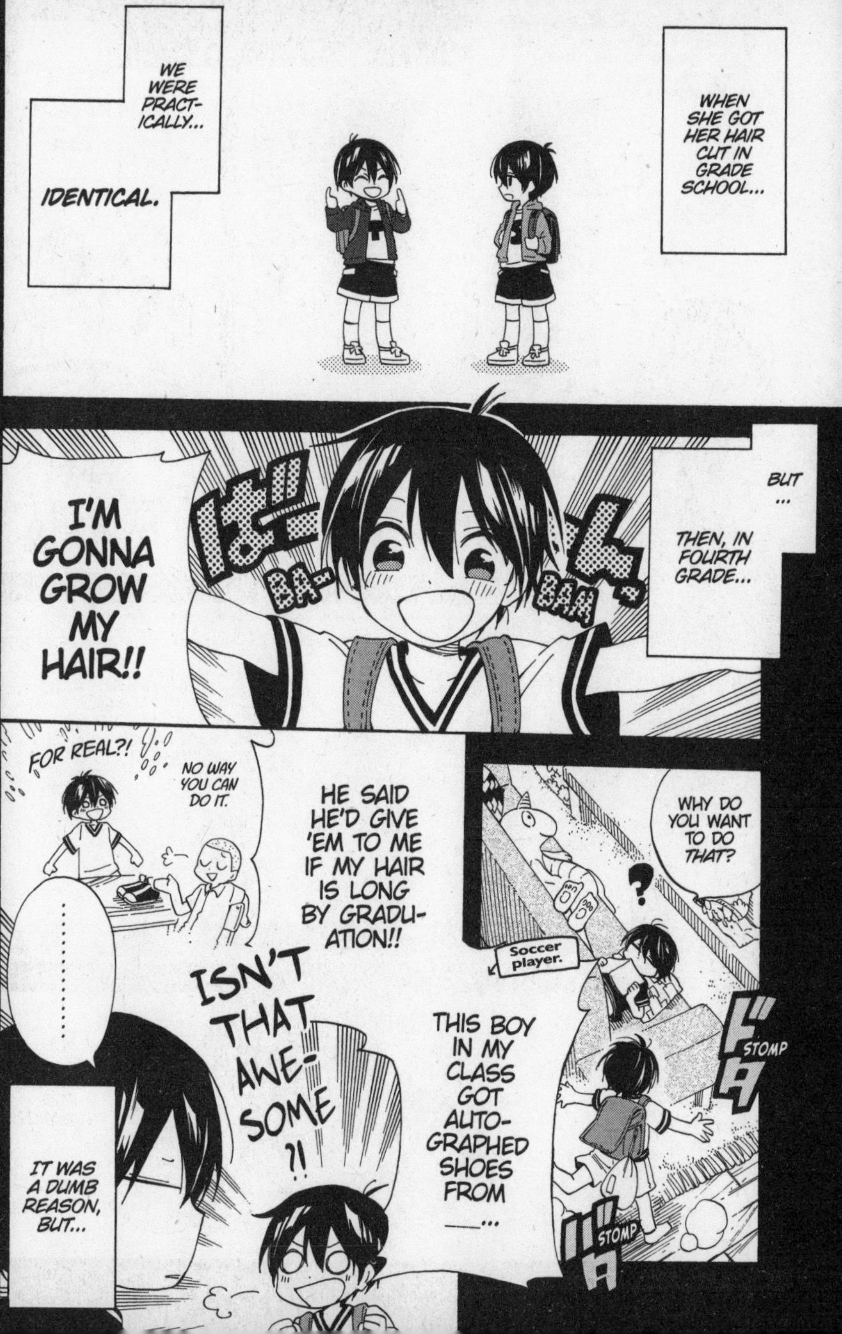

WHEN SHE GOT HER HAIR CUT IN GRADE SCHOOL...
WE WERE PRACTICALLY...
IDENTICAL.
BUT ...
THEN, IN FOURTH GRADE...
BA-BAN
I'M GONNA GROW MY HAIR!!
WHY DO YOU WANT TO DO THAT?
?
Soccer player.
STOMP
STOMP
THIS BOY IN MY CLASS GOT AUTO-GRAPHED SHOES FROM ___...
FOR REAL?!
NO WAY YOU CAN DO IT.
HE SAID HE'D GIVE 'EM TO ME IF MY HAIR IS LONG BY GRADU-ATION!!
ISN'T THAT AWE-SOME?!
......
IT WAS A DUMB REASON, BUT...

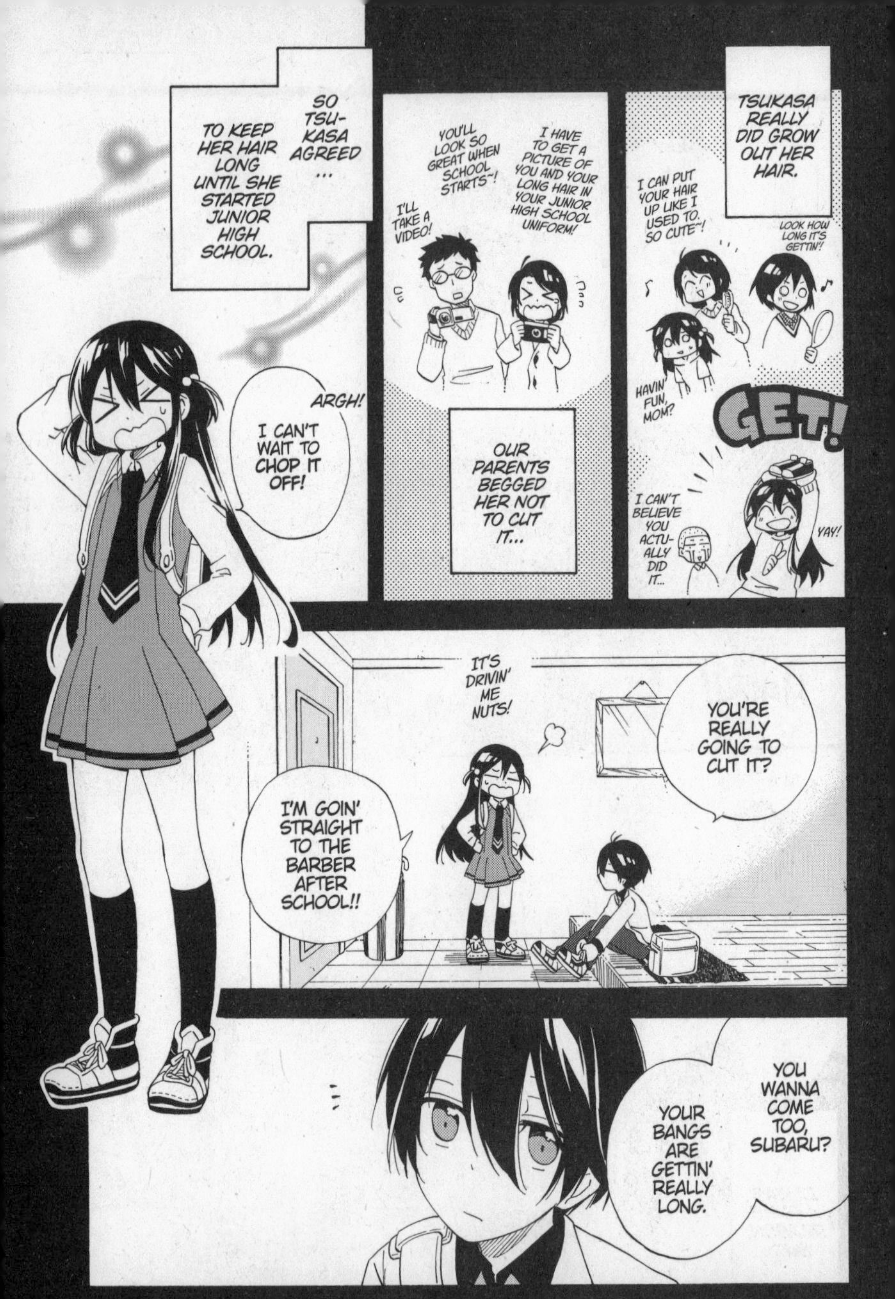
TSUKASA REALLY DID GROW OUT HER HAIR.
LOOK HOW LONG IT'S GETTIN'!
I CAN PUT YOUR HAIR UP LIKE I USED TO. SO CUTE~!
HAVIN' FUN, MOM?
GET!
YAY!
I CAN'T BELIEVE YOU ACTUALLY DID IT...
I HAVE TO GET A PICTURE OF YOU AND YOUR LONG HAIR IN YOUR JUNIOR HIGH SCHOOL UNIFORM!
YOU'LL LOOK SO GREAT WHEN SCHOOL STARTS~!
I'LL TAKE A VIDEO!
OUR PARENTS BEGGED HER NOT TO CUT IT...
SO TSUKASA AGREED...
TO KEEP HER HAIR LONG UNTIL SHE STARTED JUNIOR HIGH SCHOOL.
ARGH!
I CAN'T WAIT TO CHOP IT OFF!
YOU'RE REALLY GOING TO CUT IT?
IT'S DRIVIN' ME NUTS!
I'M GOIN' STRAIGHT TO THE BARBER AFTER SCHOOL!!
YOU WANNA COME TOO, SUBARU?
YOUR BANGS ARE GETTIN' REALLY LONG.

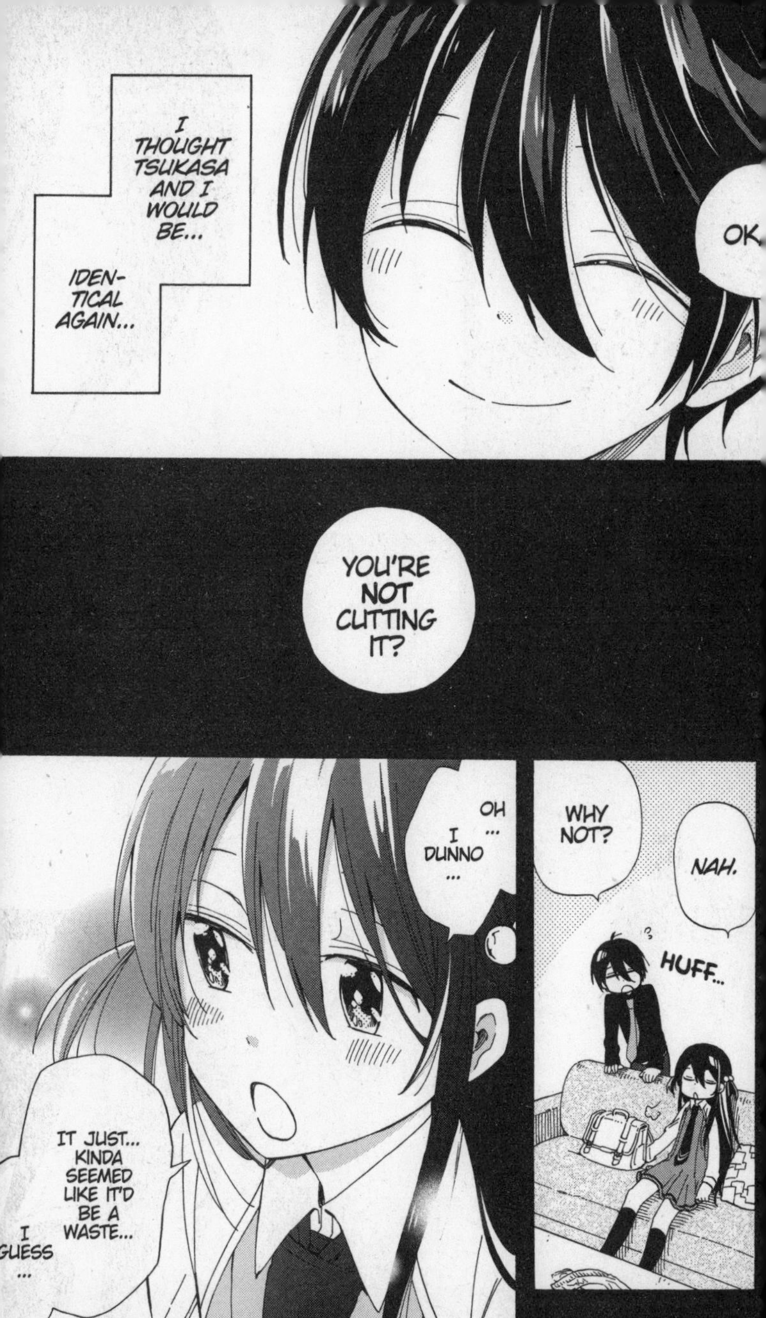

OK
I THOUGHT TSUKASA AND I WOULD BE...
IDEN-TICAL AGAIN...
YOU'RE NOT CUTTING IT?
NAH.
HUFF...
WHY NOT?
OH... I DUNNO...
IT JUST... KINDA SEEMED LIKE IT'D BE A WASTE...
I GUESS...

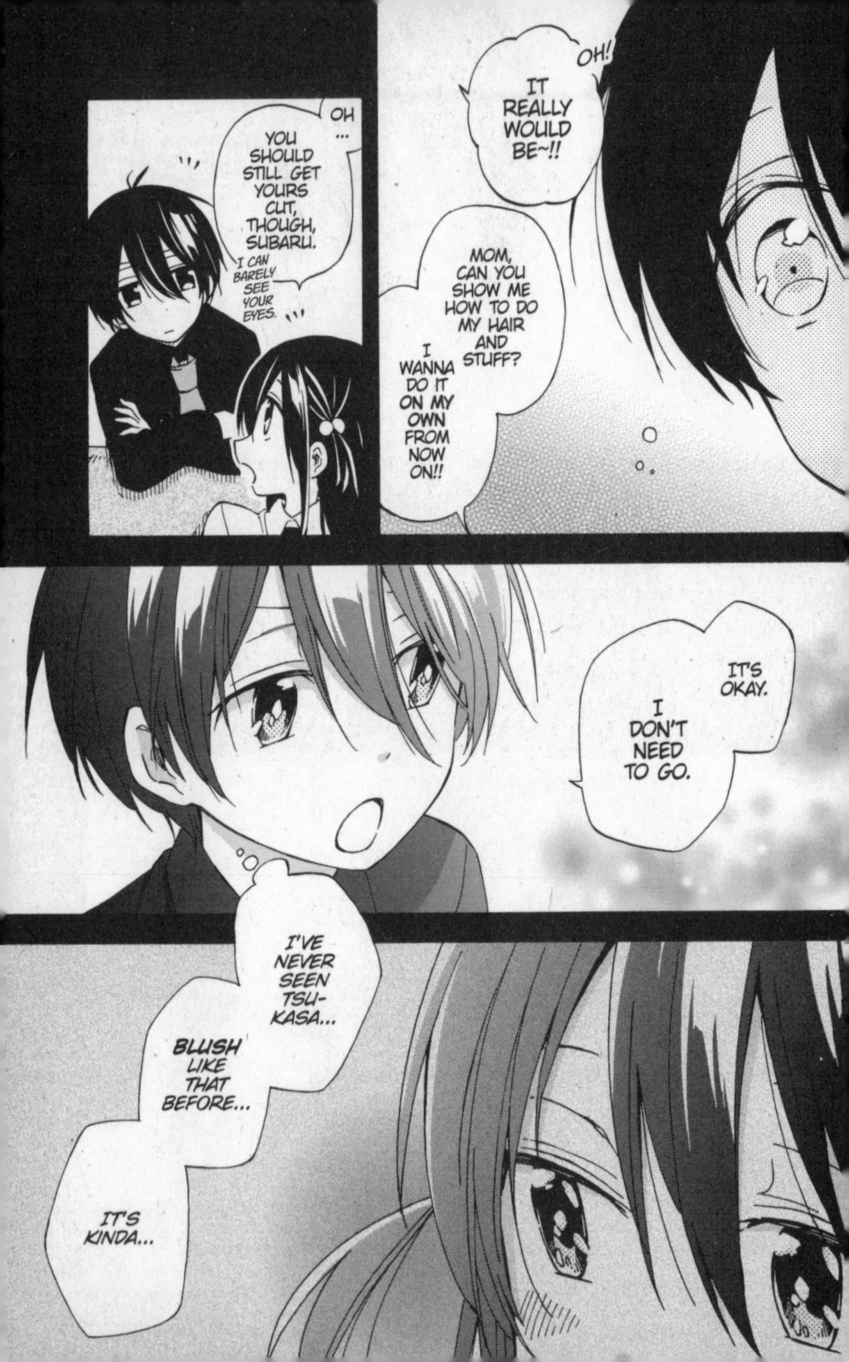
OH!
IT REALLY WOULD BE~!!
MOM, CAN YOU SHOW ME HOW TO DO MY HAIR AND STUFF?
I WANNA DO IT ON MY OWN FROM NOW ON!!
OH ...
YOU SHOULD STILL GET YOURS CUT, THOUGH, SUBARU.
I CAN BARELY SEE YOUR EYES.
IT'S OKAY.
I DON'T NEED TO GO.
I'VE NEVER SEEN TSU-KASA...
BLUSH LIKE THAT BEFORE...
IT'S KINDA...

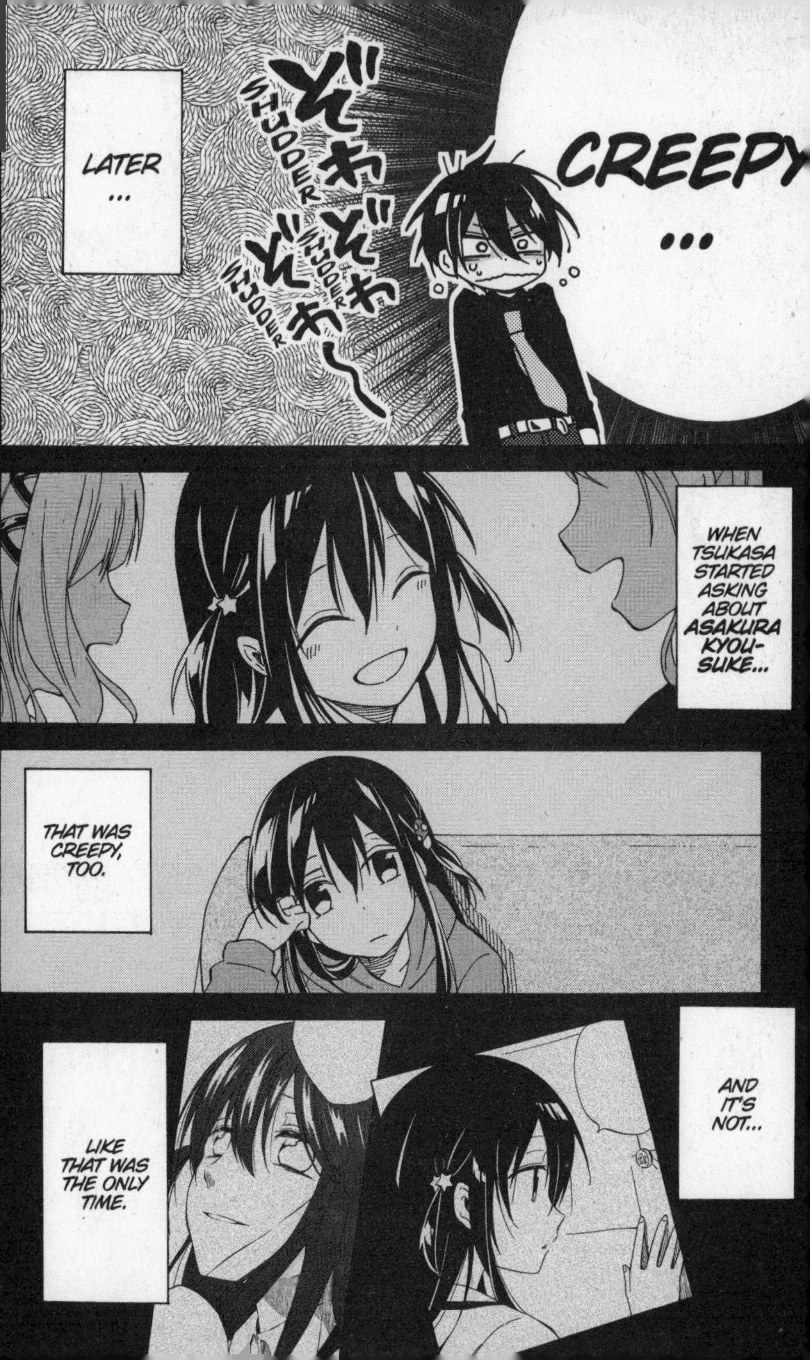
CREEPY ...
ぞわぞわぞわ〜
SHUDDER SHUDDER SHUDDER
LATER ...
WHEN TSUKASA STARTED ASKING ABOUT ASAKURA KYOU-SUKE...
THAT WAS CREEPY, TOO.
AND IT'S NOT...
LIKE THAT WAS THE ONLY TIME.

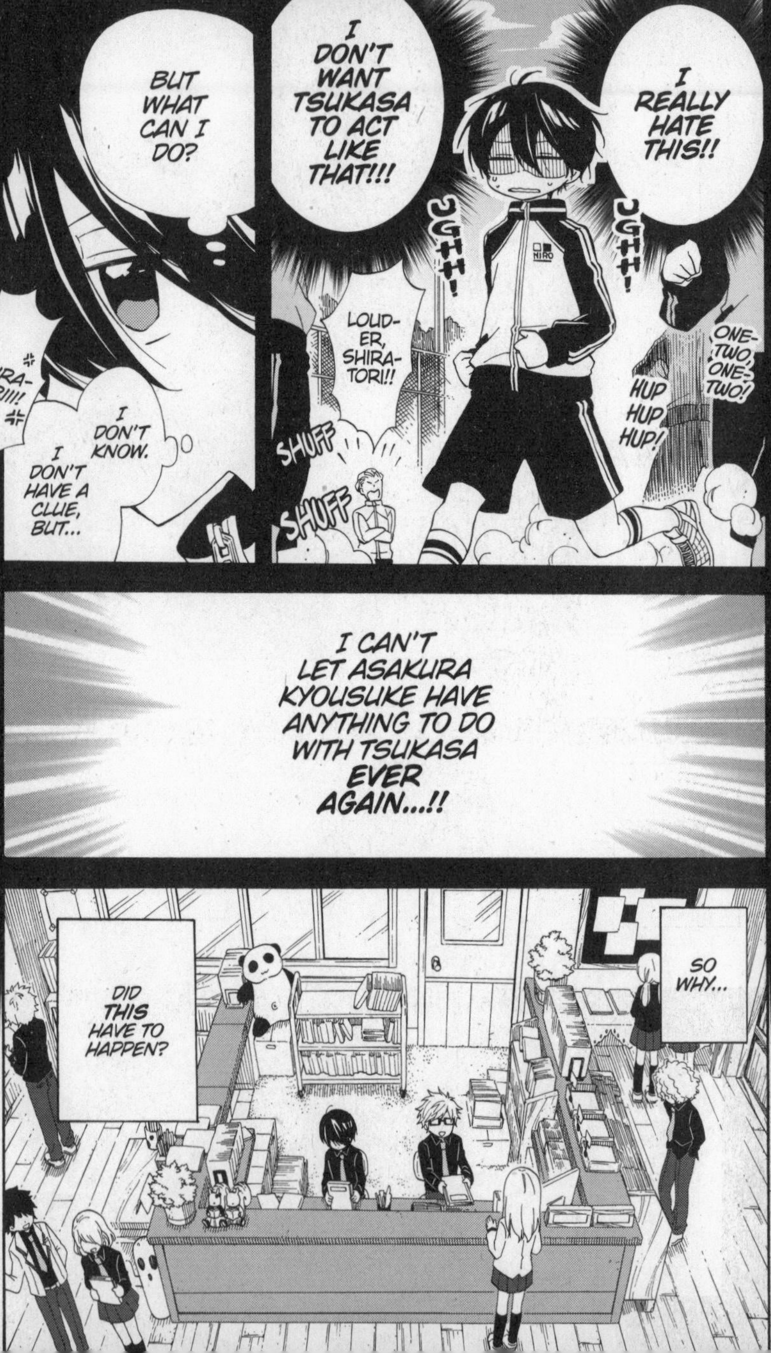
I REALLY HATE THIS!!
UGHH!
ONE-TWO, ONE-TWO!
HUP HUP HUP!
I DON'T WANT TSUKASA TO ACT LIKE THAT!!!
UGHH!
LOUDER, SHIRATORI!!
SHUFF
SHUFF
BUT WHAT CAN I DO?
I DON'T KNOW.
I DON'T HAVE A CLUE, BUT...
SHIRATORI!!!
I CAN'T LET ASAKURA KYOUSUKE HAVE ANYTHING TO DO WITH TSUKASA EVER AGAIN...!!
SO WHY...
DID THIS HAVE TO HAPPEN?

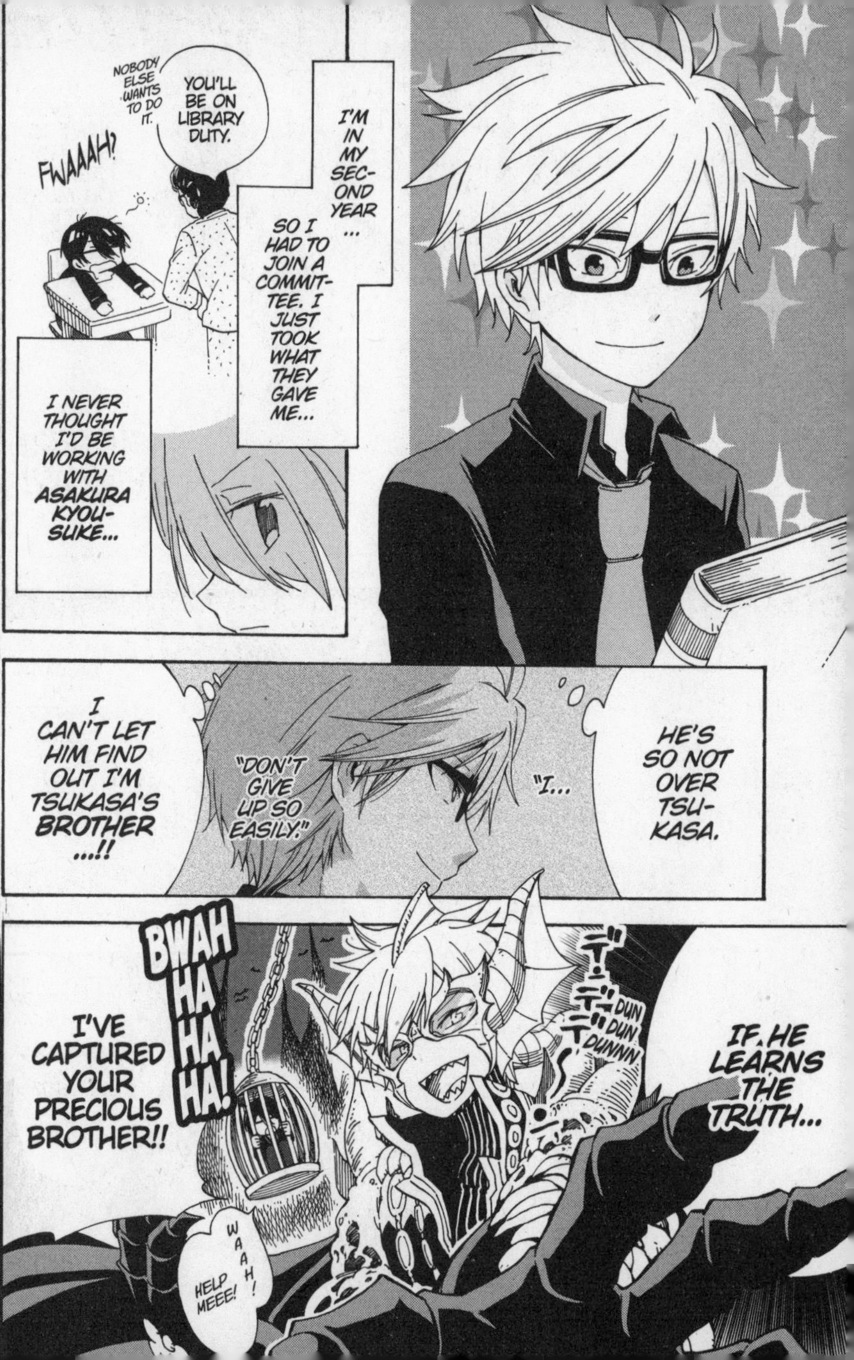
I'M IN MY SECOND YEAR...
SO I HAD TO JOIN A COMMITTEE. I JUST TOOK WHAT THEY GAVE ME...
YOU'LL BE ON LIBRARY DUTY.
NOBODY ELSE WANTS TO DO IT.
FWAAAH?
I NEVER THOUGHT I'D BE WORKING WITH ASAKURA KYOUSUKE...
HE'S SO NOT OVER TSUKASA.
"I...
"DON'T GIVE UP SO EASILY."
I CAN'T LET HIM FIND OUT I'M TSUKASA'S BROTHER...!!
IF HE LEARNS THE TRUTH...
DUN DUN DUNNN
BWAH HA HA HA HA!
I'VE CAPTURED YOUR PRECIOUS BROTHER!!
WAAAH!
HELP MEEE!

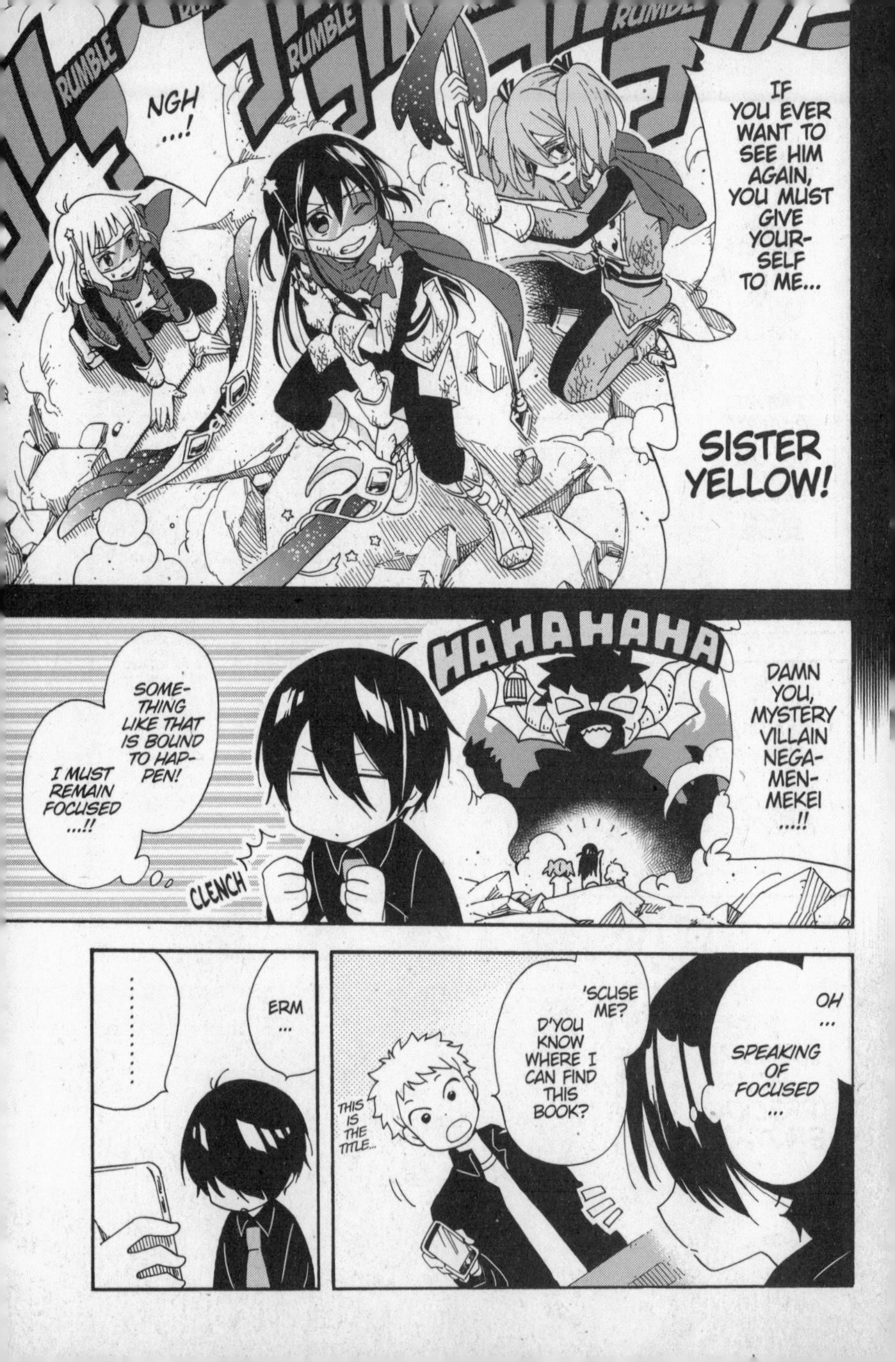
RUMBLE
RUMBLE
RUMBLE
IF YOU EVER WANT TO SEE HIM AGAIN, YOU MUST GIVE YOURSELF TO ME...
SISTER YELLOW!
NGH ...!
DAMN YOU, MYSTERY VILLAIN NEGAMENMEKEI ...!!
HAHAHAHA
SOMETHING LIKE THAT IS BOUND TO HAPPEN!
I MUST REMAIN FOCUSED ...!!
CLENCH
OH ... SPEAKING OF FOCUSED ...
'SCUSE ME? D'YOU KNOW WHERE I CAN FIND THIS BOOK?
THIS IS THE TITLE...
ERM ...
....

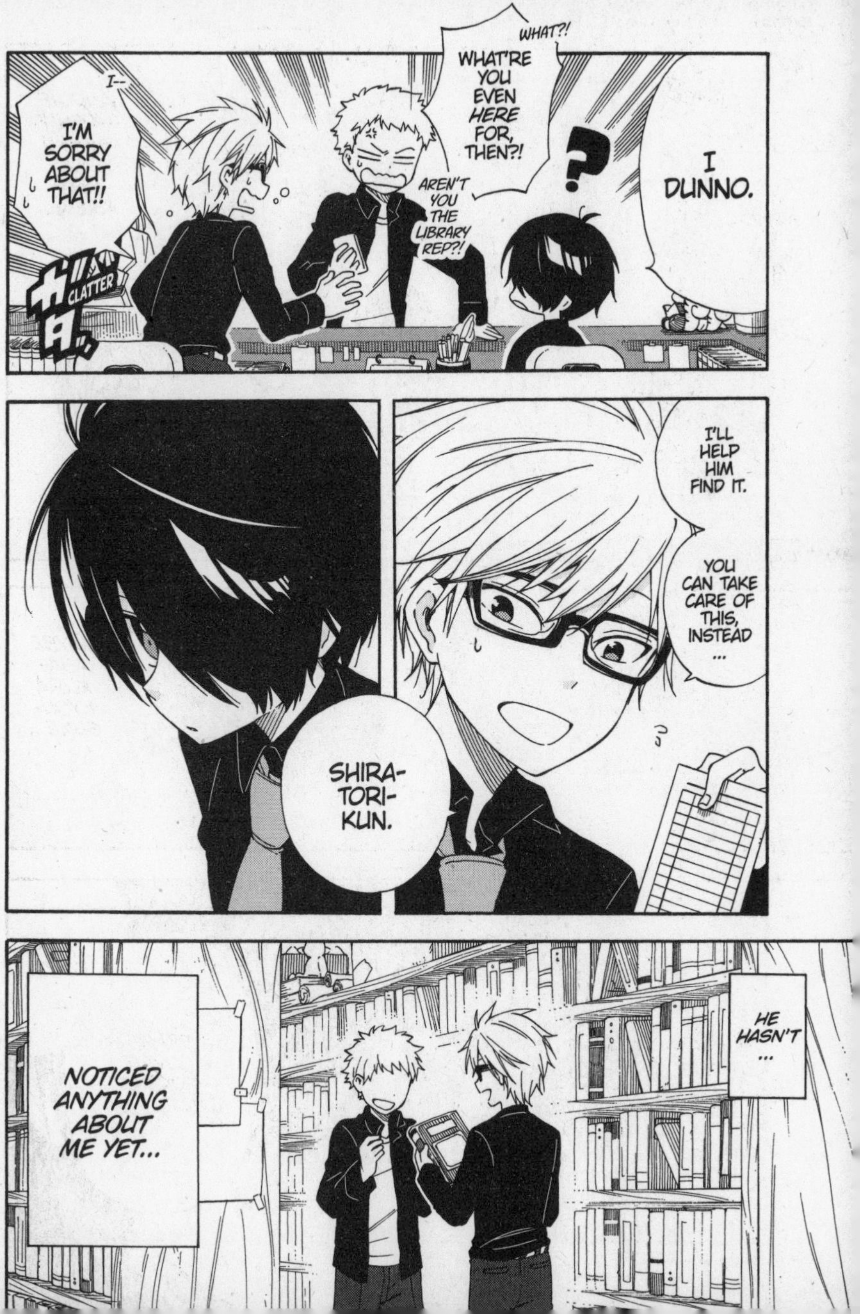
I DUNNO.
?
WHAT?!
WHAT'RE YOU EVEN HERE FOR, THEN?!
AREN'T YOU THE LIBRARY REP?!
I--
I'M SORRY ABOUT THAT!!
CLATTER
I'LL HELP HIM FIND IT.
YOU CAN TAKE CARE OF THIS, INSTEAD ...
SHIRA-TORI-KUN.
HE HASN'T ...
NOTICED ANYTHING ABOUT ME YET...

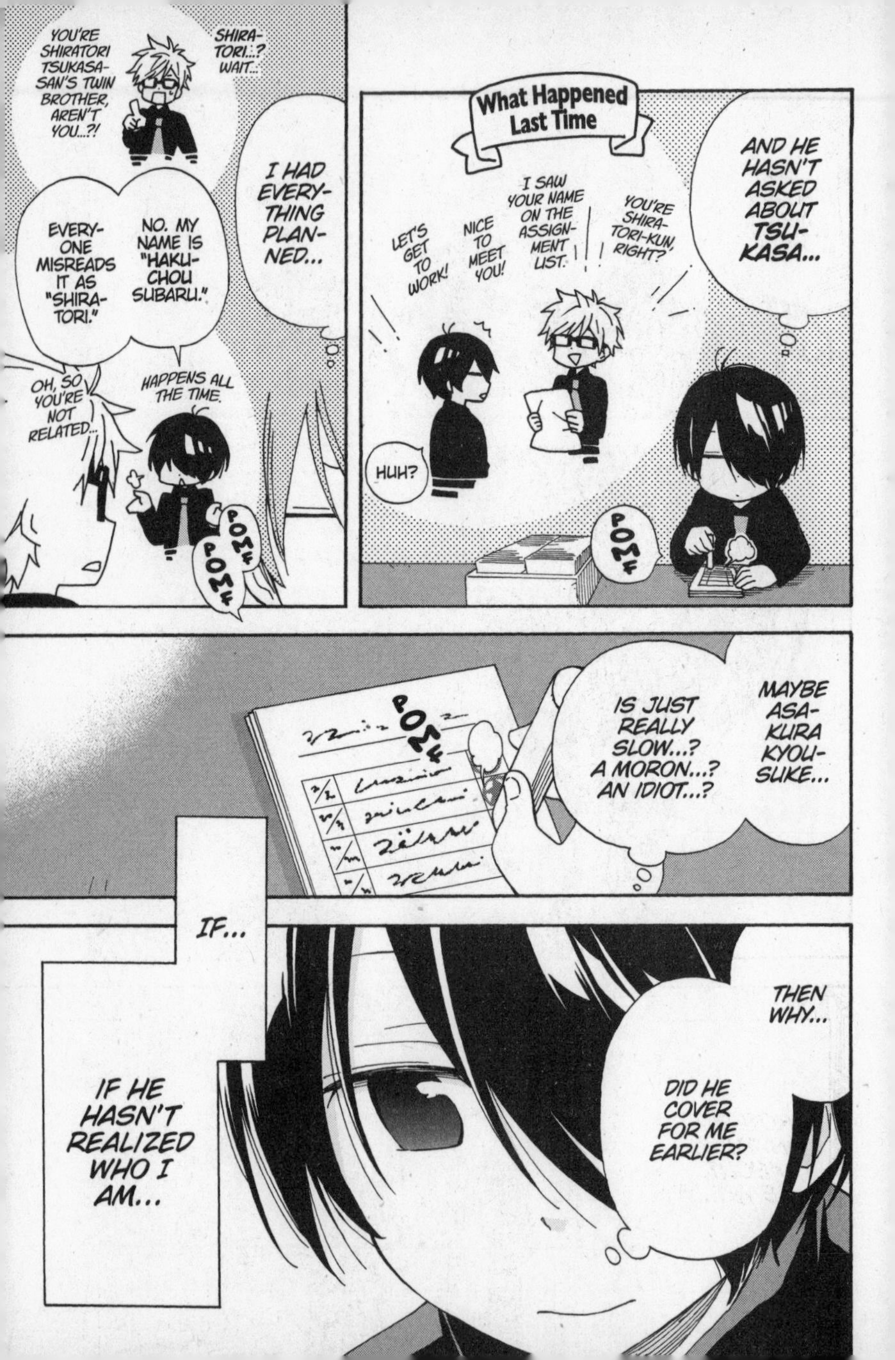
What Happened Last Time
AND HE HASN'T ASKED ABOUT TSUKASA...
YOU'RE SHIRATORI-KUN, RIGHT?
I SAW YOUR NAME ON THE ASSIGNMENT LIST.
NICE TO MEET YOU!
LET'S GET TO WORK!
HUH?
POMF
I HAD EVERYTHING PLANNED...
SHIRATORI...? WAIT...
YOU'RE SHIRATORI TSUKASA-SAN'S TWIN BROTHER, AREN'T YOU...?!
NO. MY NAME IS "HAKUCHOU SUBARU."
EVERYONE MISREADS IT AS "SHIRATORI."
HAPPENS ALL THE TIME.
OH, SO YOU'RE NOT RELATED...
POMF POMF
MAYBE ASAKURA KYOUSUKE...
IS JUST REALLY SLOW...? A MORON...? AN IDIOT...?
POMF
IF...
IF HE HASN'T REALIZED WHO I AM...
THEN WHY...
DID HE COVER FOR ME EARLIER?

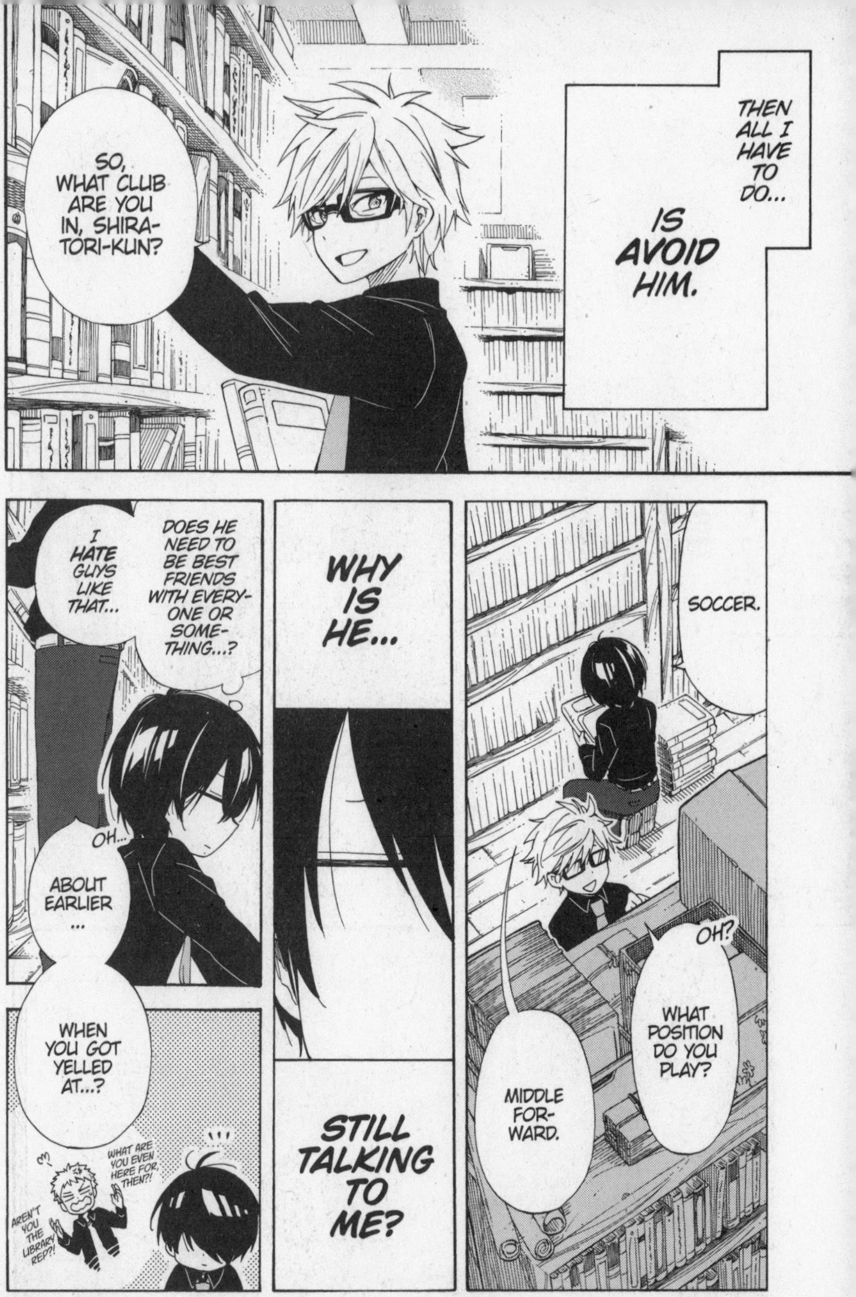
THEN ALL I HAVE TO DO...
IS AVOID HIM.
SO, WHAT CLUB ARE YOU IN, SHIRATORI-KUN?
SOCCER.
OH?
WHAT POSITION DO YOU PLAY?
MIDDLE FORWARD.
WHY IS HE...
STILL TALKING TO ME?
DOES HE NEED TO BE BEST FRIENDS WITH EVERYONE OR SOMETHING...?
I HATE GUYS LIKE THAT...
OH...
ABOUT EARLIER...
WHEN YOU GOT YELLED AT...?
WHAT ARE YOU EVEN HERE FOR, THEN?!
AREN'T YOU THE LIBRARY REP?!

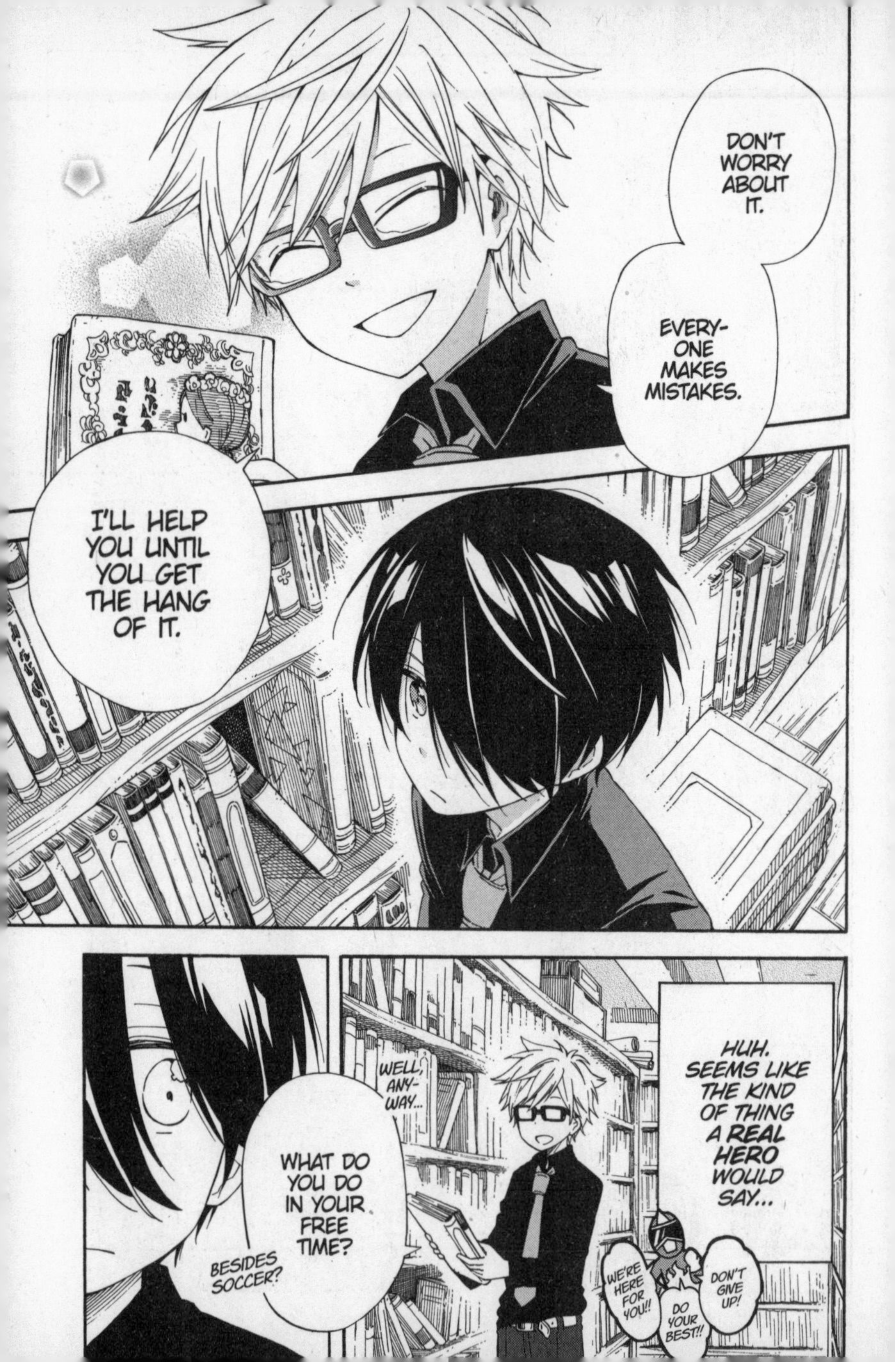
DON'T WORRY ABOUT IT.
EVERY-ONE MAKES MISTAKES.
I'LL HELP YOU UNTIL YOU GET THE HANG OF IT.
HUH. SEEMS LIKE THE KIND OF THING A **REAL HERO** WOULD SAY...
DON'T GIVE UP!
DO YOUR BEST!!
WE'RE HERE FOR YOU!!
WELL, ANY-WAY...
WHAT DO YOU DO IN YOUR FREE TIME?
BESIDES SOCCER?

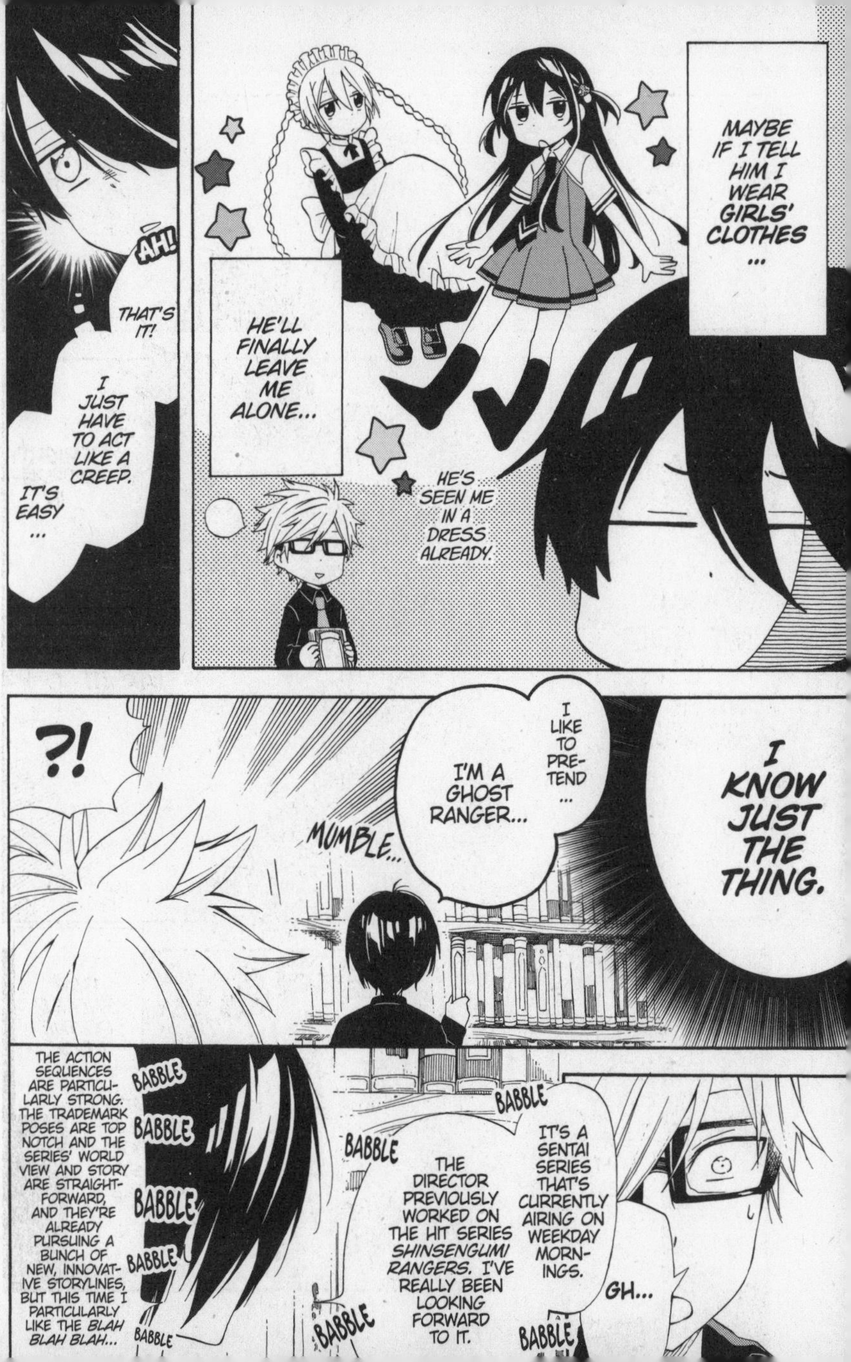

MAYBE IF I TELL HIM I WEAR GIRLS' CLOTHES ...
HE'LL FINALLY LEAVE ME ALONE...
HE'S SEEN ME IN A DRESS ALREADY.
AH!
THAT'S IT!
I JUST HAVE TO ACT LIKE A CREEP.
IT'S EASY ...
I KNOW JUST THE THING.
I LIKE TO PRE-TEND ...
I'M A GHOST RANGER...
MUMBLE...
?!
GH...
IT'S A SENTAI SERIES THAT'S CURRENTLY AIRING ON WEEKDAY MORN-INGS.
BABBLE
THE DIRECTOR PREVIOUSLY WORKED ON THE HIT SERIES *SHINSENGUMI RANGERS*. I'VE REALLY BEEN LOOKING FORWARD TO IT.
BABBLE
BABBLE
BABBLE
THE ACTION SEQUENCES ARE PARTICU-LARLY STRONG. THE TRADEMARK POSES ARE TOP NOTCH AND THE SERIES' WORLD VIEW AND STORY ARE STRAIGHT-FORWARD, AND THEY'RE ALREADY PURSUING A BUNCH OF NEW, INNOVAT-IVE STORYLINES, BUT THIS TIME I PARTICULARLY LIKE THE *BLAH BLAH BLAH*...
BABBLE
BABBLE
BABBLE
BABBLE
BABBLE

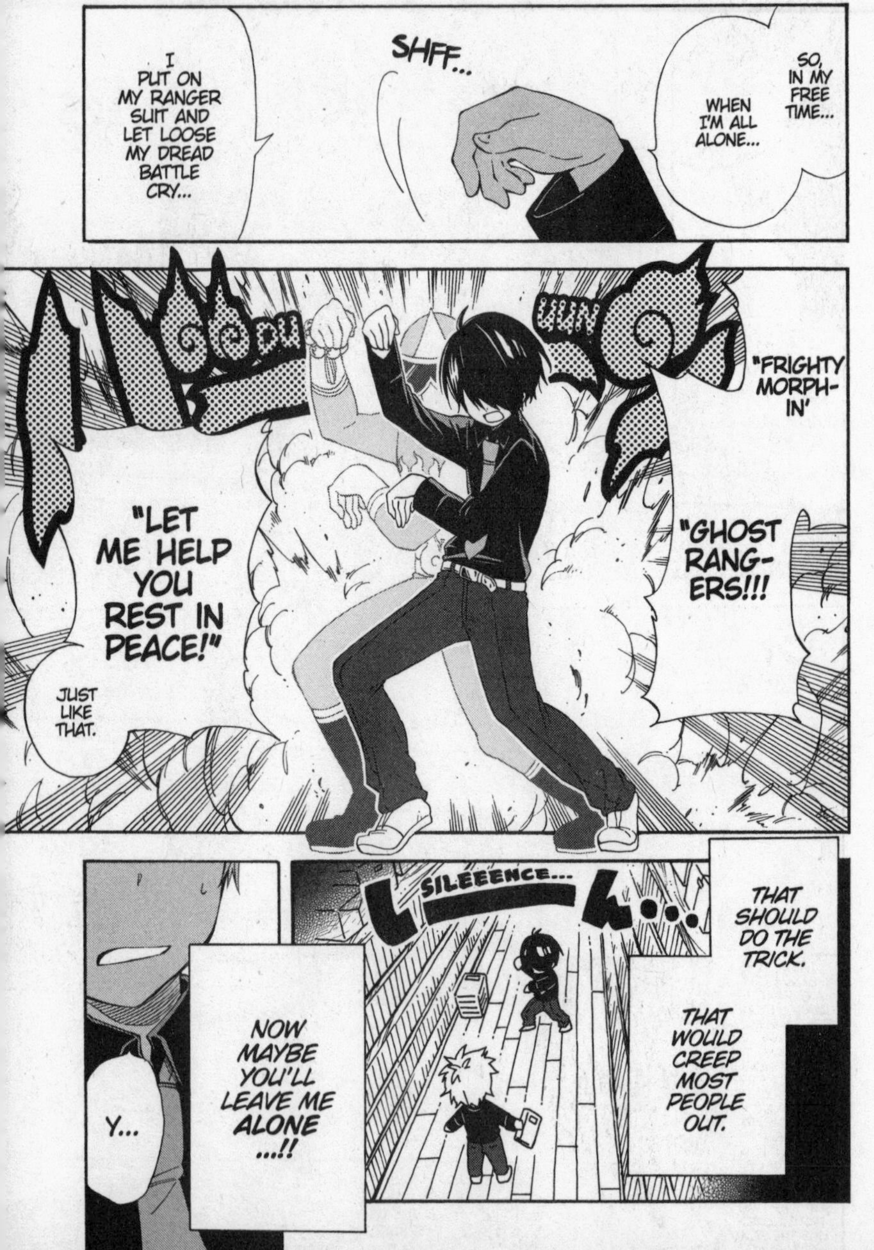
SO, IN MY FREE TIME...
WHEN I'M ALL ALONE...
SHFF...
I PUT ON MY RANGER SUIT AND LET LOOSE MY DREAD BATTLE CRY...
"FRIGHTY MORPH-IN'
"GHOST RANG-ERS!!!
"LET ME HELP YOU REST IN PEACE!"
JUST LIKE THAT.
THAT SHOULD DO THE TRICK.
THAT WOULD CREEP MOST PEOPLE OUT.
SILEEENCE...
NOW MAYBE YOU'LL LEAVE ME ALONE ...!!
Y...

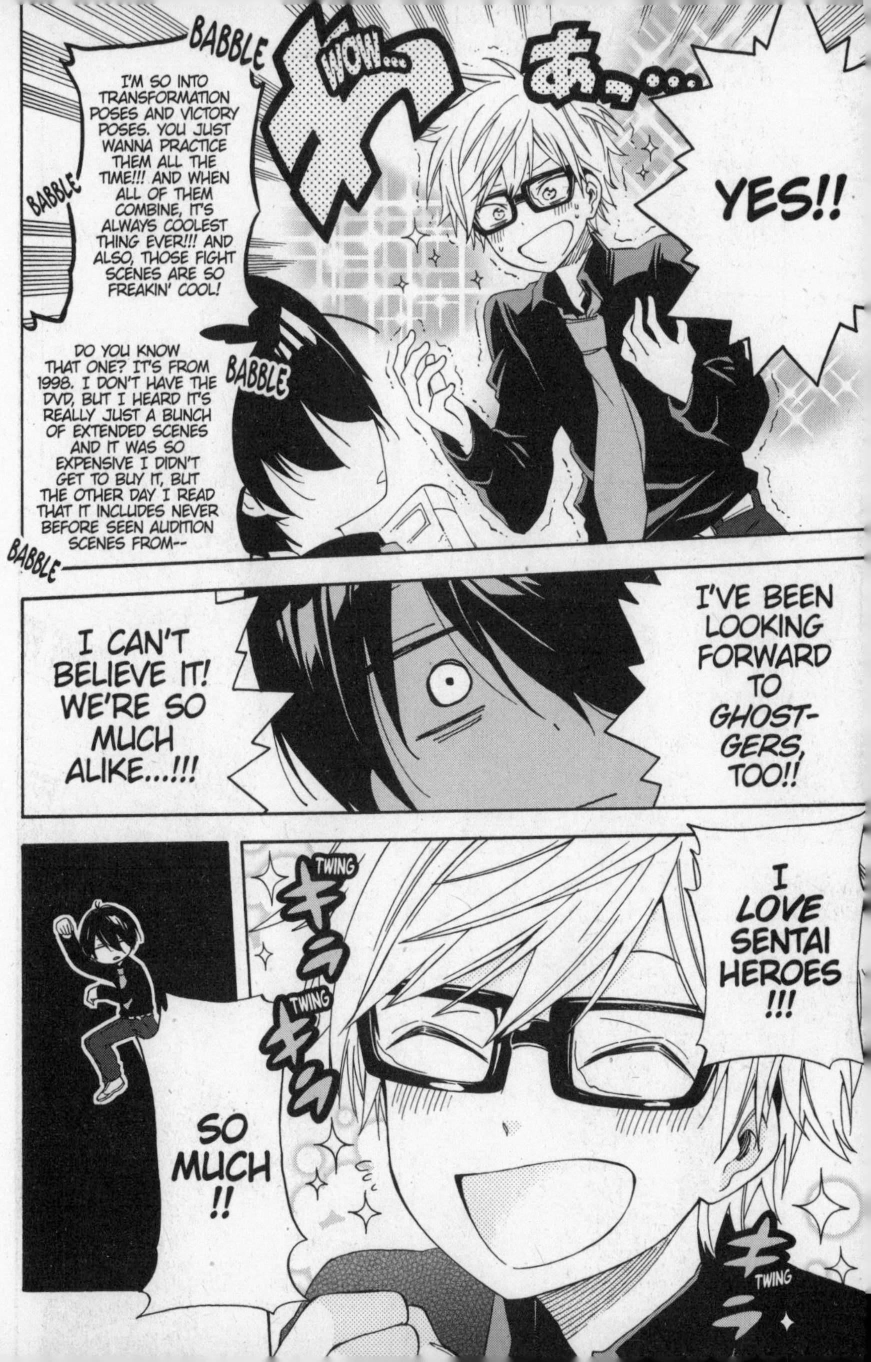
YES!!
あっ…
WOW...
BABBLE
I'M SO INTO TRANSFORMATION POSES AND VICTORY POSES. YOU JUST WANNA PRACTICE THEM ALL THE TIME!!! AND WHEN ALL OF THEM COMBINE, IT'S ALWAYS COOLEST THING EVER!!! AND ALSO, THOSE FIGHT SCENES ARE SO FREAKIN' COOL!
BABBLE
BABBLE
DO YOU KNOW THAT ONE? IT'S FROM 1998. I DON'T HAVE THE DVD, BUT I HEARD IT'S REALLY JUST A BUNCH OF EXTENDED SCENES AND IT WAS SO EXPENSIVE I DIDN'T GET TO BUY IT, BUT THE OTHER DAY I READ THAT IT INCLUDES NEVER BEFORE SEEN AUDITION SCENES FROM--
BABBLE
I'VE BEEN LOOKING FORWARD TO GHOST-GERS, TOO!!
I CAN'T BELIEVE IT! WE'RE SO MUCH ALIKE...!!!
I LOVE SENTAI HEROES!!!
TWING
TWING
SO MUCH!!
TWING

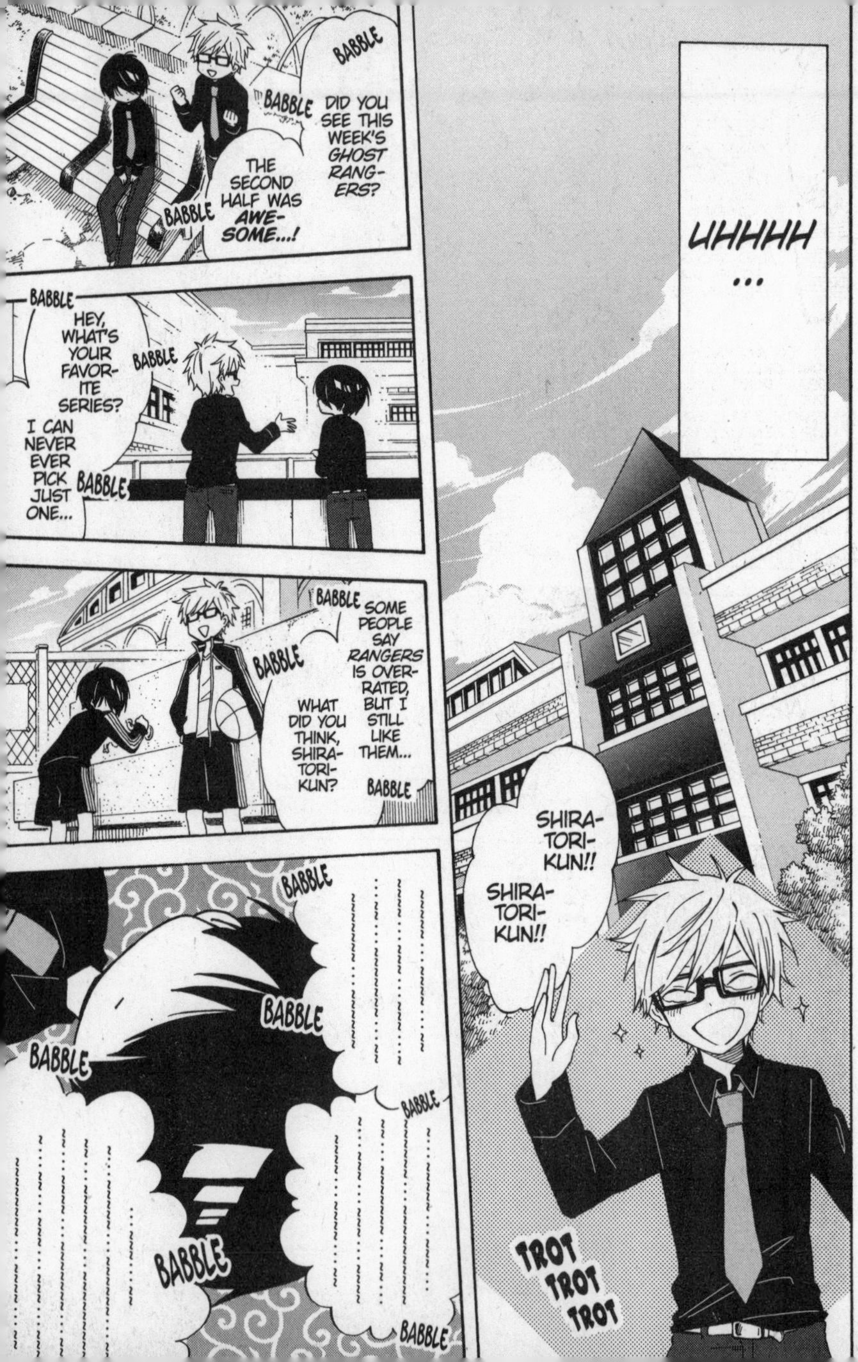
UHHHH ...
SHIRA-TORI-KUN!!
SHIRA-TORI-KUN!!
TROT TROT TROT
BABBLE
DID YOU SEE THIS WEEK'S GHOST RANGERS?
BABBLE
THE SECOND HALF WAS AWE-SOME...!
BABBLE
BABBLE
HEY, WHAT'S YOUR FAVOR-ITE SERIES?
BABBLE
I CAN NEVER EVER PICK JUST ONE...
BABBLE
BABBLE
SOME PEOPLE SAY RANGERS IS OVER-RATED, BUT I STILL LIKE THEM...
BABBLE
WHAT DID YOU THINK, SHIRA-TORI-KUN?
BABBLE
BABBLE
BABBLE
BABBLE
BABBLE
BABBLE
BABBLE

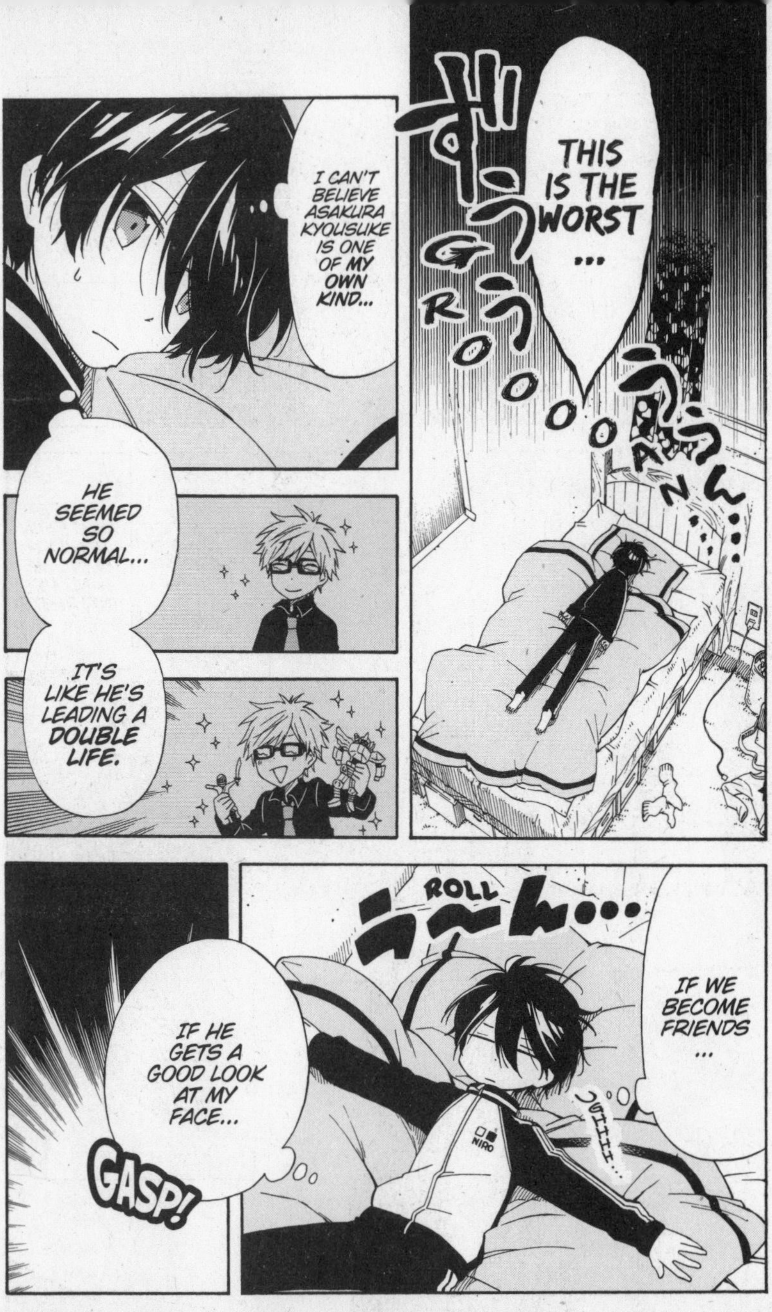
THIS IS THE WORST...
GROOOOAN
I CAN'T BELIEVE ASAKURA KYOUSUKE IS ONE OF MY OWN KIND...
HE SEEMED SO NORMAL...
IT'S LIKE HE'S LEADING A DOUBLE LIFE.
ROLL
IF WE BECOME FRIENDS...
UGHHH...
IF HE GETS A GOOD LOOK AT MY FACE...
GASP!

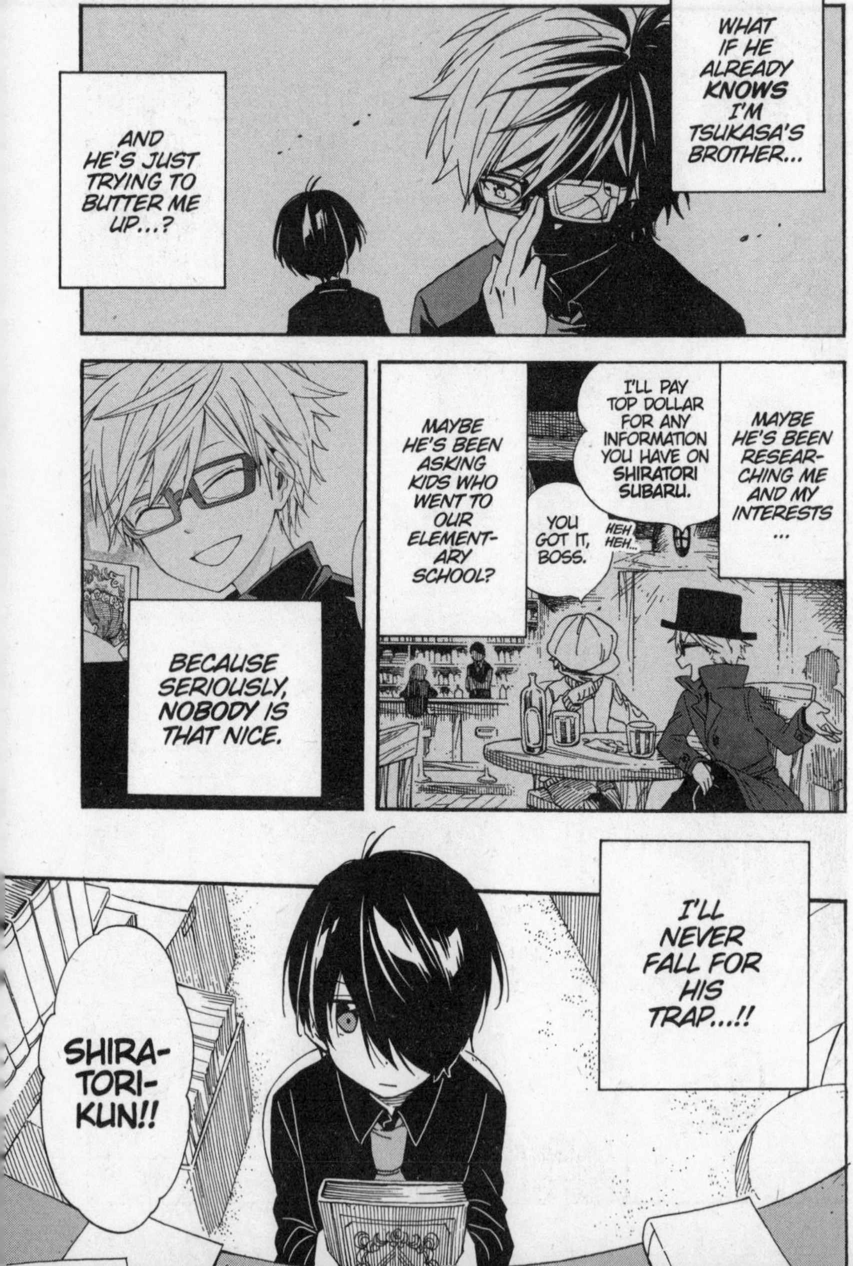
WHAT IF HE ALREADY KNOWS I'M TSUKASA'S BROTHER...
AND HE'S JUST TRYING TO BUTTER ME UP...?
MAYBE HE'S BEEN RESEARCHING ME AND MY INTERESTS ...
I'LL PAY TOP DOLLAR FOR ANY INFORMATION YOU HAVE ON SHIRATORI SUBARU.
HEH HEH...
YOU GOT IT, BOSS.
MAYBE HE'S BEEN ASKING KIDS WHO WENT TO OUR ELEMENTARY SCHOOL?
BECAUSE SERIOUSLY, NOBODY IS THAT NICE.
I'LL NEVER FALL FOR HIS TRAP...!!
SHIRATORI-KUN!!

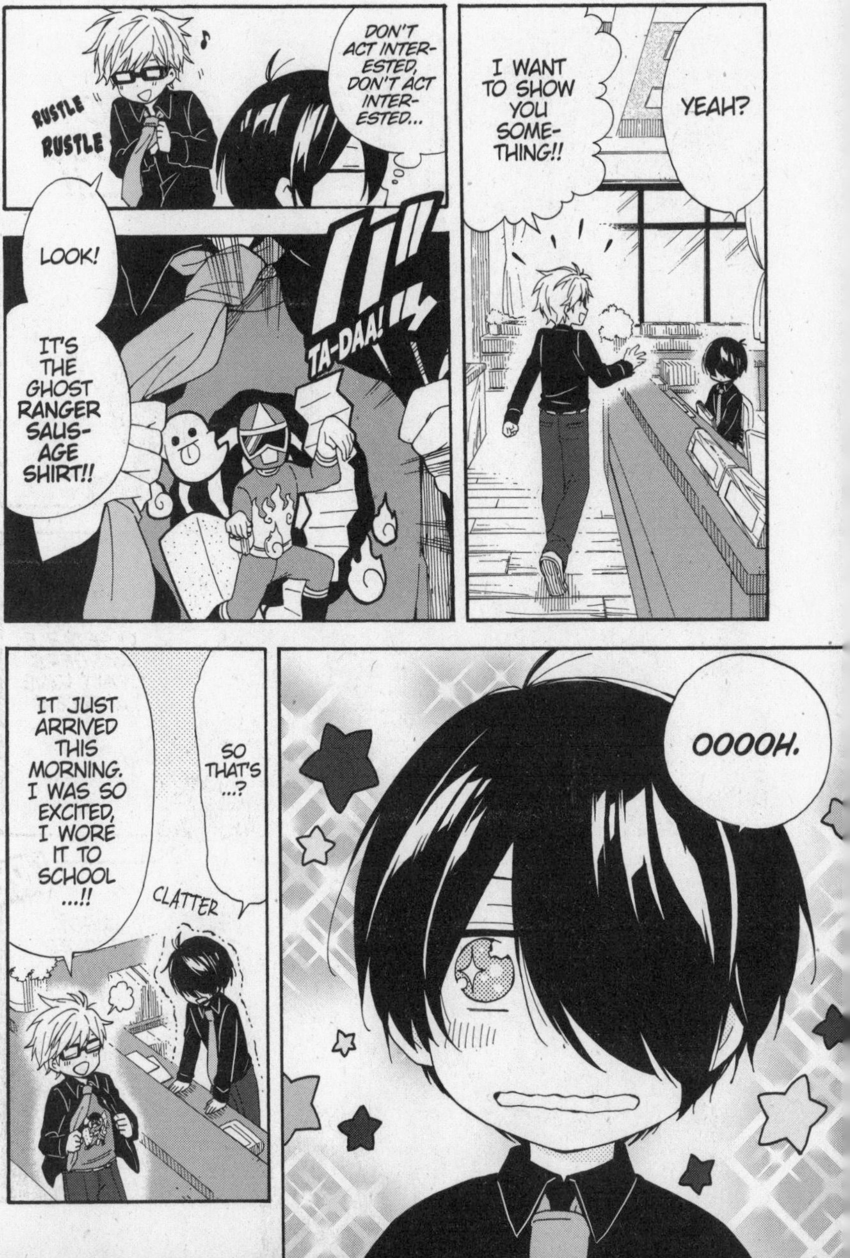
YEAH?
I WANT TO SHOW YOU SOMETHING!!
DON'T ACT INTERESTED, DON'T ACT INTERESTED...
RUSTLE RUSTLE
TA-DAA!
LOOK!
IT'S THE GHOST RANGER SAUSAGE SHIRT!!
OOOOH.
SO THAT'S ...?
IT JUST ARRIVED THIS MORNING. I WAS SO EXCITED, I WORE IT TO SCHOOL ...!!
CLATTER

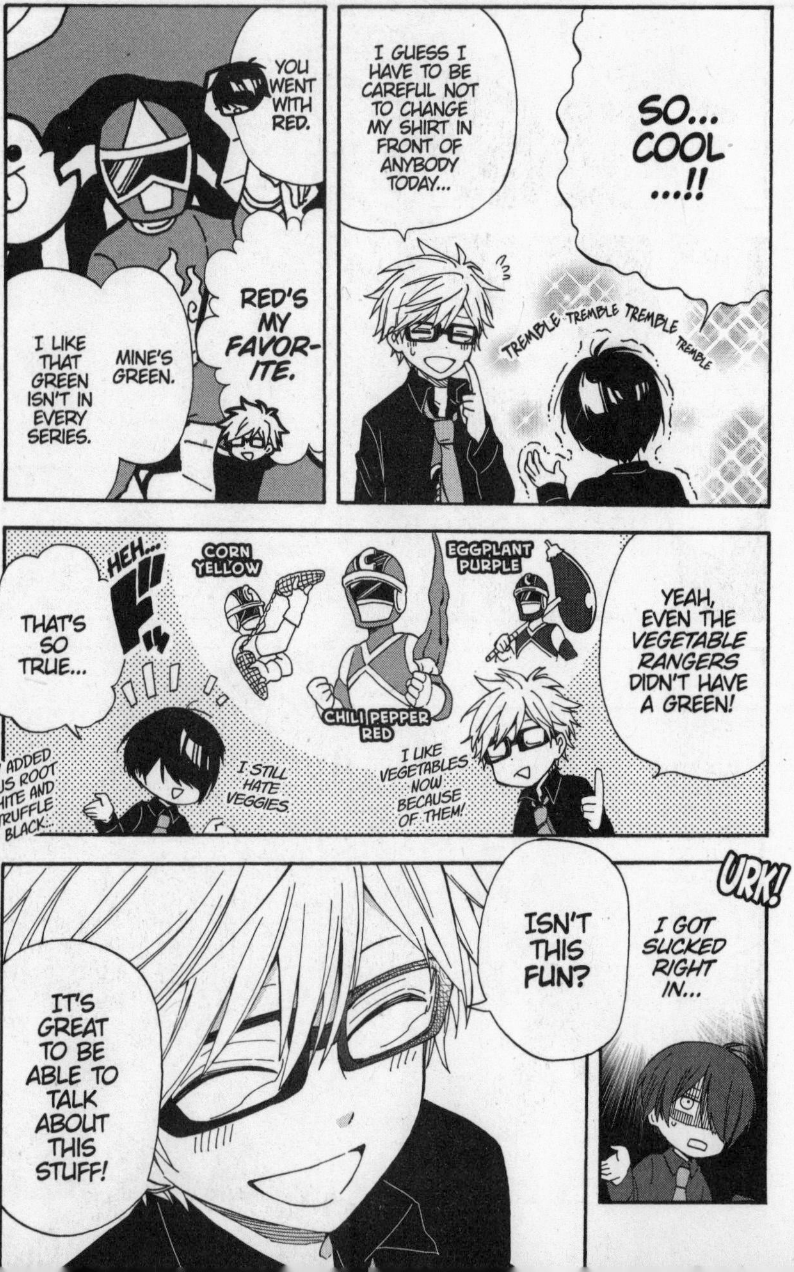
SO... COOL ...!!
I GUESS I HAVE TO BE CAREFUL NOT TO CHANGE MY SHIRT IN FRONT OF ANYBODY TODAY...
TREMBLE TREMBLE TREMBLE TREMBLE
YOU WENT WITH RED.
RED'S MY FAVOR-ITE.
MINE'S GREEN.
I LIKE THAT GREEN ISN'T IN EVERY SERIES.
YEAH, EVEN THE VEGETABLE RANGERS DIDN'T HAVE A GREEN!
EGGPLANT PURPLE
I LIKE VEGETABLES NOW BECAUSE OF THEM!
CHILI PEPPER RED
CORN YELLOW
HEH...
I STILL HATE VEGGIES.
THAT'S SO TRUE...
THEY ADDED LOTUS ROOT WHITE AND TRUFFLE BLACK...
URK!
I GOT SUCKED RIGHT IN...
ISN'T THIS FUN?
IT'S GREAT TO BE ABLE TO TALK ABOUT THIS STUFF!

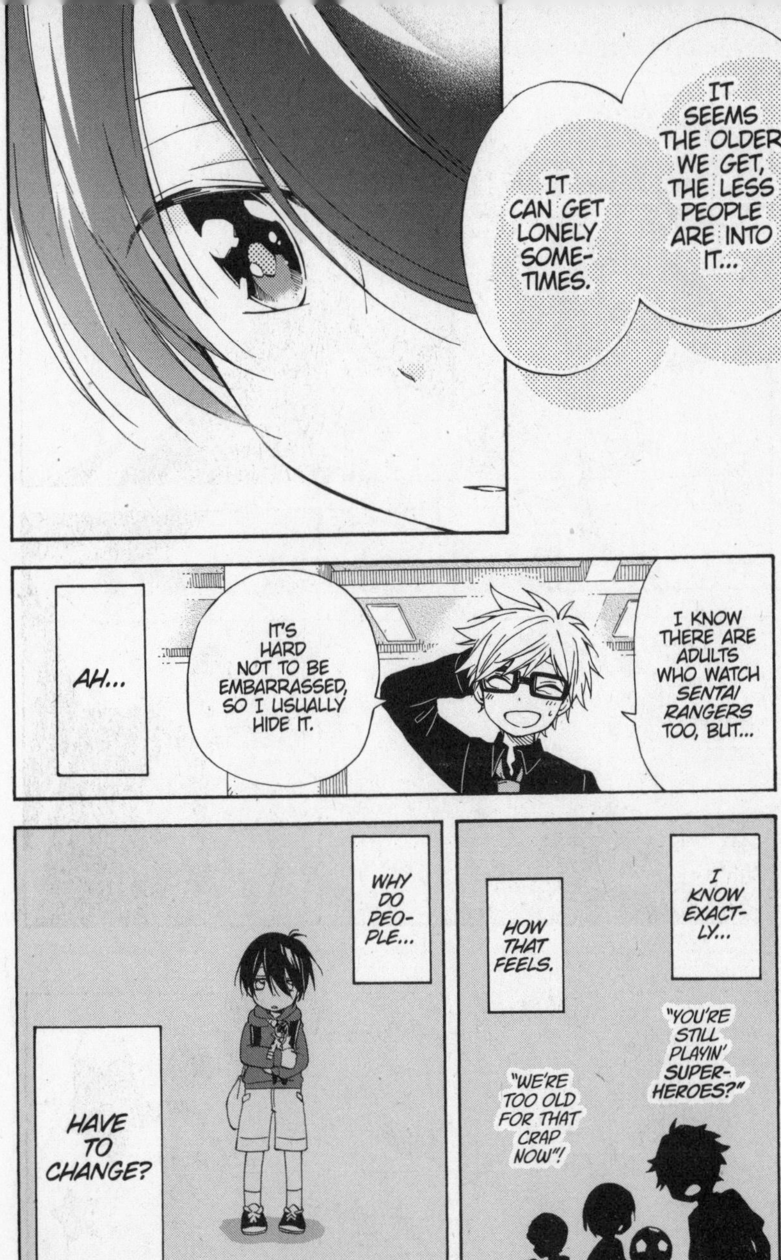
IT SEEMS THE OLDER WE GET, THE LESS PEOPLE ARE INTO IT...
IT CAN GET LONELY SOME-TIMES.
I KNOW THERE ARE ADULTS WHO WATCH SENTAI RANGERS TOO, BUT...
IT'S HARD NOT TO BE EMBARRASSED, SO I USUALLY HIDE IT.
AH...
I KNOW EXACT-LY...
HOW THAT FEELS.
"YOU'RE STILL PLAYIN' SUPER-HEROES?"
"WE'RE TOO OLD FOR THAT CRAP NOW"!
WHY DO PEO-PLE...
HAVE TO CHANGE?

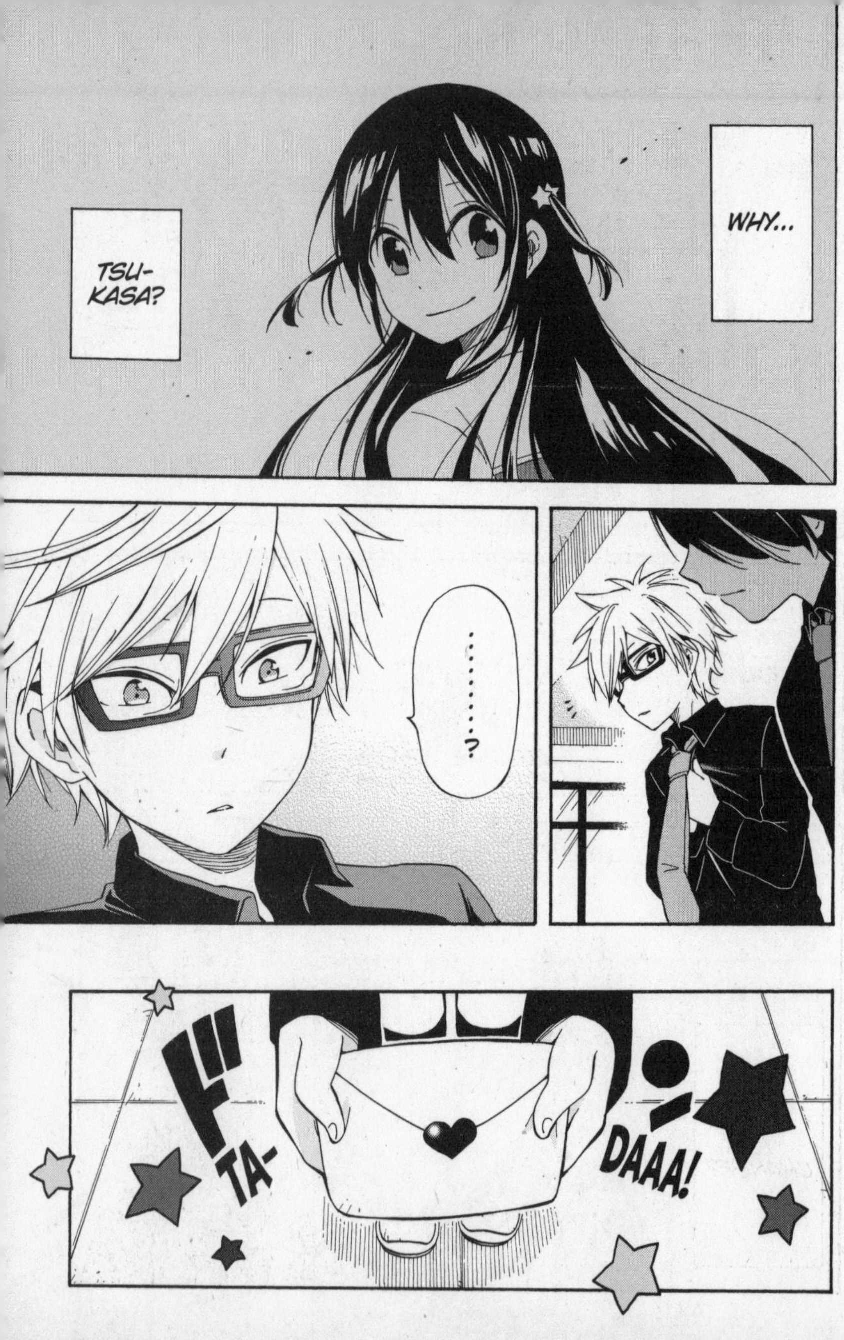
WHY...
TSU-KASA?
......?
TA-DAAA!

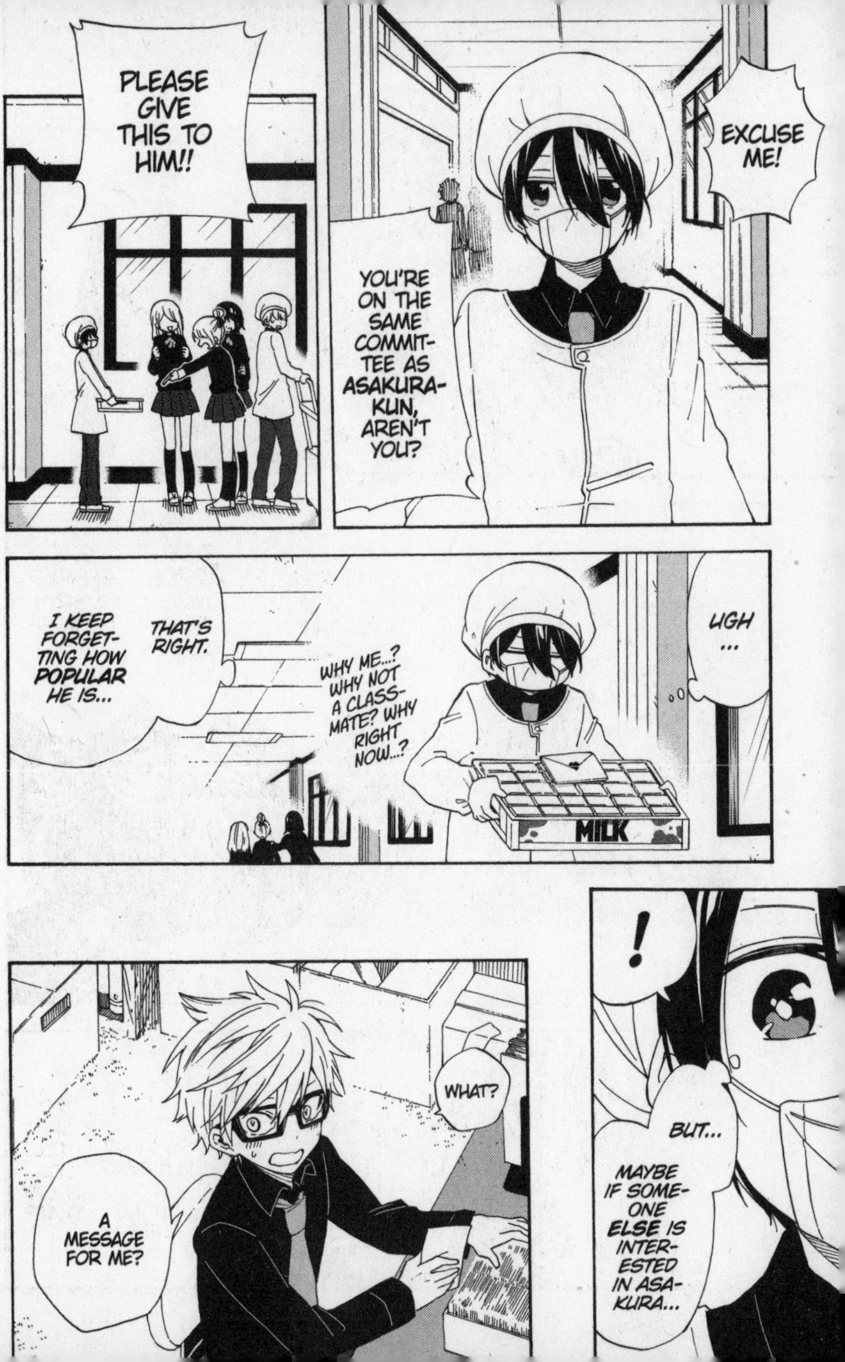
EXCUSE ME!
YOU'RE ON THE SAME COMMITTEE AS ASAKURA-KUN, AREN'T YOU?
PLEASE GIVE THIS TO HIM!!
UGH ...
WHY ME...? WHY NOT A CLASSMATE? WHY RIGHT NOW...?
MILK
THAT'S RIGHT.
I KEEP FORGETTING HOW POPULAR HE IS...
!
BUT...
MAYBE IF SOMEONE ELSE IS INTERESTED IN ASAKURA...
WHAT?
A MESSAGE FOR ME?

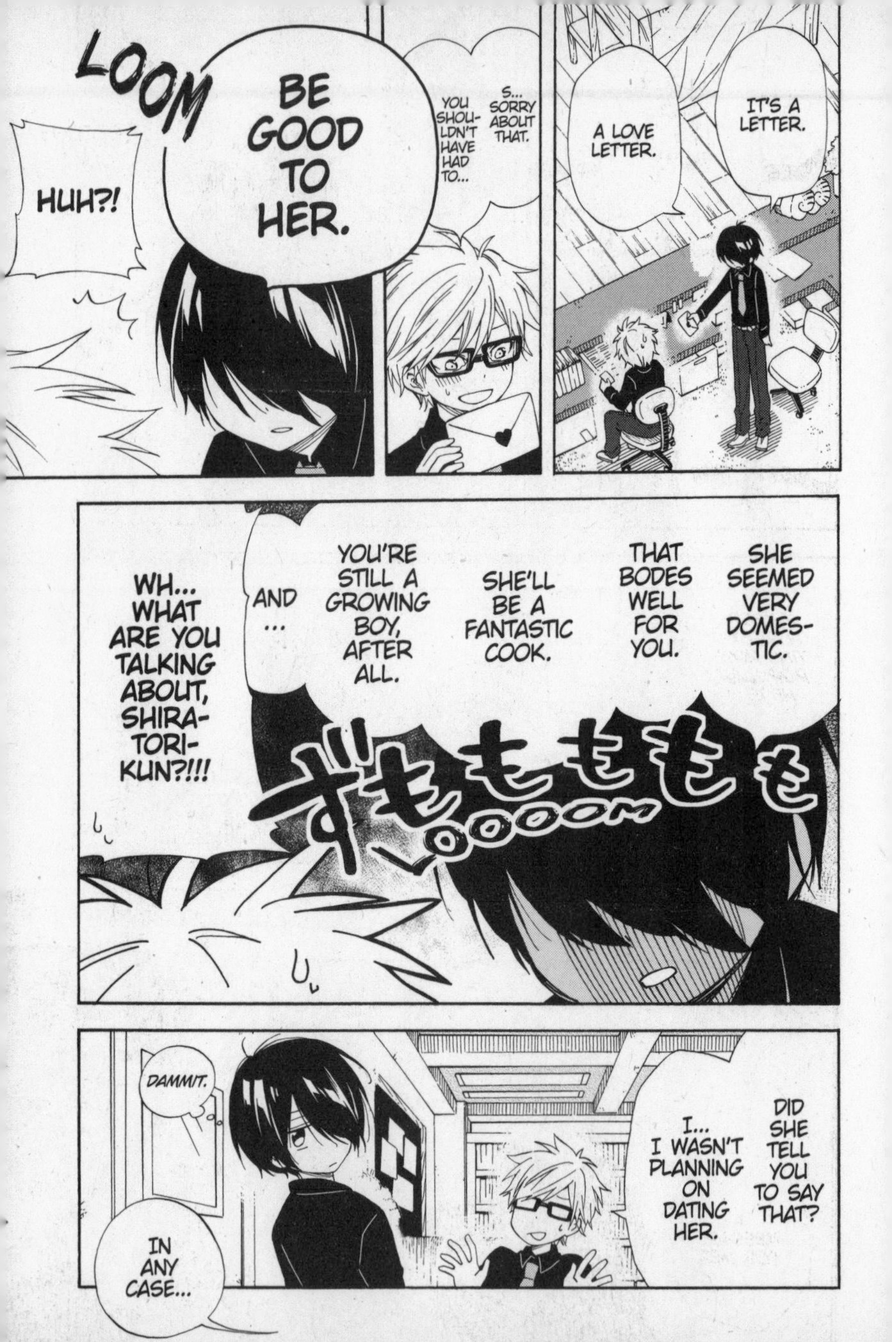
IT'S A LETTER.
A LOVE LETTER.
S... SORRY ABOUT THAT.
YOU SHOULDN'T HAVE HAD TO...
LOOM
BE GOOD TO HER.
HUH?!
SHE SEEMED VERY DOMESTIC.
THAT BODES WELL FOR YOU.
SHE'LL BE A FANTASTIC COOK.
YOU'RE STILL A GROWING BOY, AFTER ALL.
AND ...
ずもももももも
OOOOM
WH... WHAT ARE YOU TALKING ABOUT, SHIRATORI-KUN?!!!
DID SHE TELL YOU TO SAY THAT?
I... I WASN'T PLANNING ON DATING HER.
DAMMIT.
IN ANY CASE...

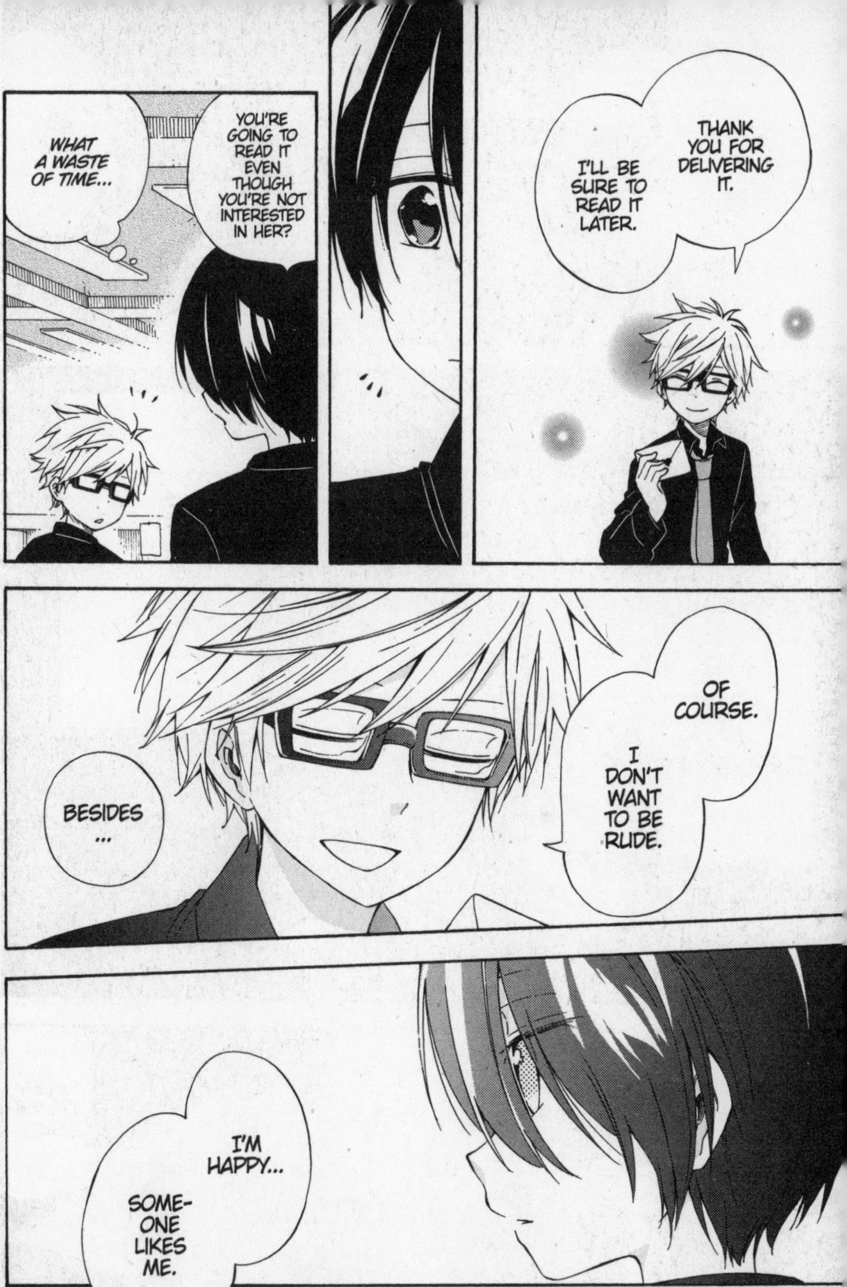
THANK YOU FOR DELIVERING IT.
I'LL BE SURE TO READ IT LATER.
YOU'RE GOING TO READ IT EVEN THOUGH YOU'RE NOT INTERESTED IN HER?
WHAT A WASTE OF TIME...
OF COURSE.
I DON'T WANT TO BE RUDE.
BESIDES...
I'M HAPPY...
SOME-ONE LIKES ME.

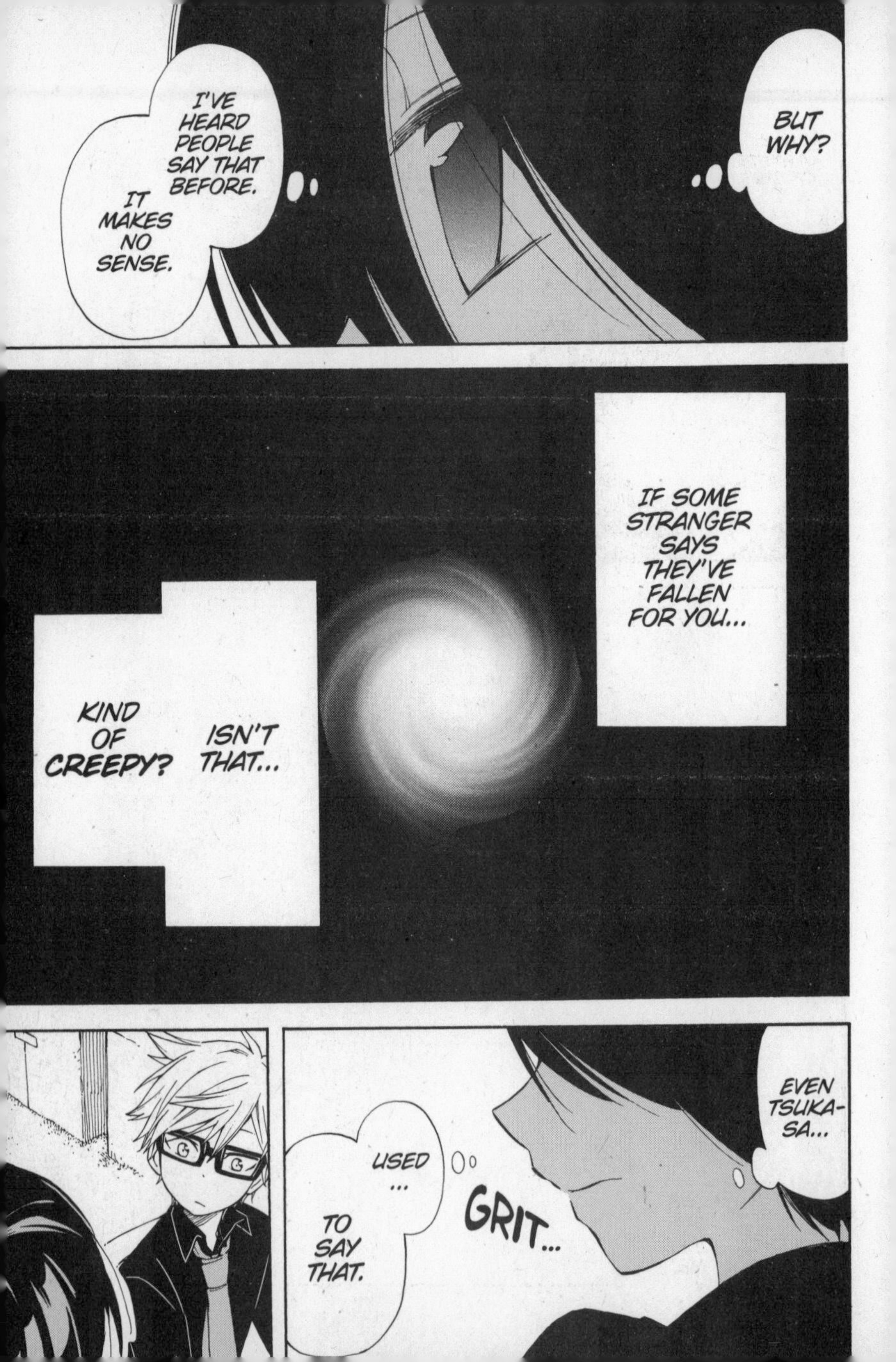
BUT WHY?
I'VE HEARD PEOPLE SAY THAT BEFORE. IT MAKES NO SENSE.
IF SOME STRANGER SAYS THEY'VE FALLEN FOR YOU...
ISN'T THAT... KIND OF CREEPY?
EVEN TSUKA-SA...
GRIT...
USED ... TO SAY THAT.

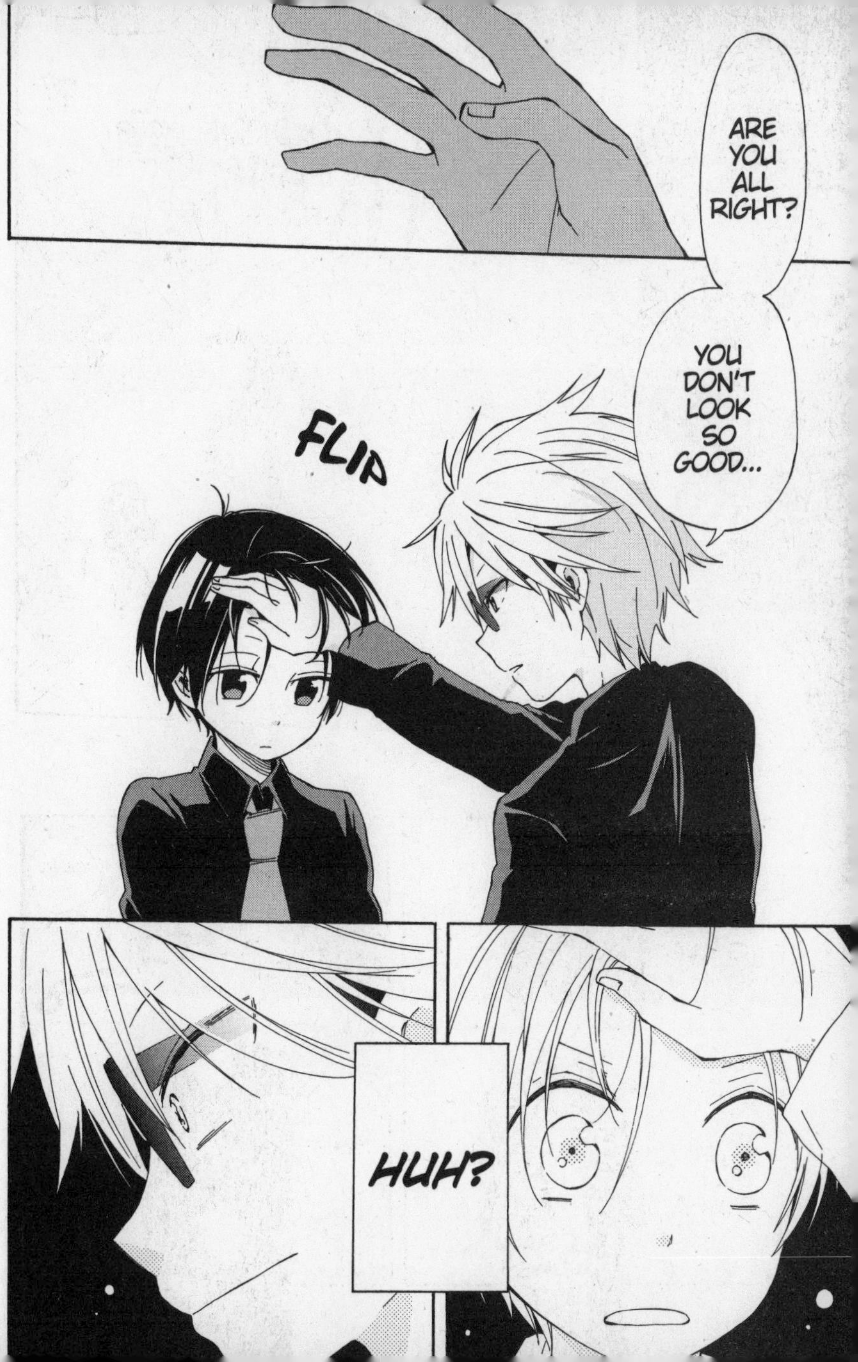
ARE YOU ALL RIGHT?
YOU DON'T LOOK SO GOOD...
FLIP
HUH?

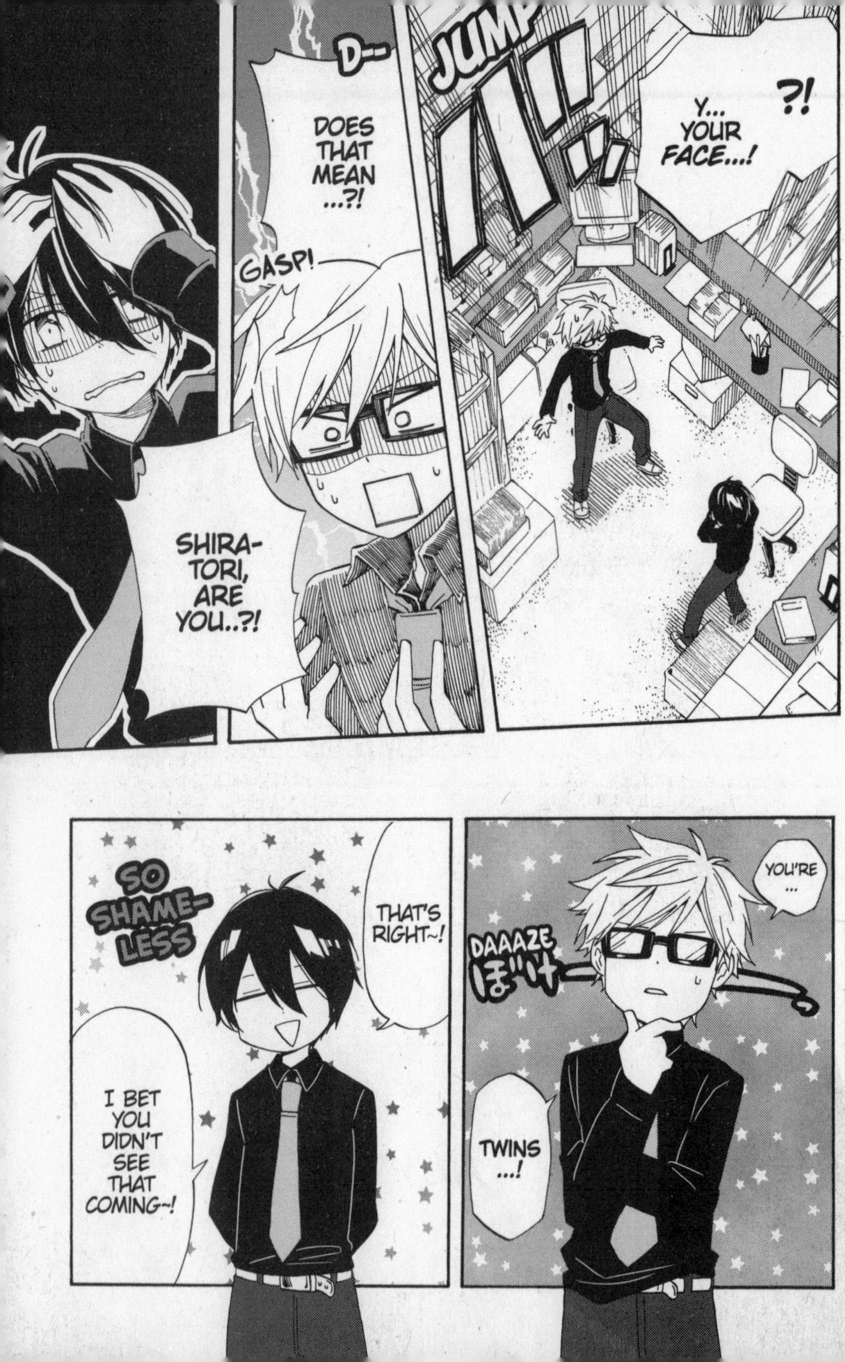
JUMP
Y... YOUR FACE...!
?!
D--
DOES THAT MEAN ...?!
GASP!
SHIRATORI, ARE YOU..?!
YOU'RE ...
DAAAZE
ぼけー
TWINS ...!
SO SHAME-LESS
THAT'S RIGHT~!
I BET YOU DIDN'T SEE THAT COMING~!

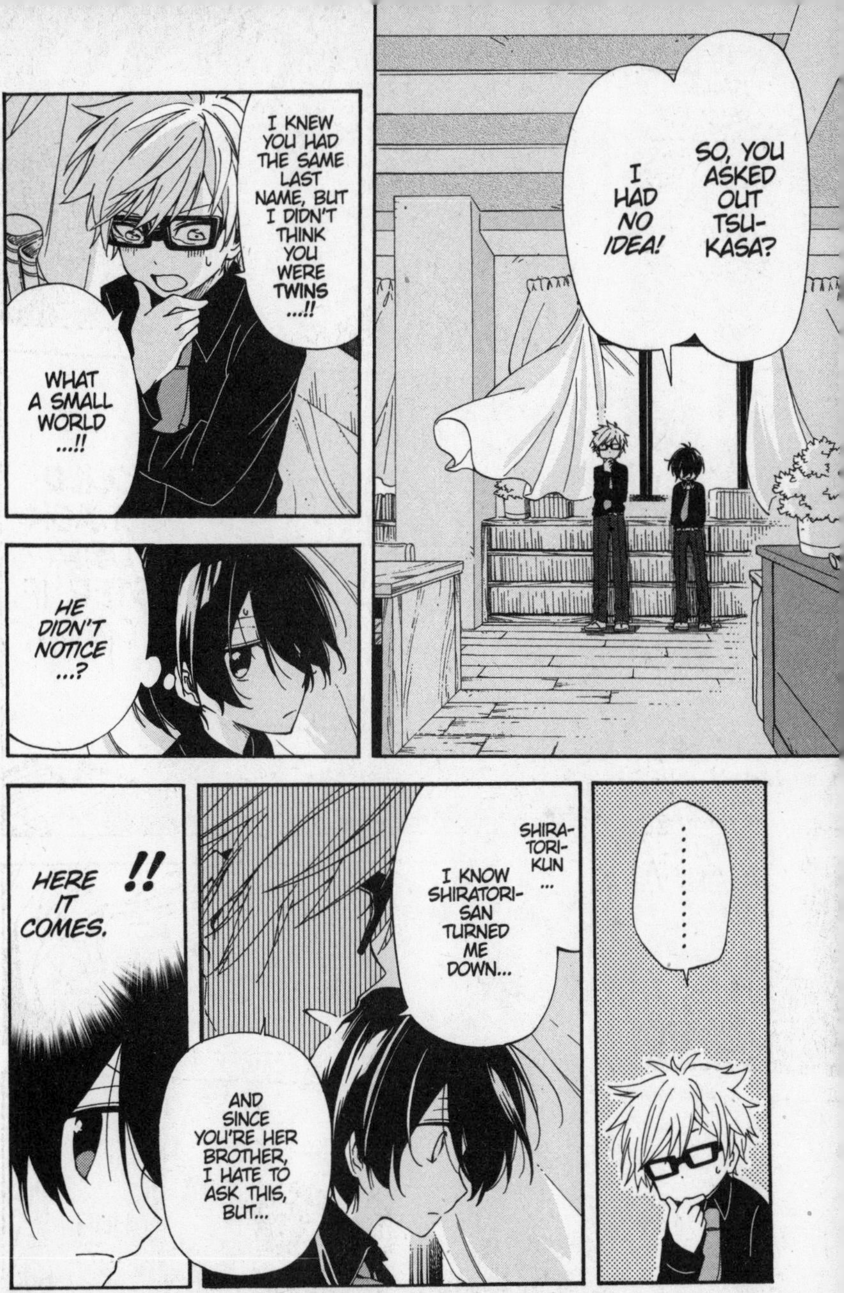
SO, YOU ASKED OUT TSU-KASA?
I HAD NO IDEA!
I KNEW YOU HAD THE SAME LAST NAME, BUT I DIDN'T THINK YOU WERE TWINS ...!!
WHAT A SMALL WORLD ...!!
HE DIDN'T NOTICE ...?
......
SHIRATORI-KUN ...
I KNOW SHIRATORI-SAN TURNED ME DOWN...
AND SINCE YOU'RE HER BROTHER, I HATE TO ASK THIS, BUT...
!!
HERE IT COMES.

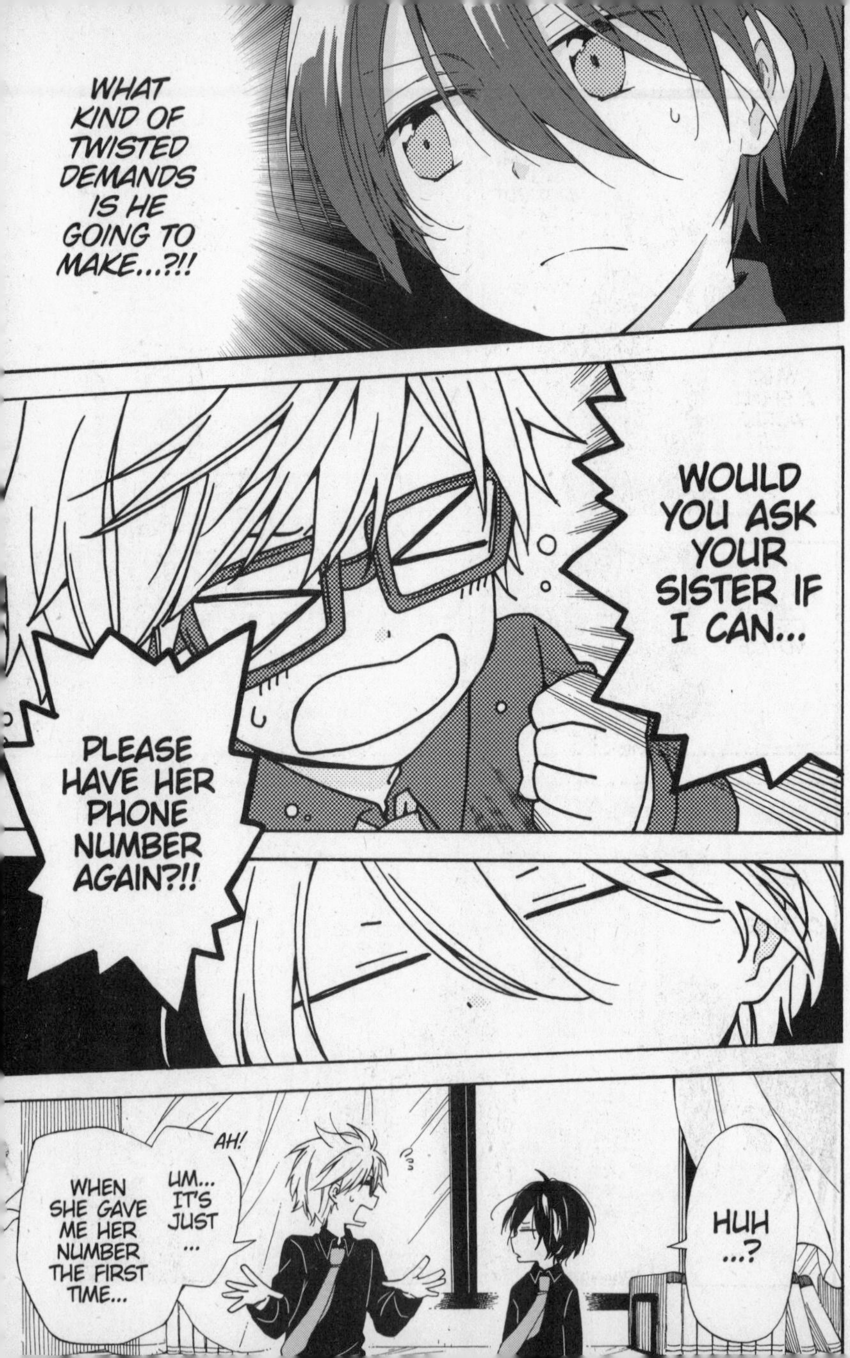
WHAT KIND OF TWISTED DEMANDS IS HE GOING TO MAKE...?!!
WOULD YOU ASK YOUR SISTER IF I CAN...
PLEASE HAVE HER PHONE NUMBER AGAIN?!!
HUH ...?
AH!
UM... IT'S JUST ...
WHEN SHE GAVE ME HER NUMBER THE FIRST TIME...

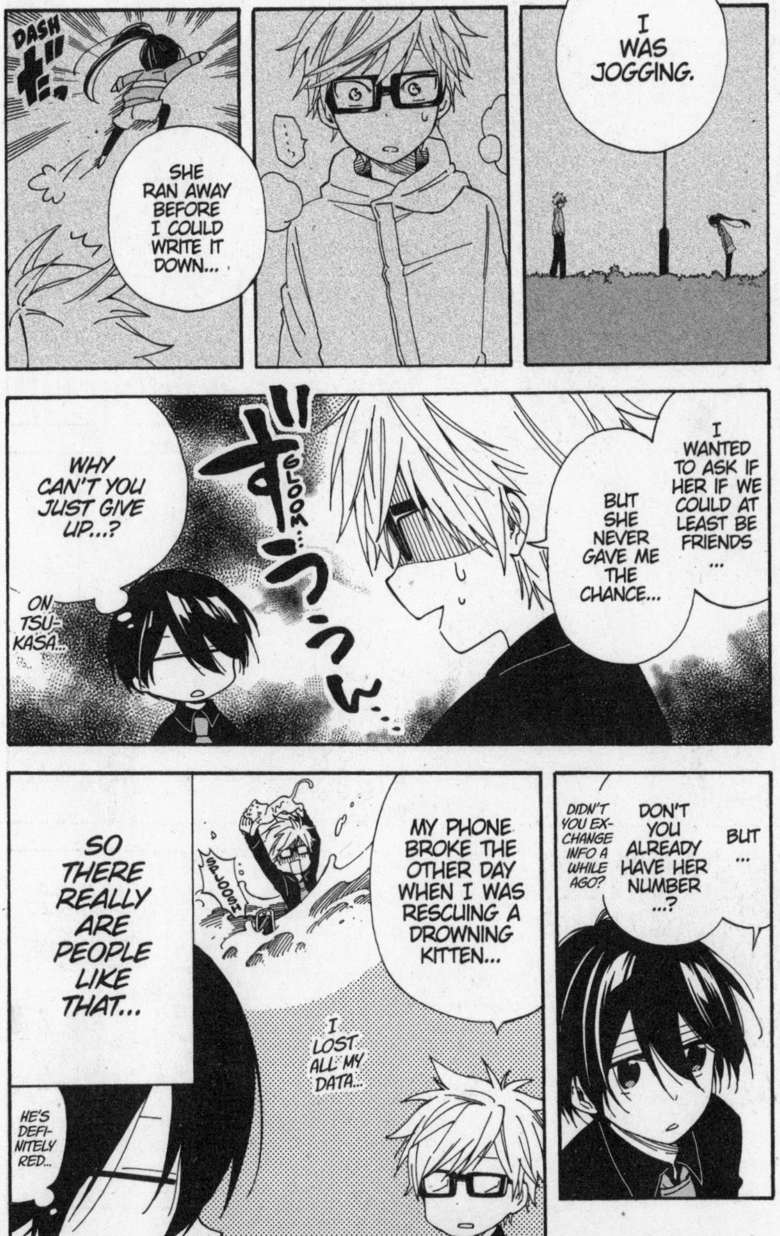
I WAS JOGGING.
...
DASH
SHE RAN AWAY BEFORE I COULD WRITE IT DOWN...
I WANTED TO ASK IF HER IF WE COULD AT LEAST BE FRIENDS ...
BUT SHE NEVER GAVE ME THE CHANCE...
GLOOM...
WHY CAN'T YOU JUST GIVE UP...?
ON TSU-KASA...
BUT ...
DON'T YOU ALREADY HAVE HER NUMBER ...?
DIDN'T YOU EX-CHANGE INFO A WHILE AGO?
MY PHONE BROKE THE OTHER DAY WHEN I WAS RESCUING A DROWNING KITTEN...
SPLOOSH
I LOST ALL MY DATA...
SO THERE REALLY ARE PEOPLE LIKE THAT...
HE'S DEFI-NITELY RED...

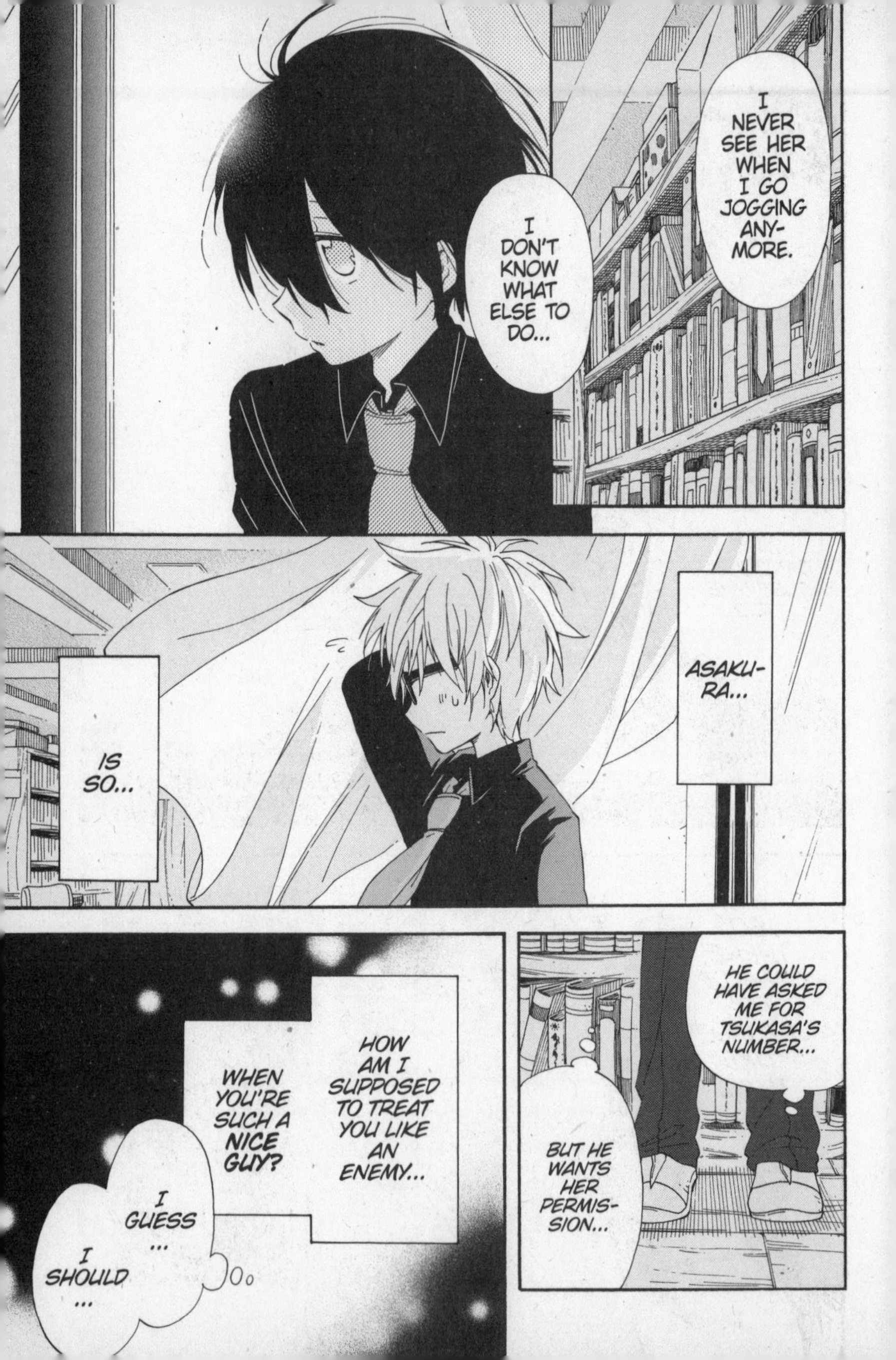
I NEVER SEE HER WHEN I GO JOGGING ANYMORE.
I DON'T KNOW WHAT ELSE TO DO...
ASAKURA...
IS SO...
HE COULD HAVE ASKED ME FOR TSUKASA'S NUMBER...
BUT HE WANTS HER PERMISSION...
HOW AM I SUPPOSED TO TREAT YOU LIKE AN ENEMY...
WHEN YOU'RE SUCH A NICE GUY?
I GUESS... I SHOULD...

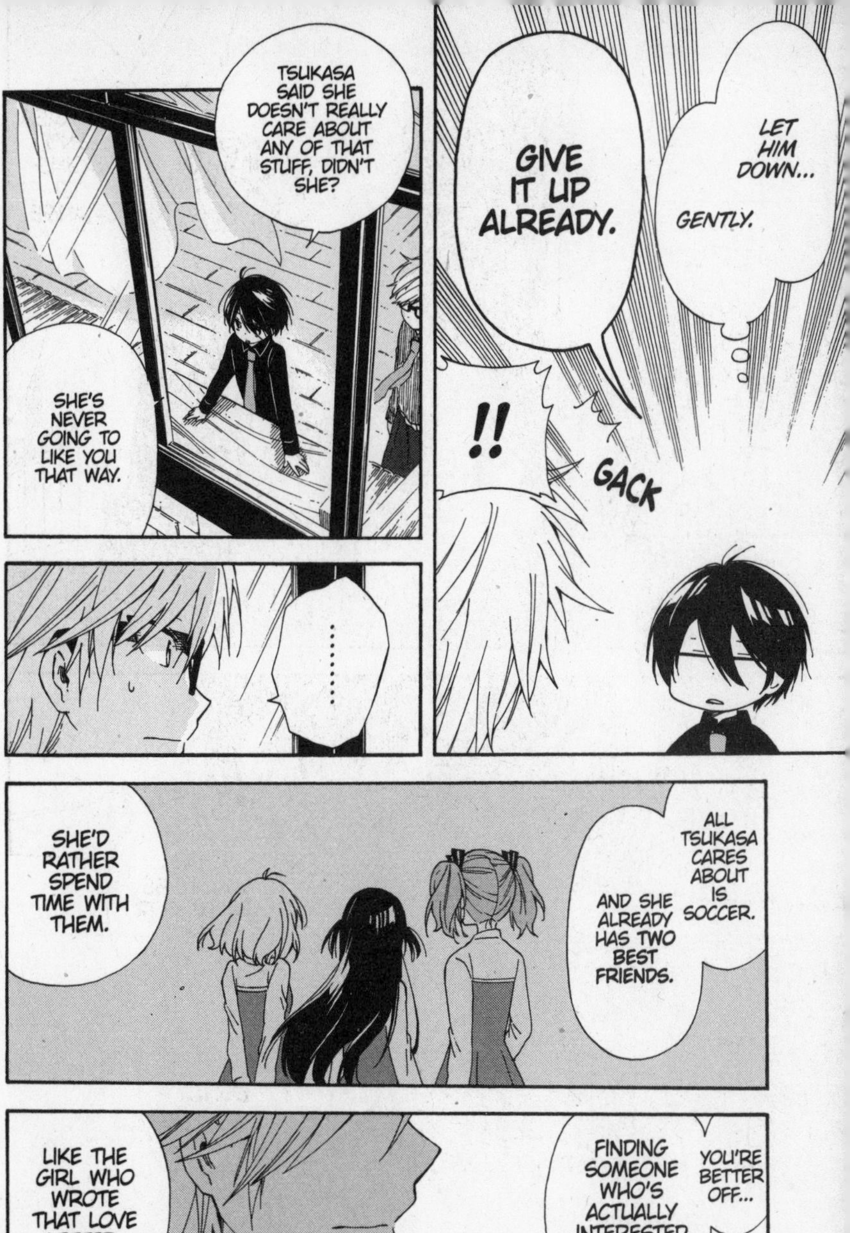
LET HIM DOWN...
GENTLY.
GIVE IT UP ALREADY.
GACK
!!
TSUKASA SAID SHE DOESN'T REALLY CARE ABOUT ANY OF THAT STUFF, DIDN'T SHE?
SHE'S NEVER GOING TO LIKE YOU THAT WAY.
......
ALL TSUKASA CARES ABOUT IS SOCCER.
AND SHE ALREADY HAS TWO BEST FRIENDS.
SHE'D RATHER SPEND TIME WITH THEM.
YOU'RE BETTER OFF...
FINDING SOMEONE WHO'S ACTUALLY INTERESTED IN YOU...
LIKE THE GIRL WHO WROTE THAT LOVE LETTER.

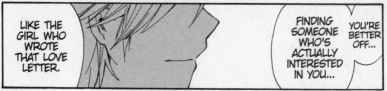

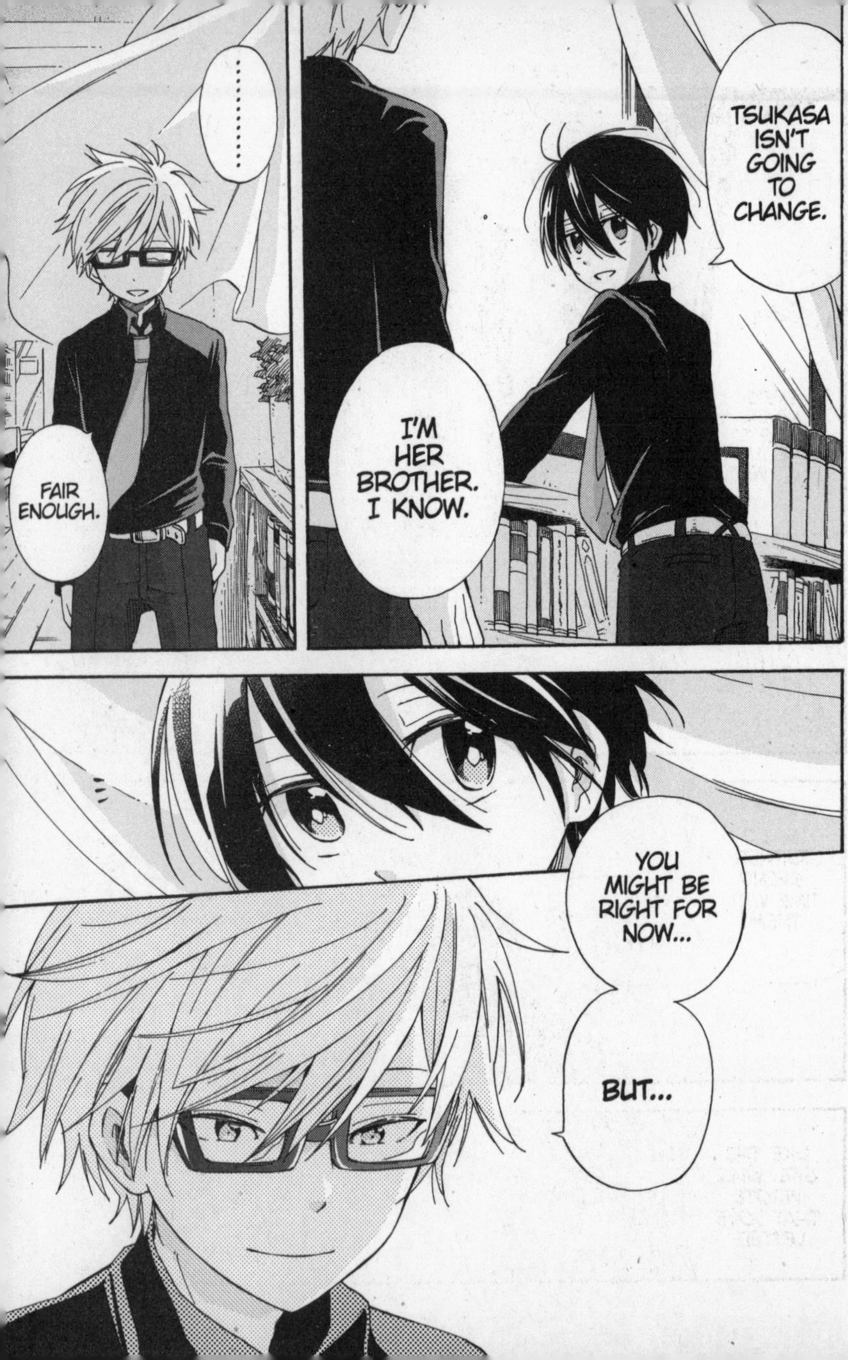
TSUKASA ISN'T GOING TO CHANGE.
I'M HER BROTHER. I KNOW.
......
FAIR ENOUGH.
YOU MIGHT BE RIGHT FOR NOW...
BUT...

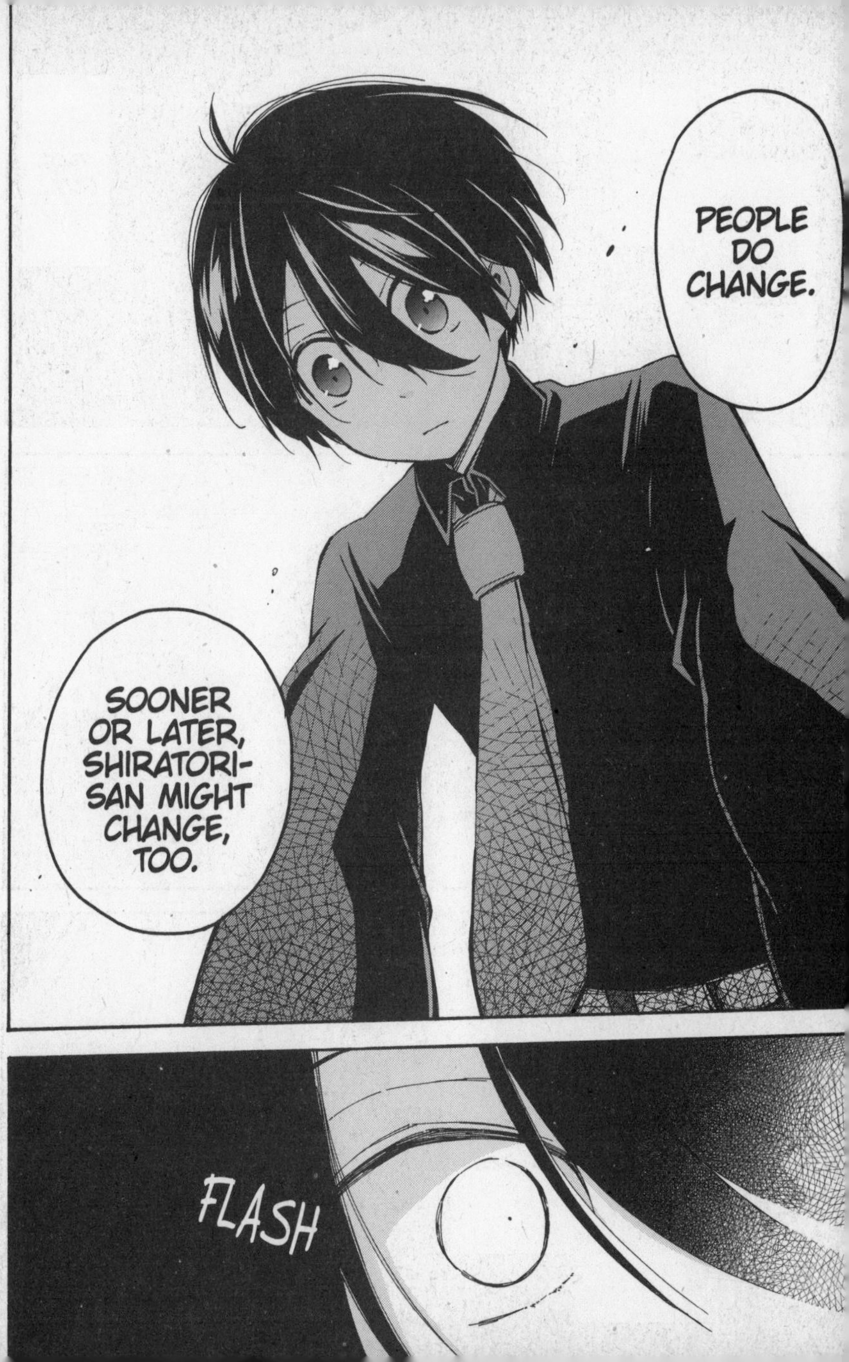
PEOPLE DO CHANGE.
SOONER OR LATER, SHIRATORI-SAN MIGHT CHANGE, TOO.
FLASH

THIS GUY...

JUST SAID ...

THE WORST POSSIBLE THING...

TSU-KASA ...

ISN'T ...

GOING TO CHANGE ...!!!

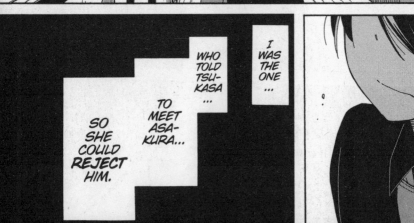

WHO TOLD TSU-KASA ...

I WAS THE ONE ...

TO MEET ASA-KURA...

SO SHE COULD REJECT HIM.

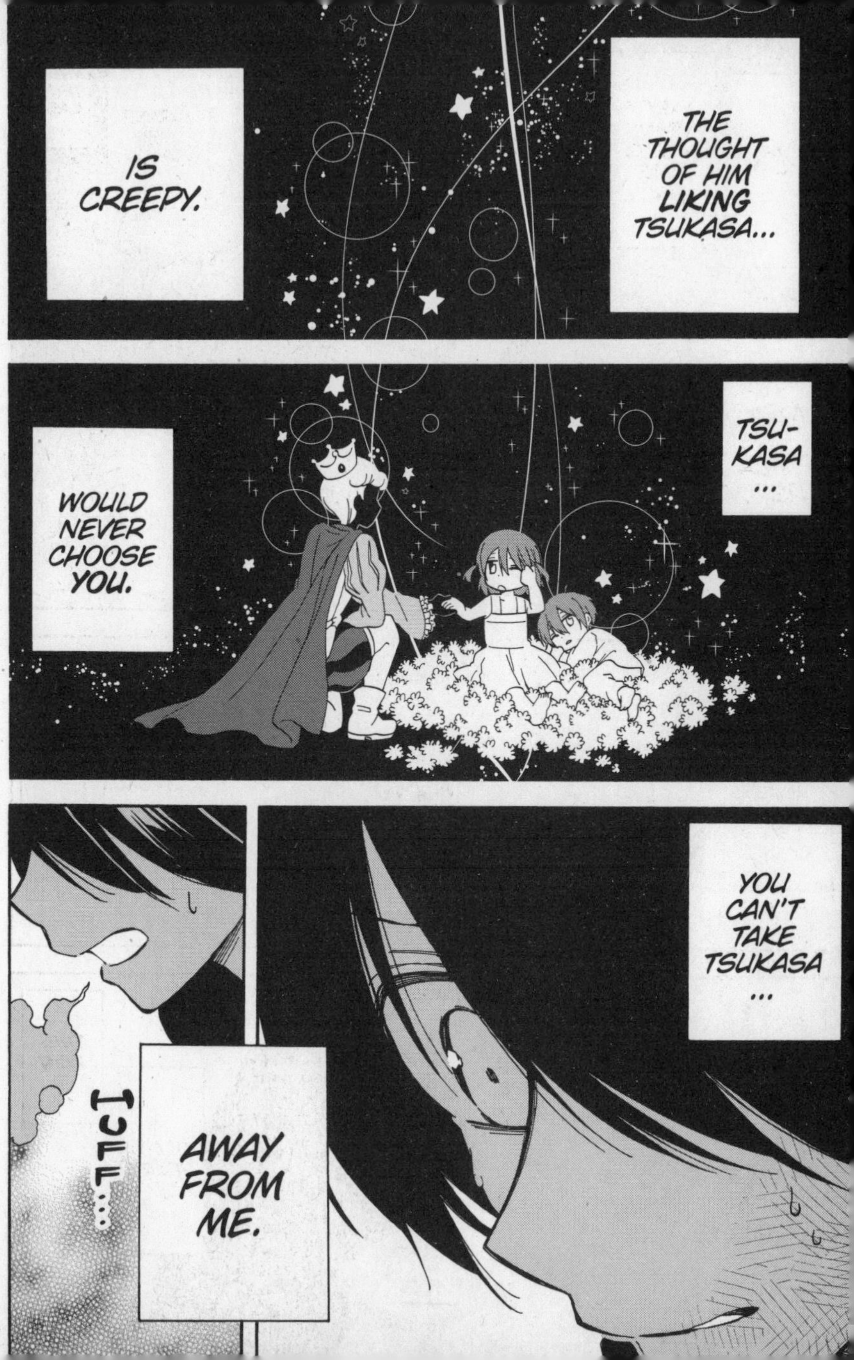
THE THOUGHT OF HIM LIKING TSUKASA...
IS CREEPY.
TSU-KASA...
WOULD NEVER CHOOSE YOU.
YOU CAN'T TAKE TSUKASA...
AWAY FROM ME.
HUFF...

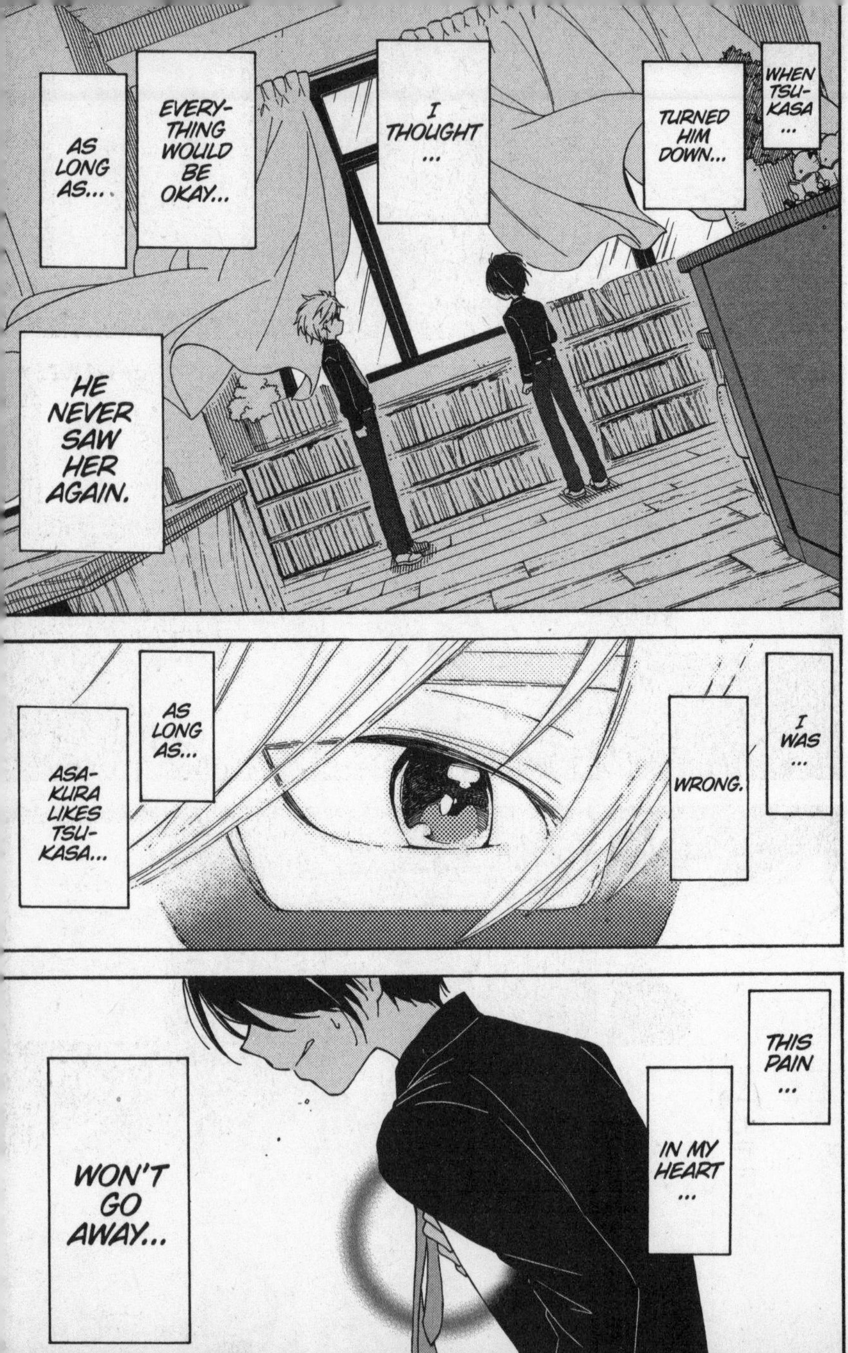
WHEN TSU-KASA ...
TURNED HIM DOWN...
I THOUGHT ...
EVERY-THING WOULD BE OKAY...
AS LONG AS...
HE NEVER SAW HER AGAIN.
I WAS ...
WRONG.
AS LONG AS...
ASA-KURA LIKES TSU-KASA...
THIS PAIN ...
IN MY HEART ...
WON'T GO AWAY...

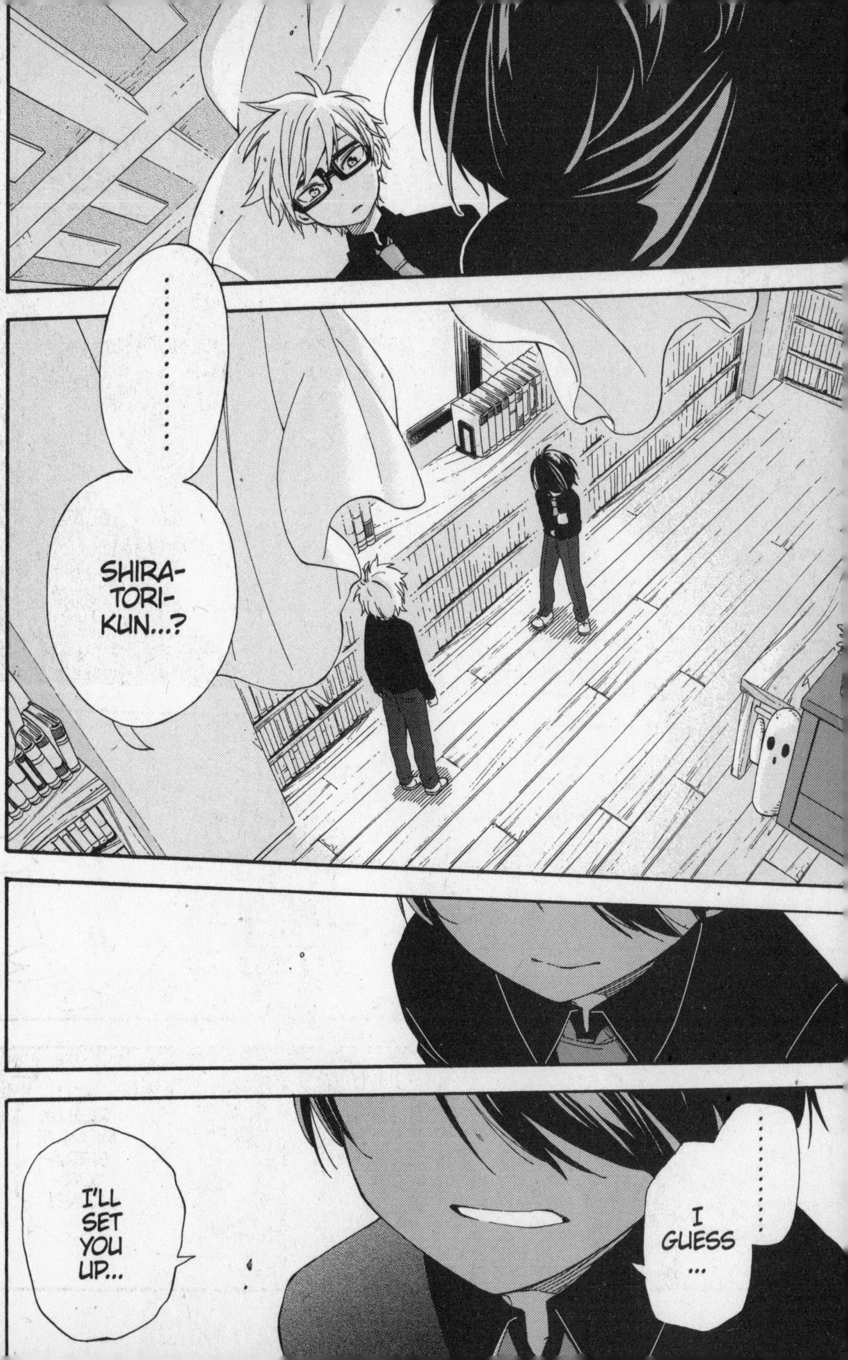
......
SHIRA-TORI-KUN...?
...... I GUESS ...
I'LL SET YOU UP...

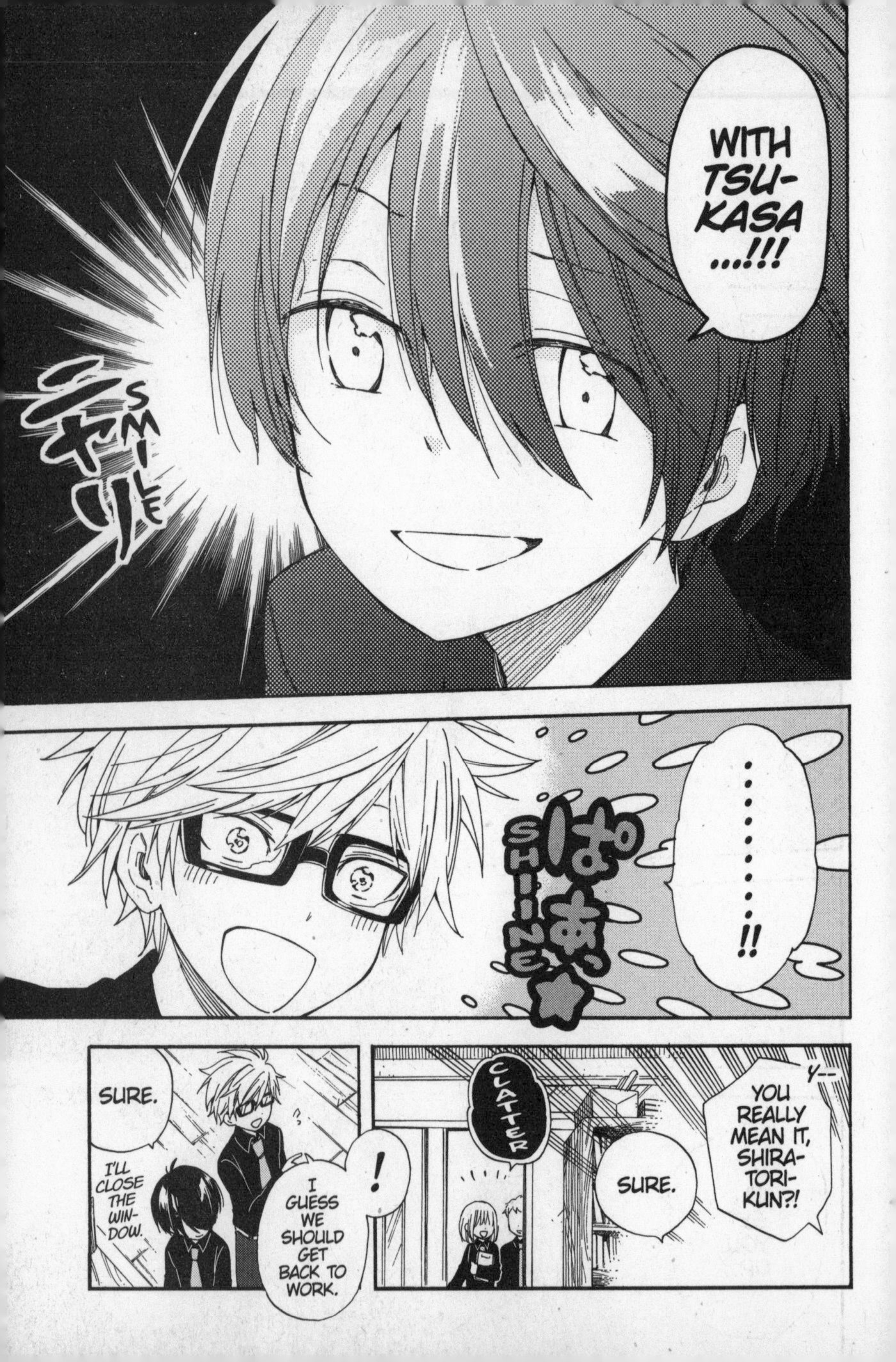
WITH TSU-KASA ...!!!
SMILE
......!!
SHINE
Y--
YOU REALLY MEAN IT, SHIRA-TORI-KUN?!
SURE.
CLATTER
!
I GUESS WE SHOULD GET BACK TO WORK.
SURE.
I'LL CLOSE THE WIN-DOW.

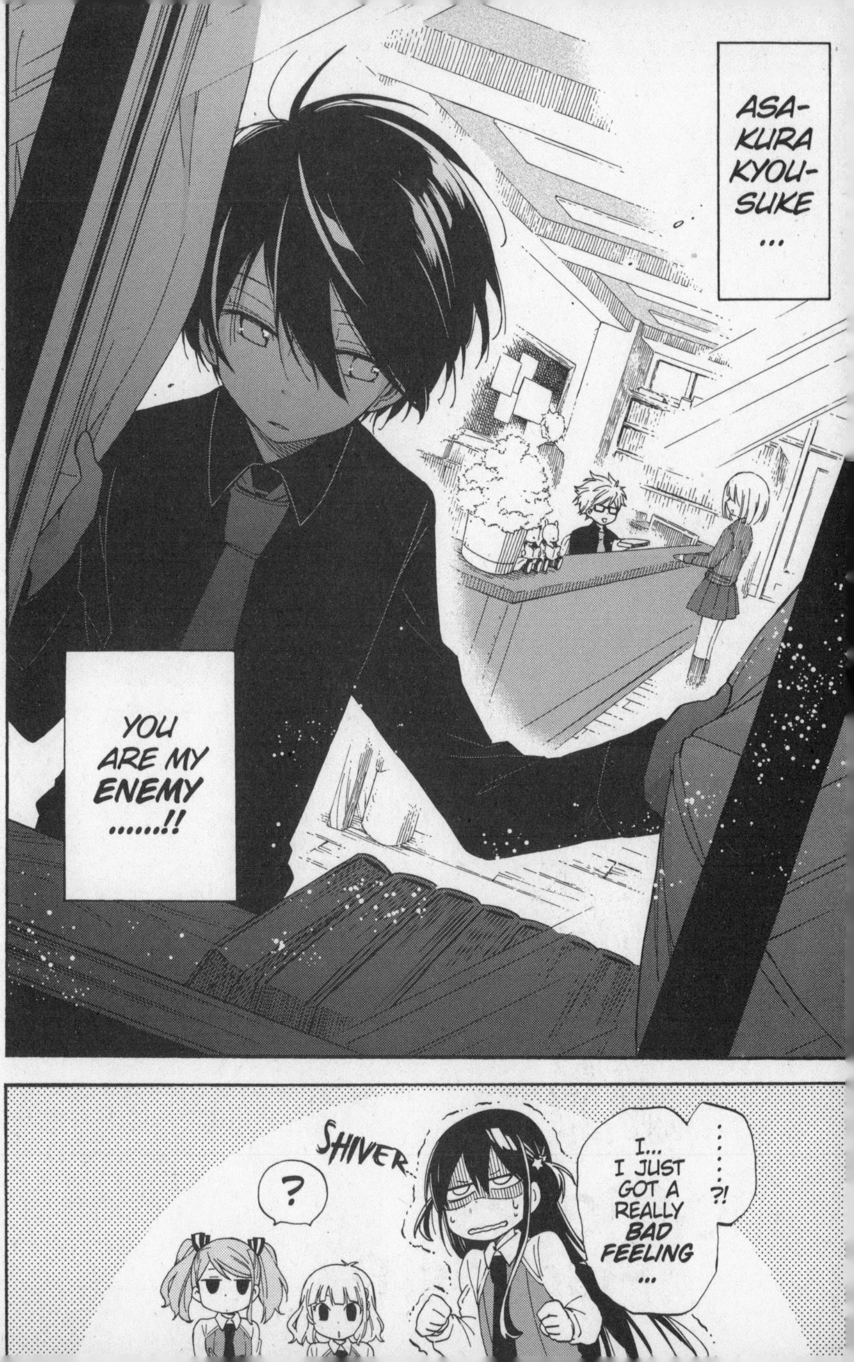
ASA-KURA KYOU-SUKE...
YOU ARE MY ENEMY......!!
......?!
I... I JUST GOT A REALLY BAD FEELING...
SHIVER
?

Nameless
Asterism

Nameless Asterism

AFTERWORD

Thank you very much for reading Volume 2 of *Nameless Asterism!*
I never know what to write for the afterword.
Thank you to all of the readers for your comments and encouragement on Twitter and the Gangan ONLINE official site!
They keep me motivated.
I hope to see you again in Volume 3...!

Kobayashi Kina

SPECIAL THANKS

Editor Ken
Nakagawa-sama
Norita-sama
Fumi Hirose-sama
Sho Nakamura-sama
Marimo Enda-sama

To all the readers

SEVEN SEAS ENTERTAINM

Nameles Asterism

story and art by
KINA KOBAYASHI

TRANSLATION
Jenny McKeon

ADAPTATION
Lora Gray

LETTERING AND RETOUCH
Ray Steeves

COVER DESIGN
Nicky Lim

PROOFREADER
Danielle King
Megan Denton

EDITOR
Jenn Grunigen

PRODUCTTION ASSISTANT
CK Russell

PRODUCTION MANAGER
Lissa Pattillo

EDITOR-IN-CHIEF
Adam Arnold

PUBLISHER
Jason DeAngelis

NANASHI NO ASTERISM VOL. 2

First published in Japan in 2016 by SQUARE ENIX CO., LTD.
English translation rights arranged with SQUARE ENIX CO., LTD.
and SEVEN SEAS ENTERTAINMENT, LLC. through Tuttle-Mori Agency, Inc.

ISBN: 978-1-626927-45-2

Printed in Canada

First Printing: May 2018

10 9 8 7 6 5 4 3 2 1

FOLLOW US ONLINE: ***www.sevenseasentertainment.com***

READING DIRECTIONS

This book reads from ***right to left***, Japanese style. If this is your first time reading manga, you start reading from the top right panel on each page and take it from there. If you get lost, just follow the numbered diagram here. It may seem backwards at first, but you'll get the hang of it! Have fun!!

1
2
3
4
5
6
7
8
9

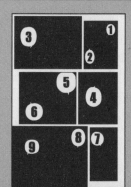